VAN VLIET'S SIAM

VAN VLIET'S SIAM

Chris Baker
Dhiravat na Pombejra
Alfons van der Kraan
David K. Wyatt

SILKWORM BOOKS

This publication was made possible by a grant from
The James H. W. Thompson Foundation.

ISBN–10: 974-9575-81-4
ISBN–13: 978-974-9575-81-9

First published in 2005 by
Silkworm Books
6 Sukkasem Road, T. Suthep
Chiang Mai 50200, Thailand
E-mail: info@silkwormbooks.com
Website: www.silkwormbooks.com

Cover: "Judea" painting reproduced with the permission from the Rijksmuseum, Amsterdam.
Set in 10 pt. Janson Text by SilkType
Printed by O. S. Printing House, Bangkok

3 5 4 2

CONTENTS

Preface and Acknowledgments ... vii
Abbreviations ... ix
Introduction: Ayutthaya, King Prasat Thong, the Dutch, and Jeremias van Vliet ... 1

The Written Works of Jeremias van Vliet ... 33

Diary of the Picnic Incident (1636–37) ... 35
Translated and edited by Alfons van der Kraan

Description of the Kingdom of Siam (1638) ... 89
Translated by L. F. van Ravenswaay, edited by Chris Baker

The Short History of the Kings of Siam (1640) ... 179
Translated by Leonard Andaya, edited by David K. Wyatt

Historical Account of King Prasat Thong (1640) ... 245
Translated by Alfons van der Kraan, edited by Dhiravat na Pombejra and Chris Baker

Appendices
- I Structure of Government ... 323
- II Table of Kings ... 326
- III Dynastic Tree ... 328
- IV Yamada Nagamasa ... 329

Glossary ... 331
Bibliography ... 333
Index ... 339

Place-names mentioned in the text.

PREFACE AND ACKNOWLEDGMENTS

BETWEEN 1636 AND 1640, Jeremias van Vliet wrote four pieces which collectively are unmatched in length and detail by anything written on Siam before the nineteenth century. They are: a section of Van Vliet's diary recounting in detail his dealings with the court at a time of crisis; the earliest lengthy analysis of Siamese society, politics, trade and religion; the earliest known chronicle from Ayutthaya; and the most detailed account of a political transition in Ayutthaya from any period. This book contains all four pieces in English translation.

Three of the pieces were published in translation in 1904, 1910, and 1975 respectively, but none is now easily available. Alfons van der Kraan's recent translation of the fourth piece (the so-called *Picnic Incident*) completes the set, but also provides a new perspective on all of Van Vliet's writings. The original 1904 translation of the *Historical Account* was incomplete and rather inaccurate; here we present a new, complete, and interestingly different version.

The *Short History* is reproduced here in the original 1975 translation by Leonard Andaya with the original introduction and notes by David Wyatt. Only a handful of small errors have been corrected, and a few inconsistencies in presentation removed. Ravenswaay's 1910 translation of the *Description* is reprinted unchanged except for the correction of a few obvious printing errors. All the notes are new. Alfons van der Kraan's translation of the *Picnic Incident* appeared in the University of New England Asia Centre Papers, 3, 2000. Here it has been slightly updated and the notes have been expanded.

The *Historical Account* is a little more complex. The original Dutch text was translated into French in the seventeenth century, and this French version was then translated into English by W. H. Mundie in 1904. In the 1930s, Seiichi Iwao discovered the original Dutch text and in the 1950s published a comparison with the French that showed some differences. Here, Alfons van der Kraan has translated the piece again, working from Iwao's facsimile and transcription of the original Dutch. Again, all the notes are new.

The major responsibility for each piece is shown on the contents page, but there has also been a lot of mutual help. Similarly in the Introduction, Chris Baker drafted the section on Ayutthaya, Dhiravat na Pombejra on the Dutch and the dynasty, and Alfons van der Kraan on Van Vliet's career, but the final version reflects some communal endeavor.

We are enormously indebted to the original translators, especially to Leonard Andaya, who consented to this republication. We would like to acknowledge the assistance of previous scholars who have helped to unearth and illuminate Van Vliet's work, including Seiichi Iwao, Han ten Brummelhuis, Kachorn Sukhabanij, F. H. Giles, and Michael Vickery. In addition we are grateful to Charnvit Kasetsiri, Piriya Krairiksh, Vinai Pongsripian, Volker Grabowsky, Iwamoto Yoshiteru, Simon Bytheway, and Songyote Waeohongsa for advice and information.

We would like to thank the Siam Society, which published all three of the pieces which appeared earlier. The Society has enthusiastically supported this republication, and has allowed us to use a very beautiful map from its collection. Thanks also to the Rijksmuseum Amsterdam for permission to reproduce the "Judea" painting.

We owe a very special debt to Bill Klausner and to the board of the James H. W. Thompson Foundation for a very generous grant to support this publication.

ABBREVIATIONS

C.S.	Culasakaraja, Lesser Era, + 638 = A.D.
f°, ff°	folio, folios
JSS	Journal of the Siam Society
KCKK	คำให้การชาวกรุงเก่า (*Khamhaikan chao krung kao*, Testimony of the residents of the old capital). Bangkok: Chotmaihet, 2001.
KKLWP	คำให้การขุนหลวงวัดประดู่ทรงธรรม (*Khamhaikan khun luang wat pradu songtham*), แถลงงานประวัติศาสตร์ เอกสารโบราณคดี (Historical reports, archaeological documents), 3, 1, (1969).
KTSD	กฎหมายตราสามดวง (*Kotmai tra sam duang*. Three Seals Law). 5 vols. Bangkok: Khurusapha, 1984.
LP	The "Luang Prasoet" version of the royal chronicles of Ayutthaya. The fullest Thai versions are reproduced in พระราชพงศาวดารกรุงศรีอยุธยา (ฉบับหลวงสารประเสริฐ และฉบับกรมพระปรมานุชิตชิโนรส) และพงศาวดารเหนือ (2 vols. Bangkok: Khurusapha, 1961), vol. I: 1–32; and, in the original spelling, in ประชุมจดหมายเหตุสมัยอยุธยา ภาค ๑. (Bangkok: Commission for the Publication of Historical, Cultural, and Archaeological Records, Office of the Prime Minister, 1967): 93–103. An English translation is provided in O. Frankfurter, "Events in Ayudhya from Chulasakaraj 688–966," *JSS*, 6, 3 (1909): 1–21; reprinted in *Selected Articles from the Siam Society Journa*l, vol. I: 38–62 (Bangkok: Siam Society, 1954).
PN	The "Somdet Phra Phonnarat" version of the royal chronicles of Ayutthaya พระราชพงศาวดารกรุงศรีอยุธยา ฉบับสมเด็จพระพนรัตน์ วัดพระเชตุพน (Bangkok: Khlang Witthaya, 1964; reprinted 1972).
RA	The "Royal Autograph" version of the Ayutthaya chronicles, edited by King Mongkut in 1855, and further edited by Prince Damrong Rajanubhab and published in 1912. The best edition, and the first to appear in a single volume, is พระราชพงศาวดารกรุงศรีอยุธยา ฉบับพระราชหัตถเลขา (Chonburi: Cremation of Tailong Phonprapha, 1969).

RCA	Richard D. Cushman (tr.), *The Royal Chronicles of Ayutthaya* (Bangkok: Siam Society, 2000).
VOC	Vereenigde Oostindische Compagnie, Dutch United East India Company

INTRODUCTION: AYUTTHAYA, KING PRASAT THONG, THE DUTCH, AND JEREMIAS VAN VLIET

THE FIRST FULL accounts of Ayutthaya and Siam were written between 1636 and 1640 by a Dutch merchant. There are some shorter descriptions from earlier dates by Chinese, Portuguese, and Dutch (and more may yet come to light). But the works of Jeremias van Vliet are both the earliest of any detail, and indeed the most comprehensive available in any period before the nineteenth century. Written in four different genres – diary, gazetteer, historical chronicle, and contemporary political narrative – these four pieces present an unusually intimate view of an independent Asian port, its rulers, and its day-to-day excitement. In this introduction, we offer some background on the setting and leading characters of Van Vliet's writings.

AYUTTHAYA

The site of Ayutthaya is an island formed by the junction of the Chaophraya and Pasak rivers, and some strategic canal building. It was probably first settled around the eleventh or twelfth century. Much earlier, the sea level had been higher and the whole area under water. The sea had fallen close to its current level by 1000 BC, but the central delta went on forming from river clay for a long time afterwards. The earliest accounts of Ayutthaya by the Chinese mentioned that the surrounding area was swampy, and in Van Vliet's time it disappeared under water for up to six months of the year during the monsoon.

Several towns around the Chaophraya delta were built or rebuilt in a Khmer-influenced style in the eleventh-twelfth centuries. Ayutthaya was probably one of these. There are traces to the east of the island, but they have never been excavated. In its early years, Ayutthaya looked outwards to the sea. For at least two hundred years – from the 1280s to the 1480s – Ayutthaya was an aggressive seaborne power (Baker 2003). Its ships traded southwards to the tip of the peninsula. On the outward journey they carried rice, other foods, gum, cheap cloth, precious metals and stones. They brought back slaves, spices, and textiles, as well as cowrie shells, which were used as currency. The Ayutthayan expeditions also repeatedly attacked other places

– down the peninsula coasts, in Champa, and in northern Sumatra – demanding submission, extracting tribute, and carrying away goods and people. These raids only ceased when a powerful Malay state emerged at Malacca (today Melaka) in the early fifteenth century, and China gave this state strong political backing.

Ayutthaya and some of its neighbors – Lopburi, Suphanburi, and possibly Phetchaburi – consolidated into some kind of federation in the mid-fourteenth century (Charnvit 1976). All these places had already opened up trade and diplomatic relations with China. By the end of the fourteenth century, Ayutthaya had become the dominant member of this federation and the spearhead of a burgeoning trade with China. The Chinese court had a huge demand for goods from tropical and subtropical forests, including aromatic wood, spices, gum bases, and exotic items like ivory and kingfisher feathers. Ayutthaya secured the sources of these goods by its expeditions down the peninsula, and later increasingly by expeditions into the interior of the Chaophraya basin. Ayutthaya became the single most important trading partner of China, and many Chinese took up residence in the emerging port city.

In the late fifteenth century, China's own traders gained the freedom to find these imports, and Ayutthaya was forced to change strategy. It seized ports on the upper western coast of the peninsula, and thereby controlled a portage route that connected the China seas to the Bay of Bengal and allowed traders to avoid the longer and pirate-infested route through the Strait of Malacca. Ayutthaya now became an entrepôt between east and west. From the east came Chinese porcelains and other goods that Ayutthaya redistributed southwards to the archipelago and westwards across the portage route to India and beyond. From the west, Arab and Indian traders brought textiles, metalware, and other items for sale in the east (Breazeale 1999). By the mid-sixteenth century, Ayutthaya had settlements of Arabs and Indians and was so prosperous that the early European travellers ranked it as one of the three great powers of Asia, alongside China and the Vijayanagar empire in eastern India (Campos 1940).

As it grew and sought more goods from the forests of the interior, Ayutthaya came into more contact with settlements to the north, especially the Tai towns that had developed along the river valleys in the foothills to the north of the delta plain. From the late fourteenth century, Ayutthayan troops raided these places to carry away people. Gradually relations became more complex. The ruling families of Ayutthaya and the main northern cities of Sukhothai and Phitsanulok became closely entwined through marriage ties. Ayutthaya established settlements adjacent to the northern cities. Warriors from the northern cities joined with the Ayutthayan forces to raid further north. More northerners gradually moved to the prospering port. In the late fifteenth century, Ayutthaya adopted some of the laws, military recruitment systems, and administrative practices of the northern cities. By the mid-fifteenth century, the Portuguese described Siam as two interlinked kingdoms, one centered on Ayutthaya and the other on the northern cities. At Ayutthaya, nobles from northern lineages became increasingly important in court politics. In 1548 they helped to overthrow a usurper and hence became kingmakers (Phiset 2003).

To the west, across the Tenasserim range of hills in the valleys of the Salween and Irrawaddy rivers, Pegu had developed on a parallel course to Ayutthaya. The two centers were natural competitors for trade and kingly dominance. In the mid-sixteenth century, the Pegu rulers gained more of the Portuguese mercenaries and guns that were a new and powerful factor in warfare. They also knew of the growing regional conflict in the Chaophraya basin. They allied with the rulers of the northern cities to take Ayutthaya by siege in 1569. The old Ayutthaya ruling family was dispersed, and the Sukhothai-Phitsanulok family was installed on the Ayutthaya throne as a tributary of Pegu.

Naresuan, the son of this family, was taken away to Pegu as a hostage. A few years later, he escaped, revoked the tributary status, succeeded his father on the Ayutthaya throne, and spent a reign of fifteen years almost wholly on horseback, holding off the Peguans and establishing military control over the lower Chaophraya basin and its borderlands. As part of this strategy, he swept people and warriors down from the northern cities to Ayutthaya, completing the city's transformation under northern influence. We have no idea what the ethnic identity of the early Ayutthayans was. The only written materials surviving from the period prior to the sixteenth century are in Khmer or Mon. But by the Naresuan era, Ayutthaya was certainly dominated by Thai, though they spoke a language that had incorporated so many Khmer words, constructions, and principles that it differed markedly from any other Tai dialect (Wilaiwan 2001) .

In the early seventeenth century, the fighting stopped. Cities had invested in stronger walls, and people had become fed up with fighting. Sieges failed, and armies deserted. Peace made way for another surge of commerce. Ayutthaya's trade had shrunk sharply after the sack of 1569, but Naresuan regained control of the portage, which rapidly became the link between two new centers of power and commercial demand.

To the west, three Islamic empires flourished: Ottoman Turkey, Safavid Persia, and Mughal India with its Golconda offshoot controlling ports on India's eastern coast. To the east, the Tokugawa Shogunate imposed peace on Japan and persuaded the western *daimyo* to turn away from warfare to trade. Ayutthaya revived again as an entrepôt between east and west. The city became yet more cosmopolitan. Islamic traders began to arrive in Ayutthaya in greater numbers in the 1600s. In the 1610s, two rich trading brothers of Arabic origin and Indian base helped reorganize the government's department of trade. Many Indian Muslims settled at Ayutthaya and were followed by Turks,

Armenians, Persians, and the Tamil Muslims called Chulia. Trade with Japan had begun by the late 1580s. Several Japanese fled to Ayutthaya after the Japanese authorities began to suppress Christianity in 1597, and others came to serve as traders and professional soldiers.

The city to which the Dutch first came in 1604 was already large, wealthy, and cosmopolitan.

AYUTTHAYA IN THE SEVENTEENTH CENTURY

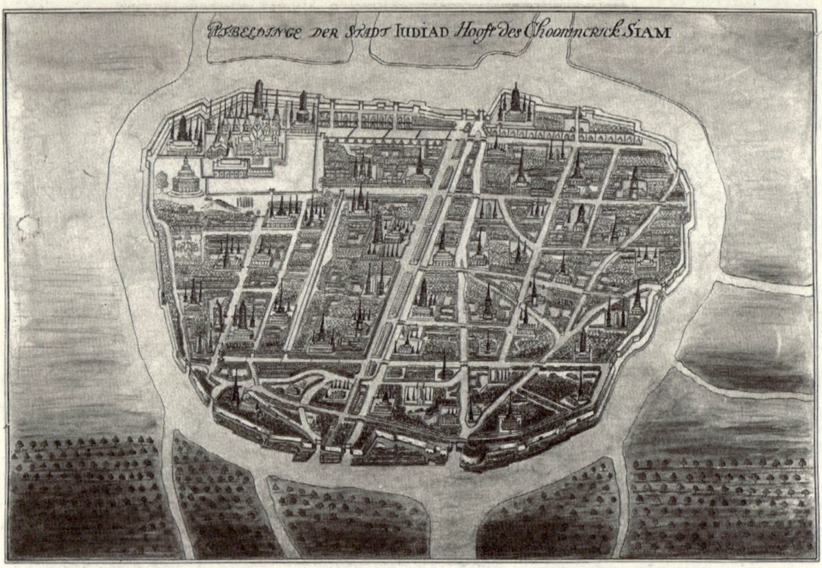

Vingboons Atlas, 1660s

But what was it like? There are a few maps and paintings of Ayutthaya executed by the Dutch, probably in the 1650s. They all seem to have been based on one original, perhaps first drawn in the 1630s during Van Vliet's residence, and seen most clearly in the version published in the Vingboons Atlas in the Hague in the 1660s. This map was adapted into the "Judea" painting hung in the Dutch East India Company's offices in Amsterdam.

The final executions of these maps were undoubtedly done in the Netherlands and hence have a lot of European influences, including some very European rendering of buildings, and, in the "Judea" painting, a background of hills. The overall ground plan of the island is clearly wrong – the shape is distorted, and the pattern of roads and waterways is impossible to reconcile with later versions. Yet in parts these maps are very detailed, and the illustration of buildings can be identified with known monuments. Most

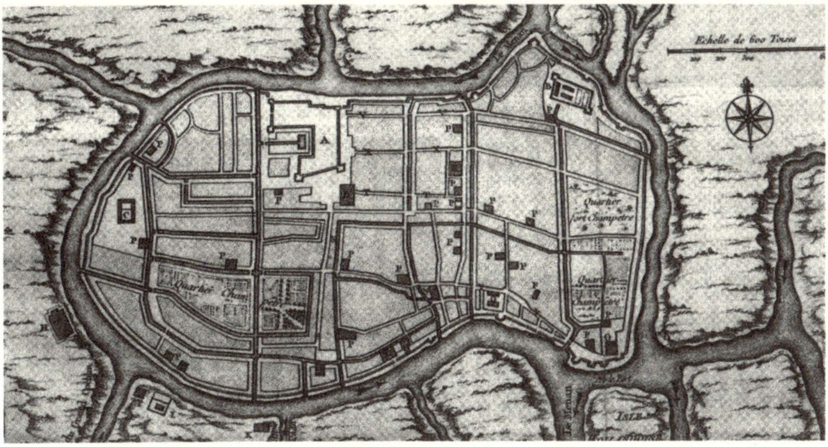

Lamare map, 1687–8

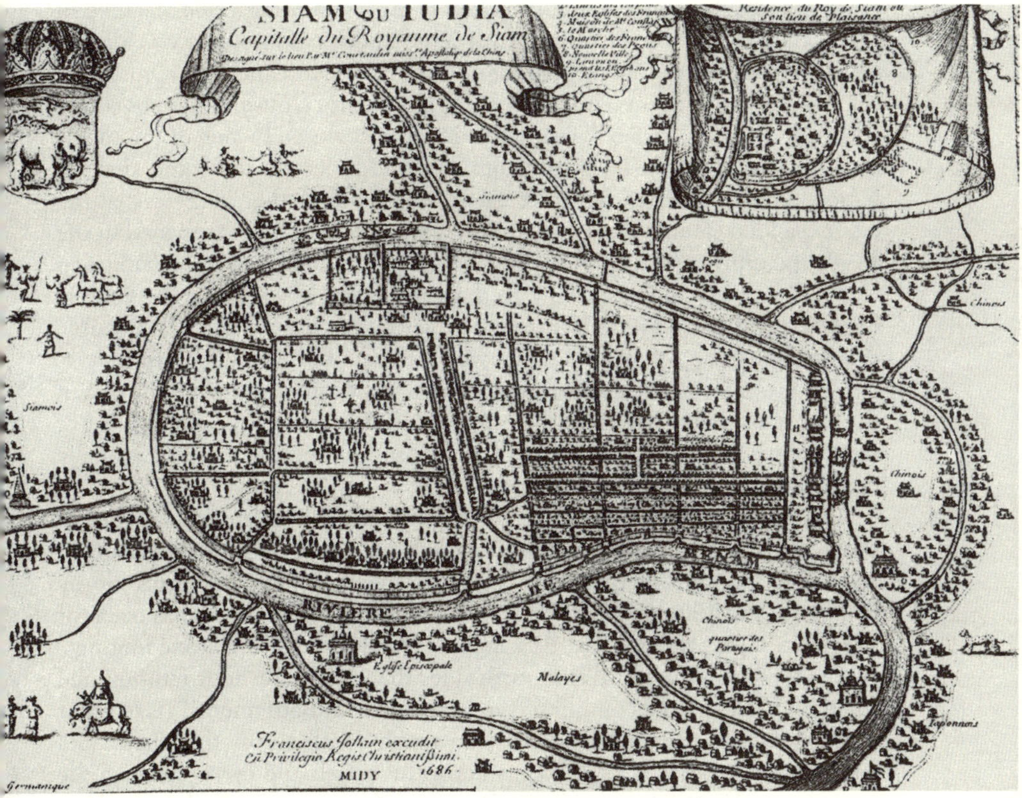

Coronelli map, 1686.

probably, these maps/paintings were based on detailed sketches done *in situ*, but these sketches did not cover the whole island, and the total composition lacked the framework of an overall survey.

A later set of maps executed by the French in 1687–8, particularly the map by Lamare, were based on an a survey by an engineer, probably Father Thomas Valgarneira, an Italian Jesuit who helped rebuild the walls from 1675 (Sternstein 1965). The ground plan fits later maps very closely, except in the southwest corner, where something in the survey seems to have been distorted, and hence a part of the plan has been tilted. Other French and Italian visitors in the 1680s drew maps (like that by Coronelli) that are cartographically very inaccurate, but convey lots of impressionistic detail.

THE MOAT AND WALLS

These maps show the city as a fortress. The area was originally a maze of waterways meandering through the swamps. The site was converted into a moat-encircled island by digging a canal to close the eastern side of a loop in the Lopburi River. By the seventeenth century, this eastern moat was formed by a canal to connect the Lopburi and Pasak rivers at the northeast corner of the city. Possibly this was done early in the city's history. But another possibility is that the original "island" was much smaller, enclosed by one of the canals that now runs north-south through the middle of the city, and that, as happened later at Bangkok, other canals were built further to the east as the city expanded (Sternstein 1965, 1966). One such extension happened in the 1550s, possibly moving the eastern moat to the line of the Makhamriang Canal. Then in 1580, according to the chronicles, "the walls of the Capital were dismantled and rebuilt up to the edge of the river" (*RCA*: 82). Possibly this was the time when the link between the Lopburi and Pasak rivers was cut. To prevent too much water now flowing down this channel to the east of the city, stakes were driven in the canal bed. But over time the old channel of the Lopburi River along the north of the city shrank and had to be occasionally dredged.

The early walls were made of earth, probably dug from the network of canals. In 1549, as the Burmese threat loomed, "the King had the walls of Ayutthaya built for the first time," probably meaning built with brick for the first time. Van Vliet notes in the *Description* (p. 110), "This wall has been for the greatest part renewed in 1634, and provided with a heavy stone footing." In the 1680s, on the south and north sides the walls were "four fathoms and a half high, clean, well condition'd and adorn'd with Battlements" (Kaempfer 1987: 42). Some five or six canals ran north-south across the island, and another two or three east-west, to drain the marsh and carry water to the settlements. Van Vliet wrote in the *Description* (p. 114): "Through Judia there are running eight rivers." At the entrance to these canals were distinctive water gates. Van Vliet counted seventeen. In a few places, the canals were crossed by stone-built bridges, but most of the bridges were narrow bamboo constructions. According to Kaempfer (1987: 44), "there are no Wagons, nor carts in this place."

THE PORT AREA

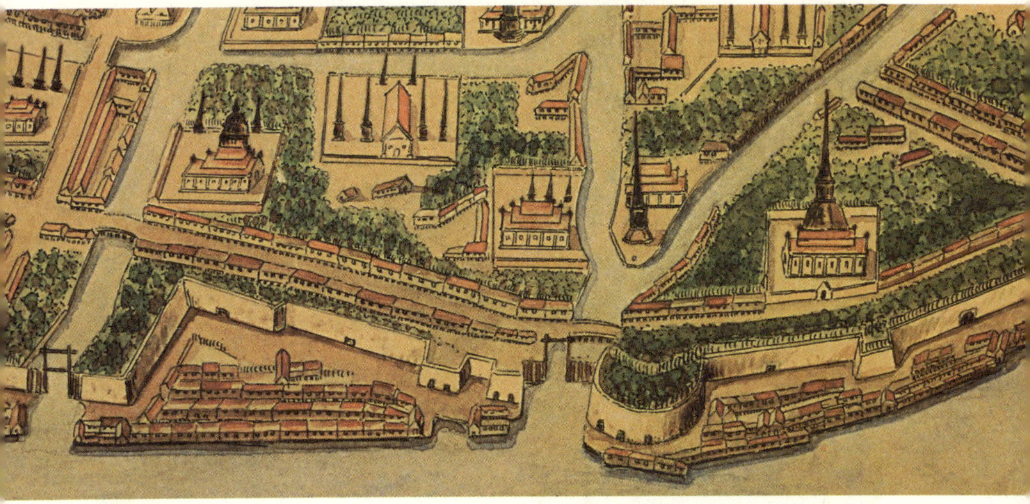

Port area on Vingboons map

The port was situated on the southeast corner of the island. Here, a jumble of houses spread along the riverbanks below and outside the walls. The houses were crammed together several ranks deep. Some jutted out over the water. Three water gates led into a network of waterways that spread westwards along the southern rim of the island. Schouten (1935: 97) noted that "the Citizens have an incredible number of small Boats or Prawes." The canals were interlaced with roads, and both were lined tightly with small houses raised on stilts. Behind these houses were areas of greenery and several temples. Wat Suwantharam (or a predecessor) is visible to the east of the port. Close by is something that may be the Chinese temple marked on Lamare's map.

La Loubère (1691: 44) wrote that only this southeastern quarter was thickly populated and the "rest lies desart where the temples only stand." But he was exaggerating a bit.

Market area on Vingboons map

THE MARKET AREA

According to Schouten (1935: 97), "The Streets of the walled Town are many of them large, straight, and regular, with channels running through them, although for the most part of small narrow Lanes, Ditches, and Creekes most confusedly placed." Some of the main streets were paved with brick. In the 1680s, two of the most important ran west from the port area and then north to the center of the island. On Lamare's map the first of these is labelled as Chinese Street. The second runs northwards alongside a canal, and is shown on the early Dutch maps lined with twin rows of continuous houses. According to Kaempfer (1987: 44) these two streets were lined by over a hundred houses "belonging to the Chinese, Hindostanians and Moors… They are all built alike of Stone [probably brick], very small, being but eight paces in length, four in breadth and of two Stories." No traces have survived, but the remains of houses that fit this description can still be seen in Lopburi.

Later maps such as Coronelli's show these houses as more of a jumble, which is probably more realistic. According to Nicolas Gervaise (1998: 33), another visitor in the 1680s, around the island center was the largest and densest settlement, mainly of Siamese "artisans":

> It has numerous wide streets with shops on both sides, and spacious squares for the markets. The markets are held every day, morning and evening, and are abundantly supplied with fish, eggs, fruit and vegetables, and an infinite quantity of other things

Remains of market houses in Lopburi

But meat is not sold there at all. The throng of people there is so great that it is sometimes very difficult to make one's way through. Most of the streets are lined with fine trees.

THE GARDEN AREA

Northwards from the port along the eastern side of the island is an area that used to be outside the walls until the rebuilding around 1580. On Lamare's

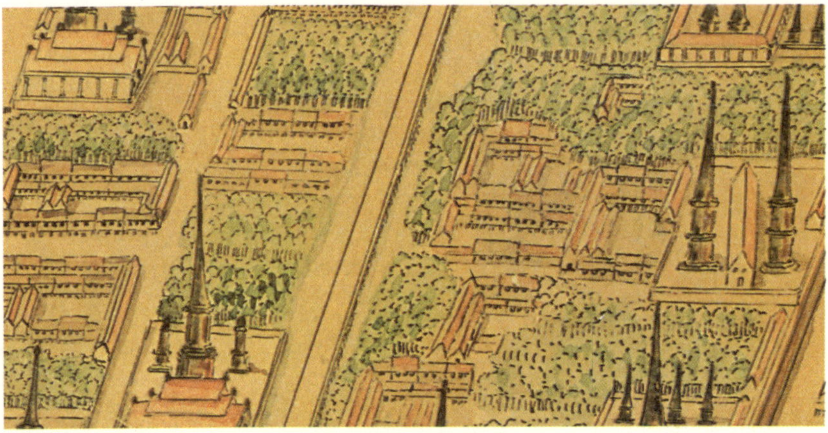

Garden area on Vingboons map

map this is marked as a rural or rather rural area (Quartier champêtre, Quarter fort champêtre). To the southwest is another area, similarly labelled, which used to be called *suan luang*, the royal park. Kaempfer (1987: 42–3) noted that the city was

> in some parts but thinly inhabited, particularly on the West side on account of its remoteness, and towards the South by reason of the morassy ground, over which people make shift to go upon planks or paltry bridges. This makes that in those parts there are abundance of empty spaces and large gardens behind the streets, wherein they let nature work, so that they are full of grass, Herbs, Shrubs and Trees, that grow wild.

The early maps and Judea painting show these areas were not totally uninhabited, but sprinkled with temples, and with village-like settlements nestling among the greenery around these temples. According to Van Vliet,

> the common and poor people live very poorly in reed and bamboo houses. The roofs are covered with cocos leaves or bad tiles, the floor of all houses is usually 4 to 6 feet above the ground and the houses have no story or garret. Most times there is a front and a back door but these are far from being good. Their sleeping rooms and resting places are bad, without any decoration and without curtains; the people sleep on stitched matrasses or twisted such. The noble, rich and poor alike, do not need more furniture than is necessary for sleeping, cooking and eating (p. 162).

In 1685, the Abbé de Choisy reported on these houses, "We entered one of them prepared to see the peasants in rags, but all was spick and span, the

Palace and stables on Vingboons map

floor covered with mats, Japanese coffers and screens everywhere. Hardly inside the door, they offered us tea in porcelain cups" (quoted in Collis 1982: 47). Possibly this was not such an ordinary household as the Abbé imagined.

THE ROYAL QUARTER

The king's palace was situated in the northwest, on the opposite corner to the port. Schouten (1935: 97) remarked it for "resembling a little Town apart, great and magnificent, many of its Buildings and Towers being entirely gilded." Van Vliet noted the palace had recently been renovated: "At the land side there is a large square which lately has been surrounded by a stone wall. Only one street and two little pathways lead to the palace: so that it is now better protected against an attack of the population during times of revolution or of neighboring enemies." On the Vingboons map, we can see roadblocks along this street, and a single narrow gate at the southeast corner of the palace compound. Tachard, visiting the palace in 1687 (after Narai had again modified it extensively), described passing through five courtyards before reaching the main audience hall. Van Vliet mentions a roofscape of five towers, and the Vingboons map shows these may be Wat Phra Si Sanpet, a main palace building with a tiered roof, a smaller hall, and two temples with *prang*-like towers at the rear.

The royal axis extends westwards and eastwards from the main palace. Lamare's map has a large compound to the west labelled as the temple where the king (Narai) was bought up. More likely this is the "front palace," the residence of the *fai na* or *upparat*, the "second king" or heir apparent. On the Vingboons map, at this site there is a compound with a palace-like building

Elephant street on Vingboons map

and an elaborate temple to its rear. Later this location became the *wang lang* or rear palace.

Around the palaces, the Vingboons map shows several areas of dense settlement, presumably the residences of those members of the palace household not housed in the outer courtyards. Just above the front palace, the map shows what looks like an artificial mound, and a cluster of wooden stakes. The mound is reminiscent of the artificial "mountains" often found in palace or wat complexes. Perhaps this was some sort of recreation area.

The royal axis also continues eastwards from the main palace across the northern rim of the island. Northernmost and nearest the river is a street that Lamare labelled as Elephant Street. On the Vingboons map this is lined on both sides by buildings that may be elephant stables. According to Van Vliet, the king had three special elephants – "the white, red, and round tailed elephants" – probably housed inside the palace. In total there were 400 to 500 elephants around the city, and over 150 used in the royal procession to Wat Mahathat.

This Elephant Street and its lining of stables stretches across to the eastern corner, passing the Chankasem Palace, the "new palace" built by Naresuan towards the end of the sixteenth century. Later (possibly during Narai's reign) this became the "front palace."

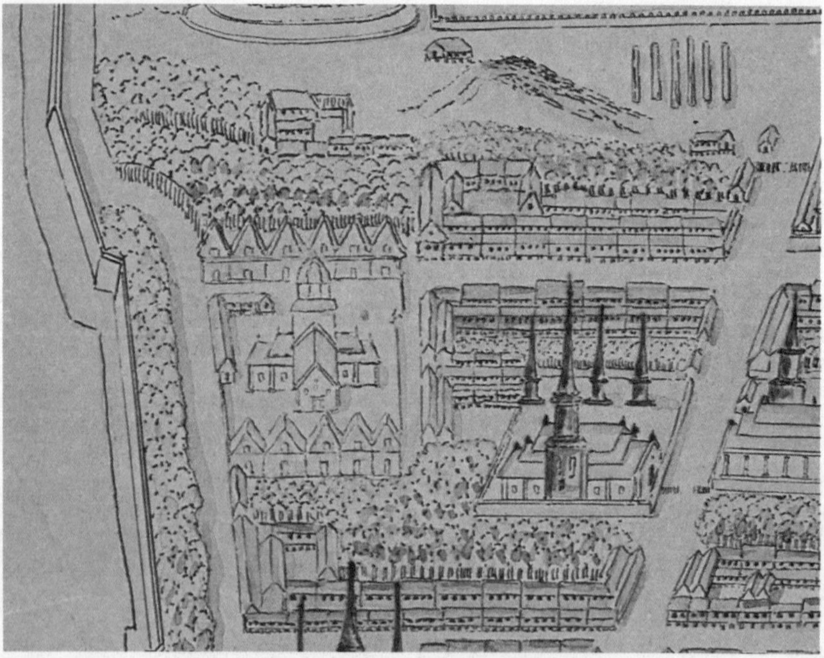

Front palace on Vingboons map

THE RELIGIOUS FOCUS

The city is dotted with temples. Schouten estimated 300, and Van Vliet raised this to 400 or 450 "which are very well built with many towers and pyramids, of which almost every one is gilded." On the maps, the *wat* are scattered throughout the island, but the main religious focus is along the central belt, which divides the royal area to the north and east from the commercial area to the south and west.

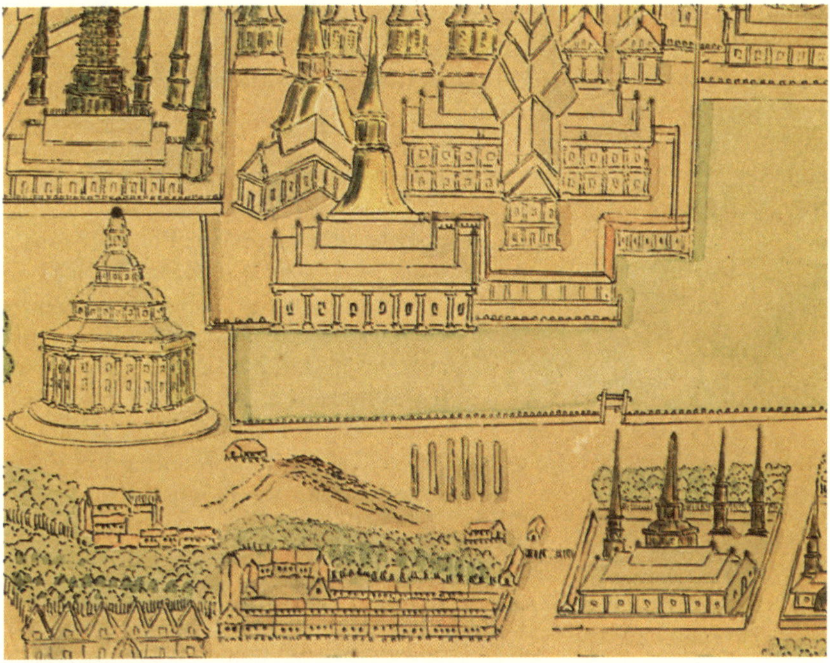

Wat Phra Mongkhon Bophit, Wat Phra Si Sanphet, Wat Phraram on Vingboons map

Towards the western end of this belt is Wat Phra Si Sanphet, the temple of the palace, enclosed within the new outer courtyard. On the Vingboons map, it consists of a single tall *mondop* or *wihan*, housing a massive Buddha image made in early Ayutthaya. Entering this temple in 1687, the Jesuit Guy Tachard (1981: 181) gulped, "There is nothing to be seen but gold.... It must needs touch one to the quick to see one single Idol richer than all the Tabernacles of the Churches of Europe."

To the west of Wat Phra Si Sanphet on the Vingboons map is a curious but large circular building. This may be the *mondop* covering the massive Phra Mongkhon Bophit bronze Buddha image. The current site of this image is actually south rather than west of Wat Phra Si Sanphet, and the building was a spired canopy sheltering the image that had earlier stood in the open;

the distortions of place and design may have resulted from the process whereby these maps were drawn. Alternatively, the image may have been moved. It had been moved once before this *mondop* was built at the start of the seventeenth century and may have been moved again when the *mondop* was replaced by a *wihan* in the eighteenth century.

A little to the southeast stands Wat Phraram, founded according to legend in 1369. One version of Lamare's map labels it the "Grand pagode." The Vingboons map shows a large central *chedi* flanked by two smaller ones, and a *wihan* beside them. Tachard visited here too and described the five central gilt *chedi*, a forest of smaller *chedi* and *prang* around the base, and a surrounding cloister with a painted and gilt ceiling housing some 400 "very well shaped" images. Tachard (1981: 183–4) noted, "We never saw a Fabrick, no not in France, where Symmetry is better observed, either for the body of the building or the Ornaments about it, than in this Pagoda." More generally, he commented: "They do not equal our churches in bigness, but far exceed them in outward beauty."

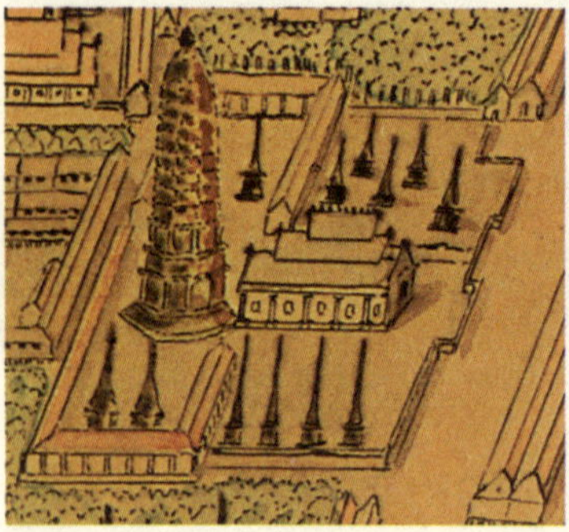

Wat Mahathat on Vingboons map

Eastwards from Wat Phraram runs a road, labelled as Wat Mahathat Road on Lamare's map. Wat Mahathat was clearly the largest and most elaborate temple complex in the city. According to legend, it was built in 1374. Its main tower had collapsed in the 1620s and was rebuilt by Prasat Thong, probably during Van Vliet's sojourn. The Vingboons map shows a single large *prang*, a *wihan*, a cluster of twelve smaller *chedi* (probably meant to stand for many more), several smaller edifices, and a large cluster of what may be *kuti* (monks' residences) to the rear.

Of the thirty or so temples marked on Lamare's map (and hence possibly the most prominent), around half lie in this central belt running from Wat Phra Si Sanphet to Wat Mahathat and further southeast towards the commercial area. Most consist of a single central *chedi* and a *wihan*. A few have a *prang* rather than a *chedi*. Some have clusters of smaller *chedi* around the main building. None except Wat Mahathat is named on the maps, and no others can be identified with much certainty. One of the complexes on the eastern side of the commercial street may be Wat Khun Muangchai, said to have been one of the city's most important temples (Tri 1972: 29).

This central belt was also the site of the great noble households. They clustered around the palaces and main temples. Lamare's map has a street running south from Wat Phraram labelled as Phrakhlang Street. In contrast to the bamboo houses of the ordinary people, "The houses of the mandarins and rich men are made of wood; the wide walls and front are provided with panels and the roofs are covered with red earthen tiles" (see *Description*, p. 162). The most important nobles had several hundred dependants, and these lived in compounds around the noble residence. Kaempfer (1987: 44) noted, "The Mandarins or Ministers of State and Courtiers live in separate palaces, with Courtyards to them, which are very dirty." On the Vingboons map, Phrakhlang Street and others nearby have clusters of houses among the greenery.

OFF-ISLAND SUBURBS

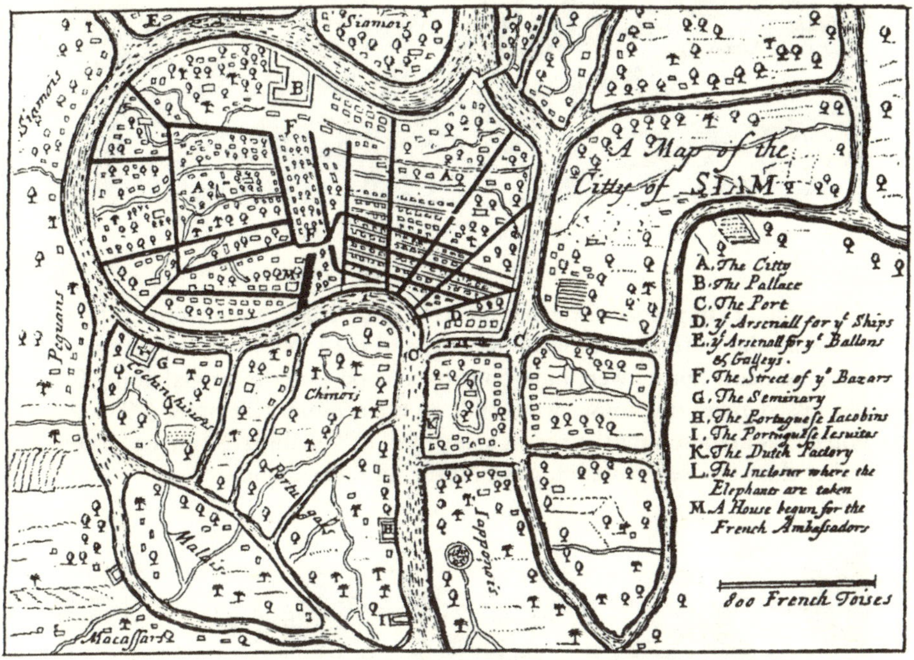

Map showing outer settlements from La Loubère, 1690

The early maps show no settlements or buildings outside the island. But Van Vliet assures us, "All round the town and on the other side of the river there are many villages, residences, houses of farmers, temples, monasteries, and pyramids, and the population here is just as thick as in the town itself." On the 1680s maps, the areas to the northwest and north are occupied by Siamese, while the remainder house the "camps" of the "forty nations," including the Dutch, Portuguese, Chinese, Cochinchinese, Mon, Malays, Japanese, Macassars, Indians and "Moors." These maps also depict patches of what may be raised gardens for growing vegetables.

Village area from Coronelli map, 1680s

Coronelli's impressionistic map, also from the 1680s, shows houses strung along all the waterways around the city, and clustered around many small temples. Most houses were built on stilts to cope with the annual flood. In a few raised areas, the houses were built on the ground. Kaempfer (1987: 49) noted that in these suburban areas many lived in "inhabited Ships, or Vessels, rather than Houses, containing two, three, or more Families each."

Village by river from Kaempfer, 1690

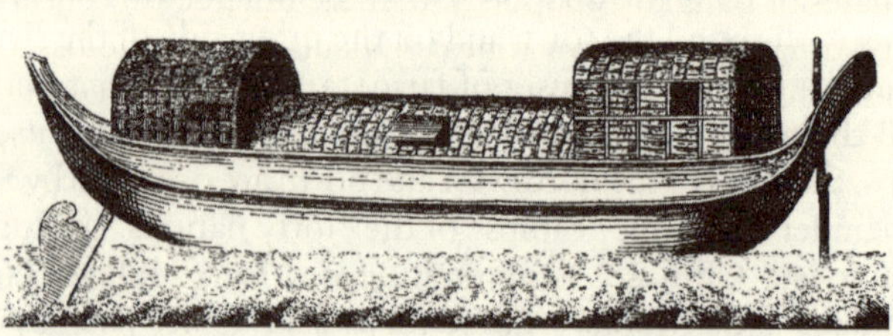

Houseboat from Kaempfer, 1690

These outer areas were also the site of many of the city's most important temples, mentioned by Van Vliet. Some (like Wat Yai) were renowned because of their great age and were located in the old settlement to the east of the island. Others were more recent like Wat Prachet, the site of the *Picnic Incident*. Several were built along the waterways, particularly the Chaophraya running south from the city towards the sea. De Choisy wandered in these suburbs:

> The streets, stretching out of sight, are alleys of clear running water. Under the great green trees and in little houses crowd the people. Beyond these camps of the nations are the wide rice fields. The horison is tall trees, above which are visible the sparkling towers and pyramids of the pagodas. I do not know whether I have conveyed to you the impression of a beautiful view, but certainly I myself have never seen a lovelier (quoted in Collis 1982: 47).

POPULATION

Visitors' assessments of Ayutthaya's size and population varied greatly, mostly according to their political views. An English visitor in 1617 reckoned it "as great a city as London," which had over 200,000 people at the time. Véret, manager of the French company, told de Choisy Ayutthaya was larger than Paris. But in 1687 Count Claude de Forbin (1996: 49) judged it "hardly so big as our towns in France of the fourth and fifth rate."

In the 1680s, Nicolas Gervaise (1928: 33), who had spent four or five years in Siam, wrote,

> The city is so densely populated that, when the king is there, it could easily supply him with sixty thousand men of an age to bear arms, and this number could be doubled, if the inhabitants of the villages on the other side of the river, which can be considered as suburbs, were included.

If that were true, the total population would have been around half a million. The French attending a river procession in 1687 argued among themselves whether the audience thronging the banks amounted to 200,000 or 600,000 (Tachard 1981: 190), but they were probably carried away by the spectacle. European estimates of Bangkok's population in the nineteenth century were also vastly overestimated (up to ten times). Calculating on the basis of the occupied area and a likely density, Anthony Reid (1993: 69–72) has suggested a more realistic figure may be 150,000. His collection of other estimates from the era show it was still probably one of the largest cities in Southeast Asia.

KING PRASAT THONG

Through the late sixteenth century, Ayutthaya was engaged in wars with its neighbors, Burma and Cambodia. These wars probably strengthened the power of the monarch, who was able to mobilize the country's manpower and other resources, but they also disrupted trade. From the accession of King Ekathotsarot in 1605, however, the Ayutthaya rulers turned their attention away from conflict and towards both the development of trade and the enrichment of the royal treasuries. The court and the city prospered, but internal struggles intensified.

At the time of Jeremias van Vliet's sojourn in Ayutthaya (1633–1641), the reigning king of Siam was Somdet Phra Chao Prasat Thong, or King Prasat Thong, also known as King Si Thammarachathirat. Born around 1599, he had come to the throne in 1629 after a violent and protracted court conflict. At the beginning of the succession conflict, he was a leading official (*khunnang*) with the rank and title of Okya Si Worawong. He was related to the royal clan, but not to the main dynastic line (see Appendix III). He then gained promotion to the ministerial rank of Okya Kalahom, in charge of the military wing of the Siamese administrative structure. Displaying a range of Machiavellian political skills, he overthrew the previous dynasty and had several members of the previous royal family executed. With no viable rivals left by 1629, he was crowned king.

The story of this seizure of the throne in 1628–1629 is told in vivid detail by Jeremias van Vliet in his *Historical Account*, one of the key documents for the study of Ayutthayan political history. Indeed, Van Vliet's writings on the king constitute a partial biography of him from his youthful days up till the end of the first decade of his reign. Van Vliet experienced the king's volatile temperament at first hand (see the *Picnic Incident* in this volume). He was also in Ayutthaya at a time when the Dutch were pushing constantly for extra trading privileges. The Dutch wanted contracts on the export of rice and animal skins, especially deerskins, and did not hesitate to ask for them at every opportunity (Smith 1977: 25–35). Such demands and requests inevitably led to tensions in the relationship between the Dutch and the Siamese court. The Dutchman's assessment of King Prasat Thong in his *Short History of the Kings of Siam* turns out to be a curious, ambiguous mixture of the positive and the negative. The king was "warlike in the Siamese fashion, of great wisdom, eloquent and friendly of speech, very religious and devout," but at the same time he was "more avaricious than any other Siamese king," "inclined toward drink and excesses," and "more feared than any other king before him."

King Prasat Thong ruled for 27 years during a time of expanding foreign trade and external relations for Siam. The Siamese crown tried to profit as much as possible from international trade, revenues from which supplemented those derived from taxation. For the Gulf of Siam and South China Sea coast, the city of Ayutthaya became an international entrepôt of regional importance. To the west, the port of Mergui on the Bay of Bengal continued to play a key part of the king's international trading activities (he sent elephants to be sold in India). The Dutch East India Company's increasing interest in the commodities found in Siam stimulated trade in Ayutthaya. The king was able to extract the maximum benefit from international commerce by a system of royal monopolies under which certain goods, such as ivory, could be bought only from the royal storehouses (Smith 1977: 74–5; Dhiravat 1984: 40–3).

The court of Ayutthaya was never free of tension and intrigue at the time when Van Vliet resided in Ayutthaya. Having risen to power from the ranks of the *khunnang* or high officials, King Prasat Thong was naturally wary of his former colleagues and even his comrades-in-arms. As Van Vliet recounts in his *Description* of Siam, the king restricted the movements and activities of the *khunnang* considerably, compelling them to come to court every day, impoverishing their families by seizing as much of their inheritance as possible, and even executing a former ally (Okya Phitsanulok) on a trumped-up charge of treason. During the 1630s the king also used the technique of reshuffling his ministers so as to make them unsure of their political footing and unable to build up a power base in any single department or ministry. King Prasat Thong also called all provincial governors to reside in or around Ayutthaya, sending substitute or deputy governors to the provincial towns instead. Although in this way the king was able to keep closer control over potentially powerful *khunnang*, political conflict was also centralized considerably. The most influential and eminent princes and high officials were concentrated in the Ayutthaya area, and so were their political intrigues.

Officials rose by attaching themselves to powerful patrons. The topmost officials rose by backing successful contenders for the throne. Hence succession struggles were about much more than just the succession itself. Similarly, the members of a deposed royal family continued to pose a threat – or were seen to pose a threat – to a usurper such as Prasat Thong. This applied especially to the princes of King Songtham's family, because Prasat Thong was able to make many of the wives and daughters of the previous king his own consorts. Van Vliet's writings about events in Ayutthaya during King Prasat Thong's reign, used in conjunction with other Dutch documents of that time (many of which were penned by Van Vliet as well), give us a fairly detailed account of the Siamese politics of that period. There was an attempt to overthrow the king in December 1642 by a son of his predecessor King Songtham, and other "conspiracies" were reported in 1636 and 1644 (Dhiravat 1984: 185–8, 216–22). It was not until a few years after Van Vliet's departure that King Prasat Thong managed to eliminate all the princes of the previous royal family.

Not all of the tensions at King Prasat Thong's court came from political issues. While Van Vliet was in Ayutthaya, the king was extremely anxious about the completion of the thousandth year of the Buddhist Lesser Era (*chulasakkarat*), a millenium which was supposed to signal the beginning of an age of calamity (see the account from the Ayutthaya chronicles in *RCA*: 221–5). The king was very active during the 1630s in building and restoring the palaces and monasteries in and around Ayutthaya.[1] As a usurper, King Prasat Thong seemed much concerned to show himself as a man of great Buddhist merit (as opposed to relying on blood claims to the throne). The principal royal monastery built during his reign, Wat Chai Watthanaram, was one of the grandest and most monumental in Ayutthaya.

King Prasat Thong died in August 1656 around the age of 57. Even though he had tried to curb or even destroy the power and influence of the high officials, a violent court conflict involving factions of princes and *khunnang* nevertheless erupted immediately after his death. This was probably because his sons had grown to a politically active age, and at the same time the king, for all his measures against the *khunnang*, was unable to rule his realm without these high officials. In 1656 the king's younger brother Si Suthammaracha and the royal sons Chao Fa Chai and Phra Narai contested the crown. The eventual winner was Phra Narai (r. 1656–1688).[2]

THE DUTCH EAST INDIA COMPANY IN AYUTTHAYA

The Dutch United East India Company (Verenigde Oost-Indische Compagnie or VOC) first entered Siam in 1604, late in the reign of King Naresuan. The initial lure which drew the Dutch to Siam was the China market, or at least the availability in Ayutthaya of Chinese goods such as silk and porcelain. The Dutch admiral Wijbrand van Warwijck, visiting the Sultanate and Siamese tributary of Pattani, was interested in finding out about the possibility of having Dutchmen accompany the annual Siamese tribute missions to the Chinese imperial court (Smith 1977: 11).

These dreams faded quickly for the Dutch, but they found enough commercial interests to keep them in Ayutthaya. A VOC *factorij* (factory or agency) was established in 1608. Initially, the results were variable, resulting in the factory being closed in 1622, reopened in 1624, and closed again in 1629 (Smith 1977: 18–22). In the early 1630s, Japan lifted a ban on foreign trade and then in 1636 forbade its own nationals from participating. This so-called seclusion (*sakoku*) policy meant only the Dutch and the Chinese were

1. VOC 1125, Van Vliet to G-G, 12 October 1637.

2. The best sources for the 1656 court conflicts are *RCA*, 227–43; and VOC 1219, Westerwolt's Report of November 16, 1656.

allowed to trade directly with Japan. The resultant rise in the Siam-Japan trade helped the Dutch to establish a near-permanent presence in Ayutthaya from 1633 until late 1765, when the city was on the verge of being captured by the invading Burmese armies (Brummelhuis 1987: 52–4). Van Vliet was in Ayutthaya during this crucial transition in the Siam-Japan trade. The VOC naturally hoped to profit from the seemingly instant elimination of its Siamese and Japanese rivals, hence its preoccupation with export monopolies and trading rivals.

The Dutch East India Company bought deerskins, rayskins, and sappanwood (a dye wood) from Ayutthaya to sell at the Japanese port of Nagasaki. It also bought forest produce in Siam, such as sappanwood, eaglewood, benzoin, gumlac, deerskins, and ivory, to resell at other ports. The VOC had to rely partly on Siamese rice to feed Batavia and other Dutch outposts in the early years of its presence in Java (Smith 1977: chap. 3–4). Later on the Dutch also bought up tin in southern Siam, trying to obtain tin export monopolies in places such as Phuket, Bangkhli, and Ligor (Nakhon Si Thammarat).

The court of King Prasat Thong had a close, if often uneasy, relationship with the Dutch. From the time of King Ekathotsarot, when the Dutch were offered the use of Mergui as a base, the Siamese had been keen to enlist the Dutch as an ally. During the 1600s the potential or perceived danger to Ayutthaya was the Portuguese adventurer Felipe de Brito and his troops based since 1599 in the port of Syriam in Lower Burma. The Dutch did not accept Siamese offers of the port of Mergui-Tenasserim, but were careful to cultivate good relations with the court of Ayutthaya. In the reign of King Prasat Thong the Dutch were considered to be the Siamese kingdom's ally against the Iberian powers and also against Ayutthaya's rebellious tributaries (Smith 1977: 13–30).

In the time that Van Vliet served at the Ayutthaya factory of the VOC, the Company was involved in Ayutthaya's attempt to subdue the Sultanate of Pattani, which had refused to acknowledge the new king, considering him to be a "murderer" and a traitor to the old royal family. In 1634, the VOC agreed to send six armed ships to help Ayutthaya conquer Pattani (which was being supported by Portuguese Malacca, Johor, and Pahang). What the Dutch wanted in return was an exclusive right to export animal skins from Siam. After negotiations conducted by the Dutch factor Joost Schouten and the Phrakhlang ministry, the VOC was indeed granted the export monopoly on deerskins, but only for a period of one year. It was not until 1646 that the Company was given a permanent export monopoly on animal skins (Smith 1977: 22–8, 61; Dhiravat 1984: 176–85).

Dutch-Siamese military cooperation during this reign did not amount to much in the end in terms of fighting. In 1634 the Dutch fleet arrived too late to save the Ayutthaya forces from defeat at the hands of Pattani. Later on, during a joint expedition proposed by Governor-General Van Diemen, the Siamese and the Dutch were supposed to attack Cambodia (then a common enemy) by sea, but the two fleets again missed each other off the coast of Cambodia (Dhiravat 1984: 223–6). But the Dutch willingness to cooperate militarily with Ayutthaya brought the Company tangible benefits, such as a piece of land on which to build a *factorij* and the export monopoly on animal skins. As the 1650s approached, the VOC changed its policy towards the involvement of the Company's military forces in "native princes'" conflicts. As the Company's resources became uncomfortably stretched owing to its expanding sphere of activities in Asia, it became much more reluctant to help out the King of Siam militarily. When King Prasat Thong attempted on several occasions to subdue Songkhla in the late 1640s and early 1650s with Dutch help, he was increasingly disappointed by the rather half-hearted assistance offered by the Dutch (Dhiravat 1984: 231–40).

During the reign of King Prasat Thong, the Dutch kept up a regular correspondence with the king. While Van Vliet was in Siam, a letter from *stadtholder* Frederik Hendrik, Prince of Orange (the "King of Holland" to the Siamese) was received by King Prasat Thong with much pride, pleasure, and, of course, the appropriate pomp. During the 1640s the Dutch decided that sending embassies bearing the Prince of Orange's letters and gifts to Siam was an unnecessarily extravagant expense. Dutch-Siamese diplomacy could be carried out equally effectively, and at much lesser cost, by the Governor-General and Council in Batavia. The prestige of the VOC Governor-General could also thus be boosted (Smith 1977: 31, 102–4; Brummelhuis 1987: 32; Dhiravat 2001: 114–6). As a result, the Governors-General of the VOC at Batavia wrote and gave presents to the King of Siam every year, and these were reciprocated.

In Ayutthaya itself, the VOC interacted with Siamese court society in order to be accepted as part of that cosmopolitan port society. The *opperhoofd* or chief merchant, having been given a Siamese rank and title by the king, would be expected to attend certain court ceremonies, such as the annual ceremonies of the drinking of "the water of allegiance" swearing loyalty to the king. The Dutch merchants also had to keep on good terms with the Siamese officials with whom they had to deal on a regular basis: translators, harbormasters, and *phrakhlang* ministers. By doing so, the VOC merchants were able to cultivate good contacts that would stand them in good stead when attempting to carry on business with the court (Smith 1977: chapter 5; Dhiravat 1992: 44–62). Without such regular bureaucratic and social contacts, people such as Joost Schouten and Jeremias van Vliet would not have been able to obtain all the data that they did concerning Siamese politics.

THE DUTCH LODGE

Dutch Lodge

In 1632–3, the Dutch received land and permission to build a lodge on the east bank of the Chaophraya River to the south of the city. The two-story structure, enclosed by a stockade, was known to Europeans as "*de logie*" or "the lodge" and to the locals as *teuk daeng*, the red brick building. Only one drawing of the lodge has survived, published in the early eighteenth century (Mandelslo 1727). Clearly finished in Europe, this drawing sets the building against a European mountainscape and a North Sea storm. A smaller representation appears on some of the French maps. During Van Vliet's time, the lodge employed 30–40 people, including merchants, assistants, surgeons, soldiers, sailors and laborers (Smith 1977: 5). Dr Gybert Heecq described it in 1655 as one of the most impressive buildings of the city.[3]

> There is an excellent building, rather large, with high ceilings, roomy and well-designed store-houses behind it. The building itself has a double gabled front with a lot of carved wood decorations over doors and windows.... protected by bars against robbers! The walls are of baked bricks and....thick,

3. This passage was quoted by de Voogd in *The Dutchmen in Ancient Ayuthiya*, tr. I. E. Eisenhofer, 1956; and in Sternstein 1965: 94–5.

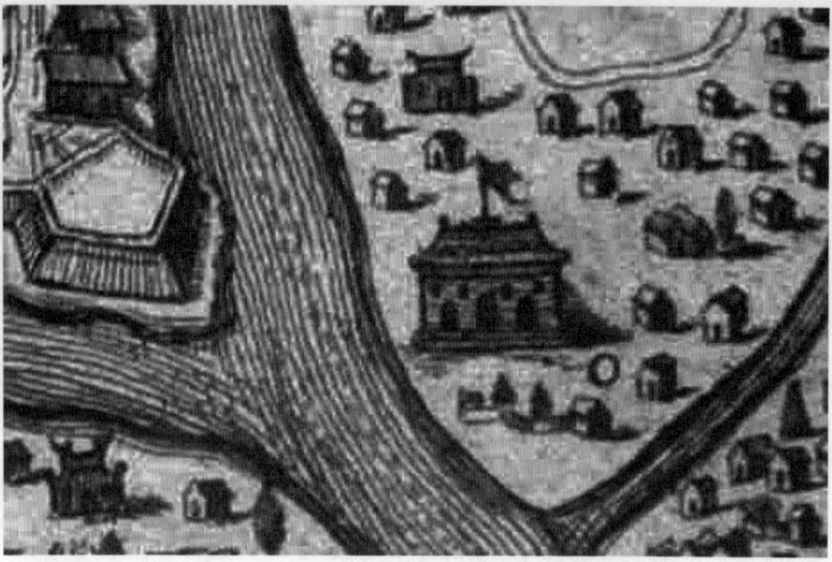

Dutch Lodge from Coronelli map, 1680s

the woodwork is carved and looks much like oak. A double staircase leads to the dining hall behind which, on each side, are smaller rooms. Here lives the manager to the right and the assistant to the left. Besides, the higher employees are accommodated here, according to their rank.

Behind the main building there are several rooms for the other assistants, the surgeon, the bottler, the cooks, the trumpeter, the wood-carvers, carpenters, two blacksmiths and several sailors, among them bookbinders, bakers, horse-grooms, and others. All the rooms are adequately equipped and furnished for the various purposes. Only the barbers – seven in number – have to content themselves with their boats as home, as they have to watch them at the same time. The *factorij* is surrounded by a high bamboo fence along which are built the bottling-rooms, the kitchen, storage rooms, and a mess; the prison, however, is built of stone. There are also stables for about 12 horses. On the other side of the fence are more stables for sheep which are bred here for export; further stables for goats, chicken, ducks, pigeons and even cranes. The last we found running around the lawn....The bamboo fence is made safe against scaling by a wide and deep moat that has a broad outlet under a fortified gate. At the landing on the Bank of the river Chao Phya there is a wide pier for loading and unloading, with comfortable benches to sit and enjoy the river view. Through a wide gate under the main building we reach the ware-houses and beyond, across a wooden bridge, a green field. In the ware-houses are large amounts of timber spread for seasoning. The stone buildings are covered with Siamese glazed tiles; only the stables and the bamboo-huts are covered with palm leaves.

> Entering the main building from the waterfront, we find a fine room with a tiled floor, airy with its many windows... Behind the storehouses there is a small garden with a few lemon, orange, and grenade trees; but it looked quite untidy and abandoned today, as some pagodas were under construction there.

JEREMIAS VAN VLIET AND HIS WRITINGS ON SIAM

Jeremias van Vliet was born in the Holland town of Schiedam in or around the year 1602. Not a great deal is known about his early life, except that he was one of the younger of the five sons of Eewout Huybrechtszoon and Maritge Cornelisdochter van Vliet, who in all likelihood were reasonably well-to-do members of Schiedam's burgher community. After trying his hand at various ventures without a great deal of success, in 1628 Jeremias decided to follow the examples of his two elder brothers, Eewout and Daniel, by enlisting with the Dutch East India Company (VOC) and seeking his fortune in the Indies. Accordingly, in May of that year Jeremias, in the capacity of Assistant (a junior clerk), took ship aboard *Het Wapen van Rotterdam* (The Rotterdam Arms) and set sail for Batavia, where, after a long and perilous voyage around the Cape of Good Hope and across the Indian Ocean, he arrived in February 1629 (*Inventarissen* 1928: 9).

After a few months in Batavia, Van Vliet was ordered to Japan, where the Company maintained an extremely profitable trading post at Hirado. In June 1629, he set sail for this distant destination in a squadron commanded by Willem Jansz, one of the most experienced sea captains in the Company's service, who was dispatched to Japan with instructions to resolve the difficulties that had arisen between the Company and the *Bakufu* (Japan's "curtain government") and to restore normal trading and diplomatic relations. Jansz accomplished this task, albeit with great difficulty, and consequently the Company was allowed to keep its Hirado trading post. Here Van Vliet spent the next three years, during which time he was promoted from Assistant to the rank of Junior Merchant. Apart from furthering his career, Van Vliet became familiar with the Japan–Taiwan–Siam trade, and he witnessed the intensifying Japanese persecution of Catholicism. He also met a number of colleagues who, like Van Vliet himself, were destined to rise to prominence in the service of the Company, people like the remarkable François Caron, one of the first Europeans to thoroughly master the Japanese language, who in 1645 became Director-General of Commerce at Batavia; and Joost Schouten, a future Councillor of the Indies, with whom Van Vliet established close personal and working relations (Boxer 1935: xv–xxx). Schouten wrote a description of Siam on which Van Vliet in part modelled his own *Description*.[4]

4. Joost Schouten was a highly talented man, yet came to a tragic end. In 1644 he was accused of sodomy, a practice which the dour Calvinist merchants at Batavia

In January 1633 Van Vliet was recalled to Batavia where he was assigned to the Senior Merchant Joost Schouten, who had been appointed Director of the Company's factory in Siam a few weeks earlier. At the same time, Batavia decided to make a greater investment in the Siam trade because it had become apparent that Siam's exports, such as deerhides, rayskins, and hardwood, provided some of the keys with which the wealth of Japan, consisting principally of silver and copper, could be unlocked. Consequently, in April 1633, when Schouten and Van Vliet left for Ayutthaya aboard the *Delft*, they carried instructions to build a permanent trading post at the Siamese capital. Upon arrival, Schouten and Van Vliet set about doing just that, and a year later in 1634, after incurring expenses of over 10,000 guilders,[5] everything was ready, enabling them to move the Company's operations from the temporary site in Ayutthaya itself to the new lodge where Van Vliet assisted Schouten in managing the Company's Siam trade. But because Schouten was repeatedly recalled to Batavia and was often away for long periods, the actual task of directing the Company's operations frequently fell to Van Vliet, who, perhaps not unreasonably, began to seek promotion to the rank of Merchant, an endeavor that was crowned with success in July 1636.

It was during one of the occasions when Joost Schouten had once more sailed for Batavia and Van Vliet was again acting Director that the incident occurred which is related in the *Picnic Incident* below. On December 10, 1636, a group of Dutchmen were arrested for acting offensively near one of Ayutthaya's major temples. The King threatened to have them executed and to expel the Dutch from Siam. Van Vliet was obliged to offer an apology, and subsequently travelled to Batavia to explain himself to Governor-General Van Diemen, who believed Van Vliet had handled the incident badly.

---

considered "a filthy and vile sin," so abominable in the eyes of God that He "had destroyed lands and cities with fire from Heaven as an example and warning to the whole world." Curiously, Schouten made no attempt to deny or contest the charges. He freely confessed and admitted to having started the practice in Siam. This meant that his fate was sealed. He was found guilty and was condemned to be burnt at the stake, but in recognition of his achievements and his services to the Company, the Court determined that he be spared the pain of a fiery death and that he first be strangled. After Schouten's strangulation at the stake, his body was burnt to ashes and all his property was confiscated. For a brief biography of Joost Schouten see Boxer (1935: 139–43).

5. This was quite a large sum of money at the time. In seventeenth century Holland, where wage rates were higher than elsewhere in Europe, a skilled tradesman such as a carpenter or stone mason earned an annual salary of approximately 400 guilders. If we assume that today a skilled worker receives about US $30,000 annually, the 10,000 guilders Schouten and Van Vliet spent on the Ayutthaya lodge would have been equivalent to approximately US $750,000.

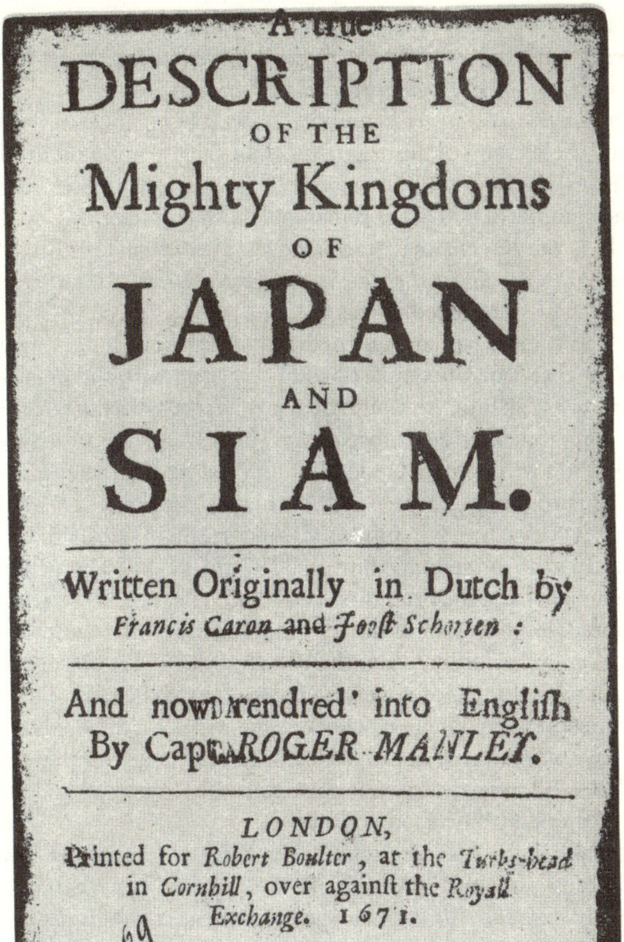

A true
DESCRIPTION
OF THE
Mighty Kingdoms
OF
JAPAN
AND
SIAM.

Written Originally in Dutch by
Francis Caron and *Joost Schouten*:

And now rendred into English
By Capt. *ROGER MANLEY*.

LONDON,
Printed for *Robert Boulter*, at the *Turks-head*
in *Cornhill*, over against the *Royall*
Exchange. 1671.

Title page of English version of Schouten.

When Van Vliet arrived at Batavia in April 1638, he learned, probably to his relief, that Governor-General Van Diemen was away in the Moluccas leading another military campaign aimed at establishing a monopoly over the trade in cloves. While awaiting Van Diemen's return, Van Vliet, who clearly was of the view that the Governor-General needed to be educated about the political realities in Siam, set to work writing a general account of Siam and the Siamese. The result was a pioneering study of the country, which he dedicated to Philip Lucasz, in Van Diemen's absence the highest-ranking official in Batavia. The study appeared in print in 1692 under the lengthy title: *Beschrijving van het Koningrijk Siam, mitsgaders het verhael van den oorsprong, onderscheid, politieke regeering, d'ecclesiastique en costuymelijke huijshoudingen van d'edelen en burgerlijke lieden, alsmede de loop der negotie en andere remarquable saecken des Koningrijks Siam* (Description of the Kingdom of Siam, and the account of the origin, the political government, the distinctive characteristics, the religion, the manner of living of the nobles and common people, the commerce and other remarkable things concerning the Kingdom of Siam). L. F. van Ravenswaay translated the *Description* into English, which was published in the *Journal of the Siam Society* in 1910. That translation of the *Description* is reproduced in this volume.

In July 1638 Van Diemen returned to Batavia from his campaign in the Moluccas, so that Van Vliet at last had his meeting with the man who could either make or break him. Although no record has survived of what transpired at this meeting, the course of subsequent events allows two conclusions to be drawn. Firstly, Van Diemen, evidently mollified by Van Vliet's intelligence, his knowledge of things Siamese, and his highly informative *Beschrijving van het Koningrijk Siam*, forgave him his alleged mishandling of the incident at Ayutthaya. Instead of sending him to Holland in disgrace, which he had probably planned to do, he promoted Van Vliet to the rank of Senior Merchant and appointed him Director of the Ayutthaya factory for a three-year period. Secondly, the discussion between the two men is likely to have centered on Siam's monarchical form of government and on King Prasat Thong. At the end of the meeting, Van Diemen, who was a man of great intellectual curiosity,[6] seems to have asked Van Vliet to inform him more fully on these subjects, a task Van Vliet did indeed carry out during his subsequent period of tenure as Director of the Ayutthaya factory (1638–42).

In accordance with this undertaking, Van Vliet in February 1640 submitted to Van Diemen a manuscript entitled: *Cort Verhael van't naturel eijnde der volbrachter tijt ende successie der Coningen van Siam, voor sooveel daer bij d'oude historien bekent sijn* (The short history of occurrences in the past and the

6. When Van Diemen assumed the Governor-Generalship in 1636, he asked the Directors of the Company's far-flung trading posts and settlements in the Indies to commit to paper some of the things they had learned about the peoples, governments, societies, etc. of the countries in which they found themselves. Some of these works have survived. Charles Boxer, for instance, in 1935 published two of these works in English translation, namely, François Caron's description of Japan and Joost Schouten's work on Siam (Boxer 1935). In addition to promoting an early version of "Asian studies," Van Diemen sponsored, much to the irritation of the Company Directors, who thought it a waste of money, a number of voyages of discovery: the voyages of Abel Tasman to the South Pacific (1642–44) which resulted in the discovery and mapping of much of Australia, Tasmania, New Zealand, and Fiji, as well as the voyage of Marten Gerritsz Vries to the North Pacific (1643), which, although failing to find the fabled Gold and Silver Islands that were believed to be situated to the east of Japan, resulted in the discovery and charting of the Kuril Islands and Sakhalin Island.

succession of the kings of Siam as far as is known from the old histories). In this study based on old Siamese records, Van Vliet explained how the Siamese kingdom had come into being and gave brief accounts of the circumstances under which each of the twenty-five known kings of Siam had come to the throne. This work was not published at the time, but lay in the archives until discovered by Seiichi Iwao in the 1930s, and translated in 1975 as the *Short History* reproduced in this volume.

Some ten months later, in December 1640, Van Vliet presented Van Diemen with a continuation of his *Cort Verhael*, a work specifically focused on King Prasat Thong, entitled: *Historiael Verhael der Sieckte ende Doot van Pra Interra-Tsia, 22en Coninck in Siam, ende den Regherenden Coninck Pra Ongh Srij* (Historical Account of the Illness and Death of Pra Interra-Tsia, 22nd King of Siam, and of the Ruling King Pra Ongh Srij). In this work, based mostly on interviews with historical actors, Van Vliet gave a detailed and compelling account of the rise to power of Prasat Thong, an account in which he demonstrated convincingly that the current King of Siam was a "treacherous usurper," who had seized the throne in 1629 with the assistance of a band of about 800 Japanese mercenaries, and proceeded to eliminate all his political opponents, including the entire legitimate royal family. A French translation of Van Vliet's manuscript by the historian Abraham de Wicquefort was published in 1663 (Herbert 1663). W. H. Mundie translated this French version into English for Prince Damrong Rajanubhab. It was published in Bangkok in 1904 and reprinted in the *Journal of the Siam Society* in 1938. Seiichi Iwao discovered the original in the Dutch archives and published first a facsimile (Van Vliet 1956) and then a transcription of both the Dutch and French versions (Iwao 1958). Iwao's publications showed that the Wicquefort French translation (and hence also Mundie's English one) had been incomplete and sometimes inaccurate. A new and complete translation is included in this volume.

In April 1642, after a term of nearly four years as the Director of the Ayutthaya factory, Van Vliet left Siam never to return. On this occasion, he abandoned Osoet Pegua (also known as Tjau Soet), his Mon concubine of long standing[7] by whom he had three daughters,[8] and on July 31, 1638, shortly

7. Soet was a remarkable woman. Before her liaison with Van Vliet, she had had a son with the Dutch free merchant Jan van Meerwijck; after Van Vliet left, she lived in "open concubinage" with Jan van Muijden, who directed the Ayutthaya factory in 1646–50. She served as the Dutch liaison with Okya Sombathiban, head of the right side of the *phrakhlang*; traded in partnership with the Okya's wife; supplied the VOC with provisions; and had good relations with one of Prasat Thong's queens. She died in 1658 and was buried in the VOC's cemetery (Dhiravat 1992: 11–2; Smith 1977: 99–102).

8. Sadly, many European men in the Company's service deserted their Asian concubines and children. In Siam in the mid-seventeenth century this was so common

after arrival in Batavia, he entered into a conventional marriage with a certain Catharina Sweers. The marriage had advantages for both partners. For Van Vliet it meant that he now had a family connection with the power elite in Batavia, because his new wife was a sister of Solomon Sweers, a member of the Council of the Indies. For Catharina the marriage meant a degree of financial security, because as her brother Solomon confided in one of his letters to relatives in Holland, Van Vliet had accumulated a small fortune estimated at about 30,000 guilders (*Inventarissen* 1928: 10), roughly equivalent to US $2 to 2.5 million in modern terms. It goes without saying that Van Vliet, who had been penniless when he came out to the Indies in 1628, could not have amassed this substantial sum from his Director's salary of 60 guilders per month.

Be this as it may, Van Vliet's family connection with Solomon Sweers, and no doubt also the goodwill of Van Diemen, who appreciated his scholarly work on Siam, stood him in good stead. In September 1642 Van Vliet was appointed to the prestigious post of Governor of Malacca, the city on the Malay peninsula that the Company had captured from the Portuguese the previous year after a long siege. During the next few years Van Vliet's good fortune continued, and in April 1645, a few weeks before the death of Van Diemen, he was appointed Councillor of the Indies. But this was as far as Van Vliet's star was destined to rise. Shortly after the death of Van Diemen, Van Vliet was accused of gross corruption and private trading on a massive scale during his Governorship of Malacca. The matter was investigated, Van Vliet was found guilty, and in August 1646 the Court of Justice at Batavia sentenced him to be suspended from his office, rank, and salary (*Inventarissen* 1928: 11).

Van Vliet, of course, protested his innocence. In October 1646 after two months of litigation, he succeeded in mustering sufficient support on the Council of the Indies to have his suspension lifted. It was, however, a Pyrrhic victory. The new Governor-General, Cornelis van der Lijn, refused to reinstate him as Governor of Malacca and decided instead to send him back to Holland. But probably because Van Vliet, through his brother-in-law Solomon Sweers, continued to have a voice on the Council of the Indies, his repatriation occurred under the most honorable conditions imaginable; in December 1646, he was appointed admiral of a richly laden, homeward bound

---

that in Ayutthaya an informal "orphanage" sprang up for abandoned Eurasian children, an orphanage that was run by a French innkeeper (Van der Kraan 1998: 59–61). Yet not all European men abandoned their Asian concubines. For instance, when François Caron was forced to leave Japan in 1636, he brought his Christian Japanese concubine, by whom he had five children, to Batavia; he recognized his children as legitimate under Dutch law, and sent at least three of them (the boys) to Holland to be educated at Leiden University. Caron married a European wife only after the death in Batavia of his Japanese concubine (Boxer 1935).

fleet of nine ships, an important and extremely lucrative assignment. And so Van Vliet sailed his fleet across the Indian Ocean, around the Cape of Good Hope to the Netherlands, where he arrived safely in August 1647. Notwithstanding his fall from grace, he could look back on his long years in Japan, Siam, and Malacca with a sense of achievement because, as he had intended when setting out for the Indies nineteen years earlier, he had made his fortune and returned to Holland as an admiral and as a man of substantial means (*Inventarissen* 1928: 10–11).

At roughly the time of his return to the Netherlands, Van Vliet's diary of the 1636–37 incident was published. The diary extract had been sent to Van Diemen to inform him of the events that had taken place at Ayutthaya. While he was still in the Indies, Van Vliet, or someone close to him, sent the manuscript to Holland where it was published in 1647 by Jan Jansz in Amsterdam under the lengthy title: *Verhael ende Historisch verhael van 't gene des Vereenighde Oost-Indische Compagnies Dienaers, onder de directie van Jeremias van Vliet, in de Jaren 1636 ende 1637 bij den Koninck van Siam, in de Stadt Judia, wedervaren is. Vervatende de Absolute regeeringe ende strenge wetten der Siammers* (Report and historical account of the events which befell the servants of the United Netherlands Chartered East India Company, under the direction of Jeremias van Vliet, in the city of Ayutthaya, in the Kingdom of Siam, in the years 1636 and 1637. Containing an account of the absolute government and severe laws of the Siamese). The small, leather-bound volume also included a piece on the tyrannical government of Shah Abbas of Persia, as well as François Pelsaert's journal of the disastrous 1628–29 shipwreck of the *Batavia* on a small island off the western Australian coast (Pelsaert 1647). Han ten Brummelhuis and John Kleinen (1980) published a summary of the diary a few years ago. The full diary extract appears in translation in this book as the *Picnic Incident*.

After his return to the Netherlands, Van Vliet largely disappeared from the historical record. A few details are known. First, he never re-enlisted with the Company, although the possibility cannot be ruled out that he may have tried. He would, however, have found it difficult to be accepted. Unbeknown to Van Vliet, the pack of missives and reports which he carried to the Netherlands on his homeward-bound voyage contained a letter from Governor-General van der Lijn to the Company Directors in which Van der Lijn detailed the charges against Van Vliet and recommended that he never again be employed by the Company (*Inventarissen* 1928: 11). Second, as far as is known, Van Vliet never again produced any work of a scholarly nature, although the VOC archives in The Hague contain a large number of highly informative missives, diaries, and letters by Van Vliet dealing with all kinds of problems and issues that occurred during his years in Japan, Siam, and Malacca.

For his remaining years, Van Vliet led the quiet life of a rentier in Schiedam, the town of his birth. During these years he tried with great persistence to gain custody of his three daughters by his former concubine, Osoet Pegua. Repeatedly, he petitioned the Company to use its influence with the King of Siam to obtain the release of the three girls, and the Company, which had a policy of trying to bring to Batavia all the offspring of "Christian" fathers, took up his case on a number of occasions. For instance, when the young Rijckloff van Goens went to Siam in 1650 to investigate reports of corruption at the Ayutthaya factory, he was also given the task of obtaining the girls' release[9] (Van der Kraan 1998: 59–69).

However, all Van Vliet's attempts to be reunited with his daughters stranded on the rock of Osoet Pegua's determination to keep her children with her. Osoet Pegua was in a position to enforce her will in this respect because she was well-connected at court and did not hesitate to use her influence to ensure that King Prasat Thong time and again denied Batavia's requests. Only after Osoet Pegua's death in 1658 did at least one of Van Vliet's daughters, Maria van Vliet, travel to Batavia to join her husband, a certain Junior Merchant de Vos, whom she had married a few years earlier. Whether Van Vliet ever saw any of his daughters again is unknown. However, the possibility cannot be ruled out, because after being elected to the Schiedam town council in 1652, Van Vliet resided in his hometown until his death in February 1663 at the age of 61 (*Inventarissen* 1928: 11).

9. Like others before him, Van Goens, in 1650, failed in his attempts to obtain the release of Van Vliet's daughters. Upon his return to Batavia, Van Goens, who certainly did not lack in courage, offered at his own risk to return to Siam and kidnap the girls. He was prepared to do this as long as the Company "compensated him for his expenses" (Van der Kraan 1998: 70–1).

THE WRITTEN WORKS OF JEREMIAS VAN VLIET

Ongeluckige Voyagie,

Van't

SCHIP BATAVIA,

Nae Oost-Indien.

Uytgevaren onder den E. FRANCOIS PELSAERT:
Gebleven op de Abrolhos van Frederick Houtman, op de hooghte van 28½ graet/ by Zuyden de Linie Æquinoctiael.

Verhatende 't verongheluckien des Schips / en de grouwelijcke Moorderyen onder 't Scheeps-volck/ op 't Eylandt Bataviaes Kerckhof; nevens de straffe der handtdadighers, in den Jare 1628. en 1629.

Nevens een Treur-bly-eynde Ongeluck, des Compagnies Dienaers in 't Jaer 1636. weder-varen, in 't Koninckliicke Hof van *Siam*, in de Stadt *Iudia*, onder den E. JEREMIAS van VLIET.

En de groote Tyrannye van ABAS, Koninck van Persien/ Anno 1645. begaen aen sijn grootste Heeren des Rijcks/ in sijn Koninckrijck Hof tot *Espahan*.

t'AMSTELREDAM,

Voor Joost Hartgerts, Boeck-verkooper in de Gasthuys-Steegh/ bezijden het Stadt-huys/ in de Boeck-winckel. 1648.

JEREMIAS van VLIET,

In den Jare 1636. ende 1637. by den Koningh van Siam in de Stadt Judia wedervaren is. Verhatende de absolute regeeringhe ende strenghe Wetten der Siammers. Gelijck sulcks by den selvigen J. v. VLIET beschreven ende herwaerts over-gesonden is.

1636. Decem. IN den Jare 1636 / den 10 December is den Onder-Koopman Reynier van Tsum met mijn consent/ neffens d' Assistenten Isaac Moerdijck, Joost Laurentsz, Jan Hart, Guiliaem uyt den Hove, Harman van Tetrode, Dirck van der Veen, Daniel Jacobsz Blijswijck, Jacob Woutersz Barbier, Item den Bottelier Gerrit Gerritsz, een blancke Jongen ende twee Swarten met een Praeuw uytghevaren / om de schoonheydt der Rijsvelden te beooghen / ende voorts weynigh vermaeck te nemen; door dien in ettelijcke maenden noch op hooghe noch ghemeene daghen hier gheen rust geweest/

Title page of the original publication of the Picnic Incident, *1648*

DIARY OF THE PICNIC INCIDENT
1636–7

Verbael ende Historisch verhael van 't gene des Vereenighde Oost-Indische Compagnies Dienaers, onder de directie van Jeremias van Vliet, in de Jaren 1636 ende 1637 bij den Koninck van Siam, in the Stadt Judia, wedervaren is. Vervatende de Absolute regeeringe ende strenge wetten der Siammers
(Amsterdam: Jan Jansz, 1647)

Report and Historical Account of the Events which befell the Servants of the United Netherlands Chartered East India Company in the City of Ayutthaya, in the Kingdom of Siam, in the years 1636 and 1637. Containing an Account of the Absolute Government and Severe Laws of the Siamese, as described by Jeremias van Vliet, the Director of the Company's Siam Factory

TRANSLATED, EDITED, AND INTRODUCED BY

ALFONS VAN DER KRAAN

INTRODUCTION

Alfons van der Kraan

THE INCIDENT

ON DECEMBER 10, 1636, a party of about twelve Dutchmen went for a boat ride on the Chaophraya River, became intoxicated, made a nuisance of themselves in one of Ayutthaya's holiest Buddhist temples, got into an altercation with some of the temple's monks, and were arrested. When King Prasat Thong heard of the incident, he became enraged and sent his guards to take charge of the arrested Dutchmen. The guards carried out the order with the greatest zeal, inflicting injuries on many of the Dutchmen before stripping them of all their clothing, tying them hand and foot, and taking them away to the King's palace. Prasat Thong sentenced all the prisoners to be trampled to death by elephants, and placed restrictions on the VOC's trading activities, including banning them from hiring labor, blockading the river, and stationing armed guards at the Dutch lodge.

At the time, Jeremias van Vliet was acting director of the VOC's operations in Ayutthaya while Joost Schouten travelled to Batavia. This document is a copy of Van Vliet's diary from the day the incident happened until the day six weeks later when it was resolved. He relates how he called on all his contacts in the court to save his men from execution; signed a pledge of responsibility for the incident, after which the restriction on labor hiring was removed; and then agreed to perform a ritual of apology before the King, after which the guards were withdrawn and the blockade on the river removed.

THE BACKGROUND

At various points in his manuscript Van Vliet mentions that the people he spoke to, mandarins as well as local merchants, were all astounded at the severity of King Prasat Thong's reaction to the incident of December 10. They were all of the view that while the behavior of the Hollanders at the temple may have been offensive, it did not warrant sentences of death and restrictions on the Company's trade in Siam. So the question arises: why did

Prasat Thong react in this way? Was his reaction to be attributed simply to an outburst of anger, or may he have had some other reasons? While the answer to these questions cannot be known with certainty, a strong circumstantial case can be made that the loutish behavior of this party of Hollanders was not the only reason for Prasat Thong's reaction. He may have harbored a prior grudge against the Company, particularly against the newly-appointed Governor-General Anthonio van Diemen, and used the December 10 incident as an opportunity to teach Van Diemen a lesson.

On September 17, 1636, a few months before the December 10 incident, Joost Schouten had led an official Netherlands embassy to King Prasat Thong. This had been a very elaborate occasion. Schouten had arrived at the mouth of the Chaophraya River with two heavy East Indiamen, the *Leyden* and *Het Wapen van Delft*, each carrying full complements of about 150–200 soldiers and sailors. On the appointed day, Schouten had come ashore at Ayutthaya with a formal guard of honor of some 100 fully armed Company soldiers. He had been received by Prasat Thong with great pomp and circumstance, and at the embassy that followed Schouten had delivered a letter from the Stadtholder of the Dutch Republic, Frederick Henry, the Prince of Nassau, a letter in which the Prince sought to confirm and strengthen the good relations between the Netherlands and Siam.[1] However, in addition to presenting Prasat Thong with various rare and expensive gifts from Frederick Henry, Schouten also gave him a letter from the newly appointed Governor-General of the Indies, Anthonio van Diemen.

In many ways, Van Diemen was a remarkable person. The son of a small town burgomaster (Culemborgh), he was bankrupted when still in his early twenties, and in order to escape his creditors, he enlisted with the Company as a common soldier and under an assumed name. Upon arrival in the Indies in 1618, his intelligence, energy and hard work earned him repeated promotions until on January 1, 1636, he reached the very top of the hierarchy and assumed the post of Governor-General. Van Diemen was a typical representative of Europe's rising bourgeoisie, a convinced Calvinist, a man of republican sentiments who throughout his life had struggled against Catholicism and the monarchical form of government, which to Van Diemen and his contemporaries was represented in its most odious form by Spain,

1. In their dealings with Asian kings and nobles, Company officials tended to ignore or downplay the fact that the Netherlands was a republic, a form of government which in any case would have been incomprehensible (and distasteful) to them. Instead, they overemphasised the powers in the Netherlands of the Princes of Orange, who were stadtholders and not kings, let alone absolute kings. The stadtholder at this time was Frederick Henry, the Count of Nassau (1584–1647), the grandfather of William III (1650–1702), who in 1688 was to realize the monarchical ambitions of his dynasty when he became King of England.

against which the Dutch Republic had been at war since 1568. It is entirely possible that in his letter to Prasat Thong of August 12, 1636, Van Diemen allowed these sentiments to come to the fore, because after the customary niceties and compliments, he took the Siamese king to task for allegedly reneging on an agreement to supply the Company with a certain quantity of rice:

> It has greatly surprised us that in the past monsoon it has pleased Your Majesty to consign to Captain Schouten such a small quantity of rice and padi. Believing the promises Your Majesty had made, we had counted on not less than 800 coyangs and in the expectation [of receiving that amount] we sent our ships to destinations [where rice could not be readily obtained]. In consequence of the unexpected shortfall in rice, the city of Batavia very nearly came to be gripped by famine, which is a most serious matter, a matter completely at odds with our long-established friendship. It is true that rice harvests can vary, but Your Majesty's country has such large stores of that grain that the promised quantity could easily have been consigned to us without exposing Your Majesty's own country, which reluctantly leads us to conclude that Your Majesty has acted against the duty of friendship, and this to such a degree that it seems as if it was Your Majesty's intention to weaken our city through famine and want. Your Majesty should understand in this regard that it was not distress which led my predecessors [as Governor-General] to request rice [from Your Majesty], but the convenient location of Siam, as well as the friendly correspondence between Your Majesty and our Prince. But when we found that Your Majesty's promises could not be relied upon, we employed the means to obtain our rice from other countries, and through God's mercy, we now have such a plentiful supply that we no longer have as great a need for Your Majesty's rice as we had before, so that henceforth we will be satisfied if Your Majesty sends us rice only in years of abundance and only in such quantity as the needs of Your Majesty's own country permit, although we would have appreciated it if Your Majesty, mindful of our alliance, had accommodated us in the past year so that we would not have been forced to obtain rice from other countries and potentates. (Brief Van Diemen, August 12, 1636)

This, of course, was no way to address the King of Siam. At Schouten's embassy on September 19, 1636, a Siamese translation of Van Diemen's letter was read out to the assembled mandarins and courtiers amidst great ceremony. King Prasat Thong had remained impassive and had not responded in any way. Nonetheless, it is almost certain that the King had been deeply humiliated by this very public dressing-down, and it is highly likely that from that moment onwards he had begun to think of ways to avenge himself on the combative new Governor-General. When a few months later a party of drunken Hollanders violated the sanctity of one of the holiest Buddhist temples in

Ayutthaya, he may have thought that the moment had come to crack down on the Company and show Van Diemen that it was unwise to criticize and scold him in this way.

But whatever motives Prasat Thong may have had, Governor-General van Diemen was simply outraged when he returned from a major military campaign in the Moluccas in August 1637 and learned from Van Vliet's report what had transpired in Siam. The principal object of his wrath was the hapless Van Vliet, who, in a very real sense, found himself between the devil and the deep blue sea. In his letter to Van Vliet of September 4, 1637, the Governor-General denied him promotion to Senior Merchant on the grounds that he ought to be content with the "honest rank of Merchant," recalled him to Batavia "to explain himself," and gave him a severe dressing-down:

> Having read your diary about the entirely iniquitous procedures that were instituted in Siam against the Company's people and its trade, procedures it must be said that had been occasioned by our licentious and debauched lads, I must confess that I am extremely upset, and all the more so when I consider the unreasonableness of the Siamese and your cowardice. I cannot comprehend what kind of blood flows through your veins when I read how you tolerated all these prejudicial and shameful affronts; how, on top of everything, you humbled yourself, and crawled along the floor like a delinquent, begging forgiveness for your crimes, which you then accepted gratefully as if it came from God Himself. In truth, I am ashamed when this history comes into my thoughts. Many valuable gifts you have carelessly thrown away, gifts which, instead of bearing fruit, will only give rise to contempt. A comedy they have played with you, and like they do with their buffaloes, they have taken you by the nose and have led you wherever they wanted you to go. (Missive Van Diemen, September 4, 1637)

In addition to scolding him in this way, Van Diemen told the unfortunate Van Vliet how he should have handled the matter:

> You should have demanded that His Majesty release the delinquents forthwith in order to do justice yourself, or alternatively, in order to send them to us together with their accusers. You were very wrong to tolerate these Siamese guards around our lodge. If it was not advisable for lack of numbers to attack them and drive them away by force of arms, you should have abandoned the lodge. That you consented to such vile conditions and that you signed a document to that effect is something I cannot approve. You were not qualified to do this, and you should have refused point-blank, come of it what may. You should have reminded the Siamese that their country is easier to reduce than just about any in the Indies.[2] If you had acted thus, all this trouble and shame

2. Here Van Diemen referred to Siam's geographical configurations. Evidently, he

> would not have come our way, but it seems that you lacked the courage to maintain the Company's rights, for which reason is mystery to me. (Missive Van Diemen, August 25, 1637)

Van Diemen also gave Van Vliet a number of instructions to carry out before returning to Batavia. First, he was to lock in chains the two young Assistants, Joost Laurentsz and Daniel Jacobsz, who had been most guilty of causing the disturbance on December 10. Van Vliet was to make sure that the two prisoners would be led chained together to the ship *Leyden* in full view of the Siamese, so that "the Berckelang and King will hear about it." If the Siamese should ask what would become of them, Van Vliet was only to tell them that he had received orders from the Governor-General to send them to Batavia. At the same time, Van Vliet was to instruct the officers of the *Leyden* that as soon as the ship was under sail, they were to release the two Assistants from their chains and set them free (Missive Van Diemen, August 25, 1637).

Second, Van Vliet was to seek a meeting with the Berckelang (*phrakhlang*). At this meeting, he was to tell the Berckelang that the Governor-General was extremely displeased, both with the way the King had treated his people and with the stationing of guards at the lodge "as if we are thieves and villains," for which reason he had not sent the King the customary letter and gifts; that the Governor-General would under no circumstances be prepared to subject his people to the laws and customs of Siam; that the Company alone would administer justice over its people; that if the King should again institute such "intolerable procedures" against his people, the alliance with the Netherlands would be deemed to have ended, whereupon the Company would withdraw its lodge from Siam and "invest the country," and, finally, that he, Van Vliet, had been recalled to Batavia in order to appear before the Governor-General and report to him in person (Missive Van Diemen, September 4, 1637).

Although it is likely that Van Vliet in his meeting with the Berckelang softened somewhat Van Diemen's ultimatums and threats, it must have been clear to the Siamese mandarin and hence to King Prasat Thong, that the Governor-General was very annoyed and that a breakdown in relations with the Company, or worse, was a real possibility. At any rate, Prasat Thong decided to withdraw from the brink. When Van Vliet left Ayutthaya for Batavia in February 1638, he carried conciliatory letters from the King and the

---

was aware of the vital importance of the Chaophraya River to Siam's communications and external trade, and he realized that by simply blockading the mouth of the river, for which no more than two or three well-armed ships would be needed, it would be possible to cut Siam off from all overseas trade. In the 1660s, when King Narai (Prasat Thong's son) occupied the throne, Governor-General Maetsuycker resorted to precisely this measure, with the result that the King quickly gave in to Dutch demands and signed a treaty favorable to the Company.

Berckelang, letters in which they wished Van Diemen "a long life" and "victory over all his enemies" and assured him that they wanted to maintain "the long-established friendship with the King of Holland and His Lordship, the General" (*Inventarissen* 1928: 10).

THE PUBLICATION

The extract from Van Vliet's diary was sent to Van Diemen to inform him of the events that had taken place at Ayutthaya. Later it found its way to Amsterdam where it was published in 1647 by Jan Jansz.

That Van Vliet's manuscript should have been deemed worthy of publication is not surprising. In seventeenth-century Holland and England, as well as in other European countries, there was a growing interest in the Orient, leading to the publication of a steadily increasing number of books on East Indian voyages and on specific Asian countries. Isaac Commelin's edited work, *Begin ende Voortgangh der Vereenighde Nederlandtsche Geoctroyeerde Oost-Indische Compagnie* (Origins and Progress of the United Netherlands East-India Company), which consisted of a collection of voyages, was published in Amsterdam in 1645–6. Francois Caron's *Beschrijvinge van het Machtige Koninckrijcke Japan* (Description of the Mighty Kingdom of Japan) was first published in book form in Amsterdam in 1648. Rijckloff van Goens' *Javaense Reyse* (Javanese Journey) was published at Dordrecht in 1666, and Robert Knox's *Historical Relation of Ceylon* was published in London in 1681. Naturally publishers, then as now, had at least one eye on market demand, and in choosing amongst the various Indies-related manuscripts that came their way, they emphasized the adventurous, the strange, and the exotic. In addition, they clearly had a preference for material that stressed the tyranny and despotism of Asian kings.

Van Vliet's piece qualified on both counts. Siam was unquestionably an exotic location, and the manuscript dealt in the main with the exercise of power of a despotic king. Again, it is not surprising that seventeenth-century Dutch and English publications should have emphasized the tyranny of Asian kings, because England and Holland at that time were at the forefront of capitalist development and republican change. In 1647, when Van Vliet's piece appeared in print, England was in the midst of a civil war that saw the overthrow of the absolute monarchy and the execution of King Charles I. Holland was already a republic in which power was in the hands of an oligarchy of merchants, an unusual (and much despised!) political formation on a continent still very much dominated by absolute monarchies, such as France, Spain, Sweden, and Russia. These accounts of Asian despotism provided the rising bourgeois classes of Holland and England with one more weapon in their ideological struggle against Europe's traditional monarchical order.

They could play this ideological role, not because they almost invariably featured cruel and sadistic punishments, since European criminal law, including that of England and Holland, was hardly any more enlightened, but because they drew attention to the *arbitrary* way in which Asian kings could exercise power. What the good burghers of Holland and England would have found abhorrent about Van Vliet's account was not so much the sentences of death in themselves (although there may have been some fascination with the unusual way the condemned men were to be put to death), but rather that the men were sentenced to death without due process, without having had a chance to defend themselves, without recourse, and simply at the whim of a king. What the burghers would have found abhorrent was the complete absence in Siam of any legally based security of life and property, so that men could be stripped of their property and be sentenced to death for no other reason than that a king, who might just be in a bad mood, decided that this should be so. Reading accounts such as Van Vliet's would have strengthened these burghers in their conviction that the freedoms and rights that they and their immediate ancestors had won at such great cost in their own countries were worth fighting for and, if need be, dying for.

Wat Worachet, Ayutthaya, 2003

REPORT AND HISTORICAL ACCOUNT OF THE EVENTS

which befell the Servants of the United Netherlands Chartered East India Company in the city of Ayutthaya, in the Kingdom of Siam, in the years 1636 and 1637. Containing an Account of the Absolute Government and Severe Laws of the Siamese, as described by Jeremias van Vliet, the Director of the Company's Siam Factory.[1]

December 10, 1636

On December 10 of the year 1636, the Junior Merchant Reynier van Tsum and the Assistants Isaac Moerdijck, Joost Laurentsz, Jan Hart, Guiliaem uyt de Hove, Harman van Tetrode, Dirck van der Veen, Daniel Jacobsz Blijswijck, Jacob Woutersz Barbier, as well as the steward Gerrit Gerritsz, a white boy, and two blacks, went sailing in a proa in order to behold the beauty of the rice fields and also to take a little pleasure. [They went on this outing][2] with my permission because for several months, on Sundays as well as on weekdays, we had all been very busy, and this day just happened to be a quiet one. But due to willfulness or wanton thoughtlessness of the Assistants Joost Laurentsz and Daniel Jacobsz, as well as the carelessness of the rest of the party (God improves), this day of merriment ended in great sadness, because before the day was done, the entire party found itself in mortal danger, while those of us who had stayed in the lodge were also in peril, as will become apparent from the account that follows.

The aforementioned persons went to Boeretiet[3] (one of the three principal temples in and around the city), which is situated on the other side of the

1. In order as much as possible to retain authenticity, all Siamese personal and place names have been left as they appear in Van Vliet's manuscript, even though it is obvious that many of these names were corrupted either by Van Vliet himself or, as seems more likely, by the clerk who made the particular copy of the original manuscript that was used in the preparation of the 1647 publication. In cases where more accurate spellings of Siamese names could be surmised, these have been indicated in italics.

2. Passages in square brackets have been inserted by the translator to improve the flow of the narrative. Passages in round brackets appear as such in the original manuscript.

3. This is probably Wat Worachet (วัดวรเชษฐ์), which is outside the moat, about a kilometer to the west. It is roughly "right opposite" the palace complex, which appears clearly on seventeenth-century Dutch maps of Ayutthaya (especially Vingboons map from the 1660s) as the largest palace after the main one; later this site was known as the Rear Palace (*wang lang*) but it may have been the Front Palace in this era (see *KCKK*: 101, which indicated the Front Palace is on the western side. In the account

river, a short distance inland, right opposite the Prince's palace. There they had their meal, and after they had made merry with a little drink, all of them except Joost Laurentsz and Daniel Jacobsz stepped back into the proa intending to return to the lodge. The two Assistants, however, (who were drunk), wanted to walk back to the river (because there was such a good footpath), and the others (not suspecting any trouble) let them go on their way. But once the aforementioned Joost and Daniel (according to the testimony of the Siamese) were under way, they behaved very willfully and spitefully against all Siamese who crossed their path, calling some of them names, hitting others, rudely entering some houses, taking food from these houses, etc. Finally they came upon the river, precisely at a place where a number of servants of the Prince were sitting, namely some proa keepers and several fellows with painted arms.[4] Also these people they rashly assaulted.

---

below, the Phrakhlang calls Boeretiet "one of the holiest temples in Siam, a temple frequented by the King himself, who often goes there to pray and to make offerings both to the temple itself and to the Religious," and the King calls it "my temple" (see p. 87). Recently restored, Wat Worachet is an impressive complex, with a large *ubosot*, a *wihan*, two *chedi*, and a *prang*. The style, especially of the central *prang*, is strikingly similar to the central *prang* of the nearby Wat Chai Wattanaram which, according to the chronicles, Prasat Thong built shortly after his accession on the site of his mother's house and hence in her honor (*RCA*: 215, ll. 42–49). The fact that Van Vliet does not mention Wat Chai Wattanaram and identifies Boeretiet so closely with Prasat Thong suggests that in 1636 Wat Chai Wattanaram was not yet built or not yet finished. Perhaps Prasat Thong initially built, or patronized, Wat Worachet and then later the grander Wat Chai Wattanaram about one kilometer away. In the *Historical Account*, in the passage referring to 1637–8, Van Vliet mentions "the King's temple . . . under construction" (see p. 318). Sources mention a Wat Worachet that was built thirty years before Prasat Thong by King Ekathotsarot to honor his predecessor, Naresuan (*KCKK*: 93; *RCA*: 199–200). Probably this was not the temple referred to here, but one now known as Wat Worachetaram, situated on the island just west of the main palace complex.

An alternative interpretation would be that Van Vliet's Boeretiet was actually Wat Chai Wattanaram, which had not yet acquired that name. Wat Chai first appears on foreign maps in the 1680s, labeled with names ("the Golden Pagoda," "the Royal Pagoda," "the King's Golden Pagoda") that suggest it enjoyed continuous royal patronage. Piriya Krairiksh (2000: 186–92) suggests it may have been called Wat Pallankara Aramwihan, and have been renovated and enlarged between the 1730s and 1750s. Perhaps it was originally called Wat Worachet (the area in which both temples are located was known as Thung Worachet/Prachet), and was subsequently renovated and renamed under successive reigns. However, the location in this passage (opposite the palace and a "short distance inland") fits Wat Worachet better. On Sumet Jumsai's reconstructed map of old Ayutthaya, there is a canal starting opposite the palace and leading directly to Wat Worachet. This could have been the picnic party's route.

4. Elsewhere in Van Vliet's manuscript, the "fellows with painted arms" are described

The Prince's slaves, however, took to flight, but once they saw that the two drunk Hollanders were by themselves, they took courage, seized Daniel and took him to the palace of the Prince.[5] Joost, however, managed to escape by running headlong into the river.

Just at this moment, the rest of the party, unaware that anything untoward had occurred, came down the river in their proa. [They sailed along] until a certain Peguan woman called out from the riverbank warning them that their companions were in trouble; but when they arrived at the place where the fight had occurred, they did not see anyone. Finally, they noticed Joost swimming in the river, but when at last they reached him, he was so exhausted that he was unable to tell them what had happened. Just then they saw that Daniel had been seized and that he was being taken away. Without knowing who had seized him or where they were taking him, they thoughtlessly decided to follow the Siamese (who had seized Daniel) in order to find out how the altercation had come to pass. And even though they saw that Daniel was being taken to the palace, they continued to follow the Siamese, [and when they had arrived at the palace] the Junior Merchant Reynier went ashore intending to speak amicably to the Siamese. But before he or anyone else had had a chance to speak to anyone, an angry crowd of Siamese began to throw rocks down at them from the city walls, which they did so fiercely that our men decided to retreat to the proa, intending to sail away.

In the meantime, the Siamese told the Prince that the Hollanders, in a strongly manned proa and armed, had attacked his people at the gates of his palace. Grabbing hold of a saber, His Highness asked them how the Hollanders had come, whether their Captain was with them and whether they had come to invade his palace? The Siamese replied that they did not know anything about the Captain, but that the Hollanders outside the palace had been playing at Boeretiet on the other side of the river, that some of them had committed wanton acts against the servants of His Highness, whereupon one of the Netherlanders had been seized and had been brought

---

by the Portuguese-language term *braspintados*, which literally means "painted arms." According to Engelbert Kaempfer (1987: 46), who visited Siam in 1690, the word *braspintados* refers to the royal guards, who were tattooed on the arms as a mark of their status and function and who, he said, carried "short, thick clubs, roving and sauntering about the palace like idle vagrants."

5. The Prince mentioned here, and elsewhere called the Crown Prince, is Prasat Thong's younger brother, Phra Si Suthammaracha, who was named the *fai na* (ฝ่ายหน้า, front prince) or *upparat* (อุปราช), implying he was the nominated heir. It appears Prasat Thong later became suspicious that his brother might plot a rebellion, and he may have been sent to reside in Phitsanulok between 1644 and 1652. By the time he returned, Prasat Thong's sons were jockeying for the succession. Si Suthammaracha succeeded to the throne in 1656 but was dislodged by Narai after less than three months and executed (see Dhiravat 1984: ch. 4).

here. It is possible (said His Highness), that they are all drunk, and that they have come to rescue their companions. Go grab them, but do not hurt or kill anyone; tie them up, take them to the Berckelang[6] and tell their Captain how unreasonably his people have behaved themselves. At this order, a host of proas immediately appeared on the river and overpowered our men. They fell upon our people and struck them with spears, bared swords, and so on as if they wanted to kill them all. Our men, who were without firearms, and who had not expected this, did not resist, so that all of them were badly hurt. [After they had been overpowered], they were stripped naked, tied hand and foot, and in this way they were taken to the Berckelang.

At nightfall, rumors reached the lodge that our men had been in a fight with the slaves of the Prince and that several Netherlanders had been seized. When our people failed to return home in the evening, we had to accept that these tidings were true, but even so, I could not bring myself to send some other Netherlanders to the palace for fear that these innocents, too, should be exposed to danger. Moreover, the river had been closed off so completely that there wasn't as much as a small proa to be seen. I consulted with Mr Verwer, and after some deliberations, we decided to send Ian Iaclijns (a mestizo, born in Paliacatta,[7] who speaks good Siamese), to the palace with one or two of our Siamese servants in order to find out what had happened. When they arrived there in a small proa, they discovered that the palace was heavily guarded and that no one was even allowed to sail past. They were seized by the people of the Prince and taken into the palace, where they were closely questioned. But unable to find them guilty in any way, they released them and allowed them to sail back to the lodge; but, nonetheless, this delay meant that it was past midnight before they returned home.

Around midnight the interpreters Omon Wytsit Bassa[8] and Olong Phit Parap[9] arrived at the lodge; they had been sent by the Oya Berckelang to tell us that what had happened, which, according to them, was the following: "That the Netherlanders, who early in the day had gone on an outing in a proa, had taken their pleasure in the temple Boeretiet; that they had entered the temple against the wishes of the monks; that the Siamese had taken great offense at this (because they regard this temple as a holy place), that there had been discord between the Netherlanders and the monks, and that they had left the temple only after many threats and the strong insistence of the

6. The Okya Phrakhlang (ออกญาพระคลัง), see Appendix I.

7. At Palliacatta (modern Pulicat in southeastern India) the VOC had a substantial presence. Some fifteen years earlier, the Company had constructed a fortress there named "Geldria," which was the seat of the Governor of the Coromandel coast and which served as the Company's principal stronghold along that coast.

8. Okmun Wichit Phasa (ออกหมื่นวิจิตรภาษา).

9. Okluang Pith Parap.

monks. That on the road between Boeretiet and the great river a few of the Netherlanders had adopted an extremely dissolute and peevish posture towards several Siamese, and finally, that they had not respected the Prince's slaves, but that they had called them names and had assaulted them, whereupon these slaves had seized some of them and had taken them to the palace of the Prince."

"That the remaining Netherlanders (on hearing that some of their companions had been seized) had wanted to force their way into the Prince's palace in order to release the prisoners and, by doing this, that they had violated His Highness, which was an extremely serious offense. That the Prince (in accordance with the laws of the country) would have been entitled to order all those who had entered his palace to be beaten to death, but that His Highness had refrained from doing this out of respect for the firm friendship between his brother, the King,[10] and the Prince of Holland[11] and His Lordship, the General[12] for which reason he had told his slaves not to hurt or mistreat any of the offenders, but only to seize them and to take them to the Berckelang. That the people of the Prince had taken the Netherlanders to the Berckelang; that the Berckelang had ordered all of them to be released from their bonds and that he had allowed them to spend the night in his pleasure garden where they would be well treated."

I replied that I was deeply saddened by these tidings and that I most strongly disapproved of the actions of our people. I told the interpreters to thank His Honor [the Berckelang] for his kindness in having released our people from their bonds and to relay my request that they be sent home during the night. [I further told the interpreters to ask the Berckelang], if it was possible, to keep the whole incident from the King, and to assure the Berckelang that I would most sharply investigate the deeds of our people, that I would punish the guilty, and that I would ensure that such mischief would not recur in the future. The interpreters seemed pleased with this reply and promised to relay everything to His Honor. They declared, however, that the Berckelang could not hide these facts from His Majesty and that our people, necessarily, would have to stay with the Berckelang until he had discussed the matter with His Majesty. But they assured me that His Honor would bring everything to a good end because, they said, he is a powerful Lord and a good friend of the foreigners, especially the Netherlanders.

10. King Prasat Thong.

11. "The Prince of Holland," or more correctly, the Stadtholder of the Netherlands, at this time was Frederick Henry (1584–1647), the Count of Nassau.

12. The Governor-General Anthonio van Diemen (1593–1645).

December 11, 1636

Before sunrise on the morning of December 11, I went to Radie Ebrehem,[13] a Muslim merchant and one of the slaves of the Prince,[14] because he was a friend who, I knew, was quite influential at the court. I told him what had happened and induced him to go immediately to the palace to ask His Highness to amicably settle the difficulties that had arisen between his slaves and the Netherlanders, to send the Netherlanders home to me, and to keep the whole incident from the King. I added that he could assure His Highness that I would most sharply investigate the whole matter, that I would punish the guilty, and that I would act in such a way that the demands of both His Highness and of justice would be fully satisfied. Radie Ebrehem promised to carry out my request.

From there I went through to the Oya Berckelang with the intention to seek the release of our people through gentle and polite persuasion. When I arrived at the Berckelang's house, I was told that he had arrived at his reception chamber at sunrise (to question our people), but that as soon as he was seated, about one hundred *Braspintados* (sent by the King) had arrived, who most unceremoniously had seized our people, had stripped them naked, had tied them hand and foot, and in this way had taken them to the court. [I was further told] that the Berckelang, the Shahbandar,[15] and the interpreters had followed the soldiers to the court — all of which, to my regret, led me to conclude that the King had learned of the incident, that he was extremely angry, and that as a consequence our people were in mortal danger.

I sent Alexander Pinieur, a mestizo[16] (one of the Berckelang's people and a very good friend of ours), to the court to tell the Berckelang that I had come to his house in person to ask His Honor's intercession and to request that our people be freed. [I further told Alexander] to remind His Honor of the long-standing friendship between the Netherlanders and the Kingdom of Siam, to ask him to soothe the King's anger, and to assure him that, if our people had offended, I would justly punish them according to their status and according to the severity of their crimes.[17] Alexander promised to relay this message in a polite way to the Berckelang.

13. Raden Ibrahim. The name suggests that this person was a Muslim merchant from Java, because "Raden" is a Javanese title. G. V. Smith (1977: 30) called him "the most important Thai Muslim merchant," and noted he was put to death shortly after this "after the King's factors made false statements against him."

14. According to Van Vliet, Raden Ibrahim was a "slave" of Okya Kalahom, which probably means that he was in some kind of dependent relationship with the Siamese Prince.

15. Harbormaster

16. Note a Portuguese descendant in the service of an Ayutthayan noble.

17. This sentence may serve as a reminder that Van Vliet wrote this manuscript before the Enlightenment, that is, before notions of the equality of man gained

In the meantime, I went to the house of Tjoucko, a Chinese (presently the chief Tonghsin),[18] who is also a long-standing friend of the Netherlanders and a person with many influential friends at the court. I told him in detail everything that had happened. Tjoucko was of the opinion that the King (in his anger) would order all the imprisoned Netherlanders to be put to death, or perhaps just some of them, even though he might regret it later on. For this reason, I agreed that he should immediately go to the court, seek an audience with the Berckelang and with the King's Chamberlain,[19] and, in my name, announce the following:

"That the interpreters, whom the Berckelang had sent to the lodge on the previous evening, had described to me how some Netherlanders had offended and how, as a consequence, they had been tied up and taken to the Berckelang's house; that His Honor graciously had released them of their bonds, had treated them well, which had given me hope that they would be released during the night. That I (seeing that our people failed to return), had appeared at His Honor's house before sunrise; and that, upon arrival there, I had learned to my regret that the *Braspintados*[20] had tied them up and had led them away in the most shameful manner. That considering the alleged offense, the King's anger at the imprisoned Netherlanders was much too severe. That the punishment would have been extreme enough if the Berckelang (who has

---

currency amongst Europeans. In Dutch criminal law of the seventeenth century (as indeed in the criminal law of other European nations) it was customary to mete out different punishments to offenders for the same crime according to their status in society. Gentlemen were punished less severely than commoners.

18. Possibly Thong Su (ท่องสื่อ), the head Chinese interpreter (*KCSD*, 1: 234).

19. Van Vliet below mentions "Oya Otheyathan, the chief Chamberlain of the King, (a powerful lord an exceptionally good friend of ours)." This must be Okya Uthaitham (ออกญาอุไทยธรรม์), the keeper of the royal apparel. In the Civil Hierarchy Law, this post is ranked Pra (พระ) with a sakdina of 5,000 (*KCSD*, 1: 244). Schouten earlier and La Loubère later both noted that this officer enjoyed more influence at court than his rank suggests, probably because of his personal closeness to the king. Like Van Vliet, La Loubère gives him the rank of Okya (Dhiravat 1984: 62; La Loubère 1693: 102).

20. In the seventeenth century, Portuguese was still the *lingua franca* of the Indies, a language used widely by the Dutch, the English, and later in the century also by the French in their communications with each other and with Asians of various nationalities. Many of the servants of the VOC spoke at least some Portuguese, and it was not at all uncommon for Portuguese words and expressions to find their way into Dutch-language documents. This is a case in point. As mentioned in note 4 above, the literal meaning of *braspintados* is "those with painted arms," and it refers to the royal guards, who wore distinctive tattoos on their arms. These guards were responsible for security around the palace. And as is apparent from Van Vliet's manuscript, they also made arrests, held prisoners captive, and carried out the King's orders in respect of tortures and executions.

authority over all matters concerning foreigners), after first questioning the prisoners, had sent only the most guilty to the King; and that, even this, should not have happened without my foreknowledge because His Lordship, the General, has appointed me as head of the Netherlanders in this Kingdom."

"That the King has acted against the prisoners as if they had already been sentenced to death, even though they had not even been questioned. That it was impossible to draw any other conclusion from these procedures than that the King no longer wished to maintain the long-standing friendship with the Netherlands because, if he had valued that relationship even in the slightest, he would not so completely have trampled under foot the honor of our nation and for such small offense have endangered the lives of so many."

"That the prisoners are in His Majesty's power and that he, being the King of his realm, is also the supreme judge, who could put to death some of them, all of them; yes, indeed, he could put to death all the Netherlanders in his Kingdom; and if he should so decide, we would be powerless to stop him. But even if all of us were to deserve the death sentence, His Majesty should refrain from taking this step on account of the long-standing friendship with the Prince of Holland and His Lordship, the General in Batavia. [Instead of ordering executions], the King should first demand advice from His Lordship, the General, or alternatively, he should send the offenders home to Batavia, like the General did four years ago in 1632 when he ordered Commander Antonio Caen to take to Siam several of the King's rebellious Chinese subjects."

"That the King should also consider all the help and assistance those of His Majesty's subjects who travel to foreign lands repeatedly have received from the Netherlanders. For instance, Commissioner Schouten[21] brought back to Siam four persons whom our people had freed from pirates. Similarly, a Netherlands Captain, named Adam van der Hoef, saved His Majesty's ship, which was coming from Bengal, from attack by the Portuguese and escorted the vessel into the port of Tanassari.[22] In addition, the aforementioned Captain saved six Siamese (who had been stranded on an island) and handed them over to Ockon Sisute Waanghsae,[23] the Anachoda[24] of His Majesty's ship, who brought them back to Siam and surrendered them to the previous Berckelang."

21. Joost Schouten was Commisioner to Siam in September 1636 when, amidst great ceremony, he delivered letters from Prince Frederick Henry, the Stadtholder of the Netherlands, and Governor-General Anthonio van Diemen to King Prasat Thong. It was on this occasion that, as a token of goodwill, he released the four Siamese persons (probably young women) who had been captured by pirates.

22. By "the port of Tennassari" (i.e. Tenasserim) Van Vliet meant Mergui, which nowadays falls within Burma.

23. Okkhun Sisut Wangsae (?), probably a Chinese.

24. From the Malay word, usually "nakhoda/nachoda," meaning a "shipmaster."

"That a proper investigation should be held of what has transpired, an investigation during which both the Prince's slaves and the accused Netherlanders should be questioned sharply. If, after this investigation, His Majesty should judge that the crimes of the Netherlanders are inexcusable and that they should be punished, that nonetheless he refrain from doing so out of respect for our nation and that, instead, he send all of them to me on the promise that I shall sharply investigate the offenses that have been committed, and that I shall punish the guilty according to their status and the degree of their guilt, and in such a way that the demands of His Majesty and of justice both will be fully satisfied."

"That if His Majesty persists in his anger and refuses to listen either to reason or to entreaties, it will be impossible to reconcile his stubborn actions with the assurances of increased friendship with the King of Holland and His Lordship, the General, which he so spontaneously and wholeheartedly made to Commissioner Schouten and myself just a few days ago in the presence of all the Lords of the Kingdom, and which he affirmed in his letter to His Lordship, the General. Moreover, His Majesty's procedures will not meet with the approval of the General; they will undermine the long-standing friendship with the King of Holland and will surely lead to great trouble. And finally, (as I have said before in audiences with the King) that His Majesty can act as he pleases, but that I am under the obligation to truthfully report everything that transpires to His Lordship, the General."

I made Tjoucko write down all the abovementioned points and induced him to go to the palace and relay my message to the Berckelang and the Chamberlain. [I impressed upon him] that he should do this with great earnestness and modesty and that he, under no circumstance, should show anger or raise his voice but that, instead, he should at all times be mindful of our principal aim, namely, to soothe His Majesty's severity, in order in that way to obtain the deliverance of our people. [I further instructed him] that if he should notice some typically Siamese selfishness on the part of either the Berckelang or the Chamberlain, he was to offer them a substantial sum of money, in which case I authorized him to issue them with promissory notes. With these instructions Tjoucko went to the palace, whereupon I returned to the lodge.

Not long after I had returned home, Tjoucko appeared at the lodge accompanied by the Berckelang's interpreters. Tjoucko told me that the Berckelang had instructed him to tell me that he, the Berckelang, was aware that, even though I was ill and could hardly walk, I had come to his house in person and that this had given him great pleasure. It showed, the Berckelang had said, that I cared deeply about my people. [The Berckelang had further told Tjoucko] that he was surprised at the King's excessive anger and that he suspected that His Majesty had been given a much graver account of the incident than that which the prisoners' confessions had shown to have actually occurred. Nevertheless, I should not despair because he, the Berckelang, cared like a father for me as well as for the prisoners, and he would do his utmost to ensure that everything be brought to a good end. [Addressing the Berckelang's interpreters], I replied in a polite way that I was sure of His Honor's favorable disposition towards us, that I had not given up hope of a good outcome, but that His Majesty's procedures were so severe as to be almost unbearable. Thereupon, I mentioned to the interpreters all the points which Tjoucko had written down and asked them to convey this message to the Berckelang and the Chamberlain, which they promised to do.

[A short time later we learned] that when the interpreters returned to the palace, the King had already in the most arbitrary way sentenced all our people to death – each one of them had already been tied to a stake within sight of the elephants, expecting at any moment to die a miserable death. The interpreters had known this, but (out of embarrassment) they had not told us, although their sad demeanor had led us to suspect that something was seriously amiss. [Not knowing that our people had already been taken to the execution ground] I decided to send Ian Iaclijns to the palace with a few medicines and such like in order to treat the wounds of the prisoners and also to find out what was going on. The aforementioned Iaclijns returned in haste and reported that the whole city was in a commotion, that the entire court was full of sadness, and that he had not been allowed near our people because they had already been tied to stakes, while the elephants that were to devour[25] them had already been led to the place of execution. [Iaclijns further reported] that many thousands of people had gathered around the palace to watch the pitiful spectacle. How these tidings made us feel is known to the Almighty.

We immediately sent a trusted friend to Radie Ebrehem, who was at the palace of the Prince, to inform him of this tragedy and to request that he do his utmost to persuade His Highness to intercede on our behalf, on the understanding that this be done in such a way as not to diminish the honor of our nation. We further sent a messenger to the Abbot of Thimphiatti[26] to request his intercession with the King, partly because this priest is a good friend of mine who is favorably disposed towards our nation, and in part also because the merciful intercession of the Religious is freely permitted in this Kingdom. The aforementioned Abbot, however, was unavailable so that we were unable to enlist his support. In the meantime, we also sent a messenger to the Priest of Wantthong,[27] a close friend of ours but not as powerful [as

25. Under the pressure of events, Van Vliet uses the word "verslinden" (devour), though he undoubtedly knew that elephants are vegetarian and perform executions by trampling.

26. Wat Chaophraya Thai (วัดเจ้าพระยาไทย), nowadays known as Wat Yai Chai Mongkhon (วัดใหญ่ชัยมงคล), situated to the east of the city, just north of the Dutch lodge.

27. Probably Wat Thong, the golden temple, which might be the unofficial name of any one of several of the gilt temples in the city.

the aforementioned Abbot], to inform him of our despair and to request that he go to the court with some influential people, which he did immediately, promising to do all he could on our behalf. Around midday Tjoucko returned to the lodge and, with great sadness, gave us the following message:

"That during the previous night the incident had been presented to the King in such a way that he had come to believe that this group of Netherlanders had unexpectedly attacked the palace of the Prince, his brother, although Tjoucko had been unable as yet to discover which person had been responsible for this misrepresentation. That when the King was told of the incident about two hours before sunrise, he had flown into a rage and had issued orders to his *Braspintados* for the evil and wanton Netherlanders to be seized at the Berckelang's house, for them to be tied up and taken into the court, for stakes to be placed in the earth, and for the elephants to be brought to the execution ground. That as soon as the prisoners had arrived at the court, they had been sharply questioned, and that after they had confessed, they had been tied to stakes, where they still sat in full view of large crowds of people, many of whom appeared to pity them."

"That he had given my message to the Berckelang and His Majesty's Chamberlain; that they had promised to submit everything to His Majesty, but that they feared that the King might not be persuaded and that he would put to death at least some of the prisoners. That all the greatest mandarins had gone to the court; that they were filled with compassion for the prisoners, and that they intended to try, in a polite way, to mollify the King's anger. [Tjoucko further reported] that he had promised the Berckelang five catties of silver, and the Chamberlain two catties,[28] if they succeeded in obtaining the freedom of our people."

After some discussion with Mr. Verwer, we decided to send Tjoucko once more to the court in order to present Oya Otheyathan, the chief Chamberlain of the King, (a powerful lord and an exceptionally good friend of ours) with a gold chain and two pieces of Chinese gold cloth (to a total value of about three catties), which the aforementioned lord, in my name, was to offer to His Majesty in order in this way to obtain the deliverance of our people. Tjoucko also undertook, as a measure of last resort, to seek the intercession of the Abbot of Mappatat,[29] one of the four greatest Religious place in the entire Kingdom. In the meantime, we secured the Company's lodge as best we could and prayed to God Almighty for a blessed outcome.

After Tjoucko had left, various people came to the lodge to tell us that Oya Pitsia Songhcram,[30] the Ney or Head of the Japanese, responding to

28. In most of the Indies the catty equalled 0.625 kg. This meant that Van Vliet promised the Berckelang about 3.1 kg of silver, and the Chamberlain 1.25 kg.

29. Wat Mahathat (วัดมหาธาตุ), often rendered by the Dutch as "Nappetat."

30. Okya Phichai Songkhram (ออกญาพิไชยสงคราม), who appears in the Military Hierarchy Law with a Phra rank and sakdina of 5,000 (*KTSD*, 1: 280).

pressure from these bald-headed villains,[31] had today suggested to the King that the crimes of the imprisoned Hollanders had given His Majesty just cause to execute not only them, but all the Netherlanders in his Kingdom. [Oya Pitsia Songhcram had added] that this was necessary so that His Majesty's Kingdom be cleansed once and for all of this wicked nation, [a desirable outcome] because the Netherlanders had spread bad rumors about the King in Japan and about the Japanese in Siam, so that Japanese merchants no longer dared to come to this Kingdom, which meant that the Siamese crown continued to be cut off from silver-rich Japan. When His Majesty had driven all the Hollanders from his Kingdom, [the Oya had concluded], Japanese junks would come to Siam once more so that the good relations between the two Kingdoms were certain to be quickly restored.[32] But even though this Oya had given his proposal a semblance of reason, the King had remained silent, which meant that the suggestion did not please His Majesty. Nonetheless, the aforementioned Oya (we have been told) raised his voice once more in order to repeat his proposal, whereupon the King interrupted him and spoke as follows:

"By my first silence, you, Oya Pitsia Songhcram, should have known that your suggestion did not please me. For what reason should I want to kill or expel from my Kingdom Captain van Vliet and his remaining companions, who knew nothing of this question and who were not even present at the places where the crimes were committed? Even though the evil acts of some of the Captain's people have angered me, I do not wish to extend my anger to his person or to the entire Netherlands nation. Even less [do I wish to extend my anger] to the General at Batavia, who is our friend and ally." After the

31. Van Vliet refers here to Japanese *samurai*, who shaved most of their heads as a sign of their warrior status, leaving some hair for a kind of "ponytail" at the back. At the time of these events (late 1636), there were still about 70–80 *samurai*, whom the King employed as mercenaries, living in Ayutthaya's Japanese quarter, which adjoined the VOC compound. Most of the *samurai* had Siamese wives with whom they had children. And since there were also some Japanese merchants residing at Ayutthaya, the total population of the Japanese quarter may have been about 400–550. For more information on the Japanese community in Siam, see Iwao (1958: v–xxviii).

32. Obviously, there was little love lost between the Japanese and the Dutch in Siam. This hostility had its roots in trade rivalries because by 1636 the VOC had largely ousted the Japanese from the lucrative Siam-Japan trade, exporting to Hirado and Nagasaki enormous quantities of deer and ray skins in return for Japanese silver and copper. In part, this Dutch success was due to events in Japan. In the mid-1630s Shogun Iyemitsu, concerned about the spread of Christianity in the southern Japanese island of Kyushu, was beginning to move towards isolationism, which meant among other things that more and more restrictions were placed on commercial contacts between Japan and Japanese living overseas, many of whom were Christian (Boxer 1935: xxxiv–xlvi).

King had spoken thus, he ordered Timon and Froskedonne, both of them Heads of the Japanese, to come to the palace.[33] [The King further issued orders] for all Japanese (residing in the Japanese quarter) to be counted and (until further notice) to be confined to their houses, and, in addition, he commanded Ockon Thip to take a proa with some soldiers and guard the lodge in order to see to it that no harm would come to us and that no armed Japanese would come anywhere near us.

After midday the interpreters returned to the lodge to tell me that the Berckelang requested that I come to his house because he wanted to let me know that the King was extremely angry, that all the prisoners remained tied up, that the King had sentenced two of them to death and that he had ordered His Honor, the Berckelang, to carry out the executions without delay. I replied that I was saddened and surprised by this message, but that it was not necessary for me to tire my sick limbs further[34] in order to hear such a message from the Berckelang himself. [I added] that the King had the prisoners in his power, that he could do with them and with all of us as he pleased, because we were unable to resist his power and we did not intend to flee. [I protested] that these procedures were far too extreme, that foreigners never before had been so badly treated in this Kingdom, but that I trusted nonetheless that His Honor, the Berckelang, would try to soothe His Majesty's excessive anger so that the honor of the Netherlands nation would be besmirched no further. In case His Majesty, [I continued], had so little regard for myself and the other Netherlanders in his Kingdom that he wished to persist in his wrath, he should think of the Honorable General and, out of respect for His Lordship, he should not treat any Netherlanders in this way, even if they had committed far graver offenses (than those of which they were now accused). The King, [I added], should have confidence in the General and trust him to be a just and severe judge who will most certainly punish the criminals according to the full rigor of the law. I ordered the interpreters to give the Berckelang this message, and I asked them to politely impress upon His Honor the importance of ensuring the preservation of good relations between the Netherlands and the Siamese nation. The interpreters seemed very pleased with this reply, and they expressed the view that it would tend towards the preservation and deliverance of the prisoners.

33. According to Seiichi Iwao (1958: xxvii), the heads of the Japanese community in Siam were named Itoya Taymon and Taramatsu Feroske.

34. Van Vliet probably suffered from beriberi, a disease that in its early stages causes the legs to swell and weaken. Although very common amongst Europeans living in Asia, the dietary causation of beriberi remained unknown until the late nineteenth century when a doctor attached to the Dutch colonial army fighting in Aceh made the simple observation that this disease almost exclusively affected the officers, who ate white rice, while the common soldiers, who ate brown rice, seemed to be immune.

Around this time Radie Ebrehem sent word that he had discussed yesterday's altercation with the Prince and that he had spoken as follows: "He had told the Prince how displeased I had been when last night I heard that our people (apparently without His Highness' foreknowledge) had approached his palace too closely, but that I was sure that none of our people had had any evil designs. [He further had told the Prince how dismayed I had been] that the Netherlanders had been seized by his slaves, had been stripped naked, that they had been tied up, and that in this way they had been taken to the Berckelang. [Radie had pointed out] that because I myself had not been present at any of these events and because I had not been permitted to speak to any of the accused, I still did not know precisely what had happened, but that I strongly suspected that the actions of our people had not been truthfully reported to the King because otherwise His Majesty surely would not have taken such severe measures against them. [He had further mentioned] that in case His Majesty was to execute all the prisoners, he would not thereby weaken the power of the Netherlands even in the slightest, but he could be sure that it would spell the end of the friendship with the General of Batavia and the King of Holland. [Radie had further pointed out] that, for all these reasons, I most urgently requested that His Honor, the Prince, use his influence with His Majesty to soothe his anger so that none of the prisoners would be executed, but instead that they all be sent to me on the understanding that I would most sharply investigate the whole incident, that I would report everything to the General, and that if the prisoners were found guilty, they would not escape the General's punishing hand. [And, finally, Radie had concluded by stating] that if our people had insulted His Highness, the Prince, or if they had offended against the laws [of Siam], I requested forgiveness and mercy for them, promising at the same time that I would see to it that such incidents would not recur in the future."

To all this the Prince had replied as follows: "I, too, am dismayed at the trouble that has arisen between my slaves and the Hollanders, and I very much regret that the incident should have reached the ears of the King. At first I considered going to the court myself to explain the matter to His Majesty, but when I heard that the King had flown into a passion, I thought better of it. In the meantime, my mother, who was very worried, sent one of her servants to the King who came back and reported that His Majesty persisted with his anger. Nonetheless, considering the reasonable arguments of Captain van Vliet, I will send one of my mandarins to the court to request mercy for the prisoners and to see to it that none of them is executed. Captain van Vliet can count on me – I will do this even if I myself have to sit in front of the elephant. It is now about four years that the Captain has lived in Siam, and during that time he has never offended against His Majesty, the laws of the land, or the Lords of the realm, for which reason His Majesty is favorably disposed towards him and is likely to seriously consider his entreaties."

Towards nightfall a messenger from the Berckelang arrived at the lodge to bring us the welcome news that the King had pardoned all the prisoners, that he had forgiven them their crimes, and that I was to come to the Berckelang's house immediately. Naturally, we were overjoyed at these tidings. I at once boarded the interpreters' proa (who, in the meantime, had also arrived with the good news) and together we made our way to the Berckelang's house. Having arrived there, His Honor addressed me as follows:

"That the King had been greatly angered by the offenses that the Hollanders had committed yesterday; that he had intended to give the prisoners their just punishment and put them all to death, but that His Majesty had learned from their confessions that their intentions had not been quite as evil as he had been led to believe, for which reason he had changed his mind. His Majesty, however, had remained resolved to have elephants trample to death the two instigators of the trouble, as well as the coolies who had called out from the proa and the Peguan woman who had called out to the proa warning the Hollanders that they should come to help Joost Laurentsz and Daniel Jacobsz when they were fighting with the Siamese. That after long deliberations and with the approval of several mandarins, the King had sentenced to death Joost Laurentsz, Daniel Jacobsz, the coolies, and the Peguan woman, while he had ordered the others to watch the spectacle. That the condemned prisoners had already been taken to the Petoutsiaey[35] (the usual execution ground), whilst the others had already been on their way to that place."

"That he, the Berckelang, had very much taken to heart the messages I had sent him via Tjoucko and the interpreters, that he had discussed these messages with some of the most prominent mandarins, and that he had asked them to help him intercede on behalf of the prisoners. [The Berckelang further told me] that at the very time the prisoners were being led to the execution ground, he had discussed the substance of my proposals with His Majesty, and that, in doing this, he had been supported by Oya Wangh,[36] a certain Braeme [*Brahmin*] named Oya Oprae Methon,[37] Oya Opheyathan, Olongh Thip Sombat (the Chamberlain of the King)[38] as well as Oya Tsy Darmart[39] (who had been sent by the Prince). Backed up by all these mandarins, the Berckelang had, in a respectful way, suggested to the King that the arguments

35. *Pradu chai* (ประตูไชย), the gate of victory.

36. Okya Wang (ออกญาวัง), see Appendix I.

37. Unidentified.

38. Okluang Thip Sombat (ออกหลวงทิพสมบัติ). It looks as if the bracketed passage is misplaced and should be linked to "Oya Opheyathan" or Phra/Okya Uthaitham, the Chamberlain mentioned earlier.

39. Possibly, Okya Chai Thammarat (?).

Captain van Vliet had advanced were so weighty that he ought to pardon the prisoners. This the King should do, [the Berckelang had said], especially because the Captain had offered to administer justice himself, because the execution of the prisoners was certain to anger the General, and because the General's anger was likely to lead to big trouble."

To these arguments the mandarins had added the following observations: "That the Hollanders have traded in this Kingdom for over thirty years, that they have always observed the customs of the land, and that irrespective of whether the mistakes some of them have now made have been due to ignorance or to wanton thoughtlessness, His Majesty should not believe that these mistakes were made intentionally. [The mandarins had further added] that one ought to be more tolerant of foreigners than of native-born people, because foreigners may not always be entirely familiar with the severity of our laws."

In response His Majesty had replied: "Captain van Vliet's suggestions and everything you have added have given me cause to think. I have decided to pardon the prisoners. Go! Release them from imminent death and hand them over to Oya Sicri[40] and Calahom,[41] who are to detain them in accordance with the laws of the Kingdom until such time as the Berckelang has consulted with Captain van Vliet."

The Berckelang further told me that the King had ordered him to most earnestly impress upon me the following: "That the offenses which these Netherlanders had committed had been very serious. They had lingered at Boeretiet against the will of the Religious, even though Boeretiet is one of the holiest temples in Siam, a temple frequented by the King himself, who often goes there to pray and to make offerings both to the temple itself and to the Religious. In addition, when these Netherlanders saw that the Prince's slaves were kicking one of their companions and were taking him to the palace, they had tried to free him. They should have known that only the King's mandarins and slaves may enter the palace. For all these reasons, they had aroused the King's wrath, which had put them in mortal danger. If one of the King's greatest mandarins had committed crimes of comparable severity, His Majesty most certainly would have punished him with death, irrespective of any attempt to intercede on his behalf."

"That His Majesty had had ample reason to put these Netherlanders to death, but that several considerations had led him to pardon them. [Firstly], for over thirty years now (to the astonishment and fear of many Indian Kings), there had been friendship between the crown of Siam and the Netherlands, a friendship that only a few days ago had been mutually confirmed with golden letters. [Secondly], the Honorable Generals have always been great friends

40. Okya Chakri (ออกญาจักรี), see Appendix I.
41. Okya Kalahom (ออกญากลาโหม), see Appendix I.

of the Siamese Kings, for which reason the [Siamese] Kings and his mandarins have always greatly esteemed the Generals, an esteem that has repeatedly been confirmed in writing, as was the case a few days ago when the General and His Majesty exchanged letters. [Thirdly], I had lived in Siam for about four years, and during that time I had always obeyed the laws of the Kingdom, and also now, in respect of this incident, I had behaved appropriately."

"That His Majesty will be pleased if I remain in Siam, but that, from now on, I had to ensure that such disorders did not recur, because if this happened again, the King's wrath would fall upon me. From now on, His Majesty would hold me personally responsible for the good behavior of all the Netherlanders in Siam. In addition, the King had warned that I was not to permit groups of Netherlanders to go out on excursions unaccompanied by an interpreter, and that I was to write to the General requesting that he send only well-behaved people to Siam, sober people of regular habits and good manners."

My reply to the Berckelang in substance was as follows: "That I was most grateful to His Honor and would always remember that he had soothed the King's excessive anger, that he had effected the pardon of the prisoners who had been sentenced to death, and that he had obtained the deliverance of the other prisoners. That the failings of my people had deeply saddened me, but that I would ensure (as much as was in my power) that such misfortunes would not occur again. That since the King had pardoned the prisoners, His Honor might want to use his influence to obtain their release so that they could return to the lodge, which was urgently necessary because I had only very few people at my disposal, and there was much work to be done in the Company's service."

"That if we had been provided with able interpreters, this whole incident could have been prevented. Our people had necessarily gone out without an interpreter because the Pecap[42] speaks neither Portuguese nor Malay, and Trompanidt[43] (who speaks only a little Portuguese) had been away for twelve days without having told us where he was going. And since it is the King's will that henceforth we rely more on interpreters than in the past, I urgently request that Your Honor see to it that we are provided with competent interpreters. I added a number of other arguments in support of these points until, in the end, His Honor replied that I could rest at ease, that he would look after everything, and that he would ensure that everything would be settled in accordance with my requests. Thereupon we said goodbye and I returned home in darkness."

42 Unidentified. We learn below that "he only knew the Siamese and the Moorish languages," suggesting he may be a translator for Arabic or Persian.

43 The VOC's translator.

December 12, 1636

In the early morning of December 12, I sent Ian Iaclijns to the Shahbandar, Oloang Tsiut,[44] with instructions to strongly urge the Shahbandar to recommend to the Berckelang the release of our people. [Iaclijns was also to prevail upon the Shahbandar] to seek permission for some of our people to immediately bring the prisoners some clean clothes and medicines, because they had all been stripped naked and most of them were injured. Around noon, Iaclijns returned to the lodge and reported that, together with the Shahbandar, he had been to the Berckelang's house, that the Berckelang had promised to look after everything, that he had given Iaclijns permission to bring our people food and medicines, but that he had advised against giving the prisoners Western clothing or money, because, so the Berckelang had asserted, the *Braspintados* were certain to take these away from the prisoners. [In support of this opinion] the Berckelang had told the story of how badly the *Braspintados* had treated him when in the previous year he, the Berckelang himself, had been imprisoned.[45]

In the afternoon, Radie Ebrehem, Tjoucko, and several other friends came to visit us. Tjoucko returned the gifts [i.e., the gold chain and the two pieces of Chinese gold cloth, which he was to present to the King's Chamberlain] because (God be praised) the Chamberlain had not deemed them suitable. These friends told us that the whole country was in turmoil, that the Muslim merchants who had been about to leave for Tanassery had had to postpone their voyage for the time being, and that they had had to unload the proas in which they had wanted to carry their return cargoes to Piply.[46] [The reason for all this commotion was] that on account of the difficulties that had arisen with our people, the King had given very strict orders that no Siamese was to perform physical labor for any foreigners, presumably in order to drive the foreign merchants from Siam, because it is impossible for merchants, and especially for the Netherlanders, to trade in Siam without local laborers and without hired Siamese proas, for it is mostly in these proas that we carry our merchandise up and down the river.

44. Below given in full as Oloang Tsiut Raymontry; probably Okluang Chularatchamontri (ออกหลวงจุฬาราชมนตรี), who appears in the Civil Hierarchy Law with a Pra rank and sakdina of 1400 (*KTSD*, 1: 233).

45. The *phrakhlang* had been involved in organizing the expedition to suppress Pattani (see the *Description*, pp. 128–32), was among those held responsible for its failure, and was imprisoned for some period between August and October 1634. The *phrakhlang*'s transition from being one of the kingdom's most powerful figures to being a victim of the *braspintados* and then back again is a nice illustration of the fragility of aristocratic power in Ayutthaya.

46. Phetchaburi.

We further discussed the King's procedures against our people and we politely asked our friends what they thought of His Majesty's extreme actions. Everyone expressed great surprise and all of them declared that they could not understand why the King had behaved in this way. But nonetheless, all the friends agreed that His Majesty may have had certain reasons, the most important of which may have been the following:

"Because the tone of the most recent letters from His Lordship, the General, had been too harsh and resolute. [These letters] had not been translated in the flattering style that is customarily used when addressing the King, and, as a consequence, the King and his mandarins had discovered to their dismay that they can no longer make us do their bidding through either granting or withholding the exportation of rice."

"Because the most recent Netherlands embassy had offended against the customs of the Siamese court. [This embassy] had been accompanied by far too many armed soldiers, and, as is well-known, foreigners are not allowed to carry weapons in this Kingdom. Moreover, even though these soldiers had come to Siam merely to add luster to the letters of the Illustrious Prince of Holland, the King had imagined that they had been sent to insult him (His Majesty is not a military man and does not handle weapons) and to frighten him with the power of the Netherlands."

"But nonetheless, the aforementioned friends were of the opinion that His Majesty is not angry with the Netherlands nation in general, and that he is not opposed to the Company's presence in Siam. Rather, he had taken this action to instill fear in all the foreigners and also in his own people, so that everyone would be more careful in the future not to offend him. If he could treat in this manner his powerful and dear friends, friends who with distinction had resided in this country for so many years and who during all this time had never made any mistakes, what, then, might he not do to others who displeased him?" But whatever his reasons may have been, the King's treatment of our people was both amazing and deplorable.

December 13, 1636

On December 13 the Shahbandar, Oloang Tsiut, came to the lodge and together with him I once more went to the Berckelang bearing a suitable gift. When we arrived at our destination, His Honor told us that several of our people, those who were imprisoned by Oya Sicry, had again been tied hand and foot, that the others were kept at the house of Oya Calahom, and that neither the interpreters nor anyone from the lodge was allowed to come near them. In a firm voice I expressed my justifiable displeasure at these Siamese procedures, suggesting that since the prisoners had been pardoned by the King, they should be released forthwith. I further pointed out that their release did not mean that they would be out of trouble, because those who had offended against Siamese customs would not escape the punishing hand of His Lordship, the General. The Berckelang replied as follows:

"That he cared more deeply for our people than perhaps I thought, and that if our people were imprisoned once more, it was not on orders of the King, but rather, it was due to the customs of the country, and possibly also to the wickedness and greed of the *Braspintados*, who might expect in this way to extort some money from the Netherlanders. That this was something that he could not have prevented because the *Braspintados* are out-and-out villains. That I should have a little patience, because as soon as a suitable opportunity arose, he would plead the prisoners' case with His Majesty. Everything, however, had to be done in a quiet and orderly fashion, because it was very important that he, the Berckelang, should not arouse the suspicion of his enemies, who otherwise might falsely claim that he, for the love of gain, had violated the customs of the country just to please the Hollanders." All in all, I was forced to conclude that I would not be able to achieve my objective, for which reason I took my leave and returned to the lodge.

December 14, 1636

In the early morning of December 14, Tjoucko came to the lodge at my request. I told him what had happened at the Berckelang's the previous day, and I asked him for advice on how to act in this important matter in order to ensure that no further harm and misery be inflicted on our people. Tjoucko was of the opinion that the Berckelang was too cowardly to argue our case strongly [with the King], because on several occasions when he had had a chance to do so, he had remained silent, evidently because each time he been overcome with fear. For this reason, the others and I immediately agreed to send Tjoucko to the court with two gold chains and two diamonds, altogether valued at 202 guilders. Tjoucko was to hand these jewels to the Chamberlain, Oloang Thip Sombat, and tell him that he, Tjoucko (in order not to arouse the jealousy of the Berckelang), presented these gifts to the King, that he requested that the Netherlanders be freed, which, he was to suggest, would be a compassionate act because I was so ill that I could hardly walk.

Around midday Tjoucko returned to the lodge to report on his business at the court. He told us that the King had accepted the jewels, that he had called the Berckelang and Oloang Tsiut, and that he, Tjoucko, was sure that before nightfall our people would be back at the lodge. Around this time I received a sad, mournful letter from Guiliaem uyt den Hove, written from prison, in which he wrote that he was held captive with five others, that they were all badly injured, that they were miserable and without any medicine, that they believed they had been forgotten, and that he did not know what had become of his companions. But even though these sad laments aroused my compassion, there was nothing I could do other than to remain patient.

Today our erstwhile interpreter, Trompanidt, was brought into the city from Bancocq in chains and all tied up because he had been too slow in the King's and in our service. [Upon arrival here], he was thrown into prison. He has been replaced as interpreter by Omon Wytsit Bassa (who is quite able, having served the Hollanders in the past), a change with which we are well pleased, hoping that the new interpreter will serve us better than Trompanidt.

In the evening I sent a messenger to the Shahbandar, Oloang Tsiut, to find out what had happened today, but the reply I received was so ambiguous that I was unable to come to any decision at all.

December 15, 1636

On December 15 before sunrise, Oloang Tsiut and I went to the Berckelang with a substantial gift. [Upon arrival], I complained in a dignified way about the harsh actions which on account of such minor faults have been instituted against our people, adding that great shame had been brought over our nation in this Kingdom; that this shame was indelible and would be remembered forever; that we have never suffered such harm in any other Indies Kingdom as we have suffered here; that none of the previous Kings [of Siam] had ever treated foreigners (especially Netherlanders) in this way; and that, whilst the King had the power to act as he pleased, I was under the obligation not only to report everything truthfully to His Lordship, the General, but also to give him my opinions about everything that had transpired. I further told the Berckelang that the prisoners held by the Calahom were badly injured, sickly, and miserable, and I requested permission to send them a surgeon to dress their wounds. The Berckelang acceded to my request, whereupon I at once sent a barber to the Calahom's house.[47] The Berckelang replied as follows:

"That the King's actions did not in any way concern the Netherlands nation in general, so that this nation cannot be dishonored thereby. [The Berckelang further said] that to be imprisoned in the Siamese way brought no shame on the victims; that [in Siam] harsh imprisonment was a common plague, a plague which frequently and for no reason befell even the greatest mandarins of the Kingdom; that I should remember that His Majesty is like a father who is wont to chastise most severely his dearest children in order to prevent them straying further from the path of virtue; and that once the King saw his children had bettered their lives, he was likely to compensate them richly for the chastisements they had suffered. His Honor further said that His Majesty had called him to the court yesterday and had asked him what faults the Hollanders had committed at the temple Boeretiet. The Berckelang had intended to reply: "Your Majesty has forgiven them their mistakes, so why is

47. It will be noted that Van Vliet used interchangeably the words "surgeon" (*heelmeester*) and "barber" (*barbier*). This, of course, is not surprising because seventeenth-century medical practitioners were multiskilled. In addition to performing such medical procedures as amputations, bloodletting, lancing boils, and the like, they also shaved their clients, cut their hair, and, if necessary, pulled their teeth.

it necessary to investigate the matter further?" But before he was able to utter these words, another Oya (whose name he did not mention), replied to the King's question. This Oya painted such an ugly picture of the behavior of our people at Boeretiet that His Majesty, clearly displeased, abruptly rose from his throne and went inside without speaking. But nonetheless, the Berckelang promised on the next occasion to raise the issue of the prisoners with the King."

After we left the Berckelang, the Shahbandar and I went to see Tjoucko. We told him what had happened, whereupon Tjoucko undertook to go immediately to the court in order to talk to the Chamberlain. [Tjoucko promised] to urge the Chamberlain to prevail upon the Berckelang once more to petition the King. He assured us that our people would be freed today, which God Almighty may grant, so that the shame may disappear and the whole matter may be forgotten.

December 16, 1636

On December 16 before sunrise, Oloang Tsiut and I once again went to the house of the Berckelang. As soon as we appeared there, His Honor ordered Oloang Pith Perap to go to the houses of Oya Sicry and Calahom with some of his servants and one of our people to obtain the release of all the prisoners, the Netherlanders as well as the Siamese slaves who had been imprisoned with them. [The Berckelang further told him] that in case the *Braspintados* or the guards, in accordance with Siamese custom, should demand lock and unlock moneys, he should tell them to come to him, the Berckelang, for payment. After about three hours they returned, bringing with them the prisoners who had been held by Calahom; namely, Guilleaum uyt den Hoven, the barber, a boy, a black servant of the lodge, the Peguan woman, and the coolies. Oloang Pith Perap reported to the Berckelang that Sicry did not want to release the prisoners before he himself had spoken to His Majesty and before he had received the compensation to which he claimed to be entitled (namely, 3.5 tael per head). The Berckelang was very angry with Sicry, saying that he would free the Hollanders from Sicry's clutches before midday and send them to the lodge, or he would not remain Kehousa Tibidy.[48] [His Honor further ordered] that the coolies and the Peguan woman go back to their masters and that the Hollanders return to the lodge. In addition, the Berckelang said that the King had instructed him to tell me once again how our people had offended against the customs of this Kingdom and why they had brought His Majesty's anger upon themselves.

That early in the morning on the day when the troubles occurred, our people had sailed past the King's palace, [on which occasion] they had refused

48. Kosathibodi, the official name (*tamnaeng*, ตำแหน่ง) of the *phrakhlang*.

to take down the cloth (which was spread like a tent over their proa), even though His Majesty's servants in a friendly manner had several times asked them to do so.

That the party had gone to the temple of Boeretiet, where they had sat down to eat, drink and make merry, even though this temple is so sacred that His Majesty, the Prince, and all the mandarins frequently go there to make offerings and to pray.

That they had refused to comply with the monks' order to leave the temple, but that they had stayed there until the Abbot came with more monks and had threatened to forcibly evict them.

That some of our people (namely Joost Laurentsz and Daniel Jacobsz) had gone on foot from the temple to the great river, [on which occasion] they had met a servant of the Prince whom they had treated very rudely, calling him names and hitting him.

That Joost Laurentsz and Daniel Jacobsz had entered a Siamese house in which there were only two sick people, whom they had treated very rudely, threatening them and stealing their last food, notwithstanding the protestations of these sick people that they needed it themselves and that they were too weak to go outside and look for other food.

That when the two Hollanders had reached the riverside, where they had encountered some of the Prince's people who were there guarding His Highness' proas, they had forcibly taken away the oars of these people, with which they (without any reason whatsoever) had begun to hit them.

That when these aforementioned proa guardians had fled into their houses to escape the trouble and violence, the two Hollanders had pursued them, whereupon at long last the guardians had seized Daniel (Joost escaped), not with the intention to harm him, but only to take him to the palace of the Prince.

That in the meantime the other members of the party had come sailing down the river and seeing that one of their companions had been seized, they had sailed very quickly to the Prince's palace, which they had entered in such an aggressive manner that the people inside had become alarmed, thinking that the Hollanders had come to fight the palace and to forcibly free their companion.

The Berckelang further said that six of these eight points were of little consequence, but that the things that had happened at the temple and at His Highness' palace were so serious as to be almost unforgivable, but that notwithstanding the gravity of these offenses, the King had released into my care all the prisoners on the understanding that I would see to it that justice be done and that the instigators of the troubles either be punished for their crimes or be expelled from His Majesty's Kingdom. [He added] that I should take great care to ensure that henceforth only people of regular habits and good character be sent [to Siam], that I was to give a written guarantee that our people would not again offend against His Majesty or the laws of this land, and that I was to be held personally responsible for any offenses which our people might commit in the future. [The Berckelang suggested] that I write to His Lordship, the General, requesting that His Lordship send to Siam only decent people (who are prepared to observe the laws of the land), and that the people he sends to Siam be allowed to stay longer and not be replaced so quickly by new people unfamiliar with Siamese laws. In years past (the Berckelang said), the Castilians and Portuguese had resided in Siam for purposes of trade, during which time (on account of the King's favorable disposition towards all foreigners) they enjoyed many privileges. However, they lost the King's favor. They were people of such bad, irregular disposition, they were so volatile and so much given to fighting, amongst themselves as well as against the indigenous people of this land, that His Majesty had had no choice but to expel them from his Kingdom. By contrast, it has usually been the case that the Chiefs of the Hollanders (who have resided in this Kingdom), have been reasonably civil and well-behaved, in consequence of which the affection of the Siamese Kings towards the Netherlands nation in general has increased steadily, so that now our two nations are as one, a state of affairs which the present King confirmed just a few days ago in a golden letter to the Prince of Holland and His Lordship, the General. And, as far as His Majesty is concerned, he will never give cause to diminish this friendship as long as the sun and moon shall shine.

The Berckelang repeated this last point several times. In addition, he earnestly recommended that I, too, commit myself to the preservation of friendship, and he urged me to write to His Lordship, the General, clearly advising him to adopt the same attitude. I replied politely in the following manner:

"That I was deeply pained and saddened that some of our people had offended against the customs of the Kingdom, but that I trusted that both His Majesty and His Honor would understand that these mistakes had not been committed intentionally. One misfortune had led to another. For some time now we had been served by incompetent interpreters who had failed adequately to instruct our people, so that many of them had not been completely familiar with the laws of the Kingdom."

"That His Honor should assure His Majesty that I will sharply question all our people, that I will obtain their confessions, and that I will send the instigators of the trouble to His Lordship, the General, so that he can punish them for their crimes."

"That it is the will of His Lordship, the General, that all Company servants residing in distant lands observe the laws and customs of these lands. They must do this because they reside in these lands to serve their masters, and if these servants should arouse the hatred of the Kings, the Company will most certainly suffer thereby."

"That I will most strongly recommend to His Lordship, the General, that he see to it that his will in this matter be observed, and that I will try, as much as is in my power, to ensure that only good people be sent to Siam. [I added] that I will set a good example by leading a sober, regular life, that I will instruct our people in the customs of the land to the best of my knowledge, and that I will issue the strictest orders to all our people to observe the laws of Siam and avoid all trouble. [But at the same time], I could not be held responsible for the behavior of all our people. If indeed I was to be held responsible, my life would be unbearable and highly uncertain. My life would then depend on a jealous tongue or on a mischievous Siamese, because as I have observed on several occasions, the Siamese, too, are sometimes unreasonable and wanton; they, too, sometimes get drunk, and they, too, have been known to attack people without reason."

The Berckelang further said that a few days earlier Tjoucko had come to his house and had very earnestly requested his assistance on my behalf, on which occasion Tjoucko had promised that when matters had been resolved in a satisfactory manner, I would pay him five catties of silver. The Berckelang said that he had refused this offer, that he did not desire anything, that my arguments alone had persuaded him, and that my gratitude was dearer to him than any amount of gold or silver.

I replied that I thanked him most kindly for his favorable assistance, that I would always remember His Honor, and that my grateful affection would never change. Thereupon I said goodbye and returned to the lodge, greatly surprised that His Honor had not desired the five catties of silver that had been promised him, because this refusal ran very much counter to the general Siamese avariciousness. I resolved, however, to more closely test His Honor on this matter, and if he persisted in his refusal to accept the five catties of silver, to send him gifts of sufficient value to ensure that we will retain his favorable affection.

Around noon the Junior Merchant Reynier van Tsum, the Assistant Isaac Moerdijck,[49] and the rest of the party (which had been held by Oya Sicry) appeared in the lodge. The interpreters reported that the Berckelang had severely reproached Sicry over the way his *Braspintados* had treated the Hollanders, and that he had also been angry with Sicry because of his refusal

49. A few years later, in 1645, Isaac Moedijck rose to become Chief of the Company's Siam establishment. He was not, however, destined to remain long in this function, because just eight months after he took up his post he was murdered by the Company's cook, a certain Anthonio Rodrigo, who in a fit of rage hit him over the head with a *galegalle stamper* (a pestle used for mixing lime and linseed oil in a mortar). Moerdijck, apparently, was very much liked by the Siamese because of his fluency in their language and his careful observation of Siamese customs. King Prasat Thong himself ordered that his body be shown special respect (Smith 1977: 175).

to release the prisoners. The Berckelang had told Sicry not to demand any money from the Hollanders, and he had warned him that if he did ask for money, he would complain to the King. I replied to all this in a way which fully satisfied the interpreters.

We sharply questioned our people over the accusations that had been brought against them, and we found (as we had suspected all along) that the Prince and also the King (presumably because their fearful Siamese slaves had told them many exaggerations and untruths) had made far too much out of the incident. We also found, however, that Joost Laurentsz and Daniel Jacobsz, unbeknown to the rest of the party, had begun a fight with the slaves of the Prince, for which reason they have been the real instigators of all the troubles.

We further found that the rest of them had been well-intentioned. Seeing that Daniel had been seized and that he was being taken away, they had wanted to find out what the cause of the problem was; they had gone in pursuit, and had unwittingly strayed into His Highness' palace. And when the Junior Merchant Reynier stepped ashore, he was pelted so terribly with rocks that he was unable to advance further, let alone speak with anyone, so that (because the proa was drifting away from the shore), Reynier had no choice but to jump into the river and swim towards the proa. After he had reached the proa, Reynier had intended to row away, but at that moment the proa was surrounded by a host of Siamese proas, and without giving any reasons, the Siamese viciously attacked them as if they were public enemies; yes, as if they were traitors. With the approval of Mister Verwer (and in the presence of the interpreters), I had Joost Laurentsz and Daniel Jacobsz clapped in irons. The interpreters highly praised my decision to punish the instigators of the troubles, saying that they would tell the Berckelang about it and assuring us that His Honor would be pleased because it showed that we strongly disapprove of their behavior.

December 17, 1636

On December 17, we sold a quantity of copper to Oprae Siverodt,[50] alias Sitong Chinese, which (as we were secretly told) was intended for the King, who needed it badly because he wanted to repair some of his idols and there was no copper left in his factory. Ockon Thip and the Pecap (who were still guarding the lodge, ostensibly to protect us from the Japanese) came to the lodge to be present at the weighing of the copper. They were displeased that I had not told them about this copper sale, and they suggested that in future I should not trade without their foreknowledge, because they said the Berckelang had ordered them to pay close attention to everything and to promptly report to His Honor all that happened at the lodge. I was very

50. Probably Okphra Siwirot, ออกพระศรีวิโรจน์.

surprised about this, and I told them that the Company would never agree to place its trade in this Kingdom under the constraint of two slaves (which is what they are), and that we would sooner leave Siam altogether than surrender our liberties to such an extent.

In the evening the interpreter, Omon Wytsit Bassa, came to the lodge to tell us that the Pecap had visited the Berckelang to tell him about the copper sale. [The interpreter said] that His Honor had told the Pecap that he did not wish to know anything about such matters, that he had been stationed at the lodge not to spy on the Hollanders, but only to see to it that they do not come to any harm. If in the meantime [the Berckelang had continued], you should notice that strangers or people who are not to be trusted wish to buy anything at the lodge, you must warn the Captain. We were very pleased with this message, and I resolved to visit the Berckelang in the morning to complain about the unreasonable behavior of Ockon Thip and the Pecap.

December 18, 1636

On December 18, the Shahbandar, Olong Tsiut, and I went to the Berckelang. Upon arrival, we (and everyone else who had some business there) were told that His Honor had gone to the temple Watmoey[51] to assist in the cremation of the mother of the deceased Oya Corassima.[52] They advised us to wait awhile, because the Berckelang was expected to return home soon. We waited until midday, when we were told that the King had summoned the Berckelang to his palace, whereupon we returned to the lodge without having attained our end.

In the evening about two hours after sunset, Boatswain Joris Dirricksz, (who commands the barge *Crooswijck*), appeared here in the lodge. He had come from Bantiauphia[53] at the mouth of the river to bring me a letter from His Honor, Joost Schouten, dated December 4, in which he informed me that he was about to leave the roads in the ship *Delft*. The aforementioned Boatswain also told me that it was rumored at Bantiauphia that the King had attacked the lodge and that, on his orders, all of us had been put to death by elephants. [He further told me] that the local Siamese people at Bantiauphia were so filled with fear that for six days no one had dared even to come close to his barge, for which reason he had been unable all this time to buy food for himself and his people. At the beginning of all these troubles, I already feared that these bad tidings would spread far and wide, and that the officers of the

51. Possibly Wat Mai (วัดใหม่), which is on the northern bank of the old Lopburi River (Khlong Muang), beside Wat Na Pramen (วัดหน้าพระเมรุ), the royal cremation site. On Valentijn's map (1726), there is also a Wat Mai just across the river from the Dutch lodge.

52. Okya Nakhon Ratchasima (ออกญานครราชสีมา).

53. Ban Chaophraya (บ้านเจ้าพระยา), a settlement on the east bank at the mouth of the Chaophraya River.

Company ships that are expected to arrive soon would hear of these rumors and refuse to come upriver. This was the reason why, on the eleventh of this month, I had wanted to send a Hollander to Bantiauphia in a small proa to warn our people there, but because everyone was fearful, I was unable to give effect to this plan. For all these reasons, I decided to go to the Berckelang in the morning and ask him permission to send the Boatswain back downriver to tell the officers of the ships (which we are expecting to arrive any day) that everything is all right at the lodge.

December 19, 1636

On December 19, I went to see the Berckelang and, at our meeting, I proposed the following points to His Honor, namely:

"That Ockon Thip and the Pecap, whom His Honor a few days ago had sent to the lodge to protect us against the Japanese, had become extremely overbearing and were behaving as if we were their servants and they our masters. They had rudely prevented everyone, especially the small merchants (who, as they well know, are fearful of them), from entering the lodge, and when they had allowed someone to come inside, they had constantly stayed at my side so that I had hardly been able to speak to anyone, let alone to buy or sell anything."

"That His Honor should rectify this situation and see to it especially that Ockon Thip be recalled from the lodge, because at present we are so closely guarded by the King's people that it seems as if we are all prisoners in our own house."

"That the Shahbandar and the interpreters have told us that the King had renewed an old Siamese custom and had issued strict orders that the Hollanders, like all other foreign merchants, be they Muslims, Japanese or Portuguese, will no longer be allowed to employ as laborers either native-born people or foreign people domiciled in Siam."

"That from this decision I had to draw the conclusion (albeit reluctantly) that His Majesty was tired of the foreign merchants, and especially the Hollanders, because this order [will make it impossible for us to trade in this Kingdom] and seems designed to burden us so much that we, of our own accord, will pack up and leave Siam."

"That last night a Hollander (who is stationed at Bantiauphia with a Company barge), had arrived at the lodge in a small proa, fearful and under the cover of darkness, because down at the mouth of the river he had heard rumors that all the Hollanders in Ayutthaya had been executed on orders of the King. That it is urgently necessary to send him back downriver quickly with a *traa*[54] from the Berckelang and a letter from me, so that the ships'

54. A *tra* (ตรา) or seal, meaning a document carrying an official seal of authentication. It is explained below that in this case it means "a permit (*traa*) allowing our ships' officers to proceed further up river."

officers (that we are expecting to arrive any day) will not be alarmed by these shameful (but untrue) rumors and resort to hostilities."

In substance the Berckelang replied as follows: "That Ockon Thip and the interpreters had been stationed at the lodge on orders of the King for reasons as have been explained to me, but if indeed they had overstepped the mark, he would punish them and instruct them not to bother us again."

"That we should have a little patience with Ockon Thip, because he would not remain at the lodge long, although the interpreters would have to stay because the King had ordered them to keep an eye on trading activities in order to guard against fraud. And if in the future (said His Honor), you should have occasion to take action against someone for nonpayment and such like, we will be able to make a sound judgment. By way of example, the Berckelang cited the case of the Japanese Faoske and Tymon, telling me how these two villains had cheated Radie Ebrehem. They had borrowed forty catties of silver from Radie Ebrehem, which they had refused to repay, saying that they were under no obligation to do so until the Japanese junks (which left here in 1634) returned from Japan, and since Radie had lent them the money without witnesses being present, His Majesty (doubting the veracity of Radie's claim) did not wish that a judgment be passed in this matter."

"That he was well aware that foreign merchants would be unable to conduct their affairs without Siamese laborers and proa hands, but that the King (in accordance with old Siamese customs) nonetheless had given this order. [Even though the order had made things difficult for us], I should believe and be assured that His Majesty had a deep affection for the foreign merchants, especially the Hollanders (on account of their courteous behavior). For this reason he would raise this issue with His Majesty when a suitable opportunity arose, on which occasion he would propose and ensure that [the order be revoked] and that everything be regulated as had been customary in the past. [The Berckelang added] that he would have been able to intercede sooner and more boldly if our ships had arrived, because he was sure (said His Honor) that with our ships at the mouth of the river, the King would neither deny nor refuse my request."

"That it was entirely understandable that I should wish to send one of my people with a letter to Bantiauphia in order to reassure the ships' officers who were expected to arrive soon, and that this would please His Majesty, who was certain to issue a *traa* later in the day." After I had attended to the Company's affairs in this way, I parted from His Honor in an amicable way and returned home.

December 20, 1636

On December 20, the interpreter, Omon Wytsit, came to the lodge to tell us, in the name of the Berckelang, that the King had been very pleased to hear that I had requested permission to send a Hollander to Bantiauphia to prevent calamities from occurring, and that His Majesty had ordered that he, Omon Wytsit, should go down river with this Hollander and remain in Bantiauphia or in Bancocq until such time as the ships appeared in order [to speak to the ships' officers] and dispel the evil rumors that have been circulating.

The aforementioned interpreter urged me write to the ships' officers advising them to give credence to his words concerning Siamese customs. I did as he had asked, whereupon I sent downriver Boatswain Joris Dirricksz (who had arrived here on December 18) along with the interpreter, Omon Wytsit. In the letter which I gave to the Boatswain, I ordered the ships' officers, who were expected to appear soon at the river's mouth, to quickly load their cargoes into the barges *Crooswijck* and *Carloys* (which are waiting for the ships at Bantiauphia) so that these goods will soon arrive here at the lodge. [I further told them] to take great care (in case they came from Japan) to secure the money, to guard it closely, and to send it to me as soon as possible.

December 21, 1636

On December 21, I sold a small quantity of cloth to Radie Ebrehem. [While this transaction was taking place] the Pecap remained constantly by our side; he counted the cloths that were sold, wrote down what types they were, and noted the prices for which they were sold. I asked the Pecap who had appointed him head of the Company's lodge and on whose authority he was acting. He replied that he had orders to act in this way. I demanded to see the written order the Berckelang had given him and found that all he and Ockon Thip had been instructed to do was to see to it that no one committed any frauds against us. Even though I clearly explained the order to this beast and admonished him to do his duty, I was unable to expel the beastliness from his head, and he remained resolved, so it appeared, to persevere in his wickedness. For this reason I began to think of ways to remove him from his service.

December 22, 1636

On December 22, I went to see Oloang Tsiut and told him about the unreasonable behavior of Ockon Thip and especially of the Pecap. I complained about the way they were constantly watching everyone in the lodge and said that under these circumstances we were unable to carry out our duties properly, so that it was inevitable that the Company's trade in Siam would suffer. I pointed out that these Siamese procedures were so difficult for us as to be almost unbearable, and I asked him to accompany me to the Berckelang in order to help me impress upon His Honor the urgency of immediate redress. Oloang Tsiut advised me to stay at home today and said that he would speak to the Berckelang first and smooth the path on my behalf. [He further advised me] to go to the Berckelang tomorrow with a valuable gift, because (said Oloang Tsiut), even if His Honor has refused to accept the five catties of silver, he will certainly be pleased if you honor him with a gift as a token of your gratitude. I was unable to reject this suggestion because we really do need the Berckeleng's help in this matter.

December 23, 1636

On December 23, I went to see the Berckelang with the Shahbandar, Oloang Tsiut, on which occasion I presented His Honor with a valuable gift, whereupon I stated my grievances as follows:

"That the annoyances which Ockon Thip and the Pecap regularly inflict upon us have become unbearable, for which reason I requested His Honor's intercession. [I added] that since we now had to rely more on interpreters, the Pecap was an entirely unsuitable person because he only knew the Siamese and the Moorish languages."

"That even though the King had released all the Hollanders and had sent them back to the lodge, he nonetheless had continued to restrict my freedom and hamper the Company's trading activities, even though I had never given even the slightest offense against either His Majesty or against the laws of the land."

"That any day now we expected our ships to arrive, for which reason we urgently required a large number of laborers to collect the wooden beams, the planks, and all the other goods, because all this merchandise needed to be shipped downriver so that everything could be loaded onto the ships. And now we were unable to get permission; yes, we were not even allowed to hire laborers for money (according to long-established practice), which is a great inconvenience because it prevents us bringing down to the lodge the sappan wood the King has granted us and which we had not received earlier on account of the high water level. All this is most unreasonable. [The prohibition on hiring labor], as well as many other intolerable rules, each day inflicts greater damage upon our trade, which means that when our ships arrive, they will have to stay here much longer than necessary to the Company's loss and to my heartache and shame."

"That we are unable to draw any other conclusion than that the King, contrary to his assertions, does not value the friendship of the Netherlanders. [If he did value this friendship] he would not, for such minor failings, have disgraced our nation and have threatened to throw some of us under the feet of the elephants."

"That His Honor please take to heart my arguments, complaints, and requests and advocate my case with His Majesty so that we may quickly be restored to our former freedoms. [Quick redress] is necessary also to avoid trouble with His Lordship, the General, because I am duty bound to report truthfully everything that happens here." I added such additional arguments as the subject matter required.

When I had finished, the Berckelang replied as follows: "I have always said that Ockon Thip would not stay long at the lodge, and if you are dissatisfied with the Pecap (because he does not know your language), I will propose to His Majesty, and if possible I will see to it, that another person be placed in his position. But everything requires time. The King does not keep you prisoner; he does not obstruct commerce; and when your ships arrive, you will be allowed to hire laborers as before. You also have the wrong impression [if you think] that His Majesty does not value the friendship of the Netherlanders, because I assure you that he esteems them above any foreign nation that frequents Siam. You also should not think that the shame which befell your people is so great. This is a common Siamese plague, a plague from which even the mandarins are not exempt. I myself have been in heavy imprisonment on many occasions, most recently in the past year. I cannot imagine wherein lies the shame. Rather than shameful, these periods of imprisonment were admonitions to better behavior and to a more careful life. The only complaint that I have is that these difficulties have arisen right at the beginning of my service [as Berckelang] and that I cannot immediately rectify everything in accordance with your wishes and my inclination. But please be patient; I shall assist you in everything." Whatever other arguments we advanced, His Honor responded to all of them in the same vein, so that it became quite obvious that there would be no redress before the arrival of the ships.

December 24, 1636

On December 24, I went to the house of Radie Ebrehim and told him what had transpired at my meeting with the Berckelang of the previous day. Radie Ebrehim agreed with me. He, too, was of the opinion that the Berckelang was a good, honest, diligent, and faithful helper of the foreigners, but that he was either too fearful of the King or simply too timid. He suspected that His Honor would not dare to raise our business with the King before the arrival of our ships, when he could not avoid speaking to His Majesty about trade issues. And because the Prince and the Berckelang are good friends, I decided, with the approval of the others, to send Radie to the Prince with a gift consisting of four yards of red cloth (super fine), which he was to present to His Highness in my name. He should then, in a mild-mannered way, restate all the complaints and arguments I had put to the Berckelang and request that His Highness assist in this matter. I also decided to send Oloang Tsiut to the Berckelang tomorrow to gently remind him of our grievances, and also in the hope that by that time the Prince would have spoken to him. [In this way] the Berckelang would be spurred on from two sides simultaneously.

December 25, 1636

On December 25, I sent for Oloang Tsiut, and when he arrived at the lodge, I suggested to him that he should try (if possible) to persuade the Berckelang to remove Ockon Thip from the lodge and grant us permission to take on workers or *coulys*. The Shahbandar undertook to go to the Berckelang immediately and to state our case to the best of his ability. In the evening we learned that the Shahbandar had been to see the Berckelang and that he had stated our requests, to which His Honor had replied that we should not be so impatient, that he would take care of us as if we were of his own family, but that it would take time.

December 26, 1636

On December 26, I went to the house of Radie Ebrehem, who told me that earlier in the day he had presented the Prince with the four yards of red cloth, that he had had a wide-ranging discussion with His Highness about the Netherlands and the commerce of the Indies, and that [during this discussion] His Highness had asked him honestly and without hypocrisy or flattery to answer the following questions:

"Whether I was personally wealthy? Whether I still kept my people locked in irons and what I intended to do with them? Whether I was displeased with His Highness because, perhaps, I felt he had been too quick to report the incident to the King and had exaggerated the seriousness of what had transpired? Whether I felt any hatred for His Majesty for the way he had treated our people, and whether I intended to report the incident to His Lordship, the General? Whether it would be more reasonable to accept my gift or to return it politely on the grounds that he had never done me any favors whatsoever?"

Radie Ebrehem had replied as follows:

"That I was reasonably well-off. That the two Hollanders (who were most guilty) were still locked in irons because that was His Majesty's wish, even though after sharp questioning of everyone involved, I had not been able to conclude that the offense they had committed deserved such severe punishment (as they had already undergone).[55] That nonetheless, it remained my intention to send them to Batavia so that their case could be judged by His Lordship, the General, and also so that the Siamese should not lay eyes on them again and, therefore, not be tempted to take revenge, because this could lead to even greater trouble."

55. Van Vliet did not exaggerate here because to be locked in irons for an extended period of time was indeed a severe physical punishment. By December 26, the two Assistants, Joost Laurentsz and Daniel Blijswijck, had been in irons for about ten days. All this time they had been kept in a sitting position in the lodge's prison hut with their wrists locked between their ankles, an extremely uncomfortable position that would have produced excruciating back pains.

"That I had not shown any displeasure with the Prince, but that clearly I wished His Highness had acted more carefully when the troubles first occurred and had refrained from trampling underfoot the honor of the Netherlands. [That I wished] that instead of sending our people to the Berckelang, he had sent them to me at the lodge, and that, if indeed he had been required to report the incident to the King, he had done so in a restrained manner, because, [I was convinced that if these things had happened in this way], His Majesty's anger would not have been aroused against our people."

"That I had repeatedly complained that the King's procedures against our people had been far too excessive, and still were, because even though His Majesty had freed the accused Hollanders and had sent them to the lodge, he still maintained guards around the Company's buildings so that it seemed as if I was being held prisoner. [In addition], I was to be held personally responsible for all the offenses which our people in future might commit against the laws of the Kingdom. [And if all this was not enough], the Company's trading activities have come to a complete standstill because we have been unable to obtain permission to hire laborers. And even though I had on many occasions sought the Berckelang's intervention on behalf of the Company, the only reply I had received (on account of his faint-heartedness) was that our ships have not yet arrived; and that when the ships do arrive, he will have occasion to discuss our affairs with the King. But since the ships evidently have been delayed, it will be expected of us to have loaded the cargoes in barges and to have them ready for shipment at the mouth of the river. That even though I am embarrassed to request His Highness' intercession with His Majesty (because I am not certain of His Highness' affection), I nonetheless make bold to do so lest His Lordship, the General, accuse me of cowardice or negligence. [This he could do] because I am duty bound to accurately report on a daily basis everything that transpires here (especially an incident of this nature), and I may propose to go to Batavia in person in order to report everything orally to His Lordship."

"That if His Highness returned the gift, he would demonstrate thereby that he bore ill will towards the Hollanders and towards me."

The Prince replied as follows:

"I regret that the Hollanders have been in a fight with my slaves and it was not my intention to send them to the Berckelang. I had wanted to send them to the merchant at the lodge [i.e., Van Vliet], but I was outvoted by all the mandarins (who were at the palace at the time). Everyone thought this was the best thing to do because the King had elevated me higher than any of the other Princes. [I had to be very careful] because, [had I acted differently], His Majesty (who is full of jealousy) might easily have concluded that I was closer to the Hollanders and to His Lordship, the General, than is warranted.[56] In

56. These fears were not unfounded, because in his bloodstained rise to power King Prasat Thong had conspired to bring about the executions of three princes,

addition, these mandarins said, Oya Berckelang, as the advocate of the foreigners, is best able to investigate the matter impartially, and either to report the incident to His Majesty or to settle matters amicably between His Highness and the Captain of the Hollanders. And even if the King should hear about the incident later, everything could then be presented in the most favorable light, and His Highness would remain beyond reproach. In the meantime, (said His Highness), my mother (who thought that the Hollanders had entered the palace bearing arms and that they had almost seized me) had told His Majesty about the matter, whereupon the King flew in a rage and condemned the Hollanders to death. [But in retrospect] His Majesty wishes (and so do I) that this matter had never occurred, or that at the beginning everything had been truthfully reported to him."

In addition, His Highness, the Prince, ordered Radie Ebrehem to bring the following points to my attention:

"That when the lodge was built [in Ayutthaya], His Highness, on three occasions had received valuable gifts from His Lordship, the General, and from Captain Schouten, an honor that he had not deserved, and, much to his regret, he had not reciprocated for fear of arousing the King's jealousy. But that notwithstanding his negligence, I should be assured of His Highness sincere and pure affection for His Lordship, the General, the Netherlands nation, the Company, and for me personally."

"That in my report to His Lordship, the General, I should guide my pen with moderation in order not to damage the friendship between the Siamese and the Netherlands nations, a friendship that not only must continue but should strengthen and deepen. His Highness is at a complete loss to understand what may have led to the distrust between our people and his slaves, so much so that he regards the discord as a work of the devil rather than of human beings."

"That I should take great care to manage everything in such a way so as not to arouse the anger of His Lordship, the General, lest the friendship diminish, troubles arise, and the seeds of war be sown, which would be to the detriment of both nations, to His Highness' eternal regret, and to my dishonor."

"That His Highness was displeased that I proposed to go to Batavia. Even if His Lordship, the General, should recall me [to Batavia] and write to the King about this matter, His Majesty would be unlikely to let me go because the arrival at the lodge of a new Captain, a Captain unfamiliar with Siamese customs, might possibly give rise to new troubles."

---

namely, the brother (and rightful heir to the throne) of his cousin, King Songtham (1610–29), and two of Songtham's sons, as well as all their followers; see the *Historical Account*.

"And finally, that I should not lose courage, and that I could rest assured that His Highness would order the Berckelang to assist me in all my requests and to restore the Company to all its former freedoms. And if His Highness should find that the Berckelang was negligent or too timid, he himself would speak to the King, in which case he had no doubt that all my requests would be granted." Radie Ebrehem repeated the aforementioned points so many times that it was very late before I returned to the lodge.

December 27, 1636

On December 27, I went to the Berckelang once again to remind His Honor of the most urgent Company issues; namely, our pressing need to obtain workers, of our objections to the continued stationing of guards at the lodge, and of our desire to be rid of the insufferable Pecap once and for all. His Honor promised to look after these matters very soon, whereupon I took my leave and went home. In the evening Oloang Tsiut came to the lodge to tell me that earlier in the day the Berckelang had been to the palace, that he had spoken to the King about our affairs, and that I was to appear at his house in the morning.

December 28, 1636

On December 28 early in the morning, I again went to the Berckelang, who told me that he had spoken to the King about our requests, and that His Majesty had made the following decisions:

"That since we are not satisfied with the Pecap, he will be removed from our service and be placed with the Muslims. Omon Trompanit has been released from his bonds and will once again be our interpreter, but, in order to keep an eye on everything, Ockon Thip will maintain his guards at the lodge for a while yet."

"That His Majesty is prepared to give us a permit allowing us to hire as many workers and proa keepers as we require in order to carry out the Company's business, but that before issuing this license, the King demanded I sign a document promising that all the Hollanders presently in Siam, and all those who may come to the Kingdom in the future, will obey its laws and customs, and agreeing that if any of them should offend against these laws and customs, I was to be held personally responsible and be subject to His Majesty's punishment."

Our reply was as follows:

"That we thank His Honor for his advocacy and that we are very pleased to be relieved of the ill-mannered Pecap, but that we would have liked to have been allocated a more able interpreter than Trompanidt (because he knows little language). However, the King's will is our command in this matter. [I also accept] that I have to be patient in respect of the guarding of the lodge by Ockon Thip."

"I am also very pleased to be allowed to hire workers once again, but the demand that I agree in writing to be held responsible for any faults our people may commit imposes a heavy and sheer unbearable burden upon me. [This burden is all the heavier] because the Hollanders are not familiar with the customs of the Kingdom and also because the Siamese laws are severe. In case the King makes this demand of me alone, I will necessarily have to obey (because I am forced to), but I would be obliged to write to His Lordship, the General, informing him that I am not prepared to continue in Siam under such harsh conditions."

The Berckelang replied that it was the clear, unambiguous will of the King that I give a written guarantee for all the Netherlanders [in Siam] and that I ought to accept this demand without protestations. [His Honor added] that His Majesty had instructed him not to issue a permit for the hiring of workers until I had well and truly given the written undertaking. I made various objections and protestations, but it was all to no avail. I had no choice but to accept this demand.

In the evening, the interpreter Omon Wytsit Bassa (who on December 20 had been sent to Bantiauphia) arrived back at the lodge. He had come from Bancocq and told us that there had been no sign as yet of any Company ships. He further reported that the Siamese guards at Bancocq had received orders to detain our ships' officers (who are expected to arrive any day) when they come upriver on the barges. The arrival of our ships has to be reported first to the Berckelang, who in turn has to report it to the King, and only with His Majesty's permission can the Berckelang issue a permit (*traa*) allowing our ships' officers to proceed further upriver. And since the interpreter had heard nothing about these orders when he went downriver [on December 20], and because he suspected that the jittery gunners at Bancocq might have made this up out of fear, he had come upriver in order to obtain certainty from the Berckelang himself.

We were greatly saddened by this report, because if these orders were indeed to be enforced, our ships' officers would have to stay at Bancocq until a permit arrived from Ayutthaya, which would take at least 5 to 6 days even if everything was handled expeditiously. This would mean a considerable delay for our ships. God grant that with the Berckelang's assistance these damaging orders soon may be rescinded.

December 29, 1636

On December 29, I was called to the Berckelang's house. Arriving there, His Honor told me that, in accordance with the old laws of Siam, the King had ordered the officers of all the ships arriving in the roads [of Bantiauphia] to wait at Bancocq until he, the Berckelang, had received written confirmation of the ships' arrival and had notified the King. The ships' officers would be allowed to proceed on to Ayutthaya only after the King had given his consent, and he, the Berckelang, had issued a permit. But since this was a new regulation with which our people were not familiar, I was to send the interpreter, Omon Wytsit Bassa, back downriver with an order to this effect, which the interpreter was to hand to the King's soldiers in Bancocq, so that these soldiers could show the order to our people when they came upriver on their barges.

I told the Berckelang that this was a most irksome law, a law which would serve to ruin the Company's trade in Siam. [I pointed out] that the ships (especially those coming from Batavia) sailing for Japan and Taiwan necessarily arrive here late in the year, because the southerly winds which are to carry them here do not blow any earlier. And because the monsoon season is very short, it is necessary, lest these ships endanger their voyages, that they be sent on their way as quickly as possible. If we were to be restricted by the necessity to have this permit, the barges would appear at the lodge at least eight days later than usual, which is an intolerable situation, because the success or failure of an entire voyage can sometimes depend on a single day. Moreover, during the additional eight days that the barges would lay idle [at Bancocq], they would be unable to provide the ships [in the roads of Bantiauphia] with water and firewood, whilst we [at the Ayutthaya lodge] would be prevented from sending the cargoes downriver.

I added a number of similar protestations, but it was all to no avail, because the Berckelang remained firm in his standpoint, declaring that this was the will of the King, insisting that I send the order downriver, and urging me to have a little patience. His Honor did mention, however, that he could well understand that merchants could not and should not be restricted in this way, for which reason he promised once again to discuss this matter with His Majesty. But he had decided to wait until our ships arrived, because with our ships in the roads, he would be able to put my complaints to the King with greater frankness. All in all, the Berckelang gave me the hope that this contrived new law will soon be nullified.

I realized, however, that I would be unable at this time to reach my objective and that the ships' officers and their barges would necessarily be delayed, much to the detriment of the Company. For this reason, I decided to ask one of the Netherlanders in the lodge to accompany the interpreter to Bancocq and to stay there until the arrival of our barges, so that I at least would quickly receive the letters, etc. which they would be carrying. The Berckelang approved this and immediately ordered Simeenraedt[57] to write out a permit. Thereupon I took my leave and returned home, where I wrote the following order addressed to the gunners at Bancocq:

> The Company servants who are about to arrive, as well as the freemen who may be sailing on the ships, are hereby instructed to obey the bearers of this

57. Probably *samian rat* (เสมียนราช), a clerk of some kind.

order (officers of the King of Siam), to lay up their barges, to tell the officers whence they came, and to remain in Bancocq until such time as the officers have sent word of their arrival to the Berckelang in the city of Judia [Ayutthaya] and the Berckelang has issued a permit to the aforementioned officers in Bancocq. This is an order from His Majesty, the King, which you people have to obey and observe in order to safeguard the Company's interests in Siam. Done in the city of Judia, at the factory of Siam, December 29, 1636.

Signed: Your well intentioned friend, Jeremias van Vliet

December 30, 1636

Before daybreak on December 30, the interpreter Omon Wytsit Bassa came to the lodge. He told me that he had waited all day yesterday for a permit to go to Bancocq (with one of our people), that the Berckelang had now given him his permit, and that His Honor had ordered him to remain in Bancocq until the Holland ships arrived. I sent the boatswain, Louis Pierre, to accompany the aforementioned interpreter, handed him the above order, and told him to give it to the King's gunners in Bancocq. I further handed him a sealed letter addressed to the ships' officers who are soon expected to appear there, in which these officers are advised to give the missives they are carrying to the aforementioned Pierre so that he can quickly take them to the lodge at Ayutthaya and let me know what the situation is with the ships, what kind of cargoes they can carry, and also what their requirements are. In this way, the time that the ships' officers have to stay at Bancocq will not be entirely wasted.

Today I presented the Shahbandar, Oloang Tsiut, with a draft of the statement by which I was to agree to be held personally responsible for the behavior of the Netherlanders in this country. The aforementioned Shahbandar did not object to the thrust of my statement, but he suggested that it should be shorter and more to the point. [He took it with him] and, after long consultations with the Berckelang, returned the statement to me with the suggestions that I put it in the Siamese script, that I have it written out neatly, that I sign it with my name and affix my seal on it.

December 31, 1636

On December 31, the Muslim merchant, Radie Ebrehem, and the Chinese, Tjoucko and Sitong, bought nearly all the Company's cloths that were available at the lodge for such prices as have been recorded in the account books. The aforementioned merchants asked Trompanidt, the interpreter, whether he wanted to count the goods they had bought and take note of their prices like the Pecap had done. Trompanidt replied that the Berckelang had not issued any orders to do this, either to him or to the Pecap, [and he added] that it was His Honor's will and pleasure (as indeed it was the King's) that our trade should be free, that the Pecap had not been sent to the lodge to place restrictions upon us, but that he had appointed himself to do this. Trompanidt further said that he had not been sent to the lodge to spy on us, but that the only reason he had come here was to prevent (as much as was in his power) troubles from arising and to settle all disputes connected with the buying and selling of merchandise. This, he said, was the only objective of the King and his mandarins.

Today I gave Oloang Tsiut the statement I had been forced to write, [the statement] by which I had to agree to be held personally accountable for all the Netherlanders residing here. It read as follows:

> On the fifth day of the waxing moon, named Deun Gy, in the year of the rat, Oya Berckelang, via the Shahbandar, Oloang Tsiut Raymontry, has demanded this statement from me, Jeremias van Vliet (Chief of the Company's lodge and trade in Siam), by which I promise, as much as is in my power, obediently to observe, in accordance with the laws and customs of this Kingdom, all the orders and recommendations pertaining to the Netherlanders residing in Siam that come from the aforementioned Berckelang and are given to us by the Shahbandar, interpreters etc., and I agree that I (being the Chief) will be held personally accountable for all offenders, to which I pledge myself. At Ayutthaya, at the Siam lodge, the last day of December 1636.
>
> At the side was my seal, pressed in red wax.
> Was signed: Jeremias van Vliet.

[Oloang Tsiut took the above statement to the Berckelang] who ordered him to keep it and safeguard it and promised to send us a permit in the morning by which we would once again be allowed to hire and use workers and proas for the Company's service.

January 1, 1637

On January 1[1637], the Shahbandar, Oloang Tsiut, and the interpreter, Trompanidt, came to the lodge to bring us the long awaited and dearly bought *traa*, with which (so they said) we would once again be permitted to hire workers and proas and deal freely with everyone without restrictions. [They further told us] that Ockon Thip would be guarding the lodge a few days longer. We told the Shahbandar to thank the Berckelang on our behalf for all his help, adding that we trusted that through His Honor's righteous assistance we would soon be restored to all our former freedoms. Oloang Tsiut further told us that the Berckelang had suggested that it would be very good under the present circumstances to present the King with a substantial gift, and that in addition we should express our gratitude to His Majesty for his beneficence (especially his merciful redemption of our people and his forgiveness of their crimes). [He added] that this was the custom of the country, that it would please the King and that, [as a consequence of His Majesty's favor], the Berckelang would dare in future to speak more freely on our behalf.

We replied that it was indeed true that the King had shown us great favor, and that we owed him gratitude, but that; at the same time I remained of the opinion that King's latest procedures against our people over such minor faults had been far too harsh. [I added] that I would leave this issue to the wiser judgment of His Lordship, the General, in Batavia, that we trusted he would be our best counselor, and that we would obey His Lordship's will in this matter. After long deliberations, the Shahbandar, the interpreter, and I agreed [on a suitable set of gifts for the King], and we made available a piece of Persian gold cloth, eight yards of red cloth (superfine), and some trifles, which they would take to the Berckelang so that he, in accordance with the customs of the court, could present them to the King along with such of our compliments as the occasion demanded.

January 3, 1637

On January 3, I was called to the Berckelang's house. Upon arrival, His Honor told me that on the previous day he had presented the gifts to the King on my behalf, that His Majesty had accepted them with pleasure, and that His Majesty had ordered him to inform me that within a few days His Majesty would call me to his court in order to appear in person before him. [The Berckelang added] that I should put my faith in this and that I should be ready to go to the court at all times. We thanked His Honor for the trouble he had taken in presenting our gifts [to the King] and said that we would be forever mindful of his efforts on our behalf. We were very surprised, unable to think of any reason why the King should wish us to appear before him. We talked about it with various friends, all of whom were of the opinion that the King wanted to show everyone that his anger had abated and that he was now completely reconciled with the Hollanders (who had insulted him). In summary, everyone was of the opinion that this could only bring honor to our nation and be of service to the Company. God Almighty grant that this may be so.

January 4, 1637

On January 4, Osoet Pegua (formerly Meerwijck's concubine)[58] informed me that earlier in the day one of the Queen's state-daughters had called her to the palace and had told her that Her Majesty for some time now had

58. Van Vliet forgot to mention that Osoet Pegua was now his concubine. In fact, Van Vliet was to have three daughters by Osoet Pegua (also called Tjau Soet) born between 1636 and 1641, the eldest of whom was named Maria. For more information on Osoet Pegua see Kraan (1998: 70–1), Dhiravat (1996: 11–12).

intended to send me one of her state-daughters. [The Queen had wanted to do this] because she was sure that my mind was troubled and my heart was pained about the King's procedures, but Her Majesty had refrained from actually sending the girl out of fear (that the other concubines, who would be jealous, should tell the King about it). [Osoet Pegua further told me] that the Queen was greatly disappointed and very displeased with the King's procedures because His Majesty had never before inveighed so severely against any foreigners, for which reason Her Majesty wanted to implore me not to think the worst and not to write to His Lordship, the General, so that great troubles might be avoided.

We could not believe that the Queen had sent this message of her own volition. We thought it much more likely that this had occurred with foreknowledge of the King, perhaps because His Majesty had come to regret his actions, or perhaps because he had been mellowed by the gifts he had received.

January 14, 1637

The 10th day after this last entry [i.e. 14 January], the Berckelang said to me: "It is now about 24 days since the Assistants, Joost Laurentsz and Daniel Jacobsz, have been locked in irons for the crimes they have committed. You have acted cautiously and wisely in punishing them in this way, because [by doing this] the King, and all of us, have become convinced of Your Honor's sincerity. His Majesty, however, has taken pity on them and has forgiven them all their failings. Release them of their bonds. And when you write to His Lordship, the General, tell him that His Majesty wishes that they be spared further punishment, which is also my earnest request to the General." We thanked the Berckelang and said that we would obey his commands. Arriving home, we unlocked the aforementioned Assistants and ordered them to stay in their room for the time being so that they would remain (as much as possible) out of the sight of people.

January 17, 1637

On January 17, around noon, I was summoned to appear at the court. When all the nobles had gone inside, the interpreter, Trompanidt, ushered me in. After we had passed through the court's innermost gate, Trompanidt handed me the base of a *pinang*-head[59] in which was placed a small wooden tray with flowers and fried rice and requested that I take it in both hands, crouch down, and in this way carry it towards the King in the audience hall. But since I knew that this was an admission of guilt, which all delinquents have to perform in this manner (when they reconcile themselves with the

59. A *pinang* is an areca palm, but it is difficult to imagine which part of the tree is indicated.

King and want to show their gratitude), I politely refused, arguing that I had not committed any offense against His Majesty. But after much consternation, I was forced to carry the unworthy token, which I did most reluctantly and under protestations of innocence.

There were more people in the audience hall than I had ever seen before. When we had approached [the throne] to a distance of about 60 meters, to the point where the mandarins were positioned, I had to crawl with the aforementioned tray in one hand until I reached the meeting. As soon as I had arrived there, the King appeared on his throne, and before His Majesty spoke to anyone, the Berckelang addressed him as follows: "Captain van Vliet appears at this meeting before Your Majesty to show his gratitude for the mercy Your Majesty has been pleased to show towards his people (who reside with him in Your Majesty's Kingdom) by forgiving them their crimes."

To which the King replied thus: "It is now about four years that you, Captain van Vliet, have resided in my Kingdom, during which time you have carried out your work in accordance with the laws of this Kingdom, for which reason I am favorably disposed towards your person. I have no doubt that you are completely familiar with my laws, and since this is the case, it will be necessary that you instruct the people who reside with you and that you govern them in such a way that the customs of my Kingdom will be observed. Some days ago, a group of Netherlanders so badly offended at my temple and at the palace of the Prince that I became enraged. I could have punished them for their deeds, but due to the long-established friendship with the King of Holland and with His Lordship, the General, in Batavia, and also due to your intercession, I have decided to forgive them and I shall not think of it again. And finally, I desire that such licentiousness be prevented, that it does not occur again so that my anger will not be aroused against you. And further, I desire that you carry the burden for your people because, henceforth, I shall hold no one responsible but you, because you are their head, and since this is so, it is entirely reasonable that you care for your people and that you are responsible for them."

After the King had spoken, I had to throw the flowers and the fried rice over my head, and after touching my head reverentially to the ground, I modestly replied as follows: "I shall set an example for my people by leading a regular, orderly life (as I have always done). I shall take care that all misfortunes be prevented, and that the laws of the land be observed as much as possible, with which I trust Your Majesty will be satisfied."

The King replied: "I love and care for all foreigners who frequent my country and come to my Kingdom to trade, but I am particularly well disposed towards the Holland nation because of their cordiality and righteousness. I love the Hollanders like my own people and I care for them in equal measure. I shall give no cause to diminish the friendship with the King of Holland and His Lordship, the General, in Batavia, as long as the sun and moon shall shine. You must also undertake to do this, and you will certainly succeed as long as His Lordship, the General, in addition to yourself (who knows the laws of this land), sends to Siam only considerate people with good manners and lets them stay longer than has been the case in the past. This you should recommend to His Lordship."

I replied reverentially as follows because there [in Siam] it cannot be otherwise: "I do not doubt that our King in Holland and His Lordship, the General, are very pleased with Your Majesty's affection, of which I during my residence here have witnessed numerous instances. Furthermore, it is the will of our principals that their servants observe the laws and customs of the countries in which they reside so that their profits will not be diminished by unnecessary difficulties."

The King had spoken the words I have related in such an emphatic and earnest manner that everyone at the court was greatly surprised. In the meantime, the Ambassador of Cotop Tsia[60] had entered the audience hall. His Majesty spoke with the Ambassador (according to the customs of the court), and after he had finished, he rose from his throne and left the audience hall without addressing anyone else. Hereupon the whole gathering rose, but I had to crawl out of the audience hall in the same way I had entered. After I left the hall, I returned to the lodge.

January 18, 1637

On January 18, the Shahbandar, Oloang Tsiut, came to the lodge with the interpreters. They told me how surprised all the mandarins had been about the King's speech of yesterday, declaring that it was a clear indication of His Majesty's sincere affection for our nation and for my person. I complained, however, that I had been wronged and that I had been deeply humiliated by having to appear before the whole gathering as if I were a criminal, even though I had never committed even the slightest offense. I also said that even though our people had been accused, it had never been proven that they were in fact responsible for the troubles. I further declared that if I had known what humiliations awaited me, if I had known that I had to crawl in and out of the audience hall, I would never have appeared at the court. Oloang Tsiut said that he had feared as much and that he had told the Berckelang of his fears, for which reason they had kept everything hidden from me. He assured me, however, that it was to the honor of our nation, that it would advance our trade, and [he assured me] that later in the day Ockon Thip and his guard proa would be withdrawn from the lodge. I was content with this news, because as long as I can advance the service of my principals, I fear neither humiliation nor dishonor.

60. See the *Description*, p. 144, fn. 116.

DESCRIPTION OF THE KINGDOM OF SIAM

1638

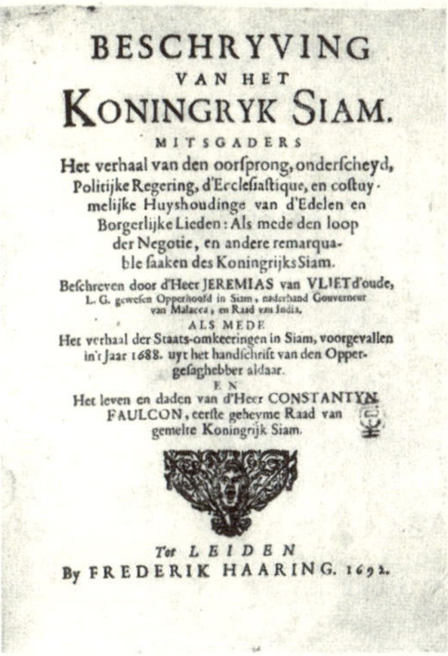

BESCHRYVING
VAN HET
KONINGRYK SIAM.
MITSGADERS
Het verhaal van den oorſprong, onderſcheyd, Politijke Regering, d'Eccleſiaſtique, en coſtuymelijke Huyshoudinge van d'Edelen en Borgerlijke Lieden: Als mede den loop der Negotie, en andere remarquable ſaaken des Koningrijks Siam.
Beſchreven door d'Heer JEREMIAS van VLIET d'oude, L. G. geweſen Opperhoofd in Siam, naderhand Gouverneur van Malacca, en Raad van India.
ALS MEDE
Het verhaal der Staats-omkeeringen in Siam, voorgevallen in't Jaar 1688. uyt het handſchrift van den Opper-geſaghebber aldaar.
EN
Het leven en daden van d'Heer CONSTANTYN FAULCON, eerſte geheyme Raad van gemelte Koningrijk Siam.
Tot LEIDEN
By FREDERIK HAARING. 1692.

Title page of original publication, 1692

Beschrijving van het Koningrijk Siam, mitsgaders het verhael van den oorsprong, onderscheid, politieke regeering, d'ecclesiastique en costuymelijke huijshoudingen van d'edelen en burgerlijke lieden, alsmede de loop der negotie en andere remarquable saecken des Koningrijks Siam (Leyden: Frederik Haaring, 1692)

Description of the Kingdom of Siam and the account of the origin, the political government, the distinctive characteristics, the religion, the manner of living of the nobles and common people, the commerce and other remarkable things concerning the Kingdom of Siam

TRANSLATED BY

L. F. VAN RAVENSWAAY

Journal of the Siam Society, 7 (1910)

EDITED AND INTRODUCED BY

CHRIS BAKER

Frontispiece of original publication, 1692

INTRODUCTION

Chris Baker

VAN VLIET'S *Description* and that of Schouten written slightly earlier are the earliest known detailed accounts of Ayutthaya as a major Asian capital and trading port. Modern scholars tend to cherry-pick these works for their information on trade, political organization, and social life. But Van Vliet's account in particular was written with a purpose. This aspect is often ignored. Here I want to elucidate Van Vliet's *argument.*

Van Vliet wrote the *Description* to save his career. He had been summoned to Batavia to explain the 1636 "Picnic Incident," which had threatened the Dutch position in Siam and resulted in Van Vliet tendering an official apology which his boss, the Governor-General, considered humiliating for the VOC. The *Description* is thus partly an attempt to explain how the Picnic Incident happened and why Van Vliet handled it the way he did. But it is more than that. Van Vliet was not only exculpating his past actions, but also hustling (successfully) for a promotion. To this end, he offered his boss a vision of what the Dutch might achieve in Siam with a little ambition.

Van Vliet wrote the *Description* between the close of the Picnic Incident in January 1637, and his presentation of the manuscript in Batavia in mid-1638. He may have written it in Ayutthaya, but according to his own claim in the opening passages of the later *Historical Account,* he wrote it "during my presence at Batavia in 1638 (upon the urging of the late Director, Phillip Lucas)" (see p. 256).

It is certain that he knew Schouten's account, written in 1636 and published in 1638. Indeed, the factual content of Van Vliet's *Description* is so similar to Schouten's that we can imagine he had either a copy of it, or a good memory of it, when he sat down to write his way out of trouble.[1] Some passages of information that Van Vliet adds to Schouten's stock of knowledge are rather garbled. For instance, the account of Siam's early history has some of the

1. Compare, for example, Schouten's definition of the extent of Siam (95), "the form of this Land is like an halfe Moon, and containeth in its circuit four hundred and fifty Dutch miles," with Van Vliet's statement, "The whole country has a circumference of about 450 miles and has the shape of a half moon."

same stories that he wrote two years later into the *Short History*, but with the details so mixed up it suggests he might have been working from memory.

Schouten's account is shorter, and more workmanlike. Its plan is as follows:

Geography
  location, landscape, main places, capital (Ayutthaya)
Politics
  king, revenues, judicial system, military resources, diplomatic relations
Elephants
  hunts, white elephants
Anthropology
  religion, gender, social divisions, housing, diet
  marriage, inheritance, education, occupation
Dutch interests
  production and trade, Iberian competitors, position of Dutch

Compare Van Vliet's plan:

Introduction
  history, location, landscape, character, laws, religion
First Part: politics
  main places, capital,
  king, revenues, military resources, diplomatic relations,
  [Iberian competitors], [position of Dutch],
  mandarins, [origins of products], judicial system
Second Part: religion
  wat, monkhood, teachings, ceremonies
Third Part: anthropology
  people, housing, diet, dress, marriage, inheritance, education, character
Fourth Part, commerce
  import market, trade decline, resources, potential exports, shipbuilding,
  weights and measures, writing and accounting
  [lack of history], [elephants and other fauna]

Overall Van Vliet's plan and coverage are remarkably similar to those of Schouten. There are three main differences. First, Van Vliet seems to have misplaced some sections (those shown in brackets). Second, he has included a few new items, the most important of which is a fuller review of Siam's resources and commercial potential. Third, the assessment of Dutch interests and prospects does not appear as the conclusion as in Schouten's work, but towards the end of the First Part. I will consider the significance of these last two differences below.

There is a another difference that is not part of the plan but of the style and approach. Unlike Schouten, Van Vliet embroiders the factual details with opinions and comments. It is these comments, rather than much additional material, which make Van Vliet's *Description* much longer than Schouten's and very different in flavor. It is these comments that add up to a very pointed *argument*.

THE ARGUMENT

As shown above, Van Vliet divides his *Description* into four parts. But the first of these accounts for 60 percent of the total length and includes the main thrust of Van Vliet's argument. The remaining three sections are more like appendices.

Van Vliet begins with a short introduction. Here he first tells the story of the origin of Siam and the fame of the first king as a great lawgiver. He then shifts into geography and general description, concluding that "Siam is a country that has more than most other countries of everything that the human being needs." His baseline thus is that Siam is an ancient and well-endowed country with a legal tradition. He then announces he will address the "character of the inhabitants." But in fact this section quickly becomes a preliminary military assessment: "the Siamese are poor soldiers ... the Siamese are poor sailors." He quickly moves on to note that the political situation has changed since the great law-giving first king: "the power of the kings became absolute, the laws were bent according to their will."

These two themes of military incompetence (and hence vulnerability) and political decline (and hence lack of legitimacy) are then expanded in the First Part, headlined to cover "the political government, statement of the principal provinces, towns and villages and population." He lists the major places, ending with the observation that their "city walls have entirely decayed." He moves to a description of the capital, remarking that the new walls of the palace "will not be able to withstand a European army," and the new "thick and heavy" city wall "has no proper foundation nor projections nor bastions like a real fortress and could be easily destroyed by artillery."

A little later in this First Part he reviews Ayutthaya's military capacity. The armed forces are large, but they have "bad weapons" and are "inexperienced." The failure of the Pattani campaign is attributed to "lack of courage and bad management." The cavalry is poorly equipped "so that an army provided with modern weapons does not need to fear an attack of the Siamese cavalry." The navy "have no experience, and they could not maintain a fight against a European navy." The Siamese kings fought successful wars in the past, particularly under King Naresuan against Pegu, but now the king is not warlike, his mandarins are "effeminate," and the country's resources for fighting have been exhausted.

Throughout this passage, Van Vliet has in his mind a Dutch military attack on Siam, and he is trying to transfer that thought to the mind of his reader.

This theme of military vulnerability is interleaved with the other theme foreshadowed in the introduction – political decline under absolute rule. Despite the excellent law-giving of the original ruler, the king has now become absolute, and the ability of the mandarins "to check him" has withered. The written law has been superseded by the exercise of arbitrary power. The king has decked himself with "arrogant titles," mounts great ceremonies during which the people are forced to venerate him with "superstitious idolatry," and is "honored and worshipped by his subjects more than a god." He is steeped in "luxury and extravagance," seizes even the "wives of the greatest mandarins" for his lust, and becomes drunk three times a day. The arbitrariness and inhumanity of such absolute rule is exemplified by the "Horrible Offerings" of pregnant women seized at random on the streets and sacrificed to strengthen the city defenses.

This decline has had several results which reinforce the earlier theme of military vulnerability. Trade has been disrupted with the result that the king "cannot possibly be very rich." The neighbors are mostly hostile. Pegu is keeping a cautious diplomatic distance. The northern Lao states have withdrawn from trading relations because of undue exactions. An expedition to force Cambodia to submit failed miserably. The attacks on Ligor and Pattani were similarly unsuccessful, and hence the court is trying to transfer the blame to the Dutch. Arakan opened diplomatic relations but they have gone cold. Relations with Aceh have soured because of dishonest intermediaries. Attempts to restart trade to Japan have failed because of "Siamese arrogance." The opportunity for trade with China has been lost because of "pride and arrogance." Failure upon failure.

Moving to the close of the First Part, Van Vliet reviews the position of westerners in Siam. The Iberians have lost ground because of pirate incidents and "will most probably not regain their former influence." That leaves the Dutch in a dominant position, but restricted because of the difficulties of dealing with this absolutist court.

Having portrayed Siam as an abundant land under an absolute rule which subjects its citizens to arbitrary tyranny, and which is militarily vulnerable because of its poor capabilities and lack of allies, Van Vliet introduces the Picnic Incident. He passes quickly over the drunken Dutch and what they did. He argues that some mandarins were out to milk the Dutch. As a result the Incident was magnified "by false accusations explained to the prince and to the king as if the men had committed an important crime. In his rage and drunkenness the king thereupon condemned all the Netherlanders to death without hearing them." Given the background of arbitrary, barbaric rule just described, Van Vliet's readiness to save the situation by undergoing humiliation becomes quietly heroic. But Van Vliet delicately underplays his role. Rather he proposes a more drastic conclusion from the whole affair:

> The friendship which always had been honored and laudably maintained by the kings of Siam, has much decreased and has almost disappeared during the rule of this king usurper. And probably this friendship will not flourish again

> as before, unless this cowardly nation is brought to better sense, and unless the disgrace which we have suffered has been washed away by the sword, in which may God Almighty help.

This is the climax of the whole *Description*. It is not clear what kind of intervention Van Vliet imagines – a brief "chastisement" or a more long-term occupation (there is some hint below). But the whole First Part is an argument that Dutch intervention in Siam would be militarily feasible, politically justified by the arbitrariness of absolute rule, probably unopposed by any of Siam's neighbors, possibly welcomed by the oppressed population, and certainly profitable in view of the potential gains.

THE RATIONALE

There are still some factual matters that Van Vliet has rushed past in his eagerness to build his argument. There are also some sections in Schouten's plan, particularly the anthropology, that he has not yet reached. These are covered rather quickly in the three remaining sections. But in these sections Van Vliet also adds a few extra touches to his main argument.

The Second Part is devoted to Buddhism. Van Vliet is very impressed by Ayutthaya's religious architecture: "The appearance of these temples is often more beautiful than that of churches in Europe." He is impressed also by the number of temples, which he estimates as 400, and of monks, which he estimates as 20,000. His Protestant sensibility is touched by the monks, the asceticism of their conduct, and their devotion to learning and education. He appreciates the simplicity and devotion displayed in ritual practice. He notes approvingly the atmosphere of religious tolerance. He also grapples gamely with the principles underlying Buddhism, in sharp contrast with the French who arrive fifty years later bent on conversion and who imagine Buddhism as a primitive totemistic cult.

But Van Vliet still leavens his appreciation of Buddhism with some examples of folly and barbarism. Despite the ascetic creed, the temples are stuffed with treasure. Funerals are the occasion for absurdly extravagant display. One fine temple is falling into decay because of a belief it is haunted. Most damning, there is worship of "the hellish devil" carried out with "such terrible abominations and incredible actions… that it is not proper for a Christian to look at them" (he seems to have seen a ritual of spirit possession).

This is the most sympathetic early European account of Siamese Buddhism, yet Van Vliet cannot resist adding touches of barbarism which reinforce his general theme. Following this section, Van Vliet adds three new points to his main argument for colonial intervention.

First, he argues that the impact of absolute rule is felt throughout society. Immediately after the "climax" passage, he turns to consider the mandarins.

He argues that Prasat Thong rules through fear, and he attributes this in part to his status as a usurper of the throne: "For as he is not an anointed David but only a little Absalom, he does not trust anybody." The king holds provincial governors at court so he can keep an eye on them. He reshuffles his major appointments every "four to eight months ... so that they could not have an opportunity to have a stronghold in one position." He has reduced aristocratic incomes. The nobles react to this pressure by tyrannizing their own subordinates and surviving "on the sweat of their slaves." Besides, "Each whose turn it is squeezes the foreigners as much as he can."

He then turns to show how absolutism affects the administration of justice. The courts are slow. Evidence is extracted by torture. "All criminal cases are usually punished more severely than usual." Banishment, confiscation, mutilation, and various gory forms of execution are the repertory of punishment. Nothing encapsulates the arbitrariness and lack of ethical principle of this regime more aptly than the practice of trial by ordeal, which Van Vliet describes twice.

He takes this argument further to a wholesale condemnation of the Siamese "character." The contents of the Third Part closely follow the anthropological section of Schouten – housing, food, dress, marriage, inheritance, education – but with an added commentary. After a few short remarks on the physical attributes of the Siamese, he announces, "Their character is volatile, cowardly, distrustful, dissembling, deceitful, talkative, and full of lies." The men "use their time very badly and idly," leaving women to do all the work. The "boasting and unfaithfulness of the Siamese" merits a subheading. They offer their services to foreigners only as long as they are paid. "These people are unfaithful, deceitful, and treacherous; yes, even the king is not upright-minded and keeps his word only as long as he is able to think with his drunken brains." He rose with the help of the Okya Phitsanulok and then had this ally "cut into two pieces." In sum, "one cannot rely upon the Siamese nation."

Van Vliet is re-emphasizing that his actions over the Picnic Incident were astute given the social and political realities. But he is also building a case that the Dutch can never prosper in Siam while they passively accept the current political circumstances.

THE REWARD

A second point that Van Vliet makes in these final sections is to emphasize that Siam can be a very valuable possession for the Dutch. This is the major theme of the Fourth Part.

Trade is not profitable at present because of the royal greed in imposing "monopolies and hindrances" which have scared away merchants both from the hinterland and overseas. Yet the interior produces many articles valued in Asian trade, and Van Vliet lists them along with their regions of origin in

Siam. He describes how the trade with China, Japan, the archipelago, and the Moors used to be much larger and more profitable. He adds that Siam can be a center of shipbuilding because of the quantity, price, and quality of its timber and other inputs. He draws up a list of the potential exports from Siam "to the fatherland," which is impressive both for the range of products and the amounts which he inscribes for each.

Van Vliet ends with some miscellaneous details on currency, writing, accounting, weights and measures, and with the obligatory passages on elephants and other curiosities. In Schouten's work, the passage on elephants is the longest section. Van Vliet is much less interested in this novelty material and apologizes for its inclusion. Rather, he uses this final section to add one final point to his argument:

> Besides Siam being very fertile and there being an abundance of victuals, there are also many other materials such as bricks, tiles, timber, a little iron (coming from the province of Corassema) and other materials in abundance necessary for the building of forts, churches, houses, vessels, junks, barges, and all other sorts of boats.

In his mind, the Dutch are already building a little colony with "forts, churches, houses… barges." Again he seems hopeful he can imprint this image on the mind of his superior. Besides, he goes on, Siam is ideal for colonization:

> For the working of these, labor can be found in Siam. Although the country is closed, as there is a sufficient provision of salt, the inhabitants can sustain themselves with the materials and fruits of their own country. They can thus do very well without the products of other countries, for a sufficient quantity of cotton necessary for the clothing of the people could easily be produced throughout the whole country.

Unlike both Malacca and Batavia, which are dangerously dependent on outside supplies of food and other strategic materials, Siam would be self-sustaining

In short, the *Description* is a proposal for colonization. Van Vliet builds his argument on many grounds. There is no military or diplomatic barrier. Absolute rule and its damaging effects throughout society deprive the existing regime of legitimacy. As a colony, Siam can be very valuable to the Dutch because of high potential profits and low costs.

We have no record of how this proposal was received, except that Van Vliet was absolved of any fault over the Picnic Incident and promoted to Senior Merchant and Director of the Ayutthaya factory. Yet of course nothing came of this proposal. Although there were regular "crises" in the relations between the Dutch and the Siamese court, there was never an attempt at colonization. This was not because the Dutch were against such a forward policy: Van Diemen gave the go-ahead for attacks on the Portuguese in Ceylon and the Spanish in Taiwan, took Malacca from the Portuguese, and in 1644 sent five ships up the Mekong River to punish the king of Cambodia (Kraan 2003). Rather it was because the Dutch seaborne empire developed in an arc running from southern India through the Straits and on to the archipelago, and colonization projects were strung along this arc. Siam remained a sideline which sometimes delivered some profits from the Asian country trade but was never important to the structure and logic of the VOC enterprise.

The nature of the *Description* as a colonialist tract must, however, affect how we read it. Sources on Ayutthayan history are so sparse that they are sometimes treated with excessive respect. The European records have proved invaluable in providing a viewpoint different from that of the royal chronicles. But, just like the chronicles, they too are political tracts.

TRANSLATOR'S PREFACE

JEREMIAS VAN VLIET was a servant of the Dutch East India Company, who in the course of his career spent some years in Siam and wrote a book descriptive of this country, its people, history, and customs for the benefit of his countrymen. It is my hope that this English version of his book may enable a number of others interested in Siamese history to add to their knowledge of the conditions prevailing here at the commencement of the 17th century and earlier.

In 1602 the Dutch East India Company established a factory in Patani, and the next year Daniel van der Leck – the chief of that station – paid a visit to Siam with the result that in 1604 he sent Cornelius Specx to establish a depôt at Ayuthia. Specx was succeeded in turn by Tourneman, van der Perre, Lambrecht Jacobs, and others, whose records doubtless afforded van Vliet much assistance when he took charge and commenced writing his interesting book.[1]

Van Vliet's immediate predecessor at Ayuthia was one Joost Schouten, who was Agent from 1624 to 1629, and himself wrote a description of Siam; and it is evident that Van Vliet derived much of his information from this source.

Van Vliet had charge of the Dutch East India Company's interests in Siam from 1629 to 1634.[2] By that time the position of the Company in this country had been established on a firm footing, and Van Vliet had excellent opportunities of making himself acquainted not merely with mercantile matters but also with the social life and conditions of the people as they existed in his time. A careful observer and diligent investigator, he made the most of these opportunities but his book was not published until after his death, a fact which probably accounts for certain vagaries of spelling occurring here and there in the text. I have explained these variations as far as possible

1. Schouten (1935). See pp. 91–92 above.

2. In fact, Van Vliet was in Siam intermittently from 1633 onwards and served as Agent in charge of the VOC's Siamese business from 1638 to 1642; see pp. 25–28.

in an appendix, but certain towns I have been unable to identify with any certainty; the locality of others it has been beyond my powers to discover.

As the translation has been from the Old Dutch into a language foreign to me, I would ask the indulgence of my readers for any idiomatic errors.

My thanks are due to Mr. René Sheridan for a translation of the paragraph relating to inheritance, which I have adopted in extenso, and particularly to Dr. O. Frankfurter, Director of the National Library, for the explanation of certain words whose orthography puzzled me and of a number of geographical names, as well as for his ready assistance in various other ways.

(Signed) L. F. van Ravenswaay
Bangkok, 28th March, 1910

DESCRIPTION OF
THE KINGDOM OF SIAM

and the account of the origin, the political government, the distinctive characteristics, the religion, the manner of living of the nobles and common people, the commerce, and other remarkable things concerning the Kingdom of Siam

Described by Jeremias van Vliet, formerly Chief of the Factory of the Dutch East India Company in Siam, afterwards Governor of Malacca and Counsellor of India.

Dedicated to
the noble, very learned, honorable and celebrated:—
Mister Feyo Johan Winter,
Doctor of medicine, formerly member of the Council of the Province of Friesland and burgomaster of Leeuwarden, and lately reappointed plenipotentiary to the assembly of the states of the above mentioned province, and member of the civic council of above named city, and its oldest medical doctor.

Sir,

Among all the prominent sciences concerning ecclesiastical as well as worldly affairs by which a man becomes famous, not the least, in my opinion, is that science which is based on the knowledge of foreign countries in regard to their origin as well as to their peculiar situation, race, government, religion, manner of living, commerce, wars, and so forth.

This science seems to me to be one of the principal means to acquire a thorough knowledge of the large as well as of the small countries.

For who can deny that, as the physician, in order to get a thorough knowledge of the fluid and solid parts of the human body, has to operate on several animals (that the health of mankind may be kept up by good remedies and health may be restored), the theologian, the naturalist, the merchant, etc. will need to his own advantage the knowledge of different ceremonies, laws, habits, and the nature of land and people of other countries (non enim omnis fert omnia tellus), their population, laws, religion, and manner of living.

They will need this knowledge in order to distinguish the true religion from the false one, to reform bad habits, to appreciate the reasons of the acts of God, to continue and to establish and to extend trade.

But why should I try with my weak pen to describe all this to you, Sir, as I am convinced that you already have a high knowledge of this science! For you, Sir, have not only held many honorable and high political offices, but you have also been occupied during many years as a naturalist and specially as a physician, to the welfare of many unhappy persons and the enrichment of our true knowledge of nature.

Shall I therefore try to recommend this book to you? No, I will not annoy you (who are occupied by more important things) by a poor explanation. Suffice it to mention that I most respectfully come to dedicate to you an account of the origin of the Kingdom of Siam, its government, the religion of the inhabitants, the manner of living of the nobles and common people, the commerce, etc., written by Jeremias van Vliet, formerly Chief of the factory in Siam, afterwards Governor of Malacca and Counsellor of India.

I hope that this service of mine, although small, will not be disagreeable to you, Sir, the more as you know how little of this matter has been described. As far as is known to me, there have been only a few Jesuits (people whom one cannot trust very much and who present things with prejudice) who have written about the Kingdom of Siam, such as P. d'Orleans, who gave an account of the life of Constantius Phaulcon, formerly Prime Minister of the King of France in Siam, and M. de Choisy and Pater Tachard, who gave descriptions of their journeys in Siam. These books have, moreover, not been translated into our mother tongue.

Therefore receive, very learned Sir, and with a favorable mind this dedication, which I offer to you to prove that I am,

Sir,
Your most obedient and obliged servant,
FREDERIK HAARING.

Leyden, at the Bookshop.
December 1st, 1692.

DESCRIPTION OF THE KINGDOM OF SIAM

with the account of the origin of the Siamese race, the situation of the country, the political government, the religious ceremonies and the manner of living of nobles and common people, the commerce, and other remarkable things concerning the Kingdom of Siam

INTRODUCTION TO THIS DESCRIPTION

The situation of the country, the government, the army in wartime, the customs in the administration of justice, the education of children, the laws of marriage, the means of existence of the population, the traffic, and other important things concerning the Kingdom of Siam have been described by some curious Netherlanders who have visited Siam; and Joost Schouten (who from 1624 to 1629 was the first representative of the Dutch East India Company in Siam) has accurately described the situation of the country and pointed out so well the most remarkable things at that time that, for his successors, there is hardly anything else to describe but the events which have occurred since he left.

However I will try to increase the information about the proposed subjects, namely, political government, religion, manner of living of the nobles and common people, and commerce as far as I could gather during the period of five years which I spent in Siam. Only such information as I thought to be true, I have mentioned in this book and beg that the will may be taken for the deed and that these few lines may be received favorably, which will in the near future encourage me to greater freedom.

In order to better analyze the proposed subjects, I will on general lines (in order not to detain the reader unnecessarily) describe the origin of the Siamese race and the situation of the Kingdom of Siam, referring the reader to the book of Schouten in the year 1632, which he has presented to the Governor-General and Council of India.

WHEN AND BY WHOM SIAM WAS DISCOVERED AND EXPLORED

More than two thousand years ago the country of Siam was an uninhabited wilderness. In a few places there lived some hermits and heathens (who had offered their bodies to the gods), and as we have heard from some reliable persons (yes, even from some learned old men), there was in China at that time an emperor's son who attempted his father's life and to take the imperial crown, in which attempt however he did not succeed.[3] The emperor intended to have his rebellious son and his followers executed for this crime, but as he suspected that the nobility and the community had taken the side of his son (who was very intelligent and had many remarkable gifts of nature), His Majesty after many supplications was persuaded not to take the life of his son and his followers, provided that they all should leave China and that they should wander as outlaws and never return again.

These exiles tried to populate uninhabited countries and to extend their power. They travelled first through the land of Chiampa,[4] after that Cambodia, from where they sailed with their boats to the Gulf of Siam. They first landed at the cape now called Cuy,[5] settled down there and built a town; and to show their thankfulness to the gods, erected a fine temple and many pyramids. Their new king sent his men from that place to look for the best lands. Some spies went to the south as far as Jamby,[6] others to the north and found a beautiful valley, which was embraced by the branches of a river. These people built the town of Picelouck[7] there with many temples, monasteries, and pyramids. The province of Poucelouck is still looked upon as being the most sacred of the kingdom. The government of this province is still only given to princes of the blood and, failing these, most prominent men in compensation for great services. At last the place Judia[8] was found where at that time there stood only a small temple (which is still existing) and where seven hermits were living who resembled each other exactly and were all children of parents who also had the same appearance. Although the town was situated amidst

3. This story has the same theme as that recounted by Van Vliet in the *Short History* (see pp. 198–201), namely a Chinese emperor's son who is sent into exile and who founds many Siamese towns including Ayutthaya. But the details are very different. In the *Short History* version, the son is chased out by the mandarins for sexual license; here he rebels against his father and has the support of the mandarins. In the *Short History* they go straight to the peninsula, make landfall at Pattani, and then work north. Here they first visit Champa and Cambodia, make landfall at Kuiburi, and then spread both north and south. In the *Short History* version, the northern cities, including Phitsanulok, are founded after Ayutthaya, but here Phitsanulok takes precedence. In the *Short History* version there is only one *rishi*, but here there are seven identical ones. The three prescriptions for a healthy life are also different. Here there is no mention of establishing trade links with China as in the *Short History*. Possibly there were several versions of this tale. Possibly Van Vliet was working from a (faulty) memory here, but with better sources when writing the *Short History*. Note the similarity with the foundation stories of many port polities in the archipelago which feature a Chinese merchant arriving by sea (Manguin 1991).

4. Champa.

5. Kui, Kuiburi.

6. Jambi in Sumatra.

7. Phitsanulok. Also spelt Poucelouck etc.

8. Ayutthaya.

fertile fields, everybody was afraid to live there, as every year a dreadful dragon appeared out of a stinking marsh which poisoned the air to such a degree that nobody except the hermits could live there. The new king (when he heard of this) consulted the hermits about the best way to get rid of this stinking marsh and to kill the dragon.

The hermits declared that according to a prophecy this was only possible if seven brothers were thrown into this marsh (being holy men, children from a father and a mother who resembled each other entirely as well as the children); but as such could not be found after the whole country had been searched for seven years, the aforesaid hermits had to sacrifice their own bodies to the marsh in order to kill the dragon. The hermits declared that they were happy to be the expiatory sacrifice to the Gods and were willing to be thrown into the marsh in order to end the life of this terrible monster and to free the whole country and so many people from such misery. When dying, they advised the king and his people that if they wanted to live a healthy life, they had to bathe every morning in the river (except in the months of December and January when the cold forbids them to do this), after this rub their bodies with sandal[wood] mixed with some betel leaf, and then eat some betel leaf rolled tightly around the betel nut. These three prescriptions have still remained unchanged to prove the truth of what has been described.

HOW JUDIA HAS BEEN BUILT AND WHERE IT IS SITUATED

On the spot thus found and on the surrounding fields the new king ordered to be built the big town now called Judia, situated 13½ degrees north of the equator,[9] about 20 miles from the sea[10] on the bank of a beautiful river which flows around the city walls, the town thus being on a flat little island. The surrounding land is entirely flat, and once in every year (as Egypt by the Nile) is flooded by the water which comes from the mountains.

This water gives fertility to the earth and enables the inhabitants to cultivate rice and fruits. This town has been and still is the principal town of the whole kingdom and is the residence of the kings. The circumference of the town is more than two miles,[11] and besides the palace of the king, the town is adorned with 350 to 400 temples which are very well built with many towers and pyramids, of which almost every one is gilded. But the houses are, after the Indian fashion, of bad construction and usually covered with tiles.

This description shows that Judia is a well-situated and thickly populated town and a worthy residence for a great king.

9. Actually, 14.3 degrees north.

10. The "mile" here and elsewhere is a "Duytsche mijl" or "Nederduytschese mijl" of about 7.5 kms.

11. I.e., over 15 kms (see fn. 10), a slight overestimate (around 12 kms).

WHAT RESPECT THE SIAMESE PAY TO THEIR FIRST KING AND WHY

The inhabitants of Siam and especially the learned men still speak with admiration and great respect of the Chinese exile, their first king. Many still worship his spirit, which they think is living amidst them. They praise him as a wonder of the world, saying that he has not only been the founder of such a powerful kingdom but that he also has ruled the entire country of Cauchenchina[12] up to Jamby, that he has subjected the inhabited countries by wars, and has ruled many years in peace. Besides this he has been the first legislator and the founder of their heathen religion, and although he kept the sovereign power over the worldly as well as over the ecclesiastical affairs in his own hands, he made orderly, excellent, and praiseworthy rules for the various branches of government as far as was necessary for a country ruled by a monarch. Also he has given rules for the administration of justice, criminal as well as civil. All these laws and foundations of religion he has written himself and has bequeathed them to his subjects. These original books, together with many others which were added in later years, are still kept in Judia in the king's finest temple, now called Wat Siserpudt,[13] and are held in great honor. At last this king, having lived more than two hundred years, came to the end of his days and died as emperor over one hundred and one crowned kings, leaving to his successors a founded and populated monarchy well provided with excellent written laws and perfect prescriptions.[14]

WHERE SIAM IS SITUATED

The Kingdom of Siam, situated in Asia, north of the equator, is an old and famous country and one of the largest in the East. In the north the boundary line runs along Pegu and Jangoma,[15] in the east Siam has as neighbors Langsiangh[16] and Cambodia, in the south there are Patany[17] and the Indian Ocean (which with a bend forms the Gulf of Siam). In the west the country reaches to the Bay of Bengal. The whole country has a circumference of about 450 miles[18] and has the shape of a half moon.

12. Cochinchina, southern Vietnam.

13. Wat Phra Si Sanphet (วัดพระศรีสรรเพ็ชญ์), the *wat* of the palace in Ayutthaya.

14. In the *Short History*, the law-giving king who lives two centuries and lords over 101 kings is a more mythical figure who precedes U Thong; see pp. 196–99.

15. Chiang Mai.

16. Lanxang. Probably Vientiane, as the capital had been moved from Luang Prabang to Vientiane in 1560.

17. Pattani.

18. I.e. over 3,000 kms (see fn. 10).

THE NATURE OF THE COUNTRY

Many parts of Siam are mountainous, others are flat, wooded, or marshy. The country is intersected by many big and small rivers, which have an abundance of fish; there are many large and middle-sized towns and villages and the country is well populated. In many places there are plenty of Indian fruits of various kinds, and the country produces many kinds of grain, especially rice, with which they could feed and still can feed several other countries. There are many kinds of birds, tame and wild animals, especially big and fine elephants, deer, and elk. In short, Siam is a country that has more than most other countries of everything that the human being needs.

THE CHARACTER OF THE INHABITANTS

In general the Siamese nation loves peace, commerce, and agriculture. At present the Siamese are poor soldiers, but during the life of warlike kings they proved to be pretty good fighters.

They used to go to war after the Indian fashion, armed with various weapons including muskets, and long and short pikes. They even had heavy artillery, which reminds us of the European way of making war, though many have only little experience (yet more than in former years) in handling these guns. Galleys and frigates were pretty well built for the sea; some of these vessels could be provided with heavy guns. But as the Siamese are poor sailors, they had little use of these boats. Although lately 120 new war vessels have been built to make an assault on Patany, the Siamese did not use them, as peace was made before these boats started.

As these boats have not been kept in repair, they are decaying and are only used for defense.

THE WRITTEN LAWS WERE NOT FOLLOWED AND BECAME CORRUPTED

The old written laws were very good and were greatly valued, but although the kings ought to have kept these laws, as they also had been made for Their Majesties' honor and fame, only few of them were followed.

By the encroachment of many prerogatives the power of the kings became absolute, the laws were bent according to their will and were changed and corrupted to their advantage and pleasure. By the natural avarice and dishonesty of the mandarins, the criminal as well as the civil justice has been very badly administered, so that (notwithstanding excellent rules have been given and pertinently prescribed in all cases) the most powerful or the richest men generally won their cases, usually by bribery or other corrupt means, and only the poor were made to suffer.

THE RELIGION REMAINED UNCHANGED

The religion remained unchanged; most of the inhabitants are very devout and superstitious heathens. Witness of that are their beautiful temples and monasteries with innumerable costly gilded images made of all kinds of materials.

WHAT THE FIRST SUBJECT TO BE DESCRIBED WILL BE

Having on general lines told much about the origin and the situation of the Kingdom of Siam, we will now describe the first subject, namely, the political government and every thing that is connected with this subject as far as we can ascertain the truth.

FIRST PART, CONCERNING THE POLITICAL GOVERNMENT, STATEMENT OF THE PRINCIPAL PROVINCES, TOWNS AND VILLAGES AND POPULATION

As has been said before, the country of Siam is large in circumference and, in general, thickly populated. There are many well cultivated provinces. The total number of towns and villages is not known for certain. But the principal towns are as follows:[19]—

Judia, which is the capital; Poucelouck, Sorkelouck,[20] Capheyn,[21] Succethay,[22] Kepenpit,[23] Conseywan,[24] Sianclangh,[25] Bonrerongh,[26] Leconsuan,[27] Poucenongh,[28] t'Siantebon,[29] Corassima,[30] Lyoure,[31] Thenau,[32]

19. It appears that Van Vliet is relaying several lists in which he has not been able to recognize the duplicates. Most of the towns appear in a similar list in Schouten which has fewer duplicates. Van Vliet repeats most of those in Schouten's list in roughly the same order but with different spelling, suggesting he may be recalling Schouten's *True Description* from memory, rather than a manuscript.

20. Sawankhalok.

21. Kamphaengphet.

22. Sukhothai.

23. Kamphaengphet (again).

24. Nakhon Sawan.

25. Sawankhalok again?

26. Unidentified.

27. Ravenswaay suggested Lang Suan but Nakhon Sawan (again) seems more likely.

28. Mentioned again below as "40 miles" east of Ayutthaya. Possibly Prachin, or somewhere close to the current Cambodia border.

29. Chanthaburi.

30. Nakhon Ratchasima, Khorat.

31. Ligor?

32. Tanao, Tanaosri, Tenasserim.

Martenaya,[33] Tanassery,[34] Lygoor[35] Bordelongh,[36] Sangora.[37]

These eighteen[38] towns are all provincial capitals and residences of the governors of the provinces.

Besides these towns there are many other smaller towns, as the Island Mirghy,[39] being the key and the mouth of Tanassery further Cuy, t'Siaya,[40] Pypery,[41] Pitsiaboury,[42] Batsjabonay,[43] Melongh,[44] Taatsyn,[45] Bannae,[46] Paranthongh,[47] Bion,[48] Banckock;[49] all which have also a local government, although of less importance. Further there are in the whole country many more towns, villages, and populated places, all the names of which we cannot possibly ascertain.

WHY MANY CITY WALLS ARE DECAYING

Some hundred years ago, during the rule of warlike kings, many of the abovementioned provincial towns and those of less importance were walled, and after the oriental method fortified and provided with a ditch around these walls. But during the reign of peaceful princes and during a period in which there were no wars with the enemies from the highlands (as the Ava, Hontscha,[50] etc.), most of these city walls have entirely decayed. Also the slowness of the Siamese must account for this, so that in the whole kingdom there is hardly to be found a single well-walled city or a good fort. Only the Island Mirghy and the town Tannassery, which are strong places by nature, were fortified a few years ago and are still occupied for fear of an attack by people from Arracand.[51] But as Siam during the yearly inundation is

33. Mautama, Martaban.
34. Tenasserim (again).
35. Ligor, Nakhon Si Thammarat.
36. Phatthalung.
37. Songkhla.
38. He has listed nineteen.
39. Mergui.
40. Chaiya.
41. Phetchaburi.
42. Phetchaburi (again).
43. Ratchaburi?
44. Maeklong.
45. Thajin.
46. Maybe Ban Nai or Noi, location unknown.
47. Maybe Pathom, Nakhon Pathom.
48. Unidentified. Ravenswaay suggests Ban Dohn.
49. Bangkok.
50. Hongsa, Hanthawaddy, Hongsawadi, i.e. Pegu.
51. Arakan entered a phase of military expansion in the 1570s which climaxed under Sirisudhammaraja (1622–38), who attacked Bengal and threatened Burma (Leider 2002).

unconquerable by the neighboring Indian kings, the walled cities or forts are not very necessary in the interior. It is sufficient to provide the biggest river "Menam"[52] and the places along its banks with means of defense.

DESCRIPTION OF THE CAPITAL JUDIA AND THE PALACE OF THE KING

We have already mentioned the capital Judia, which is the most important town of the country and the residence of the king and the most prominent men and nobles. Therefore we will describe this town in a little more detail. It is situated on the river called Menam (or in our language Mother of the Waters) and amidst a fertile plain. The town has been built on a little island of roundish shape and is surrounded by a heavy stone wall which has a length of more than two Netherlands miles.[53] This wall was for the greatest part renewed in 1634 and provided with a heavy stone footing. All round the town and on the other side of the river there are many villages, residences, houses of farmers, temples, monasteries, and pyramids, and the population here is just as thick as in the town itself. The walled city has only a few long, broad, and straight streets but several good canals. The greater part of the city is one great conglomeration of streets, alleys, canals, and ditches. During high water boats can cross most of the streets and even reach the houses.

The houses are of poor construction, but the town is adorned with about 400 fine temples and monasteries, which are all cleverly and sumptuously built with a great number of towers, pyramids, and innumerable images made of all kind of materials. The palace of the king is great and magnificent and lies on the bank of the river like a separate well-built town, embellished with five high towers and many fine gilded buildings. The palace has been very much improved by the present king. At the land side there is a large square which lately has been surrounded by a stone wall. Only one street and two little pathways lead to the palace, so that it is now better protected against an attack of the population during times of revolution or of neighboring enemies. But this stone wall will not be able to withstand a European army. This city wall is thick and heavy and built of brick and follows the course of the river. It has no proper foundation nor projections nor bastions like a real fortress and could be destroyed easily by artillery. But considering Indian conditions, Judia is a strong, beautiful, well-situated, safe, and well-populated town, and is unconquerable for hostile Indian kings as they could not stay any longer than six months, for the yearly inundation by the river would force them to leave the plains.[54]

52. Chaophraya River.

53. I.e. over 15 kms (see fn. 10), a slight overestimate.

54. This account appears to ignore the "first sack" of Ayutthaya by the Burmese in 1569. But Van Vliet's account in the *Short History* attributes this defeat to intrigues among the Siamese rather than Burmese military success. So too does the account in

THE SOVEREIGN GOVERNMENT AND POWER OF THE KING

Since the time that the Kingdom of Siam was established, the king has always had almost sovereign power, but according to the written laws His Majesty had to consult the imperial council, and where His Majesty used bad judgment, partiality, or exaggeration, the mandarins had the power to check him.

But when the empire (to which some hundreds of years ago were subjected many nations and countries) began to decay, more and more power and privileges were given to the king, as the people believed that by doing so the other nations would fear them more. The kings have ruled during a long period as monarchs with entire authority over peace, war, treaties, justice, remission of penalties, and all other affairs concerning the empire and the population. The kings could make laws and prescriptions as they pleased, and they did not consult or ask the counsel of the most influential men or nobles nor of the different classes of people, unless His Majesty of his own free will thought it advisable to consult them.

But if the king proposes important matters to his most powerful mandarins of the secret council, they usually, in conformity with the old laws, take these matters into consideration and, after thorough deliberation, demand the opinion of their inferiors, after which with humble supplications they make their decision known to the king. The king may accept, change, or reject the advice of the secret council, stating that His Majesty thought it better for the welfare of the country, but in reality to better satisfy his own will. Nobody dares to show dissatisfaction about the decision of the king, for his life and his position would be in danger.

All dignities, positions, and offices of the kingdom were given away by the king as His Majesty pleased to nobles or commoners, although in conformity with the written laws only the nobility and the most influential men had a right to such. Sometimes positions are given away to persons for promised services or in compensation for services already done by them.

But one cannot rely much on the favor of the king, and for little mistakes, sometimes even without any reason, men filling high positions were discharged and from being great men became insignificant. All the inhabitants are really the king's slaves, which name is an honorable title even among the greatest, as His Majesty is in fact the chief person and has supreme power and authority over the kingdom and the life and goods of his vassals and subjects. The king may introduce such laws as he thinks necessary in conformity with his pleasure and advantage. But by this assumed authority,

---

the early Luang Prasoet chronicle, which also dates to the early seventeenth century (*RCA*: 70, 73). The dramatic account of the Burmese assault in 1569 appears only in the later chronicles revised in the Rattanakosin era after the "second sack" of 1767.

everything had the appearance of fairness, being founded on the laws and rights of the country which formerly had been made for worldly as well as for ecclesiastical affairs.

PRAISEWORTHY LAWS AND ADMINISTRATION OF JUSTICE BUT NOT USED ANY MORE WHILE THE KING HAS ABSOLUTE POWER

The written laws of the country prescribe a certain and praiseworthy rule for the administration of justice, namely, that nobody either in criminal or in civil cases may be condemned unless his case has been examined four times by the ordinary or by the specially appointed judges.

The accused may not be punished in consequence of being accused only, but on his request the judges must allow him to defend himself against his accusers by certain ordeals, namely:— dive under water, dip the hand into hot oil, walk barefooted over red-hot coals, or eat a lump of rice over which a charm has been pronounced. These trials by ordeal were performed in public in presence of the judge, and in case the accused was not able to perform any one of them, he was punished in proportion to the importance of the case. But as the king became absolute, these praiseworthy prescriptions are now never, or very seldom, followed; everything depends on His Majesty, so that often innocent people get punished. Especially this is the case with the present king, who does not believe complaints very soon and besides this is inconsiderate and rash in his judgment. Even when the culprit's innocence is known to the most influential men, nobody dares to tell this to the king for fear of being suspected or of incurring disgrace by His Majesty's intemperate anger.

THE ARROGANT TITLES OF THE KING

The titles of the king are very bombastic and more than human, but are believed to be due to him by the great men and nobles as well as by the rich and poor people. Some of these titles we will mention here. If anybody talks to the king, however unimportant the subject may be, he never gives the king a lower title than one of these:— Pro, Boo, Dy Tsaeu kha choral, Proom Can, Sey Claen Seycke, Moom,[55] which presumptuous words are very difficult to translate in the Netherlands language but as near as possible they have the

55. Van Vliet's transliteration can be resolved as: พระพุทธเจ้าข้า ขอรับพระโองการ ใส่เกล้าใส่กระหม่อม, which is a court formula of address meaning: "Lord (lit. Buddha), let your servant receive your command to place on the crown of his head." This corresponds to the latter part of Van Vliet's translation. But the first part of Van Vliet's translation (Oh, Master … bright sun) cannot be derived from the transliteration. Probably he was working from memory and could recall only the form of address, but not the title.

following meaning:— Oh, Master of the air and the earth, whose fame is known up to the tops of heaven and who is worshipped like the bright sun, whose commands are performed by me, your poor slave, and whose words are carried by me on the crown of my head.

When His Majesty has answered the petitions or proposals, he is honored with Pon t'Yaeukhae, Chorap, Proem, Can, Sey claeu Seycke Moom t'Yaeu Yehoua,[56] which are still more proud titles than those already mentioned. In writing letters to foreign kings or princes, he assumes more than divine titles. At the Siamese court there are existing rules for titles due to foreign potentates; the greater the friendship with those foreign kings is, the more arrogant the titles become.

Usually these titles for absolute kings (after the dignity of the legation had been set forth in the introduction of the message) are the divine, illustrious, invincible, most powerful and highest Master of a hundred and one Golden Crowns and of kings adorned with nine kinds of precious stones, the greatest and highest Divine Master of the Immortal Souls, the most holy, all seeing and overshadowing supreme ruler of the most noble and great empire of Siam. His kingly throne is the beautiful and immense town of Judia. The many roads leading to this brilliant town are crowded with people. This is the supreme capital of the world adorned with nine kinds of precious stones.

The ruler of this beautiful country is more than the gods, and his house is made of gold and precious stones. He is the Divine Master of the golden thrones of the towers, of the white, red, and round tailed elephants, all three of which are excellent walkers and which the supreme god of the nine various gods has given to nobody else. He is the god-like Master of the Victorious Sword, by the perceiving of which many have become frightened and defeated. He is the greatest Master who is equal to the four-armed god of war.

The king is very fond of these arrogant titles, and as the people were told that he really deserved these titles, nobody dared to oppose the king or to resist his pride

Also one hardly dares to carry a wicked intention in his mind, as they have the idea (although this is absurd) that there is living a Divine Majesty in the king and that they for that reason ought not to do wrong.

The fear of His Majesty is so great that nobody, however powerful he may be, dares to mention his name, his head, or his royal crown in public, even when important affairs are being discussed. In cases when it is necessary to talk about him or to call his name, the people whisper the words respectfully in each other's ear. His Majesty is honored and worshipped by his subjects more than a god.

56. This is probably พระเจ้าข้า ขอรับพระโองการ ใส่เกล้าใส่กระหม่อม เจ้าอยู่หัว, which is similar to the earlier passage, with the addition of another word for "king" at the end.

HORRIBLE OFFERINGS IN BUILDING THE KING'S PALACE

By the usurped authority of the kings and by the continuous praise of the people, the pride of the former kings had reached such a height that it looked as if the king was not there for the good of his community, but that the whole country and the people were for his pleasure alone. The kings counted their subjects so little that if palaces, towers, or resting places had to be built for them, under each post which was put into the ground a pregnant woman was thrown, and the more near this woman was to her time, the better. For this reason there was often great misery in Judia during the time that palaces or towers had to be built or repaired. For as all houses in Siam are built at a certain height above the ground and stand on wooden posts, many women have endured this suffering. Although this description seems to be fabulous, these executions have really taken place.

The people, who are very superstitious, believe that these women after dying turn into terrible monsters or devils, who defend not only the post below which they are thrown but the whole house against misfortune. The king usually ordered a few slaves to catch without regard all the women who were in a pregnant state. But out of the houses no women were taken unless *in the streets nobody could be found.* These women were brought to the queen, who treated them as if they were of high birth. After they had been there for a few days, they were (excuse these rude words) thrown into the pit with the stomach turned upwards. After this the post was put on the stomach and driven right through it.

WONDERFUL ESCAPE OF SOME WOMEN WHO HAD BEEN POINTED OUT TO UNDERGO A TERRIBLE TREATMENT

Through Judia there are running eight rivers. At the places where these rivers enter and leave the town, gates have been built consisting of two straight vertical posts about eight fathoms long and one and a half fathoms thick. These posts are on top connected by two horizontal beams and the space between these beams is provided with some wooden ornamentation.

Including the Petoutsiau or Gate of the Hearts[57] (the entrance to the court), there are thus seventeen gateways. At the commencement of 1634 the present king renewed them all, and as these gates, whether they belonged to temples, monasteries, houses, or courts (however ugly or unimportant they might be),

57. Actually ประตูไชย (*pratu chai*), gate of victory, not ประตูใจ, gate of hearts. There is a gate by this name on the south side of the city. However it is probable that Van Vliet is referring to ประตูศรีไชยศักดิ์ (*pratu si chai sak*), the gate of auspicious and mighty victory, which is the "land gate" (as opposed to "water gate") of the palace, on the north side of the city (*KCKK*: 198–99; this source, dating from the end of the Ayutthaya period, counts four water gates and twenty-eight land gates).

are sacred places in Siam, His Majesty ordered two pregnant women to be thrown under each post. There were thus necessary 68 women for the 17 gates. For this purpose some women had already been brought into the palace. But at that time it happened that on each of two succeeding days five women were caught who at the same moment that they were brought inside the palace gave birth. This caused great dejection in the court of the king, and it was believed to be a miracle. Oya Sycry[58] (who has at present the title of Oya Sucethay[59] and who is a man of great self-confidence) was so bold as to tell the king that apparently the supreme god of His Majesty's gods did not approve of women being thrown under each post of the gates. But in order to reconcile the devil (who as the Siamese think has taken possession of these gates), Oya Sycry proposed to the king to perform this ceremony at the Petoutsiau only. His Majesty agreed with this and ordered the keeping of only four of the pregnant women.

The other women (those who already had given birth as well as those who had not) had their hair shaved off and received two cuts on the head, and they were told that God had given their lives into the hands of the king and that they ought to die; but as the king was merciful and more gracious than the gods, they could all go home, except the four already mentioned women, who were thrown under the posts of the Petoutsiau.

THE LUXURY AND EXTRAVAGANCE OF THE KING

With the great authority and the usurped powers of the king, we must also notice that the present luxury and extravagance even surpass those of former times. For the wives of the greatest mandarins (being healthy and of good appearance) were not allowed to stay longer than three or four days outside the court of the queen. They were brought inside the palace under pretext that they had to greet the king. Sometimes His Majesty himself selected the prettiest maidens and daughters of the greatest men, and these women were given him as concubines.

When he became king, His Majesty took also his first wife's sister and her mother as his concubines under pretext that they were too noble to be given away to others.[60] With this mother and the daughter he has had children.

58. Okya Chakri (ออกญาจักรี); see Appendix I.

59. Okya Sukhothai (ออกญาสุโขทัย); see Appendix I.

60. In the *Historical Account*, Van Vliet gives a rather different version of Prasat Thong's relations with his predecessor's women, namely that he took the eldest daughter of Songtham's sister as a fourth wife; wanted to marry Songtham's mother ("one of the most beautiful women in the kingdom") and cruelly killed her when she refused; selected the "younger and more beautiful" of Songtham's wives and daughters as concubines, again killing those who refused; and shut the older ones up in the harem (see pp. 300–1). The *Khambaikan chao krung kao* (*KCKK*: 97) records that Prasat Thong married all eight of Songtham's daughters.

The mother died in 1633, and the funeral ceremonies were more brilliant than those of any other queens during the last centuries.

Although the religion and the laws forbid the mandarins, and especially the kings, to drink spirits, and moreover this is looked upon as being very scandalous, His Majesty is usually under the influence of drink three times a day; viz., during the morning after breakfast, during the afternoon, and during the evening when he has given audience to his mandarins and has returned from his throne into his palace.

This drunkenness (which occurs very often and often reaches a dangerous limit) has caused many evils during his reign and is frequently the reason why innocent blood has been shed.

HOW HIS MAJESTY THREE TIMES A DAY APPEARS AMONGST HIS MANDARINS

His Majesty's state and suite are great and magnificent. The king appears little in public but usually receives three times a day the greatest men and officials of the country. In the morning very early His Majesty gives audience to his factors and to those who bring presents to him. In the afternoon the king consults his secret council and the greatest men, and at sunset goes to the meeting place for all the mandarins. Usually the king appears in a costly dress, sitting on a magnificent gilded throne and wearing the royal crown.

Many musicians escort the king to the throne, playing melodiously. At the front of the throne are present many nobles, courtiers, and armed soldiers, who are all respectfully kneeling. Besides this there is present a bodyguard of 30 to 40 armed men in the inner-court. As was told to me, the king is always addressed with many ceremonies, reverences, arrogant titles, and great praise. His Majesty's words are considered as those of an oracle, but by the dishonesty and avarice of the mandarins, his mandates are seldom carried out or maintained. If His Majesty appears outside the palace (which is seldom), much splendor is displayed and His Majesty is then accompanied by a great suite.

Although the king has all over the country many fine residences and resting houses where he may amuse himself, His Majesty very seldom goes outside the palace. He only visits three or four times during the year the temple, Wat Syserput,[61] to make offerings to the gods. This temple, which is of renowned holiness, is situated near the king's palace. To this temple His Majesty goes either afoot or carried by men while sitting in a little house of pyramidical shape ingeniously made of costly materials.

The men who carry this house on their shoulders are well dressed and wear golden crowns also of pyramidical shape. The greatest mandarins with their suites and some priests accompany the king to the temple. But when

61. Wat Phra Si Sanphet (วัดพระศรีสรรเพ็ชญ์).

the king leaves the palace on other occasions, His Majesty is accompanied by many great men, nobles, courtiers, slaves and bodyguards, horses and elephants. The king is then sitting on an elephant. It would be difficult to describe the whole train in detail as the number of persons and animals is not always the same, but generally there are 600 to 800 persons. Everything goes in stately order and silence and great splendor is displayed. When the king passes, all the people along the roads kneel down, fold their hands, and bend their heads to the ground. This way of greeting comes nearer to superstitious idolatry than to paying reverence to a king

THE KING COMES OUT ON WATER

Also the king appears but seldom on water. When he does go on the river, usually 12 to 16 very beautiful, costly, gilded and decorated boats, each of which is rowed by 70 to 100 rowers, accompany the king. His Majesty is then sitting in the best boat on a gilded throne surrounded by many courtiers. The other boats are for the queen and three of his principal wives. Each of these women is seated with her suite and her daughters in a beautiful boat.

These four women generally accompany His Majesty, also the suites and bodyguards of 800 to 900 men. Also several noblemen go with the king, and each of them has his own beautiful boat and sits in a small gilded pavilion. Although the total number of persons who accompany the king is not always the same, usually it amounts to about 2000.

WITH WHAT SPLENDOR THE KING APPEARS ONCE A YEAR IN PUBLIC WHEN GOING TO THE NAPPETAT[62]

It is an old custom in Siam that the king every year at the end of October or at the beginning of November comes outside the palace with the greatest splendor and followed by his whole court and all the mandarins, nobles, and officers of the country. First one procession on land is organized and after this many trips on water. A visit is paid to the principal temple to make offerings to the gods and to pray for a long life for the king and for the welfare of the country.

The procession on land is not arranged in the same way every year, but occasionally it is as follows:— First come in stately order going from the palace to the principal temple called Nappetat about 83 to 100 elephants, which are sumptuously decorated. On each of these elephants is seated, besides two armed men, a mandarin in his gilded little house having in front of him a golden basin containing cloth and presents for the priests. Then follow 50 to 63 elephants, on each of which are sitting two to three men, each of whom

62. Wat Mahathat (วัดมหาธาตุ).

is armed with bows and arrows. After this come, also seated on elephants, the five to six greatest men of the kingdom, some of them wearing golden crowns, but each with his golden or silver betel box or any other mark of honor given to him by the king. They are accompanied by their suites of 30 to 60 men afoot. Following those come 800 to 1,000 men armed with pikes, knives, arrows, bows, and muskets and also carrying many banners, streamers, and flags. Among these armed men are mixed about 70 or 80 Japanese, who are gorgeously dressed and carry excellent arms. The musicians who follow the soldiers play on pipes, trombones, horns, and drums and the sound of all these instruments together is very melodious. The horses and elephants of the king are copiously adorned with gold and precious stones and are followed by many servants of the court carrying fruits and other things to offer. Many mandarins accompany these servants.

Then follow on foot with folded hands and stooping bodies (like everyone who rides or walks in front of the king) many nobles, among them some who are crowned. Then comes the red elephant decorated very nicely with gold and precious stones. Behind this elephant follow two distinguished men, one of them carrying the royal sword and the other one the golden standard to which a banner is attached. A gilded throne follows after them showing how former kings used to be carried on the shoulders of the people, and then follows His Majesty sitting on an elephant and wearing his royal garments and his golden crown of pyramidal shape. He is surrounded by many nobles and courtiers. Behind His Majesty comes a young prince, the legal child of the supreme king, who at present is eleven years old. The king's brother,[63] being the nearest heir to the throne, follows then with great splendor, and seated on elephants in little closed houses come after this the king's mother, the queen, and His Majesty's children and the concubines. Finally many courtiers and great men on horseback, and 300 to 400 soldiers who close the procession.

Altogether about six to seven thousand persons[64] participate in this ceremony, but only His Majesty, his wives, his children, his brother, the four

63. Si Suthammaracha, the *fai na* (ฝ่ายหน้า) or *upparat* (อุปราช), who is called the Prince or Crown Prince in the *Picnic Incident*. He succeeded to the throne in 1656, but was usurped by Narai after two months and twenty days. The chronicles specifically deny that he was made *upparat*, quoting Prasat Thong as saying "This younger sibling of Ours is cruel and coarse in disposition and lacks a sense of shame. It would be impossible to appoint him deputy king to protect the kingdom far from Our holy eyes and holy ears" (*RCA*: 215, ll. 37–39). Presumably this is retrospectively legitimating Narai's superior claim to the succession.

64. Other accounts make these events larger. Schouten (128–29) estimated fifteen to sixteen thousand people. The Jesuit Father Tachard (1688: 190) was so impressed, "we judged that there could not be less than about twenty thousand *Balons*, and above two hundred thousand souls; the other French reckoned a great many more, and confidently averred that there were above six hundred thousand souls of them."

highest bishops, and other high priests enter the temple. Having stayed inside the temple for about two hours, the king and the whole splendid train return to the palace in the same order as here described. The streets are very crowded with people from the palace to the temple, but everyone is lying with folded hands and the head bent to the earth. It is forbidden for anyone to look at the king's mother, his wives, or children; and the people turn their faces when the royal family passes. Only strangers or foreign ambassadors are allowed to look at them.

THE TRIUMPHANT MANNER IN WHICH HIS MAJESTY GOES OUT ON THE WATER TO SACRIFICE TO THE GODS

When His Majesty makes his first trip on water, this is arranged as follows:— In front go about 200 mandarins, everyone with his own beautiful boat and sitting in a small pavilion which is gilded and decorated according to the rank of the owner. These boats are rowed by 30 to 60 rowers. Then follow the boats for the luggage and kitchen necessaries. After these boats come the state boats of the king, wherein nobody else but the rowers are sitting, whose number amounts to from 50 to 70 men. Each of these boats carries a little gilded pavilion of pyramidal shape or other decoration.

Then come four or five boats with musicians and finally four or five ingeniously shaped, varnished and gilded boats. Also the oars are partly varnished and partly gilded. Each of these boats is manned with 60 to 100 rowers.

In the finest boat the king is seated under a decorated canopy. His Majesty is sitting there as a worldly God hidden in all kinds of costly things, so that neither his body nor his face can be seen. He is surrounded by nobles and courtiers who pay him reverence at the foot of his seat with folded hands and with their bodies bent to the floor. In front of the boat and opposite the king is sitting a distinguished person holding between his folded hands the golden banners of the king.

Then follows the king's brother with a suite of eight to ten beautifully painted and gilded boats. He himself is seated in the best boat under a canopy less beautiful than that of the king. Opposite to His Royal Highness, in front of the boat, is sitting one of the mandarins also with folded hands and the body bent down to the floor. The king's mother, the queen, His Majesty's children, and some concubines have all their own boats and are sitting in gilded pavilions.

At last follows Oya Berkelangh[65] with all who are in his service. The total number of boats amounts to 350 to 400, and 20,000 to 25,000 persons take

65. Okya Phrakhlang (ออกญาพระคลัง).

part in this procession.[66] Along the whole way which His Majesty passes, the houses, monasteries, and temples are closed with mats, and nobody is allowed to stay in them in order that nobody may look at the king from a place higher than that of His Majesty.

Both sides of the river, for a length of two miles from the palace of the king to the temples Wat-deun,[67] Thunphiat-haai,[68] and Bankkedan,[69] are crowded with boats and innumerable persons who bring reverence to the king with folded hands and bent heads. Towards the evening the king returns in another boat. His Majesty's boat is then in front, leaving behind all the boats, which follow without any order in groups.

In the same way as has been described here, the king makes many trips on the water to the most holy temple and to bring offerings to the gods of the water. But on these occasions the crowd of spectators is not so large.

66. For a summary of the foreign accounts of these water *kathin* processions, see Dhiravat 2001: 84–90.

67. Usually identified with Wat Doem (วัดเดิม), now known as Wat Ayotthaya (วัดอโยธยา). But Piriya Krairiksh (1992: 54, fn.19) points out that Van Vliet later in this *Description* (see p. 155) says this temple is "devoted to the moon," and suggests this cannot be Wat Ayotthaya. Below Van Vliet notes that this *wat* is the location of the "highest school." According to the *Khamhaikan chao krung kao* (*KCKK*: 96), King Songtham built two schools for higher monastic study at Wat Phutthaisawan and Wat Mahathat. Since Wat Mahathat is mentioned elsewhere, "Wat-deun" is perhaps Wat Phutthaisawan.

68. Wat Chaophraya Thai (วัดเจ้าพระยาไทย), now Wat Yai Chai Mongkhon (วัดใหญ่ชัยมงคล), to the southeast of the city. A "Tianpiatay" temple is marked on a Dutch map of Ayutthaya dated around 1650 (see Piriya 1992: fig. 11). This temple was also sometimes known as Wat Pa Kaeo (วัดป่าแก้ว), the monastery of the crystal forest, after monks returned from Sri Lanka in the early fifteenth century and adopted "forest monk" practices based on meditation. In the eighteenth century, this *wat* was one of the three most important in the Sangha hierarchy.

69. This may be at the location later known as Bang Pa-in. On a 1650 Dutch map of the river, there is a Ban Kedam marked close to the position of Bang Pa-in. According to the chronicles, Prasat Thong began the royal building in Bang Pa-in early in his reign (*RCA*: 217), but the name in the form Bang Pa-in does not appear on maps until later. Perhaps the location was earlier called something like Ban Kedan (maybe กระดาน). By the 1680s, the name Bang Pa-in was in use. Engelbert Kaempfer (1987: 72) recorded that the king went on the *kathin nam* to "a stately temple call'd Banihin, situated below Judia." In his description of leaving Ayutthaya in 1690, Kaempfer (73) wrote: "having made two Leagues we arriv'd at the famous temple Banihijn, by Foreigners call'd the Golden Pagod." On Lamare's 1687 map, the location of Bang Pa-in is labelled "Pagode Royale," and on Valentijn's map (1724–26), as "S'Koning's Pagood" (the king's pagoda).

INCOME OF THE KING

It would be difficult to state accurately the income of the king. Rice cultivation produces the greatest revenue, as Siam is an excellent paddy growing country. For each plough His Majesty receives one fuangh or 3½ stuiver, and also the tenth, eighth, or seventh part of the paddy in proportion to the fertility of the fields. Besides this, the king has his own paddy fields and also gets rent from houses which belong to him. His estates yearly bring in a considerable amount of money. Sappanwood, tin, lead, and saltpeter, which are the principal products of the country, may be sold to foreigners only from His Majesty's warehouses. Also the king gets profits from the foreign as well as the native products. He also receives presents from his subjects, and the most influential men and governors of the provinces pay a certain taxation to the king. His Majesty further enjoys many profits from the trade to Choromandel[70] and China. Also the inland trade produces a large sum of money and many trading stations have been established in the various provinces. When all the boats return safely, the yearly profits are immense. If foreign traders had been treated well and if they had been encouraged to stay in the country, the profits would have been still much larger. The inhabitants of the highlands, as the Laos, the Langjangs[71] and the Jangems,[72] have left Siam for Cambodia in consequence of monopolies, rude treatment, and the excessive dishonesty of the king's factories. There they are treated well, and moreover they can bring their products, such as gold, gum benjamin and gum malacca, to the market in Cambodia by boat in a shorter time. For in going to Judia they had to cross the mountains with their wagons up to Poucelouck, and from thence they reached the capital by boat.[73] As gold is not imported any more in such quantities as before, the income of the king has grown less. The greater part of the gold used to be wasted on temples, monasteries, and pyramids.

THE TREASURES OF THE KING

Several officers are engaged in collecting the revenue for the king. Once a year or at any time wanted, these officers have to give account to Oya

70. Coromandel, Cholamandalam; the southeast coast of India in present-day Tamil Nadu.

71. From Lanxang, probably Vientiane.

72. From Jangoma, Chiang Mai.

73. This is a rare indication that Phitsanulok, apart from the strategic importance of its site, was also an important commercial center for transshipment from land to water. A source from late Ayutthaya records: "in large swing-tailed (ท้ายแกว่ง) boats, the Phitsanulok people from the north bring sugar, tobacco, beeswax, honey, and various goods from the north to sell" (*KKLWP*: 57–59)

Awangh,[74] president of the king's council, to Oya Poelethip,[75] chief purveyor of the kingdom, to Oya Sycry, chief of the army and the navy and minister of interior, and to Oya Berkelangh, chief of the king's warehouses, keeper of the great seal, and intermediary for the foreigners who are in the country. Each of these men has about one-fourth part of the administration of the country, and also receives one-fourth part of the revenue.

They make up their accounts in the presence of the representatives of the king. The moneys are deposited in the treasury of the king, but the greater part is spent on buildings and on repair of temples, images, and so on. Also His Majesty's state and court cost much money. The remainder of the moneys (which in my opinion cannot amount to much) is kept in the king's treasury for other necessities. As Siam has no gold or silver mines, and also does not receive any tributes from vassal princes, the king cannot possibly be very rich.[76]

THE ARMED FORCES OF THE COUNTRY

As already mentioned, the Siamese are more or less cowardly and by no means warriors by nature. But there is much war material in order to be able to attack on water and on land or to defend the country against invaders. Although there are few or no soldiers in actual service, within two days a force of 60,000 to 80,000 armed men can be gathered. However, they have bad weapons, such as short and long pikes, shield and sword, bow and arrow, old muskets and guns. They have good artillery, but the men who have to handle it are inexperienced and have never seen war. The soldiers are for the greater part inhabitants of the country or of the vassal states. Also foreigners join the army. The most numerous are the Pegus; further there are Moors, Portuguese mestizos, Malays, and a few of other nationalities. But the Japanese (numbering 70 to 80) are the best soldiers and have always been highly esteemed by the various kings for their bravery. The greater number of the soldiers are cowardly Siamese. Usually the king every year calls together 10,000 to 30,000 soldiers and orders the frigates and galleys to be equipped. This is done with the purpose of preventing the weapons getting blunt or growing rusty and to let the Siamese not altogether forget the idea of war. But no offensive campaigns are made. These forces the king maintains without

74. Okya Wang (ออกญาวัง), see Appendix I.

75. Okya Phonlathep (ออกญาพลเทพ); see Appendix I.

76. Van Vliet is unusually inconsistent about the royal income, perhaps torn between his intention to portray the court as grand and profligate, and his conflicting intention to portray the country as weak and vulnerable to takeover. Below he lists tributaries, in contravention of the statement here, but perhaps he means that the tribute payments were more symbolic than weighty.

any expenditure from the treasury. On the king's command his subjects must take up their arms and march, without receiving any wages. In all the provinces the necessary number of men may at any moment be called to arms. The number of men called to headquarters may amount to one-hundredth, one-fiftieth, one-twentieth, one-tenth or one-fifth of the total number of men available. The men know the company to which they belong, and if necessary can assemble within a short time in order to go to war. When going to war, the mandarins are accompanied by their own slaves and servants. In this way the king is able to call together two hundred thousand to three hundred thousand men and even more. But very seldom more than a hundred thousand men are collected, and usually not more than 20,000 to 60,000 men are sent to the field.

When the Siamese tried to subdue Patany in 1634, the army only numbered about 50,000. From lack of courage and bad management, the Siamese had to retreat. The king then ordered one hundred new frigates and galleys to be built in addition to the old war vessels. These new boats were equipped with men and weapons, and the intention was to call a large army to the field. If the king had not been persuaded by the king of Queda[77] and the predictions of the Siamese priests not to go to war, most probably an army of more than a hundred thousand men would have started for the field of operations.

THE ELEPHANTS AND CAVALRY

In Siam there are more than three thousand elephants belonging to the king. Around Judia are 400 to 500 tame elephants. Some of them are taught to fight, others to carry artillery and provisions. These elephants are attended by two or three men, are fed in stables, and get a bath every day in the river. They are highly valued for their strength, ability, and intelligence. Some are trained every day in the art of fighting; others, males as well as females, are taught to carry artillery, tents, provisions, and other necessities for the army. The army also possesses ponies but no special horsemen are provided for. The cavalry are armed with old muskets and leather shields, so that an army provided with modern weapons does not need to fear an attack of the Siamese cavalry.

THE NAVY

The king's navy consists of 130 to 140 frigates and galleys. Some of the vessels are at Siaya[78] and Sangora, but the greater number are lying in the river around Judia. These boats contain the necessary materials, excepting

77. Kedah.
78. Chaiya.

guns, and they are covered with a roof to keep out the rain. Some of the galleys are built to carry heavy artillery, but the Siamese are just as bad sailors as they are soldiers and have no experience in handling artillery. There are an incredible number of boats for use on the river, and the Siamese are expert rowers. They are, however, not well armed, they have no experience, and they could not maintain a fight against a European navy. As, however, the neighboring nations are not better armed, the Siamese navy may be of some use. During the rule of warlike kings the Siamese have fought big battles, have gained many victories, and have conquered foreign countries. As the kings had absolute power and as their rule was very strong, they could make good soldiers of their subjects. During a long period the kings of Siam have ruled over neighboring countries. Under peaceful kings the tributary nations managed to regain their independence. Although the present king is a man of courage, he seems not to have the desire to enlarge his country or to make rebellious princes pay homage to him. For his luxury and daily drunkenness have enervated his mind, and his conduct is not in accordance with what might be expected of a sovereign king. As most of the mandarins are effeminate men, they, if possible, dissuade the king from making offensive wars. But besides all this, the king has exhausted the means of the nobility and the inhabitants of the whole country by forcing them to contribute towards the erection of the city walls of Judia and towards building temples, so that a war could not be carried on without causing great misery.

FORMER WARS WITH VARIOUS NATIONS

During the past the kings of Siam, the emperors of Ava, and those of Pegu have fought many wars. They all, and especially the chiefs of Ava, have made several attempts to conquer the neighboring countries. Siam had been for many years tributary to Ava. But at last the Siamese, with the aid of a man whom they called "the black king,"[79] threw off the foreign yoke. He was the heir to the throne of Siam, and when still a youth, he was hostage to the court of Pegu. As, however, he had to endure many insults, he made up his mind to flee. One night he escaped with 300 nobles, who all belonged to his suite. They took their way back to Siam. But when the news of their departure reached the court of Ava, the king ordered the fugitives to be pursued. But the prince of Siam plundered and burned down all the villages which he passed through, and his pursuers found the country entirely desolated. Forced by famine, they had to return, and the prince arrived with his company safe in Siam. Their arrival caused great uneasiness at the court of Siam, as the king and his mandarins feared an attack of the Avas. But they all were inspired by the prince, who proposed to invade the frontiers of Pegu. As, however, the Siamese were unaccustomed to war, their arms had grown rusty and the

79. Naresuan.

other war materials were scattered all over the country, so the Pegu soldiers were ready before the Siamese and destroyed many of their towns. At last they appeared before Judia, which town they thought to conquer very easily. But the Siamese prince marched with his army against the enemy and met them half a mile[80] above the town near a ruined temple which is still existing.[81] Scarcely had the two armies taken positions opposite each other, when the Pegu prince and the young Siamese prince (both seated on elephants and dressed in royal garb) lost all self-control, left both their armies, and attacked each other furiously. The Siamese prince ran his adversary through the body with his lance and took the other's elephant. His slaves, who followed him very closely, killed a Portuguese who sat behind the Pegu prince to guide the elephant. The Pegu soldiers, seeing that their chief had been slain, fled away, but were at once pursued by the Siamese. Many thousands were slaughtered and the rest dispersed, so that only a few of the enemy's army reached Pegu again. Since that time the crown of Siam has not been tributary again to any other country. After a few years of rest Pegu and Siam attacked each other several times, but these wars were of little importance and an army of 20,000 to 80,000 men, which the Siamese kings usually sent to the frontier of Pegu in the dry season, proved to be sufficient to check the attacks of the Pegues.

THE PEGU AMBASSADOR IN SIAM

In 1634 the king of Pegu sent an ambassador to Siam in order to stop the state of war and to make a treaty of peace. But the ambassador made the condition that the prince of Siam, who is the king's only brother and heir to the crown of Siam, should marry the king of Pegu's daughter and go and live in Pegu as hostage. The king of Siam did not like this proposition at all, but treated the ambassador very well and dissembled kindness, but did not promise him anything. Soon after the ambassador had left for his country, about a hundred thousand inhabitants of Pegu fled away to Siam, as revolutions were going on in their country and times were very hard there. They were received kindly by the king and the mandarins, and although by special messenger the king of Pegu tried to force these people to go back to Pegu, His Majesty

80. Assuming Van Vliet is using the same "mile" here as elsewhere (see fn. 10), this means around 3.75 kms.

81. The Luang Prasoet chronicle dates this incident to 1592, and places it in Suphanburi (*RCA*: 123, ll. 13–39), a location that has passed into Thai history and legend. Van Vliet here corroborates the Burmese (U Kala) chronicle in locating the battle just outside Ayutthaya (see Sunait and Than Tun 1995: 43–5). In the *Short History* (see p. 226), Van Vliet specifies the location outside Ayutthaya "at a certain ruined temple (the remains of which are still visible today) called Crengh or Nong Sarai."

refused to let them go. He gave them chiefs and officers of their own nationality and also good sites for settlement.

THE AMBASSADOR OF AVA, EMPEROR OF PEGU

Last year an ambassador from Pegu or Ava [*sic*] arrived in Siam and asked assistance against Honscha, king of Pegu, who threatened Ava with a war. But as the ambassador's petition and complaints were suspected not to be founded on natural reasons, His Majesty took them for fables and thought the arrival of this man to be a stratagem to deprive Siam of war materials and soldiers in order to attack the country afterwards with the combined armies of Honscha and Ava.

The ambassador was detained a long time at the court and was treated politely, but at last his petitions were refused and he returned to his country.

So we may conclude that the kings of Siam and Pegu are not on friendly terms at present. However, it is my opinion that peace will not lightly be disturbed, because in the first place neither in Pegu nor in Siam are there enough soldiers at present; and in the second place, owing to former wars, large tracts of land along the frontiers have grown wild. A march through this country would cause much trouble, and only an army consisting of a very large force of men would have a chance of success.

HOW THE SIAMESE KING HAS TAKEN LYCOON AND HOW HE HAS TREATED THE INHABITANTS

For various reasons the Siamese kings have often attacked the neighboring countries like Jamgoma, Taiyou,[82] Langsiangh, and others. There was peace during a long period until the king of Siam, in 1632, took Lycoon[83] by stratagem, destroyed the town, and took the inhabitants as prisoners to Judia. These people came under the government of five mandarins who treated them so badly that many tried to flee away in 1633. But their intention became known before they could go. The chief conspirators were thrown into prison, some were killed by elephants, others thrown into the river and their bodies cut in two, etc.

The reason for this war was an old claim which the Siamese kings had on the province and the town. But as the chiefs and the population at the commencement of the rule of the present king refused to pay homage and the yearly taxes, His Majesty decided to force them to do so, and in order to frighten the Patanese (who were rebellious at that time), the king accompanied

82. Possibly, Phayao.

83. Probably Lampang, which was often called Nakhon or Lakhon in this era, but the northern chronicles record no attack around this time.

the army. On leaving his palace, the king swore that the four women whom he should meet first would be made an offering to the gods and that his vessels would be smeared with the women's flesh and blood. This was done; before His Majesty was out of the town he met four young girls sitting in a boat, and on these girls he fulfilled his oath.

Satisfied, he now continued his journey and imagined that victory would be his. I wanted to describe this cruelty in order to show what great authority the Siamese kings possess and how little their subjects are cared for.

DOUBTFUL FRIENDSHIP BETWEEN THE PRINCE OF JANGOMA AND SIAM

The princes of Jangoma and their neighbors were not at all frightened by the war with Lycoon. But the princes of Langsiangh sent an ambassador to the Siamese court with presents in 1633. These presents were made more or less with selfish reasons. For the ambassador brought with him many products from the highlands, such as gold, benjamin, and malacca gum, with a view to exchange these for cloth, for which there was great want in Langsiangh at that time. Many private merchants accompanied the ambassador in order to be able to sell their goods with less trouble in the name of the ambassador. But the ambassador and all the people with him had to stop about two miles above the town and were not allowed to enter the town before the day that His Majesty gave audience to him and the day the ambassador took leave. They were also so annoyed in their trade by all kinds of monopolies and ill treatment by the king's factors that they never came back to Siam again. The Siamese king, seeing afterwards that the absence of the highlanders was a drawback for him and his country, ordered Oya Poucelouck and Berckelangh to send several ambassadors to Langsiangh to invite the people to come back and promising them better treatment and more freedom than on their last visit. But no highlanders appeared in Judia (apparently kept away by distrust); some of them went as far as Poucelouck with their goods. In December last the king sent an ambassador to Langsiangh to remove any objections and to ask the king of Langsiangh to send his subjects again to Siam as in former days, promising his people many privileges and much freedom.

Up to now it is uncertain what has been the result of this mission.

THE REBELLION OF CAMBODIA AGAINST SIAM IS STILL CONTINUED

The kings of Cambodia have been from olden times vassals and subjects of the Siamese kings, but on several occasions they have revolted.

Although brave kings and powerful princes of Siam have several times subdued the vassal and with arms forced him to pay obeisance, the Cambodians did not remain in proper subjection. They made themselves ready for war and plundered the towns situated on the Siamese rivers. To prevent such from happening again and to tie Cambodia to Siam, the predecessor of the present king sent two very large armies to Cambodia in 1622.[84] One of the armies went by water and the other one by land, and the king himself accompanied the army to Cambodia. After the armada (consisting of many large armed galleys and ships of less importance) had been lying for a long time on the river of Cambodia (without going into action or doing anything), it returned again. The Cambodians, encouraged by the departure of the Siamese boats, went to meet the army which came by land. They united in the valleys and the low fields and by false guides brought the Siamese from the good roads. They attacked the Siamese and many thousands of men were slain. Many great men, elephants, and horses were killed in that unfortunate battle. The Cambodians took about 250 living elephants. After this victorious defense the one party has left the other in peace. Several times afterwards the Siamese have made preparations for war and the news spread that they wanted to attack Cambodia, but all this never had any result. I believe that the proud and thoughtless Siamese have spoiled a double chance by treating the foreign merchants and Dutch so badly a few years ago. For now not only no war vessels for the conquest of Cambodia could be expected from the Governor-General in Batavia (as was promised by letter in 1637), but also the Governor-General had established a comptoir in Cambodia, where his factors resided, so that the Siamese certainly will leave Cambodia in peace in future.

REBELLION OF PATANY, THE SIAMESE KING'S VASSAL STATE, AND THE UNSUCCESSFUL ATTEMPT TO SUBJECT PATANY

The kingdom of Patany has been subjected to Siam since olden times but was only bound every year to bring homage to His Majesty the king of Siam with the golden and silver flowers, and in times of war to send in assistance a few thousand soldiers. The princes and princesses of Patany received titles from the Siamese king. They received the title of Pra 'tJiau.[85] From that may be concluded the good right of the Siamese king over the government of Patany. But by the ambition of the late princess to obtain the highest power

84. The Thai chronicles mention no attack at this date, but Giles (1938: 191–2) found correspondence between King Songtham and the Japanese shogun which confirms this attack. In 1628, Songtham wrote that Chettha had just succeeded Suphanarat in Cambodia and refused to acknowledge Siam's suzerainty, so an expedition was in preparation. Subsequent correspondence shows the campaign lasted until 1630 (see also Kersten 2003: xv–xvii). This 1628–30 attack fits a pattern. In 1594 Naresuan sent forces by land and sea which hauled away many people. The Thai chronicles report another victorious joint land/sea attack in 1711 (*RCA*: 142–54, 401–4).

85. *Phrachao* (พระเจ้า), king.

and by the great authority of some mandarins, especially Dato Bestaar,[86] (who were not loved by most of the Orangh Cayos[87]), the people of Patany became rebellious against Siam during the change of succession in that country.[88]

The ambitious princess and mandarins already mentioned made known in public that the king of Siam did not have the right to wear the crown and that he had killed the true kings and their heirs. For this reason the Patanese regents could not recognize him as a legal king but as a tyrannic conqueror to whom the kingdom did not need to pay homage. To show their intention, the Patanese attacked the provinces of Bordelongh and Lygoor during the first year of the rule of the present king, and afterwards they took two of His Majesty's vessels which were going to Batavia and which traded with the East India Company's factors. At last they treated His Majesty's ambassador very unworthily and refused to negotiate with Governor Caan, who in 1632 was sent to Patany to promote peace. The Batavian community (burchers) could not expect any restitution and the king of Siam had given up all hope that the Patanese would be obedient to him or make friendship with him. After having conquered the provinces of Lycoon and Lygoor and after having made peace with Queda and Sangora, the king of Siam therefore wanted to force Patany to pay obeisance and to give Siam again the same power as before. To do this His Majesty called to arms in Lygoor an army of 60,000 men[89] with plenty of elephants, horses, artillery and ammunition, and placed over this army four

86. Dato Besar, a Pattani noble.

87. *Orang kaya* (Malay), "big people."

88. Pattani, a port near the midpoint of the eastern coast of the peninsula, was at the boundary between the Thai and Malay worlds. In this era both Siam to the north and Johore to the south attempted to exercise control, and Pattani played one off against the other to retain some independence. The port-state was ruled at this time by a lineage of queens, assisted by two or three male lineages of nobles. Queen Ungu, who succeeded in 1624, seems to have initiated the aggressive policy towards Siam. The Dutch also saw great advantages in gaining influence on the mid-peninsula, and hence followed Siam-Pattani politics closely, and readily offered military assistance to Prasat Thong. The *Hikayat Patani* (Teeuw and Wyatt 1970: 179–82) attributes the 1634 war to Siamese instigation. Ungu's daughter, Kuning, had been married at age 12 to a Siamese nobleman, Okphraya Decha (possibly from Nakhon Si Thammarat), who later abandoned her. The Sultan of Johore then asked for Kuning's hand and Ungu consented. Okphraya Decha then petitioned the Phrakhlang to suggest to Prasat Thong to mount an attack. The Malay Muslim states rallied in the defense of Pattani, with Pahang and Johore sending 50 galleys and 5,000 men (see also Dhiravat 1984: 177–8).

89. The *Hikayat Patani* (Teeuw and Wyatt 1970: 182) estimates the force at eighty or a hundred thousand, and taunts the Siamese for their lack of seafaring skill, which meant the main expedition had to travel by land and which caused the attack to fail for lack of supplies.

generals, namely the Oyas: Lygoor, Calahom,[90] Berckelangh and Rabisit.[91] Moreover an armada of 40 junks and galleys with ammunition and the necessary provisions were sent there. The four chiefs got the order to attack the town of Patany at the end of April or to besiege and take the town by starving it. But in order to carry on the war with more glory and to frighten the Patanese and their neighbors more, the king and the mandarins of Siam asked for the assistance of a few ships of the Governor-General and Council of India. This request was founded on various motives; namely, 1° the friendship with the Netherlands nation, which His Majesty had kept up for a long time; 2° the assistance of which His Kingly Grace, the Prince of Orange, has assured the king by various missions; 3° the assistance which the late noble general Koen had given the late king many years ago by sending two ships to fight Cambodia; 4° the assistance which the noble general Speck gave in the year 1632, without any requisition, by sending five well-armed ships under the command of Anthonio Caan, to fight against the Castilians; 5° that all relations with the Castilians and Portuguese were trade relations, but that there was great friendship with the Netherlands nation. This was proved by several actions of the Siamese government as: 1° the punishment of Don Fernando de Silva[92] by the late king for taking the yacht Zeeland and the goods of Caspir Swaris, who in 1630 came from Maccouw[93] to Siam with Chinese products; 2° the pursuit of the Maccau prisoners in 1633 by many mandarins.

For which reasons the king and the mandarins firmly believed that the requested assistance could not be refused by the Governor-General. By this assistance Patany should be forced to pay obeisance to Siam. The noble Governor-General and the Council of India have taken the claim on Patany and the urgent requests into consideration, and sent to Patany the ship Velsen ahead and afterwards six well-armed boats with a junk under the flag of Commander Claas Bruyn to assist the king of Siam. But these ships came too late as the Siamese army had already returned. The Siamese had besieged the town for about one month, had fought many skirmishes, and had even

90. Okya Kalahom (ออกญากลาโหม), see Appendix I.

91. Maybe, Okya Phrasadet (ออกญาพระเสด็จ), called the "Governor of the City of Siam" by La Loubère. G. V. Smith (1977: 180) identified Ramasit/Rabasit as "a factor of the King and usually a Muslim," but a "factor" would not be an Okya. Giles (1938: 376) identifies two posts with the title of Ramasit, but both seem too junior to qualify as Okya.

92. In August 1624, a galleon commanded by the Spaniard Don Fernando de Silva seized the VOC yacht, *Cleen Zeelandt*, in the Chaophraya. King Songtham sent a Thai-Japanese force, which seized the galleon, killed Don Fernando and 150 others, and imprisoned another thirty. The yacht was returned to the Dutch immediately, but the cargo not until years later (Dhiravat 1984: 129).

93. Macao.

been in the fortress of Patany. Oya Lygoor, who thought that the Siamese had already conquered the town, ordered that the whole town should be kept for the king and that nobody be allowed to take anything of the booty. The soldiers then retired from the town and went back to their camp. Now the Patanese regained courage, defeated the Siamese, and made them flee away. After many defeats the Siamese lost all hope of conquering Patany and returned to their fleet at Sangora. But when the chiefs of the army afterwards started to regret the mistakes which they had made, they tried to give the blame to our nation. They sent their false information to the king and made him believe that the Netherlanders, by keeping back their warships (which, as they said, were promised to them for certain), were the cause of the defeat. Without any consideration the credulous king believed all this. An immediate result of this was that we became in trouble; we were quite isolated from the outside world, lived as prisoners in the Company's house, and expected still worse things for the future. But when the king afterwards heard of the goodwill which the Governor-General had shown, His Majesty's disgrace turned from us. After the army with a loss of many thousands returned in parts to Siam, the principal officers (among whom were those who had falsely accused us) were not allowed to appear before the king to pay the usual reverence and to report of their doings. They were sharply examined about their conduct by a commission. After information had been gathered, it was found that many hundreds of Siamese had been inside the fortress of Patany, but that they had the order from Oya Lygoor, general of the army, to retire, as he feared that his soldiers would plunder and destroy the town. Having received this information, the king concluded that Patany had not been conquered on account of two mistakes of his officers; firstly, they had left the town too early and, secondly, they had not waited for the assistance of the Dutch. In his rage the king said that they all (although some had shown much ambition) deserved the severest punishment. One of the captains[94] was beheaded and his head was put on a post, and His Majesty ordered the others to sit around the post for three days under the open sky in order that they might consider whether their captain had been punished in the right way. Also His Majesty made known to them that this punishment was the best compensation for their brave deeds. In such condition the officers had to sit for two days in public as an example for everybody, though it was dangerous for their health. At last they were thrown into prison by Oya Poucelouk and Oya Sycry, but were released again with the fearful understanding that, if they should be sent for a second time to Patany and if they should return without having gained success, the king would put to death not only them but also all their relatives. The king showed thankfulness for the Dutch assistance although it came too late, and as recompense he discharged the Company for about half

94. Okkhun Sisongkhram (ออกขุนศรีสงคราม), see Dhiravat (1984: 180).

a year of the usual taxes. If Patany had been conquered by the assistance from Batavia, the Company would have enjoyed many more advantages.

GREAT PREPARATIONS FOR A SECOND CAMPAIGN BUT BY INTERVENTION OF THE KING OF QUEDA PEACE WAS MADE BETWEEN SIAM AND PATANY

After the first war great numbers of new soldiers were called to arms for the second campaign, which had been postponed for one year on account of the bad harvest of rice. In the meantime more than one hundred new vessels had been built in Siam and the neighboring countries, and the old vessels had been repaired. All these vessels were to take part in a second war with Patany, so that according to all appearances Patany would have had a hard time in 1636. But by intervention of the king of Queda, and from the predictions of the Siamese priests, the king changed his mind. By order of the king, Berkelangh sent ambassadors to Patany in order to offer peace for the last time to the queen and the mandarins (as a warning and under pretense of having pity for the Patanese). The ambassadors also had to tell the Patanese that the war had been prevented by the king of Queda and the Siamese priests, and if the Patanese would send legates to Siam to ask mercy, His Majesty without any hesitation would be very glad to grant such. In March 1636 appeared thereupon some ambassadors, who were received by Berkelangh. They were as much humble as the Siamese showed pride. The result of the preliminary negotiations was that the next August a distinguished person appeared as a legate. He presented the golden and the silver flowers to the king as a sign of subjection. This was accepted by His Majesty with great pleasure, and herewith peace was made between the two kingdoms. No claims were made from either side for insults suffered or for damages.

UNCERTAIN FRIENDSHIP BETWEEN ARRACAN AND SIAM

The kings of the Arracan and Siam have lived in peace and in alliance for a very long time without either of them being a vassal or tributary to the other. To maintain this alliance, they sent each other ambassadors every year. This was done, not only to promote commerce but also for reasons of policy. The alliance lasted until the death of the great king.[95] But as soon as this king had passed away, the friendship was finished between the two kingdoms, for the present king, having been crowned and having reached the supreme power, sent his ambassadors to Arracan as before, although no ambassadors had come from Arracan. The king of Arracan[96] did not receive the legation, saying that

95. King Songtham.

96. Sirisudhammaraja (r. 1622–38). In the early part of his reign, he took advantage of Mughal squabbles in Bengal, and a succession crisis in Ava, to expand both eastwards

he could not recognize an illegal usurper as king of Siam, and he therefore refused to give audience to the ambassadors or to pay any honor to them. The king of Arracan did not allow the ambassadors to return, but did send a boat with some of his subjects to Tannassary to trade as usual. The governors out there reported this to the Siamese king, and asked the king's advice about what to do with these people from Arracan. His Majesty commanded that their boats and their goods should be seized and the men taken prisoners and brought to Judia. For more than two years these people from Arracan have been kept prisoners, and during all this time no negotiations about these men have taken place, nor has any hostility been shown by either side, both parties keeping quiet until November last year. At that time some galleys and other small ships were sent from Arracan to the island of Mirghy and to Tannassary with a view to plunder, but as many Moors had left for Masilipatham[97] and as those who had not left were on their guard, the Arracans could do very little.

At last the people of Tannassary seized some Arracans and sent them to Judia. These prisoners after a sharp investigation confessed that the king of Arracan intended to conquer Myrghy and Tannassary, but from want of a sufficient army had postponed the expedition until he might have a better chance. In the meanwhile he wanted to make the rivers in the neighborhood unsafe in order to prevent the Moors from the coast of Choromandel from coming to Tannassary. The king had, moreover, asked the assistance of the Dutch and the Portuguese. The Dutch resident had refused such assistance, but the Portuguese had promised to help as much as they were able to. The Siamese king then released the prisoners and sent them over Tannassary to their own country. They were given a Traak'hausa Ty-bydy,[98] or missive, from Berkelangh, in which was mentioned the friendship which for so long time had been maintained between the two kingdoms.

If the king of Arracan wished to continue this friendship, the king of Siam would be very much pleased, but in case the king of Arracan did not wish to act like this, a strong Siamese army would be sent to his country. As no answer has yet been received from Arracan, it cannot be stated for certain whether the two kings remain enemies or will become friends.

---

and westwards. By the early 1630s, however, his neighbors had recovered and Sirisudhammaraja was on the defensive (Leider 2002). In the *Short History* (see p. 242), Van Vliet remarks that Prasat Thong sent embassies to Aceh and Arakan "to establish firm peace with their majesties," but without substantial result.

97. Masulipatnam, Machilipatnam; port in the Telugu region of the east coast of India.

98. *Tra kosathibodi* (ตราโกษาธิบดี), a document with the *phrakhlang*'s seal.

THAT THE PROCEEDINGS OF THE KING OF SIAM TOWARD THE AMBASSADORS OF AATCHYN[99] PROBABLY WILL LEAD TO MAKING OF PEACE BETWEEN SIAM AND AATCHYN[100]

The kings of Aatchyn and Siam have been allied friends from olden times. They never have been a vassal or a tributary to each other. To maintain the friendship, they often sent to each other their ambassadors with letters full of exaggerated titles and compliments and with presents. But during the life of the great king[101] one of the ambassadors from Siam on his own account told the Aatchynese that the king of Siam was willing to give his daughter to the king of Aatchyn in order to bind the two countries inviolably to each other. The Aatchynese listened to this talk with open ears, and as that rascal of an ambassador made himself very agreeable to the king and the mandarins, he was given a higher rank and he was respected more than all the other ambassadors. But as this rogue knew very well that his lies would lead to his ruin, he secretly fled away without taking leave. Having returned to Siam, he made a false report of the Aatchynese and the actions of his mission. The result of this was that each of the two kings kept his ambassadors at home and the mutual friendship seemed to have disappeared entirely until the great king died. The present king, however, has tried to renew friendly relations for political reasons and to satisfy his personal desire. For when he had reached the supreme power and had killed the true heirs and rooted out these relations, he found himself in the midst of revolutions and in enmity with the neighboring princes and kings like those of Ava and Pegu, whose friendship he could not rely upon any farther than he could on that of the Cambodians or the Patanese. There were further the rebellion of Lycoon and Lygoor and the doubtful attitude of Queda and Sangora. The Portuguese took a doubtful attitude and had blockaded the mouth of the river. For all these reasons and in order to make his enemies fear him more, the king sent a distinguished legation with a costly present to the king of Aatchyn and asked for His

99. Aceh.

100. As is usual with such tales of marriage negotiations, there may be a larger political context. Aceh was a rival with Johore within the Malay world. Prasat Thong sent an embassy to Aceh in 1633, ostensibly to forge an alliance against the Portuguese, but probably also to gain Aceh's help against Pattani, or at least its neutrality. Sultan Iskandar Muda of Aceh demurred (Dhiravat 1984: 17). As noted above, Pattani subsequently accepted Siamese suzerainty. It also eased away from Johore, a shift explained in the *Hikayat Patani* (186–90) by the Sultan of Johore's abandoning Queen Kuning of Pattani for an alluring head of an opera troupe. This contorted story of Aceh–Ayutthaya marriage negotiations may be designed to explain Ayutthaya's waning interest in an alliance with Aceh.

101. King Songtham.

Majesty's friendship. The Aatchynese received the ambassador and after royal entertainments sent him back with great pomp. He promised by letter the continuation of the former alliance to the Siamese king. Since then many ambassadors with letters written on gold have gone from Siam and Aatchyn. These ambassadors were usually treated with great honor so that the friendship seemed to be firm and indissoluble. But this friendship was but founded on sand, for which later events were the proofs.

In 1634, about in September, a certain ambassador from Aatchyn arrived in Siam and brought as usual a letter engraved on gold and a present for the king. In respect of this he was welcomed brilliantly, and the king gave him an audience with much pomp very soon after his arrival.

And when His Majesty brought his offerings to the temple Nappetat (as is the fashion in Siam), this was done with much splendor, and the ambassador from Aatchyn with all the other foreign ambassadors and the most prominent foreigners were also allowed to take their place in the temple. From his seat the Aatchyn ambassador had the opportunity to watch His Majesty with the women, children, and the whole suite. The ambassador having returned to Aatchyn boasted to the king and the mandarins about the unusual honor which he had enjoyed in Siam, and made his king believe that the king of Siam had made the trip to Nappetat in order to be able to show the ambassador his brilliant state, his women, and children.

From all this the king of Aatchyn and the mandarins concluded that the Siamese king would not be unwilling to give his daughter in marriage to the crown of Aatchyn. They thought that the Siamese king did not like to tell this frankly, but by the honor bestowed on the ambassador, he had clearly shown his intention. In order to know for certain what His Majesty's intention was, the king of Aatchyn sent the same ambassador with two deputies again to Siam at the end of 1636. These men were received brilliantly as before, and the letters were handed over with great pomp. This being done, the three men were asked whether besides these letters still other affairs had to be discussed. The two deputies then gave an account of what the ambassador had told to the king of Aatchyn about his last reception out here, and they also told that the king of Aatchyn had verbally ordered them to investigate whether matters were standing in conformity with the report of the ambassador and whether His Majesty was willing to give his consent to the marriage. In this case they had to send word at once to Aatchyn in order that the king of Aatchyn might make preparations to welcome the bride. But if it should prove that the ambassador had only been boasting and had been reporting things which were not true and in so doing had abused the king and the mandarins of Aatchyn, His Majesty the king of Siam was asked to put the ambassador to death in Siam. All this was told to the king by Berkelangh, and His Majesty fell into such a passion that when after a sharp examination the ambassador was found guilty, he was deprived of all his dignities and thrown into prison. He was chained in seven places of his body, and so he was kept for six months. During this time the deputies had been received in audience by the king, and they presented their letter and the presents to His Majesty. These presents were accepted with dissembled friendship and according to such the two deputies were treated. They lived out here so luxuriously and frivolously that on command of the king they also were thrown into prison. Although they asked several times to return to their country after they had left the prison, such was refused unjustly. They were neglected to such a degree that they had to live on charity.

The future will show us how the king of Aatchyn shall act on the already mentioned proceedings and detention, but many of the mandarins in Siam believe that the Aatchynese did not like this alliance with Siam as it only could be maintained by heavy expenses. They therefore thought that the Aatchynese were looking for a chance to get rid of this alliance. But as it went, the Siamese did not approve the measures taken by the king, and they wished that the king had acted more moderately against the ambassadors for they feared the Aatchynese power and the revenge of its king.

THE FORMER AND THE PRESENT POSITION OF THE JAPANESE IN SIAM

A few Japanese merchants have since long ago frequented the kingdom of Siam. They came every year with their junks, their capital, and merchandise to enjoy the profits which the Siamese deer and roeskins gave in Japan. They were so fond of this rich profit that some of them remained in Siam, and the affection of the Siamese kings (who have always favored foreign trades) for the Japanese nation (especially for the silver money which the merchants brought into Siam with their junks) became so great that they sent several legations with presents and letters full of kind compliments to the emperor of Japan. The Siamese ambassadors were usually well treated out there by the Japanese, proofs of which are the receptions which the last ambassadors to Japan enjoyed in Japan in 1629 and 1630. But as the confluence of Japanese increased considerably, their natural pride and impudence grew so great that at last they dared to attack the palace and to seize the king in his own room. They did not let him free again from their tyrannic hands before His Majesty had sworn that he would never remember the harm done to him nor take any revenge and that he would take the Japanese in his service as soldiers and as bodyguards to the end of his life. These promises remained in force, by which the rogues not only enjoyed the usurped advantages but they also practiced great impudence and violence against the natives and against the foreign traders. But fortune, which usually gives her favorites bitter compensations, made the Japanese incur the ruling king's disgrace to such a degree (notwithstanding they had assisted His Majesty very much in usurping the crown) that His Majesty, for fear of ambitious conceptions and treason (which from their impudent talk was very near) and for punishment of their disloyal deeds against the legal princes and heirs of the kingdom, has killed by trick and by force many of the Japanese, has driven the rest of them out of the country (to the gladness of the inhabitants), and in doing so His Majesty has freed and cleared Siam of them. The great men in the country and the nobles were very glad of this, as they have always suspected the Japanese for their desperate, bold, and treacherous attempt to make their king a prisoner (as was described here above).[102]

Moreover they thought the presence of the Japanese a drawback for the country. Of the 600 Japanese who were here, only 60 to 70 have returned to Japan in a junk after many miseries; the rest have been killed or have fled away to various quarters.

For good reasons we may conclude that in the future Japanese will not lightly be engaged as soldiers by the Siamese kings, nor will junks be sent from Japan to Siam for fear it occasion one party taking revenge on the other. But against the will of many persons, His Majesty, for fear of revenge of the Japanese, after a short time called those who had fled away back again, and when their number amounted 70 to 80, the king gave them a fine tract of land to live on and bestowed on the three most prominent Japanese titles of honor, appointed these men as chiefs over the others, and placed them all under one of his mandarins. Also the king ordered Oya Berkelangh on several occasions to send ambassadors with letters and presents to the governors of Naagasacque[103] in Japan in order to make good on his actions to offer friendship and to invite the Japanese merchants to come again to Siam. But the legations were never received with the proper honor by the governors of Naagasacque. They even roughly refused the last legation, saying that the master who had sent them was not a legal king, but a usurper, a traitor, and a murderer who had killed the real heirs and the princes of the blood. Although the ambassador with his junk still loaded had to leave Japan, his duty undone and an object of disdain, His Majesty decided at the time when I was going to leave Siam to send a person in his name to the emperor of Japan and the council of Japan to beg for the former friendship and to give a friendly invitation to the Japanese merchants. This request (in my opinion) was the result of many considerations and was advised to the king by some secret fortune hunters (who thought to gain much profit by the trade with Japan). Also the Japanese in Siam used their influence to the same end, as they had become poor and little esteemed. They hoped (and not without reason) that when the junks from Japan appeared, they would increase their means and would regain their lost influence and reputation. But it is against the natural

102. See *Historical Account*, pp. 294–96. See also Appendix IV.
103. Nagasaki.

course and in contradiction with the Siamese arrogance that a king for hope of a little profit should debase himself so far for people who cannot trouble him much. Also it can hardly be expected that during the life of the present Japanese emperor any Japanese should leave their country or those who are abroad should return. Why then try to gain friendship by such a humiliation? But the astute Siamese rulers know how to disguise all this and to color this case as if His Majesty feels very much attached to all foreigners, and as if His Majesty has the intention of making friendship with all neighboring kings, princes, and potentates in order that his kingdom may have rest and that His Majesty may die in peace.

THAT THE FRIENDSHIP BETWEEN CHINA AND SIAM HAS LASTED LONG AND BY WHAT MEANS

Although the Siamese nation (as pointed out by old traditions) originally descended from a rebellious Chinese who was the son of the king, who for the wicked plans of his party was expelled and banished from his country (as described and pointed out already), the kings of China and Siam have been friends and allies from olden times. In order to maintain this friendship they often have sent each other letters engraved on gold, which is considered to be the highest distinction. But the king of China in the commencement could not explain the thoughts of his heart (by lack of a man who knew the Siamese language), so he sent to the Siamese king four learned men as permanent servants for the crown of Siam in the town of Judia. These men were accepted at the court, and they were allowed to appear in audience before the king when they wanted to, just like the other mandarins. Thus they became so well acquainted with the language, the customs of the country, and the highest eloquence, that the Chinese as well as the Siamese letters could be translated thoroughly according to the original text.[104] By this, the friendship between the kings was kept up and has remained strong and durable, notwithstanding that no legation has been maintained in Siam nor in China, owing to the change in succession of the kings in the two countries. This neglect (in my opinion) has to be ascribed to the carelessness of the Siamese king. For by force of an old privilege, His Majesty has the right to send his ambassador every year to Canton, and the Siamese under this pretext may negotiate and

104. According to the Ming records, in 1487 an envoy from Ayutthaya reported: "Under the former regulations, our country's native script and Arabic script were both used [for correspondence with China]. Recently there were differences between the language of the gold-leaf memorial by which enfeoffment was requested and the tally-slips and despatch note issued. The king suspects that the people of the country who wrote the native script have engaged in fraud" (Wade 2000: 272). Ayutthaya asked for an investigation, but China simply ordered that Arabic alone be used. This did not work, possibly leading to the solution Van Vliet records here.

trade, which (as far as known to me) is not allowed to any neighboring nor to any faraway country, and this advantage is greater than the king even can perceive. But the Siamese by pride and arrogance are so blind (although His Majesty's factors believe that they are excellent merchants) that no notice has been taken of such a good opportunity that has been given to them during a long period. For by way of this yearly embassy Siam could have established an important Chinese trade in Siam and could have bound all the foreign traders to herself. But by carelessness that splendid opportunity has passed.

Sometimes the king still sends his junks to the province of Canton with a load of sappan,[105] lead, and small quantities of other products in order to change them for good Chinese merchandise. But while the embassies from both sides had stopped, the traders were to such a degree detained by monopolies and hindrances that they often had to stay very nearly two years before their merchandise could be sold properly.

Moreover they make but small profit and get no proper cargo to bring back, usually returning to Siam with a lot of paltry wares. But the Chinese from Chiuseeuw,[106] who used to appear every year in Siam with their junks and various cargoes, were detained by the deceit of the mandarins (apparently with the knowledge of the king), just in the same way as His Majesty's subjects are detained in Canton. In consequence of this, Siam (in order to escape distress as the Siamese could not make any more profitable journeys) had to admit the Chinese. So the Siamese kings have neglected a double chance; firstly, in that they let the fine chance pass by to bind the Chinese trade to their country; and secondly, in that they by arrogance did not allow the foreigners sufficient access to the court (taking also into consideration the fraud of the mandarins), by which the foreign traders were scared away and expelled from the country. But in the kingdom of Siam many Chinese are still living who enjoy reasonable freedom in trade throughout the whole country and are well respected by the previous as well as the present king, so that some of them have been appointed to high positions and offices and others are considered the best factors, traders, and sailors.

THE POSITION OF THE CASTILIANS AND PORTUGUESE IN SIAM

Many years before the arrival of the Netherlanders in Siam and in India, the Portuguese enjoyed great friendship, communications and free trade in this kingdom. They were so well esteemed by the kings that the ambassadors from the Viceroys of Goa and governors and bishops of Mallacca,[107] who

105. Sappanwood (ไม้ฝาง), *caesalpinia sappan*, also known as brazilwood, used for making red dye.

106. Chiu-chao, Swatow.

107. Malacca, Melaka

sometimes sent letters to His Majesty and proper presents, not only were entertained well and rich presents were bestowed on them, but also some of the residing Portuguese received honor and high positions. Besides free trade in the entire country, the public church and worship of the Roman Catholic religion were allowed to them; yes, even monthly salary was granted for assistance. Also His Majesty licensed his vassals to trade with their junks full with cargo to Mallacca.

Thus the Portuguese enjoyed for many years prosperity and good reputation in Siam, until the servants of the Netherlands Company also took hold of the country. From time to time on several occasions (as the taking of vessels, promoting of the trade in Santhome[108] and Negepatam[109]), they caused the Portuguese so many losses that at present the Portuguese trade has much declined. In 1624 a certain Netherlands yacht was taken in the Siamese waters by Don Fernando de Silva,[110] which deed was taken so ill by the king that His Majesty punished the Spaniards successfully by arms and returned the yacht and the cargo to the Company, for which act he became engaged in war with Manilha. And although the Portuguese did not care much for what had happened, although they continued their correspondence and remained in Siam, they were since that time in disgrace with the king and the mandarins. The vicar who had been appointed their chief by the governor and the bishop of Mallacca, could never again get proper access to the court. Then followed the hostile action of the two war galleys in 1628 under Don Jan d'Alcrassa[111] (by order of the governor and the representatives at Manilha) on the Siamese river. On this occasion not only was the Cantonese junk of His Majesty treacherously taken and after being plundered burned with many persons, but the same was done with a Japanese junk from Nagesacque. This increased the hatred of the king and the mandarins to such a degree that His Majesty not only took and confiscated the galley with the cargo belonging to Casper Swares, a Portuguese coming in 1630 with Chinese goods from Maccau, but also kept the Portuguese in strict captivity during three years and made them go about begging in the streets. Those in Mallacca sent in 1633 in the month of July a captain named Sebastiaan Moutos d'Avilla, with a galley (manned with 10 white men and 30 colored men), as ambassador, bearing a letter and a small present to the king of Siam. In this message the release of the captive Portuguese was requested, and although this embassy was not agreeable to the king, he allowed d'Avilla an audience. D'Avilla was received at the court

108. San Thome, Sâo Tomé, the supposed site of the tomb of the apostle St. Thomas, "discovered" by the Portuguese in 1518 after a long search, and subsequently a Portuguese settlement. It lies in the southern part of the modern city of Madras (Chennai).

109. Negapatam, Nagapattinam, a Portuguese settlement in the Kaveri delta (southern India) since the 1530s.

110. See note 92 above.

111. Sometimes spelt Don Juan de Alcarazo (Dhiravat 1984: 130–1).

with little honor and (after promises of friendship) was treated with dissimulation. However, the king agreed with the request and released the prisoners. But d'Avilla, seeing that he could not attain his aim and that his petition was going to be refused, fled with his galley and all the prisoners down the river in September last. Notwithstanding that he was inimically followed by many mandarins and influential men, they were just able to escape the danger and left with Siam in enmity. The discontent of the king about the sudden departure was so great that from that moment he hated the Portuguese just as much as the Castilians; also because in that same year they blockaded the river of Tannassary with two frigates, prevented the Cantonese junks from coming to Siam, and afterwards committed hostilities. The Siamese king took revenge on a few Castilians in the same cold season. For a certain Chinese named Wancangh, with some Spaniards of high rank (of whom the most prominent was Don Luis de Gusman, sergeant mayor of the Spanish fortress Illa Formosa[112]), had started from Kelangh[113] for Manilha, but during a storm lost the mast and helm and was driven to Lygoor. There they were taken prisoner by command of the king, and with their junks (containing together with some other Chinese goods about 125 piculs rough silk) brought to Judia. This cargo was kept in the king's warehouses. In 1635 some Portuguese galley was driven to Tannassary, whereupon the captain, Francisco Cotringh de Magalano, with 14 Portuguese and some slaves, was also brought to Judia. Like the Castilians these prisoners were also kept very poorly, although they were not put in chains. But as these hostilities had a bad influence on the trade with Canton and Coromandel, His Majesty, as if he wanted to show pity on the prisoners, had them all released and sent them with an ambassador and letters to Manilha and Malacca to remind the governors of these places of the former friendship. The ambassador has returned from Malacca to Siam again, and the king's letters were taken by Luis de Gusman, sergeant mayor, to Manilha and were sent to Goa by the Governor of Malacca. No answer has been received to these letters. Probably the Portuguese will visit Siam once more, but as there are in this country only a few poor Portuguese, mestizos and Indian Christians, they will most probably not regain their former influence and no great traders will appear again to settle out here.

THE POSITION OF THE NETHERLANDS COMPANY IN SIAM

It is now more than 30 years ago since the Netherlanders came to Siam. They won the confidence of the king, so that the United East India Company found it advisable to establish a comptoir for trade and to enter into an alliance

112. The name given originally by the Portuguese to the island of Taiwan. The Spanish built several fortifications in the north of the island.

113. Kelang, a port in Selangor on the lower western coast of the peninsula.

with the king. In pursuance thereof a house or factory of wood was built in Judia. In this house they traded for many years; and native products, cloths, deerskins and hartskins, sappan wood and other merchandise were sent every year to Japan. Although the Company did not make much profit by this trade (as many misfortunes happened, such as the burning of cargoes and uncompleted voyages), the Company entered into great friendship with the kings and was honored more and enjoyed a higher reputation than any other European nationalities. Many ships and junks with provisions, timber, and other necessities were brought from Siam to Batavia. This friendship was maintained for a long time, notwithstanding that many princes succeeded each other and many changes took place in the factory of the Company. Various letters from the illustrious princes of Orange, as Mauritius of Nassouw, His Princely Grace's brother Frederic Heindrik of Nassouw, and the noble generals of Netherlands India, have been sent to the Siamese kings, who in their turn replied to these letters. In this way the friendship was maintained and even strengthened.

The good reputation and friendship which the company enjoyed out here, the hatred of the king against the Castilians, the profitable trade, the fertility and the safety of the country, and the strong position of the Netherlands in India seemed to encourage the maintenance of the friendship with the Siamese kings. And the noble Governor-General and the councils of India in the year 1633 gave permission to restore the factory out here and to renew the trade with Japan. This plan was founded on good reasons, for the king had driven away the Japanese and apparently they would not return again (afterwards they came back anyway). So it was considered that from that side no hindrances would be met with. As it was found that after Japan had been opened for the trade of the Company, the Siamese products could be sold with much profit in that silver-rich country, an excellent house or lodge was erected of stone and lime in order that the Company's goods might be better secured against fire and other misfortunes and also to be able to accommodate and to manage wisely the resumed trade. This building was very commodious and large, and it proved of great advantage for the Company's trade, but (in my opinion) it was disadvantageous for many reasons. For during the change of rulers many malicious mandarins have crept in and have reached high positions, so that at present there is hardly one single distinguished person of upright mind. These jealous rascals imagine wrongly that the Company enjoys incredible profit from the trade with Japan and Tayounan,[114] and that the noble general for this reason and also in regard to the newly erected building will not lightly decide to recall the servants of the Company and the whole establishment connected with their trade. Apparently they tried to make the king (who is very credulous) believe this whenever they had an opportunity;

114. Taiwan, at that time the name of the Dutch settlement on an island off the coast of modern-day Taiwan.

also because they did not get a certain share in the profits, so they wanted to make our nation odious in the eyes of the king. Besides all this we must mention that the king did not like to sell the Siamese rice to us, particularly to the town of Batavia, unless the Governor-General by sending presents every year should ask for it; and in order to increase the dignity of his reputation, he did not want to send more rice than he thought advisable. His Majesty by doing so hoped to secretly weaken the increasing power of the government of the Governor-General. The intention of the king was shown clearly some years ago when the export of grains was very little. Quantities which had been promised were refused afterwards with frivolous subterfuges, notwithstanding from time to time many kind requests were made for the necessary quantities. All this was taken amiss by the Governor-General and not without reason. He showed his just discontent in his letters to the king. Although the tenor of the messages was unpleasant to the king and His Majesty was discontented (believing that the proper respect had not been paid to his assumed dignity), he did not show the least what he thought and concealed the poison in his murderous heart. Shortly after this it happened that some of the company's servants by dissolute lewdness offended against the Siamese laws and against the clergy.[115] These mistakes of our men were by false accusations explained to the prince and to the king as if the men had committed an important crime. In his rage and drunkenness the king thereupon condemned all the Netherlanders to death without hearing them, and proceeded so tyrannically against them and the position of the Company that the affair is almost without parallel. But when it had been pointed out what mistakes His Majesty had made, and what effect the fulfillment of his intention would cause, all the men were released and also the Company was allowed to trade with its former freedom. But although no blood has been shed on this occasion, the shame and disdain which our men have suffered are never to be forgotten. Also the Governor-General and the councils of India saw the importance of what had happened, and that it could not fail to have many bad results for us. The friendship, which always had been honored and laudably maintained by the kings of Siam, has much decreased and has almost disappeared during the rule of this king usurper. And probably this friendship will not flourish again as before, unless this cowardly nation is brought to better sense, and unless the disgrace which we have suffered has been washed away by the sword, in which may God Almighty help.

WITH WHAT NATIONS THE SIAMESE KING STILL KEEPS UP CORRESPONDENCE AND WHY HE DOES NOT CEASE TO DO SO

Having told much of the quality, authority, and state of the king, the armed forces, and alliances with far off and neighboring kings, princes, and

115. This is of course the Picnic Incident.

potentates, we still have to mention the correspondence which His Majesty maintains with some governors, as the Nawab of Bengale, the Sajachan of Coptochiae[116] and other places on the coast of Coromandel. But as the friendship with these governors did not influence matters of state and was only kept up to accommodate trade, so I do not think it necessary to describe this matter diffusively. In the next part I shall have an opportunity to talk about it "en passant," and I will now continue and describe the position of the Siamese mandarins. For this has not yet been done in the first part.

THE QUALITY AND AUTHORITY OF THE MANDARINS IN JUDIA

Besides the sovereign power and the authority of the king, the government is divided into several ranks and various departments standing under the supervision of the mandarins. These mandarins are chosen from the noble as well as from the not-noble families; but before anybody can become a mandarin, he is raised to nobility by the king, and new names and marks of honor are given to him. The nobility rises by degrees: from Opans, Omans, Ockaus, Olaanghs, Opraas, Oyas,[117] which are the highest names and the highest titles. Among this nobility everyone receives donations in conformity with his quality and his rank. The Oyas receive golden betel boxes, some Opraas silver ones, but many get only a wooden box. The gifts are kept in high honor as they have come from the king. Some of the Olaanghs and Ockans have golden swords, which is also a great mark of honor, as these are only given to persons of good standing. But the Omans or Opans seldom receive any other mark of honor than the title. In general the king gives to everybody in proportion to his state more than to human titles. Everybody is very proud of these titles as they fancy that His Majesty cannot fail; and as they receive these titles from the king, they imagine that they are men of dignity and good breeding in conformity with their titles. The marks of honor given by the king are always carried about with the owner wherever he goes, and by them he is recognized and honored. From the nobility are chosen all

116. Van Vliet mentions this place twice in the *Description*, and records its ambassador at court in the *Picnic Incident*. Below he refers to it as "Rammaradt Cotopsia, on the coast of Choromandel." In the *Short History*, he recounts how Ramathibodi established trading relations with "Rammaradt." It is very difficult to identify this place. The title "Sajachan" suggests Shah Jehan, the Mughal emperor at this time. But "Rammaradt" implies a Hindu state, and the mention below, along with the account in the *Short History*, place the location on India's east coast. That would suggest the Sultan of Golconda, which had territories on that coast, and which was a big enough state to have sent an ambassador. Yet "Cotopsia/Coptochiae" is not close to "Golconda." Possibly Van Vliet is just a bit confused here.

117. Okphan, Okmun, Okkhun, Okluang, Okphra, Okya (ออกพัน ออกหมื่น ออกขุน ออกหลวง ออกพระ ออกญา).

the regents, the king's councillors, chief of the army, judges, captains, factors, etc. I will mention here the dignities of some of these men, namely: Oya Oubrad,[118] first mandarin and *stadholder* of the king; Oya Awangh, president of His Majesty's secret council; Oya Poeletip, chief purveyor of the kingdom; Oya Sycry, chief over the political, military, ecclesiastical, and civil affairs; Oya Calahom, general over the elephants and over the armed forces afoot and on horseback; Oya Berckelangh, counsel and leader of all foreign affairs at the court and keeper of the great seal; Oya Jammerad,[119] chief judge for criminal and civil cases in Judia. These (besides some governors of quality and with high titles) are the greatest and most influential mandarins of the whole kingdom. For in case the king came to die suddenly before anybody had been chosen to succeed him and without leaving any legal heir, the Oyas Oubrat, Awangh, Poeletip, Sycry, and Berckelangh have to represent the king and have to rule under the royal standard of the kingdom until a king is chosen out of the complete assembly of mandarins and crowned as a sovereign. But the power and authority of the king do not allow anybody to perform his duty according to the written laws. For His Majesty has usurped supreme power since long ago and has taken all honor and dignity to himself, so that nobody will refer to the dignity of his position or will dare to oppose anything. Everybody must be pleased with as much influence and dignity as the king out of his own free will may allow him.

WHAT AUTHORITY THE GOVERNORS OF THE PROVINCES HAVE

The governors also have great authority, especially those of the four most important provinces, Poucelouck, Capheyn, Sorcelouck and Suckothay. These governments are due to princes of the blood and only if these fail are they given to the greatest and most influential men as a great privilege. In all the provinces, capitals, and governments there are plenipotentiary colleges and officers for the criminal and civil justice and for settling of various affairs for the welfare of the country. But the Oya or governor of the province rules with absolute power and supreme authority over justice, pardons, remittals, and other affairs concerning the province and its inhabitants. However, he is not allowed to commence wars, to break peace, or to change the written laws and the prescriptions without advice or consent of the king. But as each of these governors in his province is honored and respected as a king and is worshipped by his subjects with more than human honor, they can bend and change all laws as they please and without any danger for themselves, for nobody may leave the province or town without proper consent. So if anybody should have the intention to complain at the court of Judia or at the plenipotentiary courts about violence or any trouble, his departure would be

118. Okya (Maha) Upparat (ออกญามหาอุปราช), see Appendix I.
119. Okya Yommarat (ออกญายมราช), see Appendix I.

prevented and no consent would be given to him. And as complaints are secretly sent over by friends, the plaintiff would not be heard or received, because the mandarins are very jealous of each other and usually are political intriguers.

WHAT DISLIKE THE MISTRUST OF THE KING HAS CAUSED

Under former kings it was customary that the governors resided in their provinces and their governments, in order that everything might be done regularly and that the subjects might be ruled with proper fairness.

Those from adjacent places sometimes came once or twice to the court at Judia, and those from far-off places came once every three years to attend state ceremonies and to report about their governments. In the meantime the province or town was ruled by an influential mandarin or plenipotentiary college, and all important affairs were postponed until the return of the governor. But this custom was not maintained by the present king. For as the governors of the far-off provinces used great authority, His Majesty does not allow anybody to stay on very long. But the greatest mandarins (except Oubrat, who is incapable by old age) were all transferred after four to eight months from one office to the other, so that they could not have an opportunity to have a stronghold in one position. For this reason he does not allow them to go to their governments, except to Tannassary, where usually a competent chief has to reside on account of the foreign traders and the bad character of the inhabitants. Also Lygoor, Bordelongh, and Sangora have governors who reside out there, but the governors of the other provinces usually stay in Judia, and the government is carried on by substitutes of less quality, who have to come and report all their actions at any time the king or the master pleases. But many affairs have to suffer by the many changes of governors and by the stinginess of the substitutes; the community is troubled very much by taxes and duties. Although often well-founded complaints were made at the court against the regents, such were seldom or never accepted and remedied. The true cause of this wrong state of things is the king himself. For as he is not an anointed David but only a little Absalom, he does not trust anybody. He keeps all the mandarins under his eyes at the court, in order that they may not form a party or cause a conspiracy, knowing very well with what cunning he himself from a sharper has come to the royal crown.

HOW SLAVISH THE KING KEEPS HIS MANDARINS AND HOW HUMBLY THEY APPEAR BEFORE THE KING

A result of the king's usurped authority and distrust was that all the mandarins (particularly the most influential of them who have a state and a position) are kept very slavishly in Judia. They are entirely deprived of the former freedom. Only in the public assembly room and in presence of and the hearing of everybody, even of the slaves, are the mandarins allowed to talk to each other. Should they not follow this rule, their life and position would be in danger. The father is not allowed to visit his child, nor the child its father, without the knowledge and consent of the king, even in cases of illness or death.

By the natural stinginess, jealousy and malice have increased to such a degree that nobody spares another when accusing him before the king if they expect some profit or if they fancy that such might be agreeable to the king. But they always understand how to exalt their action with an artificial glow as if it is done for a good reason and as if the aim of it is only to increase the glory of the king and the welfare of the country. Besides this, all the influential men, namely, those of His Majesty's secret council, the governors of the provinces and of the most important towns, some officers, judges, and factors have to appear every day at court at the public audience. Three times a day, namely, at noon, in the afternoon, and towards evening, a secretary of the king writes down everybody's name; and if anybody is absent, his servants must give the clerk the reason of his absence. They have no other reason for being absent than illness, and then the suspicious king (under pretense of pity) at once sends his surgeon to visit the person who is ill and if possible to cure the illness. But this is not done out of affection for the patient but always to intrigue and to know what is going on amongst the mandarins in order that he may not be deceived by secret conspiracies and may not one day receive his reward (which he has well deserved from his real Master). Towards the evening the mandarins have to go to audience and everybody goes with his clothes tucked up, which is a sign of humility and is customary amongst slaves who appear before their masters. While going to their places, they kneel down several times, bend the head to the ground, and with folded hands pay humble reverence towards the palace and to His Majesty's seat. But while approaching the throne they creep on hands and feet. When the king appears on his throne, they all have to show humility in the way already described, and have to bend the head with the face on the floor until they are addressed by the king. All this takes place in the utmost silence, for nobody dares to move and hardly dares to breathe. Sometimes six to eight thousand persons are sitting close to each other in this assembly, and the silence is then so great that one can distinctly hear the singing of small birds and the sound of their wings. Usually the king talks with a pleasant voice, first with the four or five greatest men of the country, viz., to Oya Berckelangh, Jamerad, and the Brahman priests. If anybody else is addressed by the king or if he has received a special command, he thinks it a great honor and is very proud of it. Even his walk and bearing show this clearly, and from that date he is more honored and respected by the other mandarins.

WHAT AUTHORITY THE MANDARINS EXERCISE OVER THEIR HOUSE MATES AND OVER THEIR SLAVES

Although the mandarins in general are slavish and have to appear before the king with great humility, they are very arrogant, proud, and haughty, especially in regard to the titles and marks of honor which they have received from the king. Yes, every-one of them wants to be served, honored, and feared as if he were a worldly god. They usually practice great authority over those who are in their houses and over their slaves. Although the greater number have to live off their slaves, they have to keep up a certain state, and they do not allow themselves to be addressed otherwise than with bent body, folded hands, and with ceremonious praisings. Besides this, they often tyrannize their concubines (or small wives) and their slaves. They make them die for small mistakes or throw them into prison and treat them very harshly. For all this an excuse is very easily found for the king, and as much fault is imposed on the victim as their large conscience may care for, and in the meantime the poor victim lies smothered in his blood without being able to give account. In their houses and on the streets the mandarins are honored like small kings among their subjects, but coming to court they are only slaves.

WHAT INCOME THE MANDARINS HAVE

I have already given an account of the king's possessions and yearly income. It ought to be understood that the king enjoys profits of the rice over the whole country, without giving pensions or compensations to anybody. Only the governor of Tannassary with his council receives 6½ percent of the cloths which the Moors from Coromandel and other places bring out there or of cloths which pass that place. But on all cargo which is returned from Siam to the coasts of Bengale or Suratte, taxes are paid where the goods are bought, so the Tannassary government does not derive any other profit than that from a little tin which comes to that port. Also they rob the merchants by trick or with force, and this has often been done so roughly that serious complaints were made in Judia. The swindlers have thereupon often been punished; they were turned out of their office or they were condemned to pay a fine in money. But the greatest mandarins, governors of provinces and principal towns, and some factors receive from the king a few *bunders* or measured land, which they have to plough, to sow, and to reap with their own slaves. During fertile times they get very rich profits from their fields. Some mandarins, and especially Oya Berckelangh, get benefits from the foreign traders who frequent Siam. But as the king, in order to accommodate and to allure the foreign traders, made all taxes lighter a few years ago, and has provided the Berckelangh and each Sabandaar[120] with an official sealed

120. Shahbandar, harbormaster.

permit in proper form, the stinginess and avidity are now moderated and everyone's portion has been cut down considerably and does not amount to much. But most of the mandarins have no other profits than from their own slaves, whom they may treat kindly or harshly, just as they please. These slaves are divided into three classes, each of which has a certain position. Firstly, there are the slaves who follow their masters daily in their suite and who have to do court or private services. They get every month 50 pounds of paddy, two maas, Siamese coins (equal to 15 stuiver), and once a year a new (but common) coat. With this they have to make shift and have to provide themselves everything else which they may need for their living, or else they have to suffer want. Others have to pay their masters monthly 6, 8, 10, to 12 maas (one maas is seven and a half stuiver) in accordance with their diligence and strength and in accordance with their masters being poor, avaricious, or liberal, and besides this they have to buy for themselves everything else that they may need. Some get six months in a year to work for themselves, and what they earn during the rest of the year they have to bring to their masters. On the sweat of their slaves the master and his family are able to live, to keep up state, to offer presents to the king and to the priest. What the servant has won is easily spent by the master. From this may be judged what riches there are among the Siamese nobility. Each whose turn it is squeezes the foreigners as much as he can. Also we must mention that in the whole country the common class of people, who are not slaves, are divided under quartermasters. The latter have control over 1,000, 500, 400, 300, 200, or 100 men. This is done for the accommodation of the king, for if His Majesty needs people, these quartermasters are requested to provide the required number. From this often big profits can be made. For the quartermasters usually first force the poorest people, or those who are in worst circumstances, to leave their houses, and only by bribery are they allowed to stay at home. Also those who come from other places are divided under quartermasters, as the Pegus, who are standing under Oya Poeletip; the Lauws[121] under Oya Awangh; the Japanese under Oya Pitsjasencram;[122] the Chinese under the Oopras Sysembat[123] and Thonsuy;[124] the Malays under the Oopra Alaks Amane;[125] the Portuguese under Opraa Ray Montry.[126] These officers never let any opportunity pass of drawing profits from their subjects. Only the Moors are still free from this slavery, which is rather surprising, but it seems that they (for some special reasons) are under the protection of the king.

121. Lao.

122. Okya Phichai Songkhram (ออกญาพิไชยสงคราม); in the Military Hierarchy Law, head of a military department with a Phra rank and sakdina of 5000 (*KTSD*, 1: 280).

123 Okphra Sisombat (ออกพระศรีสมบัติ).

124. Thong Su (ท่องสื่อ), a Chinese interpreter (*KTSD*, 1: 234; Breazeale 1999: 50).

125. Okphra Alak (ออกพระอาลักษณ์).

126. Okphra Ratchamontri (ออกพระราชมนตรี).

WHERE THE PRINCIPAL PROVINCES AND TOWNS ARE SITUATED AND ALSO WHAT PRODUCTS COME FROM THE VARIOUS PLACES

Herein before we have already mentioned which are the principal fortresses, fortified places, chief provinces and towns in Siam, and we ought now to describe their situation. But this I am not able to do as I could never obtain proper information about this matter and have never seen any maps nor any sketches that could give any indications. For these reasons I will only point out from which places the most important products come, and where these places are situated.

TIMBER FOR BOATS, ETC.

Parathon and Rion[127] are small unwalled towns, are situated on a small stream east of the river, amidst many villages and populous places. As a lot of timber is growing out there, many barges and big prauws (to use on river and in the interior) are built there. Also some deerskins come from there.

AGERWOOD AND SMALL QUANTITIES OF DEERSKINS

Bannae[128] is a poor country town and is lying inside a decayed stone wall. The town is surrounded by many populous places and is close to the frontier and the mountains of Cambodia. It is the only place in the whole country which produces aguel.[129] Also deerskins are exported, but in small quantities, as it is difficult to bring them to the water side, from where they could be transported by prauws.

GITTA GOMMA

T'Siantobon[130] is a poor but unwalled town and is situated east of the river near the mountains of Cambodia. All the gitta gomma[131] produced in Siam comes from that place.

127. Possibly Prachin and Kabin on the Bang Pakong River. La Loubère's map (1688) has a place "Perion" on this river in roughly the location of Prachin.
128. Ban Nai or Ban Noi? Unidentified.
129. Eaglewood (*aquilaria*), a tree producing a core of resin used as an aromatic.
130. Chanthaburi.
131. A gum resin used as a dye and cure for toothache.

WHERE MOST OF THE DEERSKINS, DJATTIPOSTS, AND BLACK SUGAR COME FROM

Poucelouk, Sorkelouk, Capheyn, Suckothay, and Kepenpit are all provincial towns and have had good strong walls, which, however, are in decay. The nearest of these towns is more than 100 miles north of Judia, measured along the river. From these provinces and particularly from Poucelouk and Capheyn come most of the deerskins, teak posts, black sugar, and gomma malacca.[132] This wax, together with some benjuin,[133] is brought to Poucelouk by the highlanders, and from there it is transported to Judia.

BLACK WAX OR SIERAN

Loconsuan[134] is a famous provincial town and is walled. It is situated on the bank of the river about 120 miles northwest from Judia. From there comes the best sieran or vamrak[135] in Siam. But when the yearly crop is bad, no great quantities can be obtained from there, whilst in fertile times much can be got.

TIN, SAPPANGWOOD, AND RICE

Tannassary has become famous by the important passing through of foreign traders who have to visit Siam. It is one of the keys for the whole kingdom and is situated favorably for ships and junks. A great quantity of tin comes from there at a cheaper price than anywhere else in Siam. Also sappang and rice. But for the transport of rice and sappang the regents out there cannot give a license but such has to be asked in Judia from the king.

WHERE THE BEST SAPPANGWOOD COMES FROM THAT CAN BE OBTAINED IN SIAM

Poucenough[136] is a big walled (but decayed) provincial town. It is situated at the branch of the river about 40 miles east from Judia amidst a forest of sappangwood. This wood is imported in abundance and is the best which can be obtained in the whole of Siam.

132. Gumlac, a wax produced by ants and used as a sealing wax.
133. Benzoin, benjamin, a tree resin used as an aromatic.
134. Nakhon Sawan.
135. Black lac, used in making paint and lacquer.
136. Possibly Prachinburi. But if Van Vliet is here using a Dutch mile (=7.5 kms) and has got the distance right, it would be somewhere at or beyond the current Thai-Cambodia border.

WHERE A LITTLE RICE BUT AN ABUNDANCE OF SAPPANGWOOD AND SALT COME FROM

Meclongh, Pypry, Rappry, Pitsjeboury, Ratsjebeury, and Cuy[137] are all open places, situated west of the river not far from the sea. Besides rice these places produce an abundance of sappangwood. And with ships and junks these products can easily be brought from there. The Chinese and Japanese used to take the cargoes always out there in former times on account of the weight. But the license for the transport has to be asked first from the king in Judia. Also tin and lead are to be found out there, but this may not be transported from there and has first to be delivered to the king's factors in Judia and brought into His Majesty's warehouses.

TIN, LEAD, AND A LITTLE PEPPER

Lygoor, Sangora, and Berdelongh[138] are all seaports and are known by the Netherlanders since a long period of navigation. Besides tin and lead, also pretty large quantities of heavy peppers used to be imported every year from these places, so that the United Company for many years had a factory in Sangora (made of lime and stone), but as the trade did not pay sufficiently, this building was abandoned. During the rebellion of Patany against Siam all pepper plants in these places were destroyed. As the country is in peace at present, the plantations are increasing, so that now again a lot of pepper is exported and production will most probably increase.

It has also to be mentioned that from the river of Siam up to near Patany every year many deer are caught. The skins of these deer are brought to Judia by people of various nations, but afterwards they are sent to Japan and are sold there, usually at a great profit.

GARDEN FRUITS

Banckok is a small walled town situated on the river about seven miles from the sea and amidst fertile fields. The rivers Menam and Taatsyn[139] meet at this point. Around the town there are many houses and rich farms. Banckok is strong by nature and can easily be fortified. In case the little town should be taken, fortified, and kept by a prince, the supply of salt and fruits to the

137. Maeklong, Phetchaburi (twice), Ratchaburi (twice), Kui(buri).

138. Nakhon Si Thammarat, Songkhla, Phatthalung

139. Chaophraya and Thajin. The two rivers currently run parallel (north-south). There were channels connecting them around Bangkok which were widened repeatedly from the early eighteenth century onwards and eventually became the Mahachai and Bangkok Noi canals.

town of Judia would be prevented. Also all navigation on sea and passage of the Moors from Tannassary would be cut off.

There is still something more to be said about some other provinces and towns, but as the situation of those is not known to me, I will break off here and will refer the curious investigator to those who have better information about the true situation.

HOW THE COURTS AND THE HIGHEST JUDICATURE ARE COMPOSED

In the whole kingdom there are law courts of mandarins to administer justly criminal and civil cases and the written laws after the old fashion. But in Judia is a court of nine councillors, namely, five oyas, two opras (Opraa Olak,[140] chief secretary of the king, is one of them) and two olanghs. In this assembly Oya Jammerad is, in accordance with the dignity of his position, president for life. This council is the highest court of justice, and all civil and criminal cases are finally decided by it—after defense, appeal, reformation, or first instance. From the decision of this court no appeal can be made; but, at great cost, a revision may be obtained from the king or his council, who generally confirm the sentence and have it executed promptly, so that the decision of the council is seldom changed or reversed.

HOW JUSTICE IS ADMINISTERED IN CIVIL, CRIMINAL, AND DOUBTFUL CASES

Besides the court mentioned, there are still several courts of justice, as that of Oya Berckelangh, who is attorney to the court and judge for all foreigners; further Opraa Mathip Mamontry,[141] who is chief of the court where all civil questions and all ordinary cases are pleaded and decided; Oya Syserputh[142] is permanent chief of the court where all secret and uncertain cases, criminal and civil, are treated and decided by ordeal. The accusations and defenses are brought before the courts of the Berckelangh and Mathip by the plaintiff or defendant or by attorneys, verbally or in writing. Usually the case is pleaded before the commissioners, and the parties and witnesses are examined. The substantial content of the lawsuit is written in a book by the secretary, and the parties or their deputies have to sign this. The book is then sealed and kept by the judge until the next audience. But as there are no regular court days, the parties may not appear before they are summoned by a message of the court by command of the presiding judge. The books are then opened in public, the parties are heard, their accounts and debates are

140. Vickery (1996: 173) thinks this is Okphra Alak (ออกพระอาลักษณ์).
141. Okphra Mahathip Mahamontri (ออกพระมหาทิพมหามนตรี?).
142. Okya Si Sanphet (ออกญาศรีสรรเพ็ชญ์).

noted down and sealed as before. By much delay, laziness, and selfish proceedings of the judges, this ceremony has to be done so often and the progress is so slow that some cases remain undecided for many years to the great disadvantage, yes, ruin of the parties. After many solicitations the cases at last are opened and examined before the entire court. From the sentences of these courts, appeal, reformation, or revision may be obtained in the highest court after humble solicitations. When there are no witnesses or when no sufficient indictments can be obtained, the parties must undergo an ordeal; namely, diving under water, dipping the hands into hot oil, walking barefooted through fire, or eating a lump of rice which has been consecrated with an oath. This must be performed with many ceremonies before judges and people near a temple or public holy place. Also some priests are present, who with many prayers strengthen justice, and by doing so, take away all sorcery and exorcism. After this the parties take off their ordinary clothes and they are dressed with a thin linen cloth which reaches from the head to the soles of the feet, and they are washed by a priest with holy water, in order that the one might not encourage the other with conjurations and they might not abuse the judges. The diving under water is done with two sticks which are put with one end into the ground. Parties have to pull themselves down along these sticks at the same time, and the one who remains down the longest wins the case. The one who remains unburned, or who gets the least wounds in dipping the hands into hot oil, or who two or three times with four or five slow steps can walk unhurt through a glowing fire of coal, also wins the case.

The lump of rice which has been consecrated by an oath is given by a priest to be eaten. He who can get the rice into his stomach without spitting gains his case. The winning party receives a favorable and quick sentence by the judge and returns home happy. But the plaintiff who makes a wrong statement or who denies the facts in connection with criminal cases is punished according to the law for such cases. But in civil cases the false plaintiff is fined in money, and is discharged of office and dignity, thrown into prison, and has to become a slave carrying chains or is condemned to other punishments. But usually the head of the criminal is tied up and put into irons. Three successive days the criminal is conducted in all principal streets of the town to cry out his crime and his sentence in public for all the people. So long as he keeps silent or does not cry loud enough, he is made to do so by blows administered by the jailers.

THAT SINNING AGAINST THE KING AND THE PRIESTS IS PUNISHED SEVERELY

Of all crimes, none are so heavily punished as sinning against the authority of the king, against the priests, or the temples. If anybody should try to usurp any honor due to the king secretly or in public, should act against him or his state, or should show any disrespect, should treat the priests badly, rob their properties, profane churches or idols, he or the suspected would be punished with a cruel death without trial. But in case of other crimes, as injuries, adultery, murder, treachery, theft, arson, etc., the accused, after public proofs or sufficient indictments, is apprehended by Oya Jammerat, thrown into severe imprisonment, accused, sharply questioned by the court of judges, and then allowed to give account. In case, after sufficient information has been given, it is proved that the accused has given a wrong statement, he is forced to confess by cruel torture (namely, by standing on a red-hot plate barefooted, by besmearing the entire body to the feet with hot mud, by winding a rope with knots around the head, etc.). His confession is noted down in a book and presented to the assembled judges, who thereupon in accordance with this, pass sentence and see it carried out. But great crimes are submitted to the king and the condemned is pardoned, kept in prison, or executed in conformity with the sentence, which is in accordance with the rigorous or merciful nature of the king. All criminal cases are usually punished more severely than necessary. Seldom are the prisoners punished with fines or simple deportation, but usually they are banished to deserted places in the interior as slaves carrying chains, their properties are confiscated, hands, feet and tongue cut off, fried in a pan, overpoured with oil and burnt alive, quartered, beheaded, cut into two pieces, and other severe executions. But in case of adultery the accused, in conformity with the laws of the country, must be thrown in front of an elephant in order to be put to death by that terrible monster. From that moment the property of the killed person belongs to the king.

SECOND PART TELLING ABOUT THE ECCLESIASTICAL AFFAIRS, THE RELIGION, AND THE TEMPLES

The inhabitants of Siam are heathens and superstitious servants of idols. So that throughout the whole country there are many large and small temples, built expensively and ingeniously of stone, lime, and wood. The appearance of these temples is often more beautiful than that of churches in Europe, only they are dark as no glass is used. The roofs are covered with red tiles, some with planks and lead. Within the jurisdiction of Judia are the four principal temples of the whole country; namely the king's temple, Wat Syserpudt, the Nappetat,[143] Wat Deun (which temple is devoted to the moon and where the highest school is established),[144] and Thimphiathey.[145] Besides these, there are inside the town and in the neighborhood 400 other beautiful

143. Wat Phra Si Sanphet (วัดพระศรีสรรเพ็ชญ์), Wat Mahathat (วัดมหาธาตุ).
144. Usually identied as Wat Doem (วัดเดิม), but see fn. 67.
145. Wat Chaophraya Thai (วัดเจ้าพระยาไทย), now Wat Yai Chai Mongkhon.

temples, which are adorned with many gilded towers and pyramids. Each temple is filled with innumerable idols made of various minerals, metals, and other materials. Some temples are covered with gold, silver, and copper, so that they look elegant and ingenious and costly. In each temple is a big idol, 4, 6, 8, to 10 fathoms in height, usually sitting on an elevated altar. One of these sitting idols would even reach 20 fathoms or 120 feet when standing upright. Under the seats of the idols in some temples, big treasures of gold and silver have been buried, also many rubies, precious stones, and other jewels have been put away in the highest tops of some towers and pyramids, and these things remain there for always for the service of the gods. Among the Siamese fabulous stories about the immense value of these treasures are told. The people say that with the treasures lying under the idols of Wat Syser-pudt and Nappetat a ruined kingdom could be restored. As the people told me, in the pointed tower Thimphiathey there is a costly ruby, the value of which can hardly be estimated; and in order that nobody may take away the buried riches from the gods, there are many dead guards placed there. This is to be explained in the following manner. If any mandarin—he may be rich or poor—has the intention to make an offering of a human body to the temple or to the gods, he chooses one or more of the most faithful, most able, and most capable men amongst his slaves he treats this slave like his own child and shows him much friendship. By this the slave becomes so attached to his master that he cannot refuse any request. And when the day has come that the treasures will be offered, the master tells this to his slave and asks him to be the guard of the offerings. The slave has been won so strongly by the honor which he has enjoyed that he accepts the proposition voluntarily. He is then cut into two pieces at once, thrown into a pit and the money is placed on his dead body. The spirit of the killed person goes into a terrible monster, who has the power to guard the offerings so that they cannot be stolen by anybody.

WONDERS OF A RUINED TEMPLE IN JUDIA

The Siamese count the ages, or time, by thousand years and at the end of a period of a thousand years, they say that the whole country, with everything that is in it, is going to be reborn and renewed, the nature of the people as well as the customs and laws. In the opinion of the Braman priests no king nor mandarins will remain, but everything will come to an end and must be renewed. Last year[146] was the last of the previous age, and for this reason the king ordered all the Bramans and mandarins before him and requested the opinion of each of them concerning the end of the ages.[147] The Bramans

146. The Chula Sakkarat or "lesser era" completed its thousandth year in 1639.
147. This event is described at length in the chronicles (*RCA*: 221–4).

persisted in what has just been mentioned and confirmed their opinion with such strong reasons that the mandarins all kept silent and did not express their thought. This displeased the king (as he feared that he would have to lose the worldly crown), and he himself made an explanation on the prophecy of a thousand years, saying that he would be the renewer of everything, and that the people, by building and repairing many new temples, had to serve the gods so that everybody might receive rewards for his good deeds from the gods. In such a way the king thought to change everything spiritually. In view of this the king had all the principal temples in the entire country, and even in uninhabited places, repaired. In Judia, in the courtyard of the king's palace, stands a temple of such extraordinary size and height that a similar cannot be found in the whole country.[148] The pillars are more than three fathoms thick. But everything is decayed by age, and as some people say, it has been thrown down by thunder and lightning. This temple is of renowned holiness and it is said that great treasures are buried under this temple. But the priests have an old prophecy that this temple may not be rebuilt unless by the king who is a true heir and comes from the old pure stock. Many of the previous kings have commenced the repair of the temple, but everybody who worked at it died soon. The chiefs, overseers, and work-masters lost their senses, went mad, blind, and so on, so that after the loss of many persons the work had to be stopped. Although the prophecy and what has happened in connection with this temple is well known to the king and he is also convinced that he has usurped the crown unlawfully, his arrogance and pride have carried him so far that last year he had the intention to begin with the repair of the temple. But by the dissuasion of the Braman priests (who said that it was not a lucky time) and of other resolute mandarins, it was prevented. Still much more remains to be told of this temple, but as I could not guarantee the truth of everything, I hope to be excused for stopping here.

THE HOUSES AND LIFE OF THE PRIESTS

The houses and monasteries of the priests are built all round the temples. Usually they are made of wood. The front and back are ingeniously and expensively decorated with panels and relief work; the inside and outside are beautifully gilded and painted; the roof is covered with tiles; the corners are plastered with lime and are provided with nicely cut wooden decoration. In some houses the beams, roof beams, and the tile-laths are entirely gilded or painted. In these monasteries are many priests (who live in peace), who are divided under priors and other ecclesiastical officers (who rule with great

148. In the *Short History* (p. 243) Van Vliet identifies this as Wat Chi Chiang Sai, built by Chairacha in the 1530s inside the palace complex. Between 1536 and 1540, Prasat Thong razed the *wat*, moved the Buddha image, and built another *wat* over it.

discipline and have much power), and they again have to obey the highest regents, namely the four bishops of the principal temples of Judia. The bishop of the Nappetat has the supreme dignity.

The ecclesiastical power of these bishops is astonishingly great, their person is held in great respect and honor, but they have to obey the king in worldly affairs. In Judia there are about 20,000 ecclesiastics. Their number in the whole country cannot be exactly ascertained, but without doubt it is more than four times the number in Judia. All monks, without any exception, are clad in bad and common yellow linen cloth; only a few principal ones have a red cloth over the right shoulder. Their heads are shaved. The most learned become priests, and from these priests the chiefs of the temples are chosen, who are held in high honor by the people. Marriage is forbidden to the ecclesiastical persons under penalty of being burned. Also conversation with women is forbidden, but (as their weakness is well known), they may leave the priesthood, which is done by many out of sensuality. But when tired of marriage, they may put on the priestly robes again, and even persons who do so are kept in great honor. In all monasteries the head priests, priests, clerks, and temple servants read and sing during the evening and the morning; they do not accumulate any treasures, nor are they eager for any other worldly goods or riches. They live partly on what the king and the mandarins bestow on them, also on fruits and profits derived from the grounds which belong to the church. But most they receive from the common people, who furnish them with food and other necessities. From each monastery each morning some priests and clerks are sent out with a wallet. But they do not collect more than is sufficient for one day. They are not allowed to drink wine or spirits, but only ordinary water or coconut water, and they may partake only of common food, and when the sun has passed the zenith they may only chew some betel. From all this we may conclude that the priests have to live in a very modest way. Besides these male priests, there are connected with the principal temples many old women, who also have to shave their heads. They are dressed in white linen, and they are present at all sermons, songs, ceremonies, and other occasions connected with the religion. They are not, however, subject to any extraordinary rules, and they do everything out of religious fervor and free will. Also they have to live on the alms which they receive from the people. There are no young maidens or pregnant women among them.

FOUNDATIONS OF THEIR HEATHEN RELIGION

These heathens have various opinions about their religion, but in general they believe that there is a supreme god (and many other smaller gods) in the heaven who is eternal, who has created everything and by His divine power maintains everything. Also they believe that the world will once perish by

God's anger over human wickedness, but that the soul is immortal and on parting from the human body goes into all sorts of animals, as elephants, horses, cows and other cattle, and poultry, in conformity with their life on earth and what they have deserved from the gods. But after the world has been destroyed, everybody gets alive again and receives rewards or punishments in conformity with their deeds. The welldoers afterwards will live happily with the gods, and the sinners will be tortured terribly by the devils. This is the principal foundation of their religion, the rules for which, they say, were written down more than two thousand years ago and have been confirmed by many holy men. In remembrance of this, the people erected images for these holy men (as if they were small gods) and worship them superstitiously. Besides giving alms to the churches, the idols, the priests, and the poor people, they try to do works of mercy for everything that has received life. They try to please god and the heaven in order to escape from the terrible torments of the devils. The most devout and religious people, on festivals of the temples, let free many birds and fishes, which for this purpose are sold in great number. For it is sin to help only the human beings and not the animals at the end of their completed time, as it is believed that persons after their death are transformed into animals. All evils which man commits by his actions are also in the Siamese religion reckoned as sins. Notwithstanding this, such sins are very often committed. The priests are continually trying to better the people by way of precept in their way of living, preaching, teaching, and warning, but often with little success. For seldom are people persuaded to show penitence. It is more the king's strong hand and tyrannic rule which brings people to repentance and to amend their ways.

THE PRINCIPAL CEREMONIES AND THE DEVOTION

On new moon, full moon, and quarter moon the people very devoutly visit the temples, usually four days a month. Several times in the year (particularly in March and October) there are extraordinary and large festivities, which are celebrated very solemnly by a great many people (yes, even by women and distinguished mandarins who else go out seldom). The principal ceremonies of this heathen religion (which is read by priests from printed [*sic*] books) are doctrines, as pointed out here afore, concerning the praise, the life, and the deeds of famous old kings, songs, morning and evening tides, offerings to the priests, which is done in the temples with many torches, candles, incense, herbs, and flowers. Before the commencement and the end of the sermon, a great number of people walk with folded hands and bent bodies around the temples and pay great respect to the idols, who represent their Opuis [*sic*] the supreme god, the smaller gods, and holy men. By doing so the people believe to keep off the ire of the gods against human wickedness.

In order better to chastise themselves, they refuse to take several kinds of food every year for three successive months. But the present king is so devout that he has added to this another three months of fasting, during which time nobody (on penalty of his life) may catch any cattle or fish, and especially he is not allowed to kill any living being or to drink spirit. They have to subsist simply on the products which God and nature have made grow in the fields. This, of course, is a wrong compassion and a strange superstition, as man has to suffer in order to protect the animals. They also pray for the souls and worship the people who have passed away. These are superstitiously washed, shaven, anointed, prayed over, lamented daily, and preserved with many ceremonies until the best friends and slaves (men and women) have shaved their heads and have prepared everything for the burning ceremony. This ceremony which has to be done in conformity with the position of the deceased, takes much time, so that sometimes the deceased remains 12 to 13 months above the earth in a box. At last the deceased is burned near the temple, with prayers of the priests, theatrical performances, music of many melodious instruments, fireworks, and other demonstrations, in conformity with the importance of the deceased. The ashes are then collected and kept in a little box. After being anointed, this box is then buried near the temple. On these burying places wealthy people build elegant and costly gilded pyramids. From the above we may conclude that great riches are spent and thrown away. There is no other thing in the world for which the Siamese care more than the burying of the body after death. However poor and foolhardy they may have been during their life, they will always try to keep something that they may be burned. But those who get drowned by accident, who get killed, or who die of smallpox may not be burned, but must be thrown in the river or in the wilderness. But sometimes they are secretly burned (without the presence of anybody and far from the temples), which the priests connive at.

ABOUT THE MODERATE RESPECT FOR OTHER RELIGIONS

Although among the clergymen and worldly persons there are opinions prevalent about their religion, they live very quietly and there are no disputes, quarrels, ruptures, or sects. They behave very moderately, even against the Christian and Mahomedan religions, without blaming anybody's opinion, and even less do they try to force anybody's conscience. But the present king has tried to force some Moors (of Mahomedan parents, born in Siam) to embrace the heathen religion. The priests opposed this, saying that one can come into heaven in various religions and that many religions are agreeable to the Supreme Master. However their own religion is the best of all, of which they are firmly convinced by laws and books, and changes will not easily be made. And to prove this, they refer to the attempts with little or no result of the Portuguese, who with several of their priests have tried to introduce the Roman Catholic religion. Also the Mahomedans did not have any success, notwithstanding they as well as the Portuguese were allowed free execution of their religion. The little success of the Portuguese we cannot ascribe to the little ardor of their priests, but principally to the old customs and the obstinacy of the Siamese.

TERRIBLE SACRIFICE IN ORDER TO GET RECONCILED WITH THE DEVIL

As already described, these heathens are very superstitious and devout; however, they serve (against the opinion and the learning of many priests) in public the hellish devil, who is (in the opinion of the priests) the cause of the evil, like the Gods of the good. In case of sickness they have strange feasts with many ceremonies, gambling, drinking, dancing, jumping. Several fruits and animals are offered and when these animals die when the dancing and singing is going on, this is a sign that they have reconciled the devil and that the sick will recover. When sacrificing to the devil, often such terrible abominations and incredible actions are done that it is not proper for a Christian to look at them. For at these feasts sometimes women are engaged, who by old age are bent and stiff and who are incapable of dancing, but who by influence of the devil are able to make such demonstrations and strange jumps as is not in accordance with their weak nature and high age. If young maidens are taken to dance, it is believed that the devil gets more pleasure out of it; yes, even that he has also carnal intercourse with them. With such offerings and sacrifices the poor, strayed people try to reconcile their mighty Master and for this reason we may conclude that they are delivered entirely to the wickedness of the devils, and that the Almighty has been rejected entirely.

THIRD PART TELLING ABOUT THE LIFE OF THE NOBLES AND THE COMMON PEOPLE, GOOD BREEDING AND CONDITION OF THE SIAMESE

In general the Siamese are well proportioned, their stature is pretty long, brown between black and yellow. They are cowardly soldiers, but cruel towards the subdued enemy, or to those who are rejected by the king and who are found guilty by justice. Also they are proud and fancy that no other nation can be compared with them, and that their laws, customs, and learning are better than anywhere else on earth. Their bearing and face are proud and they are decent in conversation. Their character is volatile, cowardly, distrustful, dissembling, deceitful, talkative, and full of lies. Besides this, the men are in general lazy and slow, so that the women, (who are well built and pretty), do most work in the fields. These women also row the boats on the river and besides many other things and (contrary to other nations) do the same work as their slaves and take care of their family with great diligence. On the other hand, many men do nothing else but attending at court, and army services or walk idle in the streets. They love to sit chatting in the public court, in the public houses, or in their houses, and they use their time very badly and idly.

THEIR HOUSES AND HOUSE FURNITURE

The houses in Judia are not built along both sides of the streets; and after the fashion in India they are not placed in proper order. The houses of the mandarins and rich men are made of wood; the wide walls and front are provided with panels and the roofs are covered with red earthen tiles. Nothing on these houses is gilt or painted, for to such only the king and the priests are competent. But the common and poor people live very poorly in reed and bamboo houses. The roofs are covered with cocos leaves or bad tiles, the floor of all houses is usually 4 to 6 feet above the ground, and the houses have no story or garret. Most times there is a front and a back door, but these are far from being good. Their sleeping rooms and resting places are bad, without any decoration and without curtains; the people sleep on stitched matrasses or twisted such. The noble, rich, and poor alike do not need more furniture than is necessary for sleeping, cooking, and eating.

THEIR DAILY FOOD AND WITH WHAT FOOD THEY ENTERTAIN THEIR FRIENDS

They are not excessive with their food, but usually only take ordinary rice, dried as well as fresh and salt fish, and vegetables. As sauce or dessert they take bladsjan[149] (prepared of shrimps, crabs, mussels, and fish mixed with some pepper and salt), fish and pepper sauce, which has a very bad smell, but which they find delicious. They have no knowledge of cakes or other dainties. Their drink is usually ordinary or cocos water; during recent years, however, the habit of drinking arak has increased among all classes, very much by the bad example which the king has given in drinking so much. For towards evening both the common and the high class of people usually drink, filling their stomach. But after dinner they don't use any spirits, as such would be sinning: for rice is one of their sacred things and may not be made heavier by arak. During fasting time they have to be very modest with food and drinks,

149. Van Vliet uses the Malay word, *blachan*, for the fish paste normally called *kapi* in Thai.

but during festivities they eat and drink lavishly. The rich people treat each other with good food, but the cakes of sugar and cakes fried in cocos oil are bad. Also there are all sorts of native fruits and Chinese sweets and distilled water, which is strong but not delicious.

The common people treat each other with their ordinary food, tobacco, betelnut, and fruits; but they also drink so much arak or wine until they are full and drunk.

THEIR DRESS

As the climate of this country is hot, the people dress lightly. Men as well as women cover the lower part of the body with a painted cloth, and they pay much attention to this part of their dress. The men wear also a short shirt with half sleeves. The feet are not shoed nor the head covered. The hair is carefully cut all around the head up above the ears, getting shorter close to the neck, and the lower part is shaven. They have no beards, and when the mandarins go to the palace or to the court, they put on a fine linen cap of pyramidical shape and bind it with a twisted string around the chin, in order that it may not drop when they pay reverence to the king.

The women hang a thin cloth with both ends over the shoulders so that the breasts are covered. As decoration they wear a golden pin in their hair and a few golden rings on the fingers. This is the common dress of the rich and the poor, and no difference in the value of the cloth and the number of rings can be noted. But the powerful and rich people are easily recognized by their suite of servants, of which they are very proud. The nobles and mandarins and also their wives are accompanied by 10 to 40 slaves, male or female (the number is in accordance with their state); the wealthy people go out with fewer servants, while the common men and women take one to three servants along.

MARRIAGES AMONG PEOPLE OF QUALITY AND MATRIMONY

Although the Siamese are luxurious and voluptuous, they keep marriage in high value. The adulterers (men or women) are, in conformity with the written laws, condemned to die and must be killed by elephants. There are various customs with regard to matrimony, for the children of the most influential men when coming of age are often by the will or the consent of the king married to each other. Also widows of deceased or punished mandarins have been given to other mandarins as first or principal wife, or as small wife, and for fear of the king they will not easily leave their new husbands and marry somebody else. But usually marriages are made with the consent of the parents or friends, and among powerful people, people of quality, and the rich it is customary that each of the two parties gives the other goods to a certain value.

The marriages are performed without religious ceremonies, but there are always music and wedding festivities. It is always possible to divorce by partition of goods and children for various reasons, and this can be done without scandal or punishment by the magistrate for unlawful acts. The husband may, besides the woman whom he has married (even when a wife has been given to him by the king) without asking anybody's consent, take as many small wives in his house as he likes, but all these women must be obedient to the principal wife, who is satisfied with having power over the other women and with the idea that her children will be the heirs of their father's goods, for the children of the concubines have to be satisfied with only small portions.

MARRIAGES OF THE COMMON AND LOW PEOPLE

Among the low people there are other customs. The bridegroom comes first to an understanding with the parents and the friends of the bride, and buys her for a certain sum. The daughter is then given away and a small feast is arranged. The marriage can always be dissolved with consent of both parties and with partition of the children. This always is done with sufficient reasons and without scandal. After the death of the parents, each of the children takes the same part of the goods, only the eldest son enjoys some advantages. But the low class of people very seldom leave any means, for if they have some fortune, they use it in order to receive some honorable title from His Majesty. They offer the king all that they possibly can spare in exchange for his favor. With what remains, they entertain the priests and make offerings to the temples and the idols. If after this something still remains, this is spent for the burning ceremonies of their dead bodies. There are many other customs in connection with marriages, but they are not nice to describe and they would be too tedious for the reader, and for this reason I break off here.

INHERITANCE

According to Siamese laws the property of the aristocracy is divided upon death in three parts.

One part goes to the king. Another part goes to the priests and cremation ceremonies. The third part goes to the principal wife and children, and out of this last part a small share is given to the concubines and their children. But this rule is not strictly followed. As a rule it is left to the discretion of the heirs and also depends on the number of concubines and children.

As to this last third part, the concubines and their children having received their shares, the remainder is divided into two equal parts, of which one goes to the mother and the other to the children.

This only holds good when the father has not disposed of his property by will. But owing to the avarice of the king, the old laws have little effect.

When the king hears of the death of any mandarin or other high class person who is rich, the principal wives and the principal persons of the deceased's household are arrested and minutely questioned as to the estate of the deceased, and they are often brought to confess by horrible tortures. Then, deceased's property goes to the king, only a small portion being given to the wives and children.

If any person of the rich or middle class (not being a slave of the king) dies without having made a will and being childless, his heirs are his children [*sic*]. If there are no children, the heirs are the brothers and sisters.

In case there are neither brothers nor sisters, the parents receive half of the estate, the other half going to the husband or wife, whichever survives the other. If it is the husband who is still living, a small portion of the estate is given to the concubines and their children with the consent of the friends, but if the husband dies, first the concubines and the children receive a small share of the joint property [?].

In case there are no heirs as above mentioned, the heirs are the children of brothers and sisters. No relatives of a more distant degree can inherit. In such case everything goes to the king.

It happens very often that married people having no children set apart their personal property and earnings, each of them providing for himself or herself; he or she dying intestate, the heirs get the property which deceased had amassed and earned in his lifetime.

EDUCATION OF THE CHILDREN

The Siamese have several ways of educating their children, and I will only describe briefly how the children of decent people are educated. The sons are kept idly in the houses of their parents until they have reached their fifth or sixth year, and then they are sent to the priests in order to learn to read, to write, and other necessary things. These boys have also to assist the priests during their services, and during the time that they are under the control of the priests they very seldom go to their homes. As soon as they know to write and read fairly well, they take up a profession or any other business. But usually the ablest, in order to learn more (the priests are the teachers for both the secular and the religious learning), are kept in the monasteries and they continue their study. When they have learned enough to fill government positions, they are glad to put off the yellow robes. But many bright boys and those who hope to be promoted remain in the monasteries in order to become chiefs of the temples or of schools or to become priests. The daughters stay continuously in the houses of their parents; they very seldom learn to write and read, but in their youth they are taught good sewing, spinning, etc.

THE BOASTING AND UNFAITHFULNESS OF THE SIAMESE

In general, the Siamese—they may be nobles, influential men, common, or poor people—are boasting among each other as well as against strangers about their good nature, uprightness, love for truth, and faithfulness; and how honored and loved they are by the king, and how feared they are by their equals, and honored and loved by their inferiors. The prominent men also have the peculiarity that they are very quick in offering their services, especially to foreigners, if these have to go for important matters to the king or if they have petitions to send to the king. This friendship lasts as long as some presents are received, but after the petitioners have been kept in uncertainty for a long time, they impudently acknowledge their incapability with many excuses. With pretense of good reason, they say that in consequence of many considerations they are sorry not to be able to fulfill their intention. These people are unfaithful, deceitful, and treacherous; yes, even the king is not upright-minded, and keeps his word only as long as he is able to think with his drunken brains, as has been shown clearly in the case of Oya Poucelouk,[150] who has placed the crown on the king's head and who has helped him to become from an insignificant man king of such a powerful kingdom. The king has often drunk the blood of Oya Poucelouk, and with an oath promised that nobody could do any harm to this oya, and no hair on his head would be hurt. But notwithstanding his oath, he had him thrown into prison for a simulated reason. After many supplications (yes, even of Poucelock's child), His Majesty pardoned him in the morning and promised that he would be taken out of the prison before the evening. But the very same day he ordered the oya to be cut into two pieces. Many more such examples could be told, but as I am sure that the reader would not care to read them, I will not write them down; and in conclusion I will only mention that one cannot rely upon the Siamese nation, and that nobody can be trusted or believed.

150. This man had been *phrakhlang* during 1628–29 and played a key part in Prasat Thong's seizure of the throne. According to Van Vliet (see *Historical Account*, p. 316), he aspired to be *fai na*, which suggests he might have been related to Prasat Thong, perhaps by marriage. But Prasat Thong gave the *fai na* role to his own brother, and rewarded the *phrakhlang* with the prestigious governorship of Phitsanulok. The *fai na* and Okya Phitsanulok became rivals at court. In March 1636, Phitsanulok was executed for having falsely accused the *fai na* of "aiming at the crown" (Dhiravat 1984: 173–4, 185–7).

FOURTH PART CONCERNING THE COMMERCE, FURTHER WHAT TRADE IS DONE IN SIAM AND BY WHAT NATIONS

In several provinces, towns, and small places of the kingdom, trade with various merchandise is transacted, and especially in Judia. There we find cloths from Choromandel and Surratte, made and painted after the fashion in Siam. These goods are in great quantities imported by the Moors, the Gentiles, the Siamese, and other nations at Tannassary. The trade in these goods did not bring much profit to the Company, and as long as the Netherlands comptoir is established in Massulipatan, this cannot be remedied. If this comptoir could be transplanted to a more favorable place, Siam would prove to us to be a splendid market for cloths. Rough and fine porcelain and a few other Chinese goods are every year brought by the Company's ship from Tajouan and with two to three junks from Chiuscheeuw. By this continuous supply and the little demand, the market was to such a degree overstocked with these goods that nobody could make sufficient profit. Further there are in Siam ... mace, light and heavy peppers, sandalwood, Japanese copper, iron, and some small miscellaneous goods, but European manufactures or other goods are not in favor, except red cloth, and small mirrors in small quantity. But the king is a fervent lover of jewels, especially big, nicely watered, pointed diamonds, while tables or diamonds cut in facets, however beautiful they may be, are not in favor and cannot fetch the market value.

THE INLAND TRADE AND WHY IT HAS DECREASED CONSIDERABLY

Also in native products, such as sappan and ager wood, a great trade used to exist, and the king still enjoys great profits from this trade as only the king's factors may sell these products. In former times a trade also existed in black sugar, roeskins and a great quantity of deerskins, but principally in all kinds of provisions, so that yearly more than two thousand loads used to be exported to the neighboring countries. In consequence of the flourishing trade, Judia was frequented by land and by water by many nations from Asia and also by European nations and by heathen, Moorish, and Christian merchants. But during the negligent rule of the present king the trade has suffered much by monopolies and other hindrances. Also the bad crops of some time ago had their influence on trade. But the main cause of the present state of things is the king, who in consequence of his usurped power and ideas has kept his country closed, so that during the last five years not even 2000 loads of grains have been exported to foreign countries. This quantity is very small in comparison with former years. Through the strange actions of the king and many vexations, many foreign merchants left the country while some of them were sent away or expelled, so that at present there are in Siam only a few rich merchants (two or three rich Moors and a few rich Chinese).

WITH WHOM AND WHAT TRADE HIS MAJESTY'S FACTORS DID IN FORMER TIMES

In former years the king's factors used to trade with Pegu, Ava, Jangoma, Langhsiangh, and other neighboring places in order to exchange cloths against jewels, gold, benjamin, gomma malacca, and wax. This trade produced immense profits, so that throughout the whole kingdom there was a flourishing trade. However the trade has decreased considerably by the uncertain friendship of the Prince of Ava and by the fact that the highlanders do not come any more. This state of things was caused through the Siamese king himself, but notwithstanding this, Siam is a country where much trade is still done.

EARNINGS OF THE INHABITANTS

Inside the towns and other centers of population, the people earn their living by trade, court services, navigating with junks, barges, and prauws, fishery and industries, and handicraft by making ingeniously worked golden and silver objects. The inhabitants of the villages and the country do slave services, work their fields, cultivate all sorts of grains, especially rice, and also great quantities of wet indigo.[151] Further they plant all sorts of fruit trees and especially the cocos, siri, and penang trees.[152] They also keep ponies, cows, pigs, goats, geese, ducks, chickens, doves, and many other tame animals. All provisions (during fertile years, because eatables are dependent on the high or low price of the rice) are very cheap, and in consequence with the abundance of products, much can be exported to neighboring countries.

THE MATERIALS OF THE COUNTRY

Besides Siam being very fertile and there being an abundance of victuals, there are also many other materials, such as bricks, tiles, timber, a little iron (coming from the province of Corassema), and other materials in abundance necessary for the building of forts, churches, houses, vessels, junks, barges, and all other sorts of boats. For the working of these labor can be found in Siam. Although the country is closed, as there is a sufficient provision of salt, the inhabitants can sustain themselves with the materials and fruits of their own country. They can thus do very well without the products of other countries, for a sufficient quantity of cotton necessary for the clothing of the people could easily be produced throughout the whole country.

151. Plant used for production of blue dye.
152. Coconut, betel, and areca palm.

THAT SIAM HAS NO GREAT NAVIGATION OF ITSELF

Although Siam is favorably situated for navigation and the kings (including the present one) have been great traders, the Siamese during the past and present ages have never traded to faraway countries. The king and his brother, the prince, every year send a ship with a valuable cargo over Tanassary to Choromandel, also to Canton, and two or three junks to other places in China (for which His Majesty by an old treaty has the privilege from the Chinese kings). Also to Couchinchina, Benjermassingh,[153] Jamby, and Lygoor little junks were sent from time to time, principally for the import of the black pepper of good quality for the use of the Chinese inhabitants. This trade does certainly give off big profits to the king and His Highness; but on the other hand it is a hindrance for the private merchants. Also every year one to three small junks, loaded with sappan, lead, rice, paddy, and other products are sent to Couchinchina by the Chinese in Siam.

From the above may be judged the amount of trade done by the Siamese themselves.

THAT IN FORMER TIMES FOREIGN TRADERS USED TO FREQUENT SIAM FREQUENTLY AND THE REASON WHY THIS HAS GROWN LESS

Siam used to be visited pretty frequently by foreign ships, namely from Jamby, Malacca, Patany, Borneo, Makkasser, and most all southern places. Especially ships from Jamby, Malacca, and Patany frequented Siam for provisions and good commodities. But within a few years the navigation has grown less by the quarrels with the Portuguese, the rebellion of Patany, and by the fact that the king gives licenses very sparsely for export of grains and has vexed the foreign traders covetously. Also the Japanese used to appear yearly with a large supply of money, which they spent in buying deer and roe skins, sappanwood, ager wood and other merchandise. But also this trade was stopped by the hostile action of the king against the Japanese in 1630 and by the proclamation of the emperor of Japan.

The Chinese from Chincheeu and Couchinchina were trading in former days to a greater extent to Siam than at present. They used to bring pretty large cargoes of all kinds of Chinese goods to this country, and returned with big loads of sappanwood, lead, and other merchandise. By the trade of these nations to Siam the income of the king and the welfare of the people increased and trade flourished. But as the present king preferred to force the market by his factors and the prices of the goods which are imported by the Moors, the Chinese, etc., and further lays taxes upon them and does not pay market prices, nobody comes to Siam unless compelled to do so. This is the reason that the king's resources have grown less and that all trade has suffered.

153. Banjarmasin, in south Kalimantan (Borneo).

WITH WHOM THE SIAMESE KING KEEPS CORRESPONDENCE TO PROMOTE HIS TRADES

The Siamese king has during his reign made alliances and has kept up friendship with the kings of Rammaradt Cotopsia,[154] on the coast of Choromandel, and with the Nawab of Bengal. Every year ambassadors are sent out from both sides with letters full of praisings and compliments and also with small presents. This is only done to promote trade, for the Moorish and Gentile merchants often try to secure the assistance of the embassy in order to pay less duties and to become more free in their trade. The Siamese subjects in the above named places try to get the same advantages. So that this friendship is not kept up for political considerations, but only to get more profits. The governors of Paliacata,[155] seeing that their neighbors through the gorgeous embassy had gained the king's favor and enjoyed many profits, have imitated the same comedy and have abased themselves so far that besides a rich present, they offered the king during five successive years the golden and silver flowers. This means that the town Paliacatta is subjected to the Siamese Crown. The principal object was to get a few elephants. It was dishonor for the towns and Moorish castes, and by this action great disrespect was also shown towards the (Dutch) Company's servants. For now the arrogant Siamese believe that they have the supreme power not only over Paliacatta but also over the Netherlands fortress and everything connected with our trade. It means also that the Company's servants reside out there under the shadow of the king. Notwithstanding their humbleness, the ambassadors from Paliacatta were so little respected that they have never been allowed to appear in audience before the king or His Majesty's council, but they have only been received by the Berckelangh in the public court.

THE EXPORTS

On several occasions we have spoken about the fertility and the products of Siam. During good crops two thousand loads of rice and even more can be spared and exported. Also we have mentioned that peas, beans, bacon, arak, butter, sugar, tamarind, dried and salt fish, and many other things are in abundance in Siam. We have already pointed out from which provinces or towns the most common necessities come, but we still have to note down what export cargoes to the fatherland Siam can produce.

2,000 to 3,000 picul lead in small pieces
1,500 to 2,000 picul tin

154. See fn. 116.

155. Pulicat, just north of Madras (Chennai), a Portuguese and then a Dutch trading base, mainly for export of textiles.

30,000 to 40,000 picul sappanwood
50 to 60 picul elephant tusks
60 to 70 picul ager wood
10 to 12 picul gitta gomma.
70 to 80 picul tsieran or black wet wax
3,000 to 4,000 picul black cane sugar
600 to 800 picul Cambodian nuts
120,000 to 130,000 pieces deer skins[156]
35,000 to 40,000 pieces roe skins
200 to 300 buffalo skins
2,000 to 3,000 buffalo horns
200 to 300 rhinoceros horns
1,500 to 20,000 pots of coconut oil
150 to 2,000 pots of cow butter
5,000 to 6,000 pots of wet indigo
400 to 500 pieces teak posts
800 to 1,000 pieces of teak planks
Quantities of bent wood
3,000 to 4,000 pieces of bird skins
1,500 to 20,000 coyang salt

For gold, benjin, gommemalacca, heavy peppers, and much other merchandise no reliable account can be given, because these are products which mostly come from far away places.

THAT SIAM IS FAVORABLY SITUATED FOR SHIPBUILDING

Taking into consideration that Siam has a river and as there is an abundance of timber, moss, cotton, galla galla, etc., small as well as large ships can be launched successfully. The free people build their ships, junks, and other vessels, and also the Company has often ordered boats to be built.

THE MONEY, THE MEASURES, AND THE WEIGHTS

The Siamese money is made of very fine silver, has the proper weight, is cast in round shape, and is minted with the king's seal. The common people are very curious about such seals, so that one has great trouble in paying it out, for out of ten pieces they sometimes do not want to take a single one, not because the silver alloy is not good, but because the seal of the king is not according to the rule. There are three kinds of coins, namely ticals, maas,

156. This enormous quantity, which is confirmed in several other sources from the period, indicates how numerous deer must have been in the Siam of this period, and how relentlessly they were slaughtered.

and foeanghs,[157] which in Netherlands money are worth 30, 7½, and 3¾ stuiver. Usually the Siamese make their accounts in catties of silver; each of which is worth 20 tayls of 6 guilders, or 48 reals of 50 stuiver each. Each tayl is worth 4 ticals, each tical 4 maas or 8 foeangs. Only these coins are used in trade and for payment. But for the use of the common people, small shells are used, which come from Manilla and Borneo. 600 to 700 of these are worth one foeang, and the daily provisions and other little necessaries are paid with them. With 5 to 20 of these shells, or even with less, the people may buy on the market sufficient supplies for one day.

All grains as peas, beans, paddy, and rice are measured by coyang, sat, and sioup.[158] One sioup of rice is almost one catty weight, one sat is equal to 64 sioup, and one coyang is 40 sat. One coyang of Siamese rice weighs about 3000 Dutch pounds. But there are two kinds of coyangs, namely sombrat (which is the king's measurement) and sarra[159] (with which all grains are sold among the common people and to the foreigners). Also the sat and the sioup are much used for measuring rice. One sat sombrat holds 40 sioup, so that 8 coyangs sombrat are equal to 5 coyangs sarra.

All liquids such as black wax, butter, oil, indigo, etc., are also measured by the sioup. One Siamese pot is equal to 45 sioup, and in buying, care must be taken not to be deceived with too small pots. When measuring lands, towers, temples, monasteries, or things which are sold by measure, the fathom, asta, and inch are used. 24 inches is one asta (sok), and 4 asta one fathom (wa).[160] One fathom is equal to about 5½ Rynland feet. All timber, as posts, planks, etc., is measured by canat[161] and Siamese inches. One canat is long 3½ fathoms, thick 12 and broad 14 Siamese inches.

But all rough materials like sappan, tin, and lead are weighed by picol (118 Dutch pounds).

THE MANNER OF WRITING OF THE SIAMESE. THEY HAVE NO FUNDAMENTAL KNOWLEDGE OF ORTHOGRAPHY[162]

The Siamese do not write with characters like the Japanese and the Chinese, but in lines, and form the words with their A. B. C. of 46 letters. Although they are very fond of their way of writing, they have no fundamental

157. Normally expressed in Thai as *baht* (บาท), *salung* (สลึง), *fuang* (เฟื้อง).

158. *Koyan* is a Malay measure of between 27 and (usually) 40 pikul (5320 lbs). A *sat* (สัด) is 20 litres. A choup, tsioup, or sioup is a Portuguese measure of volume.

159. Unidentified.

160. A *sok* (ศอก) is 50 cms and a *wa* (วา) is 2 meters.

161. Probably ขนัด.

162. This passage has a bearing on the question whether Van Vliet read Thai sources, particularly for composing the *Short History*. It is unlikely someone who could read Thai would make his comments about masculine and feminine genders, or would

knowledge of orthography. Only at the end of the words they use the correct characters [according to grammar] but they do not make [in the middle of the word] any difference between vowels and consonants. They have also no knowledge of proper names and do not begin sentences with capital letters. When writing they do not use signs such as apostrophes, full stops, colons, parentheses, or hyphens, but they know how to express the past, the present, and the future time. They also make difference between the masculine and the feminine. God, emperor, king, and everything that is procreating and not generating is masculine; the moon, the earth, the sea, and everything that is producing and not multiplying is feminine. A difference is also made between the singular and the plural.

Many of their characters are not unlike the Roman characters, so that the Siamese writing is elegant to look at.

THE WAY OF WRITING IN ORDINARY CASES

All daily happenings (messages, sessions of the court, etc.) are written as open letters on bad paper with a little round pen of soft baked earth. The signature is wanting, but the letter is confirmed with a mark or with a seal with which the king has honored the writer. Those who have not received any mark from the king use a little cross or stroke where the name ought to be.

THE WAY OF WRITING FOR IMPORTANT CASES

Everything concerning the trade, the courts, and other public places is daily noted down in books of black paper, and every day these books are closed and sealed. But all definite and important affairs, such as letters from the king and mandarins, commands, ordinances, sentences of law, contracts, prescriptions, obligations, and so on, are written on fine Chinese paper with black ink. When the letter consists of more than one sheet of paper, each sheet is signed at the corner, so that it cannot be changed for another or forged.

THE SIAMESE HAVE AN INGENIOUS BUT LONG METHOD OF WRITING

When writing letters in common as well as for important cases, they use a flowery but long-winded style, which does not in the least resemble the Netherlands way of writing. This of course causes much difficulty when

---

note the existence of plurals without describing how they are constructed differently from European languages. The overall impression of the passage is that he may have tried to learn to read Thai but become discouraged by the differences from European languages.

transacting business. Another difficulty is that every time a name is written, the various titles are also added, so that the letters are often filled with arrogant titles.

THE MANNER OF BOOKKEEPING

Although much trade is transacted in this country, and although there are among the king's factors very good merchants, they have a complicated and difficult method for making entries in their books. They have no knowledge of the Italian bookkeeping. Some have books according to the letter of their alphabet A, B, C, and others make all entries together in the form of a memorandum, so that when errors creep in, they have much trouble in looking through their accounts, and the books are corrected with much trouble.

ABOUT THE ARITHMETIC

The Siamese have a fairly good knowledge of geometry and arithmetic, and they also know five rules, but they do not use them in the same way as the Europeans. They calculate by units, tens, hundreds, etc., and multiply and subtract by a cross, but this is done in such a peculiar way that it cannot be very well described. Also the method of dividing is not the same as ours, for instead of crossing the figures, they are rubbed out. The method of addition is almost similar to ours and the units, numbers of ten, etc., are added separately, but the Siamese begin from the left side. Taken as a whole, the method of figuring is very correct, but slow.

HISTORICAL DESCRIPTION OF THE SIAMESE

However much old chronicles and trustworthy historians of the past are witnesses of the times, councillors for the present, and signposts for the future, the Siamese have little knowledge thereof. The position, government, power, religion, manners and customs, and other remarkable things of foreign or outlandish nations are unknown to them; they have also no curiosity to inquire into them. Of antiquities of their country, of the beginning of war, of the conclusion of peace, of the loss of countries and towns, victories or defeats in battles, famous heroes or excellent persons in virtue and knowledge, etc., they have few descriptions. Thus their principal descriptions consist in the laws of the country, the fundaments of their religion, the lives, deeds and praise of some dead kings whose fame was not so much based on royal respect as on service rendered to the gods, temples, and priests living in their country; and these descriptions were mostly committed to the care of the priests, by whom also their ceremonies, punishments, exhortations, consolations, and instructions are formed. Thus amongst the nobility, the rich, or civil population, not many chronicles or historical records are known, with exception of those which are reported verbally or are related in discourses.[163]

CATTLE AND SOME STRANGE STORIES ABOUT THEM

Although I have already described shortly what cattle and what wild and tame animals there are in Siam, I will extend this account in conformity with what I have seen and with information which I know to be reliable.

There are fine and big elephants in great number; some reach a height of 6 to 7 asta (9 to 10½ feet). I will not describe how these elephants are caught by artifice, are tamed, are fed, are housed, and are made to do several services; nor what power, intellect, and other extraordinary qualities these animals may develop, as much has already been told about all this by others. I will only remark, that the king's elephants are held in such high value, that in case they get sick or if they have met with an accident, they have to be guarded and fed by the most prominent mandarins. Sometimes a white elephant is caught in Siam, and such an animal is considered as a *wonder* of nature by the Siamese and the neighboring nations, and is honored as a prince of the elephants.

Usually the Siamese kings have one white elephant in their court, which is there well lodged, ornamented, well treated, and provided with attendants and a suite; the king often pays it a visit and the mandarins honor it; and it is fed from plates of pure gold.

In the commencement of the reign of the present king, a young white elephant was caught, which suddenly died in 1633. His Majesty was so upset by this that all the slaves who had guarded and assisted the animal were executed. Besides this, the king paid reverence to the dead animal, ordered it to be buried near one of the most famous temples, and a small house of a pyramidical shape was built over the grave. But after it had been buried a

163. Here Van Vliet indicates the existence of both oral and written chronicles, although he suggests the written are few. He makes a distinction between royal chronicles and others kept among the nobility, usually in oral form. His brief description of the royal chronicles – kept by the monks and concentrating on religious matters – suggests the *phongsawadan wat*, known today mostly from Lanna examples, rather than the *phongsawadan wang* or court chronicles, into which category fall the Ayutthaya chronicles which are known today. It is worth noting that Van Vliet's *Short History* has much of the flavor of a *phongsawadan wat*. It passes judgment on each king according to his character, achievements, and contributions to religion. This suggests that Ayutthaya used to have such chronicles, which have since been lost. Michael Vickery (1976), in his review of the *Short History*, noted that the chronology and certain sentences are similar to the *Sangitiyavansa*, suggesting they may be based on the same sources.

short time, it was dug up and was burned with a splendor even greater than that which ever has been displayed for the most famous mandarins. All remains which had not been consumed by the fire were collected in a box, buried at the temple, and a beautiful pyramid was erected over it. The Siamese pretend that besides royal dignity there is also something divine in these animals.

The people know how to appreciate the qualities of the white elephant; for not only is it respected for its white color, but also for its natural intelligence and for its sensitiveness for honor and treatment. It becomes sad and melancholy when not properly honored and treated, in which case the black elephants do not respect it like formerly. This seems fabulous, but long experience has taught the Siamese to believe it. In 1635, in the month of May, a miracle happened. It was reported to the king that about 20 miles up the river north of Judia a white elephant was born in the jungle. His Majesty thereupon sent Oya Poucelouck with four of the greatest mandarins to the spot at once in order to ascertain the facts. The men, having reached the indicated place, found the animal of the same appearance as had been reported to the king, and they at once sent word to Judia. His Majesty (thinking that great fortune had been bestowed on him) was very happy, and went accompanied by many mandarins and a brilliant suite to the place in order to see the honored animal and to bring it with much pomp to the town. But as soon as he had left his boat to inspect the elephant, it turned black. The mandarins became thereby deadly frightened, as they expected that the king would say that they had deceived him. But Oya Poucelouck regained his courage and reported what had happened. The king was as much surprised as astonished and had the animal brought to Judia. After it had been out there for one night, it became copper red and it kept this color for its life.

Oya Poucelouck himself has told me everything that has been described above.[164] Although the story seems fabulous, I could not refrain from noting it down because it was related to me by such a trustworthy man.

Last year a young white elephant was caught in the neighborhood of Corassima (near the mountains of Cambodia) and the king was much rejoiced. As the animal was still too young to be sent down, it was nursed there.

Besides the white elephant, the king has also in his court a full grown copper red one, which for its extraordinary size and beauty is honored almost like a prince of the elephants. However it has less value than a white elephant, but it has a beautiful stall assigned to it and is often visited by the king and the mandarins. Also this elephant is fed from golden and silver plates, and when it comes out, it is beautifully ornamented with gold and precious jewels, so that those who have never seen it themselves would hardly believe it. Wonderful stories are also told about the red elephant, but as they are more or less like fables, I deemed it better not to note them down.

164. Here Van Vliet indicates something about his sources.

There are also a great number of rhinoceros in Siam; they are very seldom caught alive, but are caught in snares and shot with a silver or tin musket bullet. Everything from these animals is held to be good medicine. The Siamese even collect their sweat. Further there are tigers, buffaloes, bulls, cows, cats, elk, deer and hinds in abundance, each of which is caught in a different way. They are killed on account of their skin. The Siamese told me that the farmers, who are used to go into the forest every day, are intrepid and do not fear the wildest or most cruel animal, and after avoiding the attack of the elephant or the springing of the tiger, they attack in their turn. There is also a multitude of buffaloes, oxen, cows, goats. The Siamese are also fond of riding. The tame buffaloes, oxen, and cows usually graze near the temples as they are dedicated to the gods. These animals are neither killed nor milked, so that only a small number of milk-producing animals are raised and fed by the farmers. The Chinese and especially the Peguans keep many pigs. Of these pigs, the following fabulous story is known. When the boars are two to three months old, the testicles are cut out, so that nothing is left but the rod, but in spite of this, and taking into consideration the fertility of the country, they are still fit for procreation, and if anybody should inquire after an uncut boar, he would be sneered and laughed at.

The country is also full of all kinds of birds, as eagles, peacocks, geese, ducks, chickens, doves, sparrows, parrots, and others with beautiful feathers of various colors. The skins of these birds are very much in request by the Chinese. Crows are there in such an abundance as to my knowledge in no other place of the world, and these birds are so impudent as to take their food often out of shops and boats, yes, even from one's hands. This the owner allows willingly, as the idea is prevalent in Siam that the soul of man lives in these birds, and for this reason the people only in case of necessity will do them any harm.

THE CROCODILE

I have never heard about strange sea monsters in the sea around Siam, except that in the gulf and on the bar of Siam sometimes big fish, very much like whales, are seen. But in all small waters throughout the whole country, and particularly in the big river Menam, there are many crocodiles. The Siamese firmly believe that in the neighborhood of Judia no crocodiles or beasts of prey may live, but that they are banished by the priests below Bangkok, outside Ban-thiau-phia. When it becomes known that a crocodile has killed and eaten a person, the animal is compelled by incantations to come to the surface to receive its punishment. In case it refuses to do so, other crocodiles are caught in such numbers that the others force the evildoer to appear.

The Siamese catch a crocodile in the following way. They take a dog, which by incantation of the priests has been prepared, bind a chain with a hook, through which a piece of bacon has been put, around the hind legs, hang its body with bells, wind around it some ropes, and pull it forward and backward, until the crocodile seduced by the sound of the bells goes eagerly towards the groaning dog, and devours the bacon. The hook remains in the throat and then the monster is seized, tied, and killed like a worthless person. Many witnesses maintain that the people living along the river feed the crocodiles themselves. A result of this is that the crocodiles become very tame and do not do harm to anybody. When the people bathe in the river, they often play with them. But it has happened often that cattle have been surprised and devoured by them while drinking out of a small stream. In case an unknown person drops into the water close to some crocodiles, he will not be spared.

Many persons pretend that there are crocodiles with four eyes, of which two are in the front of the head and two at the back, and these monsters never go straight for their prey, but pass it by and bring it with the tail, in seizing it, to the mouth.

Although this description about the crocodiles may seem fabulous, all that has been told here is believed to be true by the Siamese.

For this reason I could not keep quiet about this matter, and I beg the willing reader not to take offense at it and to believe as much of what has been told as he may judge in conformity with the truth.

CONCLUSION OF THIS DESCRIPTION

Thus I have tried to give an account, in conformity with the truth and to my best knowledge, of the origin, the situation, and customs in Siam, which I have studied with ardor during my stay in this country. If the reader does not find enough information in this book, I kindly refer him to the better and more detailed descriptions of other writers about these subjects.

THE END.

THE SHORT HISTORY OF THE KINGS OF SIAM 1640

Cort Verhael van't naturel eijnde der volbrachter tijt ende successie der Coningen van Siam, voor sooveel daer bij d'oude historien bekent sijn

The Short History of Occurrences in the Past and the Succession of the Kings as far as is Known from the Old Histories.

BY

JEREMIAS VAN VLIET

TRANSLATED BY

LEONARD ANDAYA

FROM A TRANSCRIPTION BY

MIRIAM J. VERKUIJL-VAN DEN BERG

EDITED AND INTRODUCED BY

DAVID K. WYATT

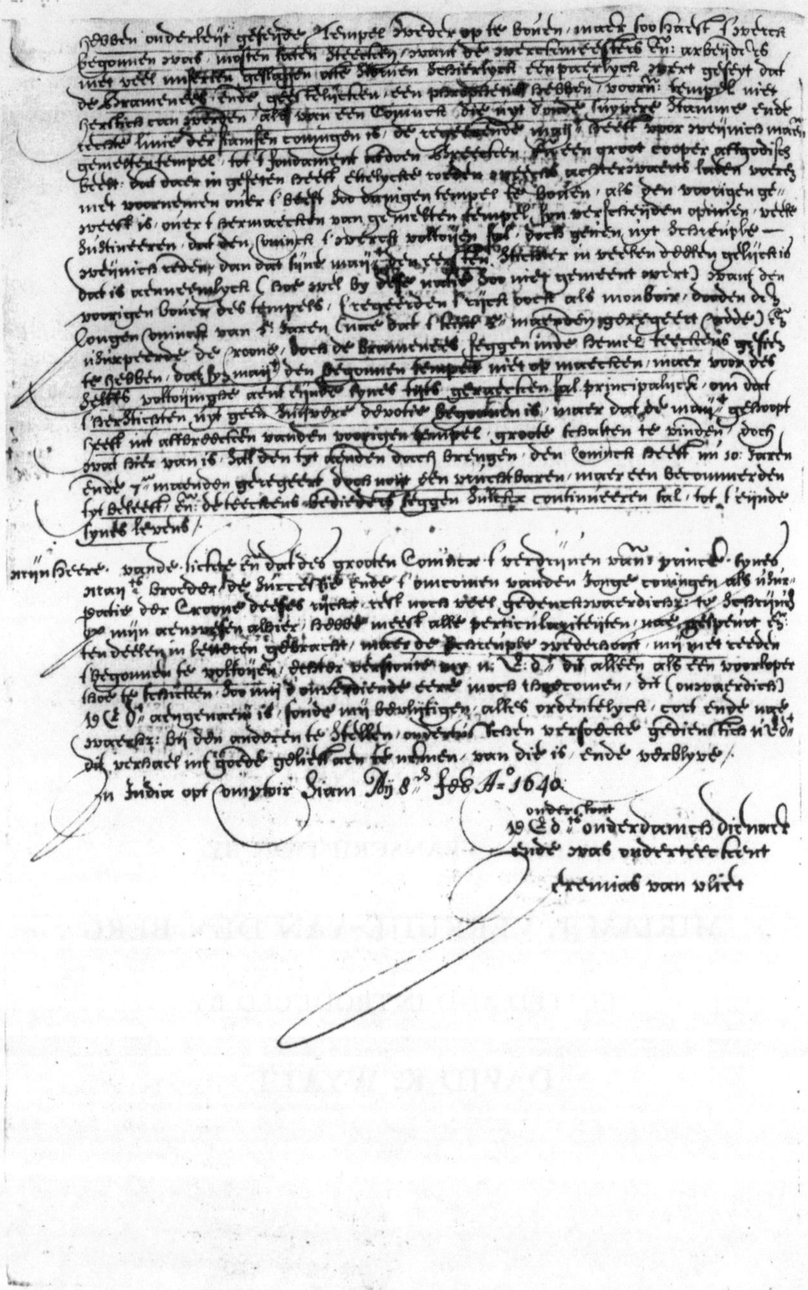

Last page of the manuscript

INTRODUCTION

David K. Wyatt

THE DISCOVERY OF a new account of the history of the Kingdom of Ayutthaya is a notable event of rare occurrence. The last major such finds came with the unearthing of the "Luang Prasoet Chronicle" in 1907, and Kachorn Sukhabanij's discovery of the "British Museum Version" in 1958. These earlier finds each made a distinctive and important contribution to our knowledge of Ayutthaya history: the "Luang Prasoet Chronicle" at last provided a reliable chronology of events, and the "British Museum Version" an almost unique linking of Ayutthaya history with the earlier history of the Menam Chaophraya Basin.

Jeremias van Vliet's "Short History of Occurrences in the Past and the Succession of Kings of Siam as far as is Known from the Old Histories" first came to light in the researches in the 1930's of Seiichi Iwao, Professor of Japanese History at Tokyo University; but its existence did not generally become known until the publication in 1958 of his edition of Van Vliet's better-known "Historiael Verhael." Iwao's brief description of the "Short History," or "Chronicle," generated some enthusiasm among students of Thai history, and with his kind assistance a microfilm copy of the text was obtained by Dr. Kachorn Sukhabanij, of the College of Education at Prasanmit, Bangkok. For lack of a translator the text remained unnoticed for some years until Professor Alexander B. Griswold, with his accustomed enthusiasm and generosity, transmitted it to the present editor in 1970 with the request that he attempt to arrange for its translation. The task consumed almost two years. Miss Miriam J. Verkuijl-van den Berg agreed to undertake the task of transcribing the original manuscript from the archaic script in which it was written into a clean typescript. On its completion, Dr. Leonard Andaya, of the Department of History, University of Malaya, was prevailed upon to translate the whole into readable English, a task he performed splendidly. In preparing it for publication, the editor has compromised between the minimal annotation that would serve merely to explain the most obscure references in the text, and the full-scale annotation that would seek out the most subtle points of the text and relate its evidence fully to all that has ever been written on the Kingdom of Ayutthaya.

The "Van Vliet Chronicle" presented here is unique in several ways. It is, first of all, the earliest connected account of Ayutthaya history yet to have been discovered, antedating the "Luang Prasoet Chronicle" by forty years, for it was compiled by the Dutch merchant Jeremias van Vliet in 1640. Furthermore, it includes important new information concerning early subjects and episodes about which there has long been considerable controversy. This brief introduction is a modest attempt to describe the text, to comment on its possible origins and sources, and to begin to assess its significance.

The text termed here the "Van Vliet Chronicle" is included in bundle number 7 of the Sweers and Van Vliet Collection of the Algemeen Rijksarchief in The Hague, inscribed on both sides of eighteen folio pages (32.5x21 cm.) numbered from 70 to 87. The hand is not Van Vliet's own, but rather that of a clerk or scribe, and seems identical to that in which his well-known "Historical Account," on folios 88 to 137 of the same bundle, is written.[1] The script is that typical of early seventeenth-century Dutch records, and to the uninitiated seems as legible as Cyrillic or Arabic. The transcription included in this volume, done by Miriam Verkuijl-van den Berg, was done from the original in the Algemeen Rijksarchief.

The provenance of the manuscript, its date, and its origins are closely bound up with the life of its author, a figure already well known in the history of Siam, both as an actor in Thai–Dutch relations of the early seventeenth century and as one of the classic chroniclers of his day. Little can or need be added to the account of his life provided by Professor Seiichi Iwao in his modern edition of Van Vliet's "Historical Account."[2]

> Jeremias van Vliet was a scion of Eeuwout Hybrechtz van Vliet and Martige Carnelisd. One of five sons, he was born in 1602 at Schiedam, west of Rotterdam. Three of the sons, Eeuwert, Daniel and Jeremias went to the East Indië.... When he was still young, Jeremias squandered his time at the place of his birth, but once having made up his mind to find his way to the other hemisphere, he entered the East India Company at Rotterdam. Leaving for Batavia on board the ship "'t Wapen van Rotterdam" as an assistant in May 1628, Jeremias arrived in Batavia the following February.
>
> Soon thereafter, still holding the same position, he proceeded to Japan where he worked very diligently for more than three years and a half during the difficult days following the conflict between the Dutch and Japanese in

1. This has been reproduced in facsimile: Jeremias van Vliet, *Historiael Verhael der Sieckte ende Doot van Pra Interra Tsia 22en Coninck in Siam & den Regherende Pra Onghsry*, Toyo Bunko Publications, Series C, No. XIV (Tokyo: Toyo Bunko, 1956). Van Vliet's own signature is reproduced on the reverse of the title page of this volume.

2. Seiichi Iwao (ed.), *Historiael Verhael der Sieckte ende Doot van Pra Interra-Tsia 22en Coninck in Siam, ende den Regherenden Coninck Pra Ongh Srij*, The Toyo Bunko Publications, Series D. No. 5; (Tokyo: The Toyo Bunko, 1958): vii–ix.

Formosa. In January 1633 he left for Batavia. During his residency at Hirado [the Dutch Factory in Japan], he was promoted to the rank of sub-merchant *(onderkoopman)* by the Governor-General Hendrick Brouwer. Soon after returning to Batavia in April 1633, he was assigned to Siam. He arrived in that country for the first time aboard the ship "Delft." In Siam he served under Joost Schouten,[3] Cape-Merchant of the Factory at Ayuthia, but as Schouten frequently went to Batavia, the business of the Factory was almost entirely managed by Van Vliet as though he were head of the Factory. During his residence there, some of the merchants of the Dutch Factory were arrested by the Thai Authorities. These incidents were reported by him in detail to the Governor-General.[4]

As a result of a resolution taken by the Governor-General and Councils on July 23, 1636, he was promoted to the rank of Merchant *(Koopman)*. Believing that he deserved to be Cape-Merchant *(Opperkoopman)*, he went to Batavia in order to present a petition to this effect. But as Antonio van Diemen, the Governor-General, was absent on his inspection journey to Amboina, Van Vliet met Philips Lucasz, Directeur-General, to whom he offered his *Description of the Kingdom of Siam*. This narrative was not published in Leiden until 1692, many years after his death.[5] On August 17, 1638, having been promoted to the rank of Cape-Merchant in place of Joost Schouten, he returned to Siam. During his tenure of office, in addition to the above book, he wrote several other books and reports relating to Siam. First of all, we must mention the *Chronicles of the Ayuthian Dynasty* [the subject of the present book], written on February 8, 1640, which he presented to the Governor-General and Councils of India. It was received with great thanks and praise. Secondly, we should note the *Historical Account of the War of Succession Following the Death of King Pra Interajatsia, 22nd King of the Ayuthian Dynasty*,[6] which was written by him

3. See C. R. Boxer (ed.), *A True Description of the Mighty Kingdoms of Japan and Siam Written originally in Dutch by Francois Caron and Joost Schouten* (London: Argonaut Press, 1935). (Note from Iwao)

4. Jeremias van Vliet, "Een Treur-bly ende Ongeluck, des Oost-Indische Compagnies Dienaers in't jaer 1636, weder-varen, in't Coninckliјcke Hof van Siam, in de Stadt Judia, onder de directie van den E. Jeremias van Vliet," included in, *Ongeluckige Voyagie, van't Schip Batavia, Nae de Oost-Indien* (Amsterdam, 1648): 40–71. (Note from Iwao)

5. Jeremias van Vliet, *Beschryving van het Koningryk Siam, Mitagaders Het verhaal van den oorsprong, onderscheyd, Politijke Regering, d'Ecclesiastique, en costuymelijke Huyshoudinge van d'Edelen en Borgerlijke Lieden: Als mede den loop der Negotie, en andere remarquable saaken des Koningrijks Siam* (Leiden, 1692). See also "Translation of Jeremias van Vliet's Description of the Kingdom of Siam, by L. F. van Ravenswaay," *JSS*, 7, 1, (1910).

6. The work cited in notes 1 and 2, above. This was first published as "Relation historiqve de la maladie et de la mort de Pra-Inter-Va-Tsia-Thiant-Siangh Pheevgk, ou du grand & juste Roy de l'Elefant blanc, & des revolutions rrivées (sic) au Royaume de Siam, jusqu'à l'advénement à la Couronne de Pra Ongly, qui y regne aujourd'huy...,"

> in the Dutch Factory at Ayuthia at the end of that year, and afterwards also presented to the same official. This work was translated into French by Abraham de Wicquefort, historian and author of the *History of the Netherlands*. . . .
>
> In May 1641, Van Vliet went again to Batavia and offered several reports on Thailand, probably including the said *Historical Account*. He returned to Thailand on September 23 of the same year as a Commissioner. This was his last visit to Thailand. In the same year, in order to enable four Dutch children to learn the spoken and written language, and customs of that country, he accompanied them to the Dutch Factory. There they were welcomed by the King. On May 28 of the following year, he went to Batavia and married Catharina Sweers, sister of Salmon Sweers, one of the councils of the East India Government. In a letter to his relatives, Sweers wrote that his brother-in-law was clever and facile with his pen, and that his riches were calculated at more than 30,000 guilders.
>
> Then Van Vliet was appointed to the head of the Factory in Persia, as a successor of Wolbrandt Geleynsz de Jonge. However, due to sickness, he remained in Batavia. On September 6, 1642, instead of going to Persia, he was appointed to the Governorship of Malacca to succeed Johan de Twist. During his stay there, he was promoted to the position of alternate member of the council of the East Indies. But while he was at Batavia, Dirck Snoeck, a Cape-Merchant immediately subordinate to Van Vliet at Malacca, began court proceedings charging that Van Vliet had committed fraud while in office.
>
> On August 18, 1646, both Van Vliet and Snoeck were summoned to Court and sentenced to temporary suspension of their ranks and salary. When Cornelis van Lijn took the post as Governor-General, they were released on October 20, 1646, but Van Vliet never returned to Malacca. On December 11, he was appointed the commander of the return fleet, which reached his native land safely on August 10 of the following year. He lived quietly at his boyhood home as town councillor until his death in February 1663.

A substantial portion of Van Vliet's Asian career was spent in Ayutthaya: allowing for several absences in Batavia, he was closely involved in Siamese

---

in Thomas Herbert, *Relation du Voyage de Perse et des Indes orientales. Traduite de l'Anglois de Thomas Herbert. Avec les revolutions arrivées au Royaume de Siam l'an mil six cens quarante-sept. Traduites du Flamand de Ieremie Van Vliet* (Paris, 1663). The first English translation was by W. H. Mundie: *Historical Account of Siam in the 17th Century* (Bangkok, 1904). This was reproduced, under the title "Van Vliet's Historical Account of Siam in the 17th Century," in *JSS*, 30, 2 (1938): 95–154, and also in *Selected Articles from the Siam Society Journal*, 7 (Bangkok, 1959): 31–90. Both these latter are followed by Francis H. Giles' extremely useful "A Critical Analysis of Van Vliet's Historical Account of Siam in the 17th Century," *JSS*, 30, 2 (1938): 155–240; 30, (1939): 271–380; also *Selected Articles*, 7: 91–176.

affairs from late 1631 until mid-1642. He is almost certain to have learned the Siamese language early in his stay, for he lived in Ayutthaya with a Thai wife who bore him three children.[7] His writings, and his "Chronicle" in particular, suggest that, in addition to speaking the language, he may also have been able to read it, for he refers to written sources and their authors.[8] Van Vliet was more than moderately successful in the service of the Dutch East India Company: his promotions came relatively rapidly, and had he not come under a cloud for his financial dealings in 1646, he might have ended his service in the Indies as a number of the Council that ran the Company's affairs from Batavia. He was very much a man of the world, who had a great deal of contact with the Thai both in his official dealings and during the long intervals between sailing seasons. His business and political responsibilities required of him considerable sensitivity to the politics of the Siamese court and to the intricate commercial relationships that underlay them; and his "Historical Account" in particular shows his considerable mastery of such detail. However, Van Vliet was also a very intelligent man of inquiring mind, curious about all that went on around him. His "Description of the Kingdom of Siam" reflects this wide-ranging intellect, dealing quite early in his stay (1638) with an enormous range of subjects, from the origins of the kingdom, the housing of the capital, geography, administration, civil and criminal law, royal ceremonies, crown finances, military organization, foreign relations, the civil hierarchy of officials, social organization, ecclesiastical affairs and religious beliefs, marriage, inheritance, education, and commerce.[9]

Van Vliet seems to have discovered quite early in his service in Ayutthaya that his natural proclivities could be turned to good account in the service of his ambition. It is noteworthy that Van Vliet gained appointment as Senior Merchant and Director of the Ayutthaya factory after offering to the Batavian government his first major work on Siam, the "Description."[10] His two works of 1640, the "Chronicles" and the "Historical Account," immediately preceded his final promotions. Both were dedicated to Governor-General Antonio van Diemen (1636–45), and both baldly suggest that their author be rewarded.[11] The narrow interpretation of these correspondences between writing and promotion would suggest simply that Van Vliet's motives in writing had less to do with the advancement of knowledge than with his personal fortune; and, indeed, it is noteworthy that Van Vliet apparently ceased writing when he left the Company's service in 1647.

7. Iwao, *Historiael Verhael* (1958): xiv–xv.

8. See, for example, ff 73 and 74^v of the "Chronicle," below pp. 202, 207.

9. See note 5 above.

10. At this time Van Vliet also submitted his diary of the "Picnic Incident" of 1636, which was published eleven years later, and which is reproduced in this book. See the biographical sketch of Van Vliet in the Introduction of this book.

11. Iwao, *Historiael Verhael* (1958), 2, 4; "Chronicle," below, f 70, p. 195.

In the preamble to his "Chronicle," Van Vliet offers the reader four separate motives that impelled him to write that work. Two support the interpretation given above, and two run in quite a different vein. He first suggests that Van Diemen in particular appreciated historical writing, citing his "inclination for things worth remembering"; and then expresses his hope that Van Diemen might "favorably recompense" him. His fourth reason for writing seems amusing only at some distance from "The Protestant Ethic and the Spirit of Capitalism": "in order that the rest of the time would not be squandered in idleness, because idleness is the root of all evil, says Basilius."

It is Van Vliet's third suggested motive that most nearly approaches the intellectual thread which underlies such of Van Vliet's work as has survived to the present day. There he states that he writes "because the number, succession, names and nature of the Siamese kings (to our knowledge) have never been brought to light by our predecessors" – in short, he writes to bring knowledge "to light." This is not a self-indulgent quest for personal understanding and intellectual satisfaction, but rather the responsible man-of-the-world sharing his hard-won understanding with others. Would that his successors were similarly motivated!

This somewhat generous interpretation of Van Vliet's motivation for writing gains some added weight with a consideration of his writings as a whole. Previous scholars, excepting Iwao, dealt with his works one at a time, and none considered his "Chronicle" as part of the corpus. With its addition, we now have three substantial works by Van Vliet, each revealing a separate facet of his mind and interests, the three forming a coherent whole. The "Description," written first (1638), was a general overview of his subject undertaken to acquaint his readers (and himself) with the Kingdom of Siam as he saw it around him in the 1630s. His second, the "Chronicle," written early in 1640, was an effort to explain in succinct terms how the kingdom had come to be what it was, tracing the history of Siam from earliest times down to his present. Van Vliet apparently was not completely satisfied with this account, for on the very last folio he indicates that he had already begun to investigate and write a more extensive account of the political events of his own day.[12] That was to become, at the end of December, 1640, his "Historical Account," which, in effect, elaborates considerably upon the account in the "Chronicle" of the reigns of King Song Tham (1611–28) and his successors, in the course of which it becomes a treatise on contemporary politics.

The material and information necessary to the composition of the "Historical Account" must have been relatively accessible to Van Vliet through his contacts and acquaintances in the Siamese capital; and a good deal of what he reports there he may himself have witnessed or learned from the participants themselves. His sources for the "Chronicle" are, by contrast, much less clear.

12. F° 87^{v}, p. 244.

In the course of the "Chronicle," Van Vliet makes less than a dozen direct references to his sources, most of these in its early pages. All suggest a multiplicity of sources, both oral and written.

To begin with, in discussing the origins of the Siamese kingdom, Van Vliet states that "There is no unanimity with regard to this but several fables (some of which are reasonable and have the appearance of truth)."[13] A reference just a few lines further on indicates that these "fables" were embodied in oral tradition, for Van Vliet reports that "Many of the Siamese, especially the learned monks, *spoke* very attentively and respectably of their first king."[14] The same impression of reliance upon oral tradition for his account of the origins of the kingdom is conveyed by several later references:

> "Although many are able to *speak* thus about the above king... nevertheless this is greatly doubted by others, who *say*. . . "[15]

> "A few people *say*. . . "

> "Others *say* that they have no knowledge of the two former kings Phra Thammikarat Chao, nor Phrommathep: they consider such to be fables or embellished explanations. However, they *say* . . . "[16]

Finally, he suggests that such oral accounts are quite widespread:

> "This story is considered to be the most certain by the largest majority...

> "Many and varied are the opinions which can be brought forward concerning the beginning of the Siamese nation and kingdom."[17]

In addition to indicating the source of his alternative accounts of the origins of Ayutthaya, these remarks also suggest something about Van Vliet's historical method and attitudes. He seems to have spoken to many about Siamese history, including "learned monks" – the only group he specifically mentions by name – and tested his information against his own rational ideas of natural plausability. Of the various accounts of Siamese origins, he notes that "some are too fabulous and their veracity cannot be determined by argument"[18] – presumably meaning "reason." Having determined, however, the veracity of one particular account of the origins of the kingdom, he proceeds "to tell in

13. F° 70, p. 196.
14. F° 70ᵛ, p. 196; italics added.
15. F° 70ᵛ, p. 196; italics added.
16. F° 70ᵛ, p. 197; italics added.
17. F° 71, p. 198.
18. *Ibid.*

a reasonable manner who restored the Siamese kingdom and which kings have ruled since then."[19]

In the course of this early section, Van Vliet inserts a remark that suggests that he worked entirely from oral sources: ". . . the Siamese are not curious enough to investigate events of ancient times and there are no relevant histories which have appeared publicly for posterity . . ."[20] However, two subsequent remarks belie this initial impression. First, in treating the reign of Thao U Thong, King Ramathibodi, he mentions that "The old Siamese histories testify. . . "[21] Later, he is quite specific in mentioning his dependence upon written sources when dealing with the reign of King Borommatrailokanat: "He died a monk. However, the history writers do not mention how long he lived as a monk."[22] Conclusive evidence is provided by the very title Van Vliet gave his work: "Short History of Occurrences of the Past and the Succession of Kings of Siam *as far as is known from the Old Histories*."

Taken together, these few assorted references do not say a great deal about Van Vliet's sources, but they do tell us something when carefully interpreted. First, Van Vliet unquestionably did employ written historical materials: the three references cited in the preceding paragraph so indicate. Should his word be insufficient proof, three examples may be cited which demonstrate close congruency between Van Vliet's "Chronicle" and various extant written sources. (1) There are some interesting parallels between Van Vliet's account of pre-Ayutthayan relations with China and a tale which appears in the Nakhon Si Thammarat chronicles.[23] (2) There are even stronger similarities between a long tale told by Van Vliet of King Ramathibodi II and another told of the same king (or Ramathibodi I) in another Nakhon Si Thammarat chronicle.[24] (3) Finally, it is highly suggestive that Van Vliet's account of the reign of King Chaiyaracha begins in the same manner as the account of the same reign given in the Luang Prasoet and Royal Autograph Version chronicles of Ayutthaya.[25] Although these congruences may, at least in part, simply derive from oral traditions available both to Van Vliet and to later chroniclers, their appearance here in conjunction with explicit references to "Siamese histories" and "history writers" is sufficient to establish the fact of Van Vliet's dependence to some degree upon written sources.

Several additional points concerning Van Vliet's written sources are implicit in the statements quoted above. It is clear that he employed more than one written source, for his several references in this regard are always in the plural.

19. *Ibid.*
20. F° 70ᵛ, p. 197.
21. F° 73, p. 202.
22. F° 74ᵛ, p. 207.
23. See below, f° 71ᵛ, pp. 198–99, and note 14 to the translation.
24. Ff° 75–76ᵛ, pp. 209–12, and note 54 to the translation.
25. Ff° 77ᵛ–78, 215, and especially note 68 to the translation.

In addition, these sources appear to have been manuscripts of some age, if one may take literally his remark about "the *old* Siamese histories...." The reconciliation of these remarks with his first, concerning the fact that "there are no relevant histories which have appeared publicly for posterity," would seem to lie in his choice of words. He may be considered to be arguing that the written sources that he has used are not the product of serious "investigation," but consist only in the recording of stories about former times by private individuals who have not "published" the results of their labors.

It is strange that, for all his use of written sources, Van Vliet never mentions a single date, save for his incomplete reference to the date of the foundation of Ayutthaya: "On the fifth day of the waxing moon of the fourth month (in our reckoning being the month of March) in the Year of the Tiger."[26] He does not lose any great accuracy thereby, for, if all his regnal periods are totalled, from the accession of Ramathibodi (1351) to the time Van Vliet wrote (1640), they come to about 307 years; and the totals come out much closer to the accepted chronology if figured only to the first Burmese capture of Ayutthaya in 1569. The absence of actual dates in Van Vliet's account would seem to suggest that he worked from non-official sources, perhaps popular histories of the sort that have survived in the oral testimony taken by the Burmese on the sack of Ayutthaya in 1767, where dates are very sparingly given.[27]

Taken together, such information and inferences as can be gleaned from the "Chronicle" indicate that Van Vliet definitely did not translate his account from a single text, nor base it primarily upon a single source. He appears to have combined oral and written sources of information, and to have bound them into a chronological framework provided by an informal, non-official history or histories, perhaps some sort of a "king list."

In dealing with his sources, Van Vliet begins with an attitude basically sympathetic to the Siamese. Early in his account, in conjunction with a reference to his sources, he writes, "I would like to say that in my opinion Siam is an old kingdom, more so since this nation is provided with good laws and policies, and the common man is very modest, civil and upright in his daily life."[28] He reports Thai Buddhist religious belief without passing moral or rational judgment upon it.[29] Rarely does he qualify some more fanciful tales with any words of skepticism though he does indicate that he has decided

26. F° 72ᵛ, p. 201.

27. See คำให้การชาวกรุงเก่า ฯลฯ (Bangkok: Khlang Witthaya, 1964); and Prince Vivadhanajaya (tr.), "The Statement of Khun Luang Ha Wat", *JSS*, 28, 2 (1935): 143–172; and 29, 2 (1937): 123–36.

28. F° 71, p. 198.

29. Ff° 70ᵛ–71, pp. 196–97.

to omit the more "incredible" and "fabulous."[30] He gives the impression of having already made up his mind as to the veracity of his sources, from which he has chosen the information he reports. In short, he is "reporting" his considered version of Siamese history.

There are five broad sections to Van Vliet's text. The first consists of his introduction and dedication, the single short paragraph on folio 70 (see below p. 195). The second section, folios 70–72ᵛ (pp. 195–201), sets forth four alternative versions of the origins of the Siamese kingdom, the last of which he considers most worthy of credit. His sources for all four appear to be oral tradition, although there are echoes of at least two of them in some written sources. The third section, folios 72ᵛ–79 (pp. 202–19), covers the early reigns of the Ayutthayan kings, from Ramathibodi I to the first Burmese sack of the capital in 1569. With a few exceptions, each king is treated briefly, almost as if to a set formula. The first sentence on each reign states the name of the king, his order in the succession, and the length of his reign. There follow a few sentences giving the age of the king upon his accession to the throne and the circumstances under which he succeeded. Brief references are made to a few notable events or laws of the monarch's reign, and then Van Vliet adds an assessment of the character of the ruler and his reign. The account of each reign then concludes with the circumstances under which the reign ended, usually with the death of the king, and the age of the king at the time. The most notable interpolation, and break in this set pattern, comes with the reign of King Ramathibodi II (?1491–1529), with the insertion of a lengthy story already noted.

The fourth section of Van Vliet's text, folios 79–84 (pp. 219–33), covers the period of warfare with Burma in the last third of the sixteenth century, during the reigns of kings Mahin, Thammaracha, and Naresuan, up to 1605. Events are recounted here in considerable detail, and require close checking against the Ayutthaya and Burmese chronicles. A preliminary check suggests that both chronology and sequence are awry: and some of the toponyms mentioned have resisted positive identification.

The fifth and final section of the text, folios 84–87ᵛ (pp. 233–44), deals with what, to Van Vliet, was "recent history," the reigns of kings Ekathotsarot (perhaps misnamed?), Songtham, Chettharacha, Athit Surawong, and Prasat Thong, from 1605 to 1640. Most of the material covered here is given in greater detail in Van Vliet's "Historical Account." This section is perhaps the least interesting, or original, of the "Chronicle," not only because Van Vliet himself gave it more extensive treatment elsewhere, but also because so many other Europeans were contemporary recorders of the events he reports here.

30. For example, fº 75, p. 209.

In writing the "Chronicle," Van Vliet seems to have consciously tried to keep his narrative brief and to the point. One can see something of the historian's human impulses coming forth when, on two occasions, he cannot refrain from inserting lengthy digressions: the long story about Ramathibodi II, already cited (folios 75–77, pp. 209–12); and then concerning King Naresuan, when Van Vliet first determines to omit a story, and then changes his mind:

> "Many memorable things are told about this king, but they will not be mentioned here to avoid going on too long. Although brevity has been promised, another thing must be added. One evening…"(f° 83, p. 230)

Both stories certainly deserve the preservation Van Vliet afforded them!

It is much too early to begin to assess the full value of the version of Siamese history that Van Vliet presents in his "Chronicle." A great deal more work remains to be done in comparing his version with that of the several versions of the Royal Chronicles of Ayutthaya and other documents and records that have survived from that early period. A preliminary assessment would conclude that Van Vliet's account must be taken seriously, at least as representing the earliest known report as to what some Siamese (and not just Van Vliet) *thought* the earlier history of Ayutthaya had been. This conclusion is drawn from a variety of considerations. First, the early date of Van Vliet's "Chronicle" alone, forty years prior to the skeletal Luang Prasoet Chronicle, demands that his evidence be carefully weighed, all the more so because he has depended to some degree upon written Siamese sources probably no longer in existence. Secondly, the several points of correspondence between Van Vliet's "Chronicle" and other written sources strengthens the veracity, although not conclusively so, of both. Undoubtedly points of correspondence additional to those already signalled in the notes to the translation will emerge as the text is studied further. Thirdly, the chronology implied in Van Vliet's "Chronicle" should lend additional weight to the opinion that a reconsideration of the Luang Prasoet chronology is now in order. Points of particular stress within the accepted chronology seem at present to fall especially within the reign of Ramathibodi I, where Van Vliet reinforces the Royal Autograph Version's dating of the first Thai attack on Angkor, as against the later date of the Luang Prasoet Chronicle; the reign of King Borommatrailokanat, confusing in most versions of the chronicles; and the period immediately following the Burmese sack of Ayutthaya in 1569. These dates will not be easily established with any certainty, but Van Vliet's "Chronicle" at least should assist in opening, and hopefully settling, the question of their validity. Fourthly, there is at least one point on which Van Vliet provides information available in no other Thai historical source. This occurs quite early in his text in his detailing of the events leading up to the foundation of Ayutthaya. However much one may be inclined to discount the legends he reproduces here, he does both mention and accurately locate the early state of Lankasuka precisely where, on the basis of Chinese evidence, Paul Wheatley suggested it should be more than a decade ago.[31] One may note, in addition, that Van Vliet, uniquely among sources dealing with the history of Ayutthaya, routinely records the ages of rulers upon their accession to the throne. It is hard to believe that he simply invented these figures. Similarly, his rendering of the names of Thai kings, in particular, is so consistently close to the versions of their names that have come down to us in the chronicles that we may be confident that we have here a source whose author took his own sources seriously and reproduced their evidence faithfully.

It is difficult to explain why a source of such importance as Van Vliet's "Chronicle" was ignored for so many years, especially when the two other segments of Van Vliet's *magnum opus*, the "Description" and the "Historical Account," have been so well-known for so long. The explanation may derive in part from the simple fact that both the "Description" and the "Historical Account" were published in the seventeenth century, though in both cases after the death of their author: the "Historical Account" in 1663 and the "Description" in 1692. Subsequent scholarship picked these up more readily than the original manuscripts, perhaps due to the inclusion of both in Cordier's *Bibliotheca Indosinica* (1912). One notes that the original version of the "Historical Account," as opposed to the abridged French translation, was properly edited only in 1956–58 by Seiichi Iwao; and that, for all Giles' work on that text in the 1930s, he could not at that time locate the original.

It was Iwao who indirectly led to the discovery and, ultimately, the publication of the "Chronicle," though his initial reference to it may have deterred some. In referring to it among "Van Vliet's Other Works Relating to Thailand," he simply notes that "These *Chronicles* contain 26 pages in folio and are found in the same bundles as his *Historical Account*; they are numbered from 69 to 87. They were written by another hand and some pages are now damaged in their entirety."[32] Unfortunately, those most vitally interested in consulting Van Vliet's "Chronicle" have lacked facility in reading late-medieval Dutch, or even modern Dutch, and their appearance has been long delayed.

The pages that follow contain Leonard Andaya's English translation, based on Miriam J. Verkuijl-van den Berg's transcription of the original Dutch text, with the editor's rudimentary annotations. The translation bears marginal annotations of the pagination of the original folios.

The reader now has before him what may be considered the earliest known comprehensive version of Siamese history to have been based on indigenous

31. See below, f° 71v, pp. 198–99, and note 10 to the translation.

32. Iwao, *Historiael Verhael* (1958): xiv.

sources. As the "Chronicle" in coming years begins to be assessed in the context of Siamese historiography, we would do well to bear in mind the conditions under which Van Vliet labored in the 1630s on his three accounts of old Siam, probably ill-taught if at all even in his own history, and without any printed European sources to direct his researches. With the publication of his "Chronicle," he surely must be given a place among the pioneers of the modern study of Thai history.

1975

THE SHORT HISTORY OF OCCURRENCES IN THE PAST AND THE SUCCESSION OF THE KINGS OF SIAM AS FAR AS IS KNOWN FROM THE OLD HISTORIES* 70

To be presented to the noble, generous, wise, sober lord, the noble Lord Antonio van Diemen, Governor-General of the state of the United Netherlands in India Orientalis.

Sir, the opportunity demands that I put on paper (and as far as possible with the wisdom that God Almighty has seen worthy to bestow on me) in a reasonable fashion what has been mentioned above. There are various reasons for this: Firstly, in order for me to satisfy Your Lordship's inclination for things worth remembering; another, in order that Your Lordship would be pleased not only with the ordinary services but also with the special obligations of the Company's subjects and favorably recompense them, [that] in this way they will be encouraged always to try harder to fulfill their duties in an honest fashion; thirdly, because the number, succession, names, and nature of the Siamese kings (to our knowledge) have never been brought to light by our predecessors, nor been shown to Your Lordship in any extensive fashion; and finally, in order that the rest of the time would not be squandered in idleness, because idleness is the root of all evil, says Basilius. It is therefore fitting to do our normal duties quietly, and, for the present as well as the future, to demonstrate our humble obeisance in serving you in every way, not only for the good but also for the profit of the Company. I am thus (of the intention, as mentioned) moved and encouraged to reverently present this treatise to you with this request, that Your Lordship kindly focus not on the unembellished style but on the truthful history. It is hoped also that everything will be pleasing to you as we trust Your Lordship's usual mercy, on which foundation the following was dedicated and presented.

As an introduction to this work, I will in passing (only when necessary) touch upon those matters which have been investigated and researched with

* In this English version of Van Vliet's text, all proper names have been rendered in a simplified form of the General System of transcription of the Royal Academy. In few cases is there any doubt as to the appropriate form such names should take; but where there is any doubt, the question is taken up in the footnotes, where Thai forms of the name are also provided.

great curiosity in order to discover the origin of the Siamese nation, who brought the country into being, who established the kingdom, which king was first to rule, and who the successors were from that time to the present day. There is no unanimity with regard to this but several fables (some of which are reasonable and have the appearance of truth). Therefore, the closest that one could establish and which accorded most with reason is that about 2000 years ago a son of the Emperor of China was exiled because he tried to kill his father and seize the kingdom. He and his followers after many wanderings finally landed in the Bay of Siam at the Hook of Kui[1] and there
70v established themselves. After he had the land spied out by several of his men, he discovered that it was fruitful but sparsely populated. He therefore resolved to develop the Siamese land in order to extend his power properly without danger.

Many of the Siamese, especially the learned monks, spoke very attentively and respectably of their first king. Yes, they consider him to be a wonder of the world and say that he was not only the founder of a great kingdom such as this, but also the first lawgiver and founder of their religion. This king wrote down the law of his land and the principles of religion with his own hand. They say that he was an upright, mild-tempered, liberal, wise, prudent, and victorious prince, who brought many lands and cities under his authority, who lived more than 200 years, and was emperor over 101 kings. When he died his successor inherited a mighty monarchy with good laws and religious institutions (although heathen). This king was named Phra Thammikarat Chao.[2]

Although many are able to speak thus about the above king Phra Thammikarat and probably with good reason, nevertheless this is greatly doubted by others, who say that a Brahman named Phrommathep[3] was the founder of the Siamese kingdom, the first king, lawgiver, and founder of their religion. But the abovementioned Phrommathep abandoned the kingdom and the crown because of the wickedness and stubbornness of men and fled to the mountains where he died. After his death the kingdom began to decline, indeed, so much so that it once again became a wilderness.

1. In Prachuap Khirikhan province. Its original site, dating from the early Ayutthaya period, is about 600 m. from the modern *amphoe* center of Kuiburi.

2. The "Just King." Cf. "พงศาวดารเหนือ," in พระราชพงศาวดารกรุงศรีอยุธยา (Khurusapha edition; Bangkok, 1961): II, 371; and C. Notton, *Légendes sur le Siam et le Cambodge* (Bangkok, 1939): 110.

3. I.e., Brahmadeva (พรหมเทพ). Might some connection be implied with King Phrom (พรหม), founder of the Chiangsaen line into which most chronicles place the founder of Ayutthaya? See ตำนานสิงหนวติกุมาร in ประชุมพงศาวดาร pt. 61 (2nd ed.; Bangkok, 1972): 75 ff.; and Prince Damrong Rajanubhab, "Siamese History prior to the Founding of Ayutthaya," *JSS*, 13, 2 (1919); reprinted in *Selected Articles from the Siam Society Journal*, 3 (Bangkok, 1959): 69–74.

A few people say that Phrommathep learned that the Chinese Phra Thammikarat Chao (who was mentioned above) had entered the country with a large number of people. He fled out of fear of being besieged and conquered, and so Phra Thammikarat Chao took over the kingdom. But because the Siamese are not curious enough to investigate events of ancient times and also because there are no relevant histories which have appeared publicly for posterity, this point cannot be disputed and [it] is even more difficult to determine its veracity.

Others say that they have no knowledge of the two former kings Phra Thammikarat Chao, nor Phrommathep: they consider such to be fables or embellished explanations. However, they say that Phra Phuttha Chao[4] was the first founder of the Siamese kingdom, king, lawgiver, and founder of religion; that he was the most merciful, wise, rich, liberal, fortunate, and most invincible. Till today in Siam one hears more of the godlike qualities he possessed than of the human ones. He is said to have been reborn 500 times, each time entering the world in the country of Siam in another form; first, in
all states of the human condition, from the most dignified to the most 71
miserable depths, and once again from the most miserable state to the most supreme power and honor. After that he appeared as all kinds of forms of cattle, birds, and fish. He also appeared once as a white, then as a red, and the third time as a round-tailed elephant.

But this Phra Phuttha Chao died, was brought into heaven among the gods because of his righteousness, and did not again return to Siam. After Phra Phuttha Chao went away, the kingdom went 713 years[5] without a king and the kingdom decayed and nearly reverted to wilderness.

This story is considered to be the most certain by the largest majority, and it still applies to this day because the Siamese kings are not addressed with anything less than with the name of Phra Phuttha Chao. And in their religion they are true Pythagorians, because they do not believe that when they die their souls go to God, who had given it to them, nor that the body returns to the earth from whence it came. Instead, they believe that the living spirit moves from one body to another in men as well as in beasts, and that they finally return to the world without knowing how long they have been away, what state they were in previously, nor how often they must die, move away, and return again.

4. I.e., the Buddha. Note, however, that this name frequently was used to refer to Thai kings: see *RA*, 232.

5. As Ayutthaya was founded in the year 712 of the Lesser Era *(Chunlasakkarat)*, implied here is an old Siamese belief that the Lesser Era begins with the Nirvana of the Buddha. However, the Buddhist Era was employed in inscriptions both at the time Van Vliet wrote and as early as the fourteenth century.

Many and varied are the opinions which can be brought forward concerning the beginning of the Siamese nation and kingdom. However, I consider that unnecessary, since some are too fabulous and their veracity cannot be determined by argument (as mentioned). Finally, I would like to say that in my opinion Siam is an old kingdom, more so since this nation is provided with good laws and policies, and the common man is very modest, civil, and upright in his daily life.

In order to deal with this material, it will be necessary to digress and to tell in a reasonable manner who restored the Siamese kingdom and which kings have ruled since then.

More than 300 years ago there was a king of several provinces in China (whose names, however, are unknown to the Siamese) who had a son named Chao Ui.[6] This son was so lustful that he violated the wives of the most important mandarins,[7] and those he could not coerce were secretly killed. The mandarins complained to the king of his son's unbridled way of life and threatened to depose and kill His Majesty if the latter refused to kill his son. The king agreed to this and intended to take his son's life, but the queen (mother of the accused) prevented it by remonstrating with the king and saying that it would be best to send him out of the country. His Majesty consented and informed the mandarins, who agreed to this and were satisfied.

71v This decision was announced to the son, but it did not astonish him greatly. He said, "Have the mandarins considered my behavior so bad that they would like to kill me or kill My Lord Father the king? Has His Majesty decided to send me away? If so, I will accept this decision."

The king had many junks outfitted and supplied them overabundantly with food, ammunition, and everything which was necessary for a long voyage. He presented his son with 200,000 persons and bestowed upon him great wishes, and with these he left China. He intended to settle wherever the gods and winds should take him. The elder son[8] of the king accompanied his brother because he loved him.

Quite by chance the aforementioned Chao Ui appeared with his fleet at Pattani, where he landed with his people. But since he found it to be a populated city, he did not want to stay there, but travelled several miles inland to Ulu Pattani.[9] He established a city there and called it Langkasuka.[10] After

6. VV: t'Jaeu-ou-e; i.e., probably something like เจ้าอุย.

7. The original text speaks of "mandarins" whenever referring to the officials of the kingdom (Note by Andaya).

8. This individual does not figure further in the story.

9. I.e., upcountry or interior Pattani, up the Pattani River.

10. This is a startling piece of information, given a century's controversy over the location of the kingdom known to the Chinese as Lang-ya-hsiu from the seventh century onwards. After careful study of the problem of its identification and location,

he had supplied the newly-built city with inhabitants, occupied it with soldiers, and given it laws and ordinances, he went overland to what is now called Ligor.[11] Since it was only woods and wilderness,[12] he took this opportunity to build a city and called it Ligor. He also occupied Ligor, provided it with everything and went forth to Kui (and although he found it to be a wooded place, he nevertheless built a city and remained there).

Meanwhile, there appeared at Kui two Chinese junks from the Chinese Emperor. The Chinese *nakodas*[13] and merchants were pleased to obtain sappanwood, and this came to the notice of Chao Ui. He liberally presented them with as much sappanwood as their two junks could carry. They thus departed for China greatly pleased. Upon arrival they made a report to the Emperor concerning what had befallen them, with an account of the gift of sappanwood. The Chinese Emperor was so delighted with the sappanwood that as a reward he gave his daughter, named *nang* Pacham Thong, to Chao Ui in marriage.[14] He then sent her off with great ceremony. In addition, he rewarded him with a royal title Thao U Thong.[15]

After the aforementioned Chao Ui, now called Thao U Thong, lived at Kui for a short time with the Chinese Emperor's daughter, he decided to better populate the country of Siam. After having received information about the opportunities to do so, he left Kui and built other cities. The first was Phetchaburi.[16]

While digging, the laborers found a copper image about ten fathoms high lying under the earth, which was a great surprise to Thao U Thong. But after an explanation had been given to him concerning the image and foundations of the Siamese religion, he left the Chinese religion and accepted that of the Siamese. 72

After that Thao U Thong built the cities Chongh, Cout-Thiam,[17] and Bangkok. Meanwhile, he received information about the island where the

---

Paul Wheatley in 1956 proposed to locate it in the vicinity of modern Pattani. See his "Langkasuka," *T'oung Pao*, 44 (1956): 387–412; and the same author's *The Golden Khersonese* (Kuala Lumpur, 1961): 252–67.

11. Nakhon Si Thammarat.

12. This hardly jibes with Nakhon's long early history: see D.K. Wyatt, *The Crystal Sands. The Chronicles of Nagara Śrī Dharrmarāja* (Ithaca, N.Y., 1975).

13. "Shipmasters."

14. Compare a similar tale in "ตำนานเมืองนครศรีธรรมราช" in รวมเรื่องเมืองนครศรีธรรมราช (Bangkok, 1962): 52–55; translated in Wyatt, *Crystal Sands*,102–105.

15. The title by which the founder of Ayutthaya was known: see also *ibid.*, 51–52, 84–85; "พงศาวดารเหนือ," 388 ff.; and Notton, *Légendes sur le Siam*, 90–94, 97–104.

16. Phetchaburi was in existence by the reign of Jayavarman VII of Angkor (A.D. 1181–c.1218); see the Prah Khan inscription, in *BEFEO*, XLI, fasc. 2 (1942): 296, line CXVII.

17. Both unidentified.

city of Ayutthaya is built, and appeared surprised that such a beautiful site was not inhabited nor built upon. But he met a hermit (called *rishi* by the Siamese) who informed him that previously there was a city there called Ayutthaya. But how it declined he had not knowledge and added that no other city could be rebuilt there. The reason was that at a place Wo Talenkang,[18] now in the middle of the city, there was a pool in which there was a voracious dragon, called Nāgarāja[19] by the Siamese, who on being disturbed blew poisonous saliva from his mouth. This brought about such an epidemic that everybody around there died of the stench. Thao U Thong asked the *rishi* whether the dragon could not be killed and the marsh filled in. The *rishi* answered that this would not be a remedy, but that a *rishi* (like him in every respect) should be thrown in. Thus Thao U Thong had the whole country searched to find such a person.

The *rishi* further declared that Thao U Thong, after killing the dragon and filling in the marsh, should do three things if he wanted to live in that place in health: shoot an arrow and catch it again in his quiver; smear his body daily with cow dung; and blow on a horn every day, just as the Brahman priests do when they go to their temples or places of devotion.

Thao U Thong said that he knew how to fulfill these conditions and went with a *perahu*[20] to the middle of the river, shot an arrow upstream, and as the arrow came down the quiver went to the water and received the arrow. In place of cow dung he covered his body with rice meal every day mixed with a little *seruijs*,[21] saying that the rice could not grow unless the land had been fertilized. By this he meant that the cow dung is also part of the rice. With regard to the blowing of the horn, he had *sirih* leaves rolled close together and ate it as *pinang*,[22] which had some similarities with the blowing of horns.

The *rishi* replied, "Since thou hast made the arrow return to thee, thy people shall be united with each other and thy kingdom freed from internal wars.

72v "Secondly, because thou so cunningly applied the cow dung, thou and thy people shall suffer little from smallpox.

18. Unidentified. Note, however, the reference in *RA*, 77, in connection with a fire in Ayutthaya, to a Talaengkaeng (ตะแลงแกง).

19. นาคราช.

20. A *perahu* (proa) is a small boat usually propelled by oars. This is the Malay word often used in seventeenth and eighteenth-century Dutch East India Company reports to refer to small native boats. (Note by Andaya)

21. *Serious* or *cerius*, an unguent or powder with styptic powers, originally made from lead oxide, and later from the non-poisonous zinc oxide. (Note by Andaya)

22. *Pinang* is the Malay word for betel nut, which is prepared with lime and *sirih* leaves. (Note by Andaya) Is there a double ambiguity here; a play on words with *PI-nang*, as well as a visual pun?

"Thirdly and finally, because thou has rolled the *sirih* which had a likeness to a horn, the gods shall have great love for you and bring you great fortune."

In the meantime, the messengers sent out returned to Thao U Thong with the tidings that a *rishi* like that which they were ordered to look for could not be found. Thao U Thong kept this message secret, went to speak with the *rishi* at the mouth of the marsh where the dragon was, and without warning threw him in and filled in the marsh. Since then the dragon has never again appeared, and the land has been free from epidemics.

Then Thao U Thong began to re-establish the city on the fifth day of the waxing fourth moon (in our reckoning being the month of March) in the Year of the Tiger and called it Ayutthaya.[23] He also built three temples which are still considered to be the most important in the whole kingdom: the Nopphathat,[24] the most holy; Ratchaburana,[25] the same size and shape as the Nopphathat but not visited by the kings because of a prophecy that the first king who goes in there will die shortly thereafter; and Wat Doem,[26] still the foremost [monastic?] school. After Thao U Thong had built the aforementioned city, he had the entire population called together and declared himself king. He also ordered them, on pain of extreme punishment, to show him royal honor, and took the following titles to enhance his glory: Somdet Phra Racha Ramathibodi Sisurintha Borommachakkaphat Thianracha Ramesuan Thammikarat (thi) Chao Si Aiyaborommathip Siphuwanatthibet Borommabophit Phra Thao U Thong.[27] These titles are so full of pride and vanity that after that time they were never assumed by any other Siamese kings.[28]

23. The date universally given in the chronicles and astrologers' notebooks (ปูม) is Friday, the sixth day of the waxing moon of the fifth month of the Year of the Tiger, C.S. 712, which is equivalent to March 4, A.D. 1351. The date given here would be equivalent to February 2, 1351.

24. VV: Nappetadt and (f° 86^{v}) Nappetat. The *RA* (68) and other chronicles (s.v. C.S. 715) mention King Ramathibodi establishing a *vihāra* and พระมหาธาตุ as a monastery and naming it Wat Phutthaisawan. However, since a reference below (f° 86^{v}, p. 242) to Wat Nopphathat can be checked against the *RA* and other chronicles' references to Wat Mahathat, these have to be identical. Note, however, that Wat Mahathat is thought to have been built by King Ramesuan or King Borommaracha I: see ราชวังและวัดโบราณในจังหวัดพระนครศรีอยุธยา (Bangkok, 1968): 31–35.

25. Wat Ratchaburana (วัดราชบูรณะ) was, however, constructed only in or shortly after 1424: see *ibid*, 37–38.

26. Wat Doem (วัดเดิม), i.e., Wat Ayotthaya (วัดอโยธยา): see *ibid.*, 89–98, which argues for its construction prior to 1350.

27. Or, in Thai script, สมเด็จพระราชารามาธิบดีศรีสุรินทรบรมจักรพรรดิ์เทียรราชาราเมศวรธรรมิกราชธิเจ้าศรีไอยบรมทิพศรีภูวนาธิเบศร์บรมพิตร์ พระท้าวอู่ทอง.

28. Hardly true: virtually all the elements in this particular royal title appear in the titles of various kings of Ayutthaya and even later. See, for example, Rama I's title in

THAO U THONG, THE FIRST KING OF SIAM AFTER PHRA PHUTTHA CHAO ABANDONED THE THRONE, REIGNED NINETEEN YEARS.[29]

After Thao U Thong established his seat in Ayutthaya, he declared himself king and founded the cities Nakhon Chaisi, Phitsanulok, Sukhothai, and Kamphaengphet, which are still the most famous provinces in the Siamese kingdom.[30] The Chinese Emperor, having heard of the settlement and the whereabouts of his son-in-law Thao U Thong, was so pleased that he sent his ambassadors to Siam with letters engraved in gold.[31] Such a firm alliance was made with Thao U Thong that it is still maintained by the Chinese and Siamese kings to this day. These are the reasons why the kings of Siam are singularly privileged in being allowed to send their junks to Canton and
73 ambassadors to the Chinese kings. Thao U Thong had resided in Ayutthaya for about ten years, when the 73 astrologers and soothsayers announced that they had seen in the movement of the stars that an imminent calamity would befall the city. It seemed that it would be a great catastrophe in which all the people would die. Consequently, Thao U Thong commanded that everyone bury his gold, silver, etc., and flee with him overland to Cambodia. They found a small little city in the forest, but since it did not please His Majesty, he built another city of stones created by nature, which he called Nakhon Luang.[32] The old Siamese histories testify that the abovementioned city was so exquisite and ingenious that no human being could possibly have built it. Therefore, they say that angels from heaven came to help in building this magnificent city in Cambodia. Many Siamese also say that Thao U Thong himself built it.

Thao U Thong remained nine years in Cambodia with his followers, but since his city was far from the sea and no junks from China or other place appeared there,[33] and since the astrologers told him that the imminent disaster

---

the foreword to the Prince Ratburi edition of the Three Seals Code, กฎหมาย เล่ม 1 (Bangkok, 1970): 1–2; or that of King Borommaracha II in *ibid.*, 465; and Ekathotsarot's in *ibid.*, 536.

29. King Ramathibodi I, whose reign universally is attributed to the years C.S. 712–731 (A.D. 1350/51–1369/70), a span of nineteen years.

30. It is more than unlikely that any of these cities was founded by the first Ayutthaya ruler: all except Nakhon Chaisi are mentioned in the 1292 inscription of King Ramkhamhaeng of Sukhothai.

31. On Ayutthaya's early relations with China, see T. Grimm, "Thailand in the Light of Official Chinese Historiography: A Chapter in the 'History of the Ming Dynasty,'" *JSS*, 49, 1 (July 1961): 1–20.

32. The term by which Angkor usually was referred to; see D. K. Wyatt, "The Thai 'Kata Mandiarapla' and Malacca," *JSS*, 55, 2 (July 1967): 285.

33. This "Cambodian" episode is tantalizing, especially in the light of O. W.

had occurred in the city of Ayutthaya, he left his son there in Nakhon Luang to rule the country while he himself returned to the city of Ayutthaya. There he died at the age of fifty-seven, after having reigned for nineteen years. Ever since then the Siamese kings have claimed to be the highest governing power and authority over Cambodia. This king was wise, eloquent, careful, courageous, active, liberal, solicitous towards his soldiers and people, and devoutly religious. Although he had many titles he was not inflated but humble, familiar with his people, and merciful. He was not rash or inconsiderate in his punishment, but was a strict upholder of justice. Because he possessed so many great virtues, he was loved by everyone.

PHRA RAMESUAN, SECOND KING OF SIAM, REIGNED THREE YEARS AND WAS DEPOSED.[34]

The son of the dead king succeeded his father in the kingdom peacefully when he was thirty years old. He was called Phra Ramesuan. He was of little wisdom, was bad-natured, cruel and bloodthirsty, choleric, avaricious, greedy, gluttonous, and lustful. He did not hesitate to dishonor anyone's wives and have them brought to him by force. He was careless in everything concerning the welfare of the kingdom and the peace of the community. No warrior by nature, he did not love his soldiers at all, things spiritual and religious very little, and the poor even less. That is the reason that after he had reigned for three years he was deposed by his father's brother.[35] He was pursued far and wide so that for a long time no one knew where he had taken refuge.[36]

Wolters' "The Khmer King at Basan (1371–3) and the Restoration of the Cambodian Chronology during the Fourteenth and Fifteenth Centuries," *Asia Major*, n.s. 12, 1(1966): 44–89. It runs parallel to what is printed as the third paragraph of *RA*, 67, recounting an expedition sent by King Ramathibodi against Cambodia, headed by then-Prince Ramesuan, which had to be rescued by Phra Borommaracha of Suphanburi. In the chronicle, this is placed before C.S. 715 (A.D. 1353/54). It is not mentioned in the Luang Prasoet Chronicle.

34. พระราเมศวร (VV: Prae-rhaem mijsoon), the son and heir of Ramathibodi, is assigned a reign of one year, C.S. 731–732 (A.D. 1369/70–1370/71) by all other versions of the chronicles. No other source gives his age at accession.

35. All other sources indicate that his successor was the elder brother of Ramathibodi's queen from Suphanburi, Khunluang Pha-ngua. See, for example, the opening paragraph of *RA*, 67.

36. The chronicles all agree that he went to govern Lopburi. See, for example, *RA*, 68.

73v CHAO KHUNLUANG PHA-NGUA, THIRD KING OF SIAM, RULED EIGHTEEN YEARS.[37]

The uncle was declared and crowned king by agreement of the entire royal family in place of the one who was driven out. He was sixty-three years old and was called Chao Khunluang Pha-ngua. Since that time there has been a law in Siam that at the death of the king, his brother inherits the crown and must rule instead of the son. Sometimes it happens to the contrary, but then the old laws have been corrupted.

The aforementioned king was wise, eloquent, devout, religious, liberal toward the ecclesiastics and the poor. By nature a war-minded ruler, a lover of weapons, he took great care of his soldiers and the community. The land was blackened with civil war under his rule, but he settled everything with little bloodshed, bringing everyone under submission and under one head. This king ruled eighteen years and died in peace in the eighty-first year of his life. It was a time of great prosperity during his regime and nothing was lacking in the land, nor was there scarcity. This the Siamese kings consider a great blessing, which is also attributed to the glory of Their Majesties.

PHRA THONG CHAN, FOURTH KING OF SIAM, REIGNED SEVEN DAYS.[38]

The son of the late king Chao Khunluang Pha-ngua succeeded his father in the kingdom (since there was no brother available) at the age of seventeen years.[39] He was named Phra Thong Chan, and was a prince of little promise. He reigned seven days and was killed by Phra Ramesuan (who had previously been driven out by Chao Khunluang Pha-ngua).

ONCE AGAIN PHRA RAMESUAN CAME TO THE THRONE AND BECAME THE FIFTH KING OF SIAM, REIGNING ANOTHER SIX YEARS.[40]

During his eighteen years of exile this Phra Ramesuan had been living a lonely life without luxuries. The forests, meadows, fields, and woods were

37. VV: TJaeu Couloangh Phongh Wo-Ae; เจ้าขุนหลวงพงั่ว. The *LP* chronicle assigns his reign of eighteen years to the period C.S. 732–750 (A.D. 1370/71–1388/89), while other versions, e.g. *RA* (68–69), assign it to the years C.S. 732–744 (A.D. 1370/71–1382/83). Again, VV uniquely records his age at accession, 63 years.

38. VV: Prae Thongh t'Jan, to whom all the chronicles assign a reign of seven days. The usual form of his name is Thong Lan (ทองลัน), although at least one other chronicle, *RA* (69) terms him Thong Chan. *LP* dates his reign in C.S. 750 (A.D. 1388/89), while all the others date it in C.S. 744 (A.D. 1382/83).

39. *RA*, 69, gives his age as 15 years.

40. *LP* assigns this reign to the years C.S. 750–757 (A.D. 1388/89–1395/96), a span of seven years; while others, of which *RA* (69–71) is representative, assigns to it

his companions most of this time, but poverty brought him enlightenment. He always followed closely the doings of the reigning monarch and the character of his son who was to succeed him. (But since he noticed that so many virtues and excellent qualities resided in the king, he kept in hiding. However, learning that His Majesty was ill, delirious, and that there was little hope of his recovering, he showed himself in the plains.) He assembled secretly as many followers as he could, and after the son was crowned king, he entered the city of Ayutthaya in stealth at night. He stormed the court, attacked the young king, killed him in a fury, and once again made himself king. At this time he was fifty-one years old. However, he had entirely abandoned his former character and during his second reign displayed more outstanding qualities than those evil ones which had blemished his previous reign. He was merciful, full of pity, modest, punished without haste, but forgave easily. He was wise and prudent, brave in the handling of weapons on 74
elephants and horseback, as well as on foot. He gave many alms to the ecclesiastics and to the poor, building and repairing many temples and monasteries. Because of his devotion, he often went to sacrifice to the gods, not so much like a king, but more like a monk. He was much loved by the mandarins and the common man. He reigned six years and died at the age of fifty-seven. The second reign of this king was a prosperous one.

PHRA RAM, SIXTH KING OF SIAM, REIGNED THREE YEARS.[41]

The son of Phra Ramesuan became king at the age of twenty-one and was named Phra Ram. He reigned for three years. He was of little wisdom and judgment because he sent the brother of Phra Thong Chan (killed by his father Phra Ramesuan) as governor to the province Suphanburi and gave him so much power that the aforementioned governor defeated and killed him, and made himself king. There is nothing more to write about this king Phra Ram, since, as was mentioned, he reigned a short time and did nothing notable.

---

the five or six year period C.S. 744–749 (A.D. 1382/83–1387/88), ending the treatment of his reign with the statement that he was "on the throne for 6 years."

41. VV: Prae Rhaem; พระรามราชาธิราช. *LP* calls him "Chao Phraya Ram" and assigns his reign to the fourteen years C.S. 757–771 (A.D. 1395/96–1409/10); while other versions, e.g. *RA* (71), term him "Somdet Phraya Ram" and give him a fourteen-year reign C.S. 749–763 (A.D. 1387/88–1401/2). *RA* gives his age at accession as 15 years.

PHRA NAKHON IN, THE SEVENTH KING OF SIAM, REIGNED TWENTY YEARS.[42]

The aforementioned governor (being the son of Chao Khunluang Phangua and brother of Phra Thong Chan) became king in the seventieth year of his life. He was named Phra Nakhon In, and was a wise, prudent, and merciful king; he was liberal and took great care of his soldiers, subjects, and the welfare of the country. He was a worldly prince, liking clerics little. He loved weapons so much that he sent various missions with junks to other countries to buy weapons.[43] During this king's reign the land was burdened with internal wars, but he conciliated the two parties.[44] After he had reigned twenty years, he ended his days in peace. It was a fruitful and not a difficult time under his government.

PHRA BOROMMARACHA THIBODI, THE EIGHTH KING OF SIAM, REIGNED TWENTY YEARS.[45]

The son of Phra Nakhon In followed his father in the kingdom and inherited the crown in the thirty-fifth year of his life. He was named Phra Borommaracha Thibodi Phrachao Sam.[46] By nature a warrior, he was also wise, eloquent, prudent, merciful, and clement. He took great care of his soldiers and subjects. He was liberal, building and improving many temples. He gave much assistance to the priests and the poor. He was the most benevolent king that has ever been in Siam, for every ten to fifteen days His

42. VV: Prae Nae-choon In. *LP* terms him พระอินทราชา, and dates his reign in C.S. 771–786 (A.D. 1409/10–1424/25) while *RA* (71–72) calls him สมเด็จพระนครอิน, and assigns his reign to the years C.S. 763–780 (A.D. 1401/2–1418/19). The *LP* count of the length of his reign, 15 years, is echoed in *PN* (10), though *PN*'s dates are the same as *RA*, which gives a length of reign of 18 years.

43. The Dutch text has *geweer*, "guns, rifles," but a broader meaning is less anachronistic here.

44. Apparently further confirmation of the bi-polar interpretation of Thai politics in this period that has featured in the recent work of A. B. Griswold, O. W. Wolters, and others, who have seen a continuing struggle between the houses of Ramathibodi and Suphanburi for political supremacy in the first century of Ayutthaya's history. See Charnvit Kasetsiri, *The Rise of Ayutthaya: A History of Siam in the Fourteenth and Fifteenth Centuries* (Oxford, 1976).

45. VV: Prae Borromma raet Jae Thijbo-dij; พระบรมราชาธิบดี (II). *LP* assigns his reign to the years C.S. 786–810 (A.D. 1424/25–1448/49), a span of 24 years; while *RA* gives him the sixteen/seventeen years C.S. 780–796 (A.D. 1418/19–1434/35).

46. The last element in his name, Phrachao Sam, is a reference to his being the third son of his predecessor; his two elder brothers (Chao Ai and Chao Yi) having duelled to the death over the succession to the throne, a story not repeated here.

Majesty went into the city asking how everything was, whether everyone was getting his rightful due and was being helped. This king reigned twenty years and died without children. He had a fruitful life and never suffered hardships. His subjects were also rich and prosperous.

PHRA BOROMMATRAILOKANAT, THE NINTH KING OF SIAM, REIGNED TWENTY YEARS.[47] 74v

The brother of the late king, by right of Siamese laws and consent of all the mandarins, was chosen and crowned king when he was 48 years old. He was called Phra Borommatrailokanat. He was the most liberal king that Siam has ever had because His Majesty demanded tribute, imposts, and gifts from no one. He built walls around and fortified many principal cities, such as Phitsanulok, Sawankhalok, Kamphaengphet, Sukhothai, etc. He also founded many temples. He used laborers as workers with daily wages and not as slaves as most Siamese kings have done and still do. His Majesty lived a fruitful life, which his forebears had not experienced. He was very merciful and solicitous towards the welfare of his people and the peace of the land. He was a lover of justice, and if any judge let himself be corrupted with gifts, he had him severely punished. He ruled twenty years. He lay down his royal functions and became a religious person to the grief of his subjects. He did not encumber himself any more with worldly affairs, but remained studious, religious, and devout. He died a monk. However, the history writers do not mention how long he lived as a monk.

47. VV: Prae Boromma Thraeijlock Chanaet; พระบรมไตรโลกนาถ. The dating of this reign is confused and complex. *LP*, in effect, gives him fifteen years as king in Ayutthaya (C.S. 810–825, AD. 1448/49–1463/64), and then a twenty-five year period as king in Phitsanulok (C.S. 825–850, A.D. 1463/64–1488/89), and states that another ruler, Borommaracha (III) began rule in Ayutthaya in 825, and continued to rule there (as sole monarch from 850) until 853 (A.D. 1491/92). By that reckoning, Trailok's reign would extend to the conventional forty years. The *PN* chronicle obviates the question, simply assigning Trailok a 38-year reign from C.S. 796–832 (A.D. 1434/35–1470/71), leaving blank, however, the years 832–835, and beginning the reign of Borommaracha, under the name of Ramathibodi (II), in the latter year. *RA* adds yet another variant, according to which Trailok reigns for only fifteen/sixteen years, C.S. 796–811 (A.D. 1434/35–1449/50), to be succeeded upon his death in 811 by his son, Phra Intharacha (II), who then reigned until 835 (A.D. 1473/74), a span of 24–25 years.

PHRA INTHARACHA, THE TENTH KING OF SIAM, REIGNED THIRTY-SEVEN YEARS.[48]

After the aforementioned king set down his crown, he was succeeded in the kingdom by his son who was a young man of sixteen years. He was called Phra Intharacha. This king was in no way as merciful as his father, for he was by nature no warrior and was not studious. He had little to do with spiritual life but lived a lustful one. He found great enjoyment in sailing, in the hunt, in horseback riding, and in elephant fights. He traveled often from one place to another. This practice was very expensive for the mandarins, because it is a Siamese custom that if the king leaves the palace, the mandarins must accompany him with great pomp. This is the reason that His Majesty was secretly hated by the royal family but greatly loved and admired by the common man (who did not feel the burdens).

This king fortified many cities, repaired some ruined works, and greatly improved His Majesty's palace. However, he obtained large subsidies for this purpose, especially from the mandarins, but little from the community. In addition, he introduced a practice in which, after the death of the mandarins, one tical weight of go1d[49] had to be paid from every ten measured lands from their estate. This was a very damaging principle as will appear in the following.

In the thirty-seventh year of his government, His Majesty went to Chong Chalung[50] to enjoy himself and to have fun. He died there suddenly, much to the joy of the mandarins. His reign was not prosperous but a troubled one.

We mentioned previously that the king set a value to the measured lands. Regarding this matter, one should know that in Siam no one but His Majesty owns any land or estate. But if the kings choose someone to become a member of their mandarins, they reward him with a court name or a mark of honor, whether it be a gold sword or a silver or gold sheath. These marks of honor then bring with them hundreds or thousands of measured lands in their new role as feudal lords. Each measure is twenty fathoms square, as you well know.[51]

48. VV: Prae Inthaeraetsiae; พระอินทราชา. See note 47 above.

49. One tical weight equals 236 grains troy weight, nearly half an ounce avoirdupois or 15 grams.

50. Unidentified.

51. A categorical answer to the perennial question of the significance of *sakdi na*: compare H. G. Quaritch Wales, *Ancient Siamese Government and Administration* (London, 1934: reprinted New York. 1965): 49–50.

PHRACHAO RAMATHIBODI, ELEVENTH KING OF SIAM, RULED THIRTY-EIGHT YEARS.[52]

The brother of the late king succeeded in the kingdom and inherited the crown when he was twenty-one years old. He was called Phrachao Ramathibodi. He was the most fortunate king[53] (after Phra Phuttha Chao) in Siam. Many incredible things are said about him which, because they are too fabulous, will not be mentioned. Although the following also does not appear to be true, I have nevertheless decided to make note of it, principally because with the Siamese as with us evangelism was maintained. I pray that Your Grace will not take offense or be grieved in reading it. At the time when Phrachao Ramathibodi [II] ruled in Siam, there was also a king on the Coromandel Coast in Ramaradt[54] who was honored with the same name and title. This king thought in his heart that he alone had the greatest dignity, honor, and territory on the earth. When he learned that the Siamese king also bore his name and title, he became angry, saying with great gravity: "Under heaven I alone am worthy of this dignity, and whosoever wishes to rob me of this I will kill." Taking an assegai[55] he cast a spell and then threw it with all his strength saying, "Go, kill the Siamese king."

This assegai fell in Siam at the feet of the king's throne, where His Majesty was holding audience. Seeing the assegai, the king asked that it be brought to him, but no one had the power to do this. The king left his throne, grabbed the assegai, and found a letter attached to the spearhead written in Brahmanic [Devanagari] with these contents: "The gods have made no one under the heavens who is my equal. But since you, King in Siam, have taken my name,

52. VV: Prae t'Jau Rha Mathij Bodij; รามาธิบดี (II). Only with this ruler does VV get back in phase with other lists of the kings of Ayutthaya. The corresponding ruler in *LP* is assigned a reign of 38 years, C.S. 853–891 (A.D. 1491/92–1529/30); while *PN* and *RA* give him a 36–37-year reign, C.S. 835–871 (A.D. 1473/74–1509/10).

53. The Dutch word in the original text is *geluk*. I have translated it as "fortune" whenever it appears in different forms throughout the text. The Siamese may have used a word which has a much wider connotation than either the Dutch word *geluk* or the English equivalent "fortune" [such as the word *chok—Ed.*] From the context in which this word is used, it seems that what the Siamese may have had in mind was the whole spectrum of beliefs in luck, stars, and the sacred auras surrounding leaders of extraordinary qualities. (Note by Andaya)

54. In a Thai version of this tale, (ตำนานพราหมณ์เมืองนครศรีธรรมราช, Bangkok. 1930), this place is identified in a footnote as the palace quarter of the holy city of Benares in India. The Thai version of the tale, however, is set in the reign of Ramathibodi I, not Ramathibodi II.

55. An assegai is an African spear, but the seventeenth-century reports of the Dutch East India Company often used the word to refer to spears of various Asian countries. (Note by Andaya)

I am angry and send this assegai from my hand to kill you." The Siamese king tied a letter to the assegai with the words: "The gods have made you the greatest in your land and me in mine. If you think that you are greater than I, choose a place where we can war with each other. The winner shall indeed be the greatest and the vanquished will be the other's subject." He also sent the assegai with great force from his hand, charging it to go and seek its master once again.

When the king in Ramaradt received the assegai and letter, he was amazed that his spell had been rendered powerless. Although the Siamese king had
75v presented his demand, he could not resolve to do battle with him. However, he decided to kill him by means of spells. He had a large wooden image made in the form of a bird, cast a spell over it, and had his brahmans and sorcerers do the same so that his wish could be fulfilled. He selected four brave soldiers, commanding them to go to Siam with the bewitched image and kill the king. One evening these soldiers arrived at the court of the Siamese king and through some spell put the guards to sleep and made the doors open for them. Finally, one of them went to His Majesty's bedchamber in order to carry out his orders. But when he entered, he was immediately transfixed, not being able to move forward or backward. The second and third followed after him, and the same happened to them. The fourth, seeing that none of his companions had returned, thought that they must have been held back by devilish tricks. He exorcised the Siamese devil and went to the king. He drew his sword to kill His Majesty, whom he found asleep, but when he tried to strike, he found himself rooted to the spot with his arm raised but unable to change his position. When the king awoke in the morning, he was surprised to see this stranger in this position and three others like him at the exit of his bedchamber. His Majesty had his mandarins and all foreign interpreters summoned and commanded them to ask these strangers how, whence, and why they had come. They answered: "Have the king first release us, then we will tell everything truthfully." His Majesty commanded that they be brought to the following angels: Phra Trong Müang, Phra Cena [?] Müang, and Phra Canoolij [?] at the Pratu Chai, that is, the Heart Gate,[56] where (so claim the Siamese) many angels lived, and that they should honor them in the Siamese way in order that through their prayers they might be freed.[57] After they had paid homage at this place, they were released and were able to move. They told His Majesty which king had sent them, and why and how they had come to court. Because of the king's mercy, no harm came to the attempted murderers, but His Majesty sent them back with a letter to the king in

56. The major gate on the south side of the city. Cf. the map of Ayutthaya in Tri Amatayakul, *Guide to Ayudhya and Bang Pa-In* (Bangkok, 1957), at end. This is, however, ประตูไชย ("Victory Gate") and not, as Van Vliet thought, ประตูใจ ("Heart Gate").

57. Some sort of guardian spirits of the capital city are clearly indicated here, although their identification is problematic.

Ramaradt with the following message: "If you are of manly courage and a lover of fortune, then come and do battle with me. He who is vanquished shall be the subject of the other."

The king in Ramaradt, having learned what had happened from the men he sent, and having read the contents of the letter, tried to kill the king in Siam by other means. He sent four brave soldiers, who could shave splendidly, with a junk to Tenasserim and then to Siam. Their orders were to cut the 76
throat of the Siamese king when he came to be shaved. As a reward they would enjoy great honor and riches. In addition he gave them a locked chest and a letter full of compliments to be given to the king in Siam, saying: "The gods have given us both equally great fortune and honor; therefore, let us be as brothers. These four men are excellent shavers and accustomed to shaving kings. Take them into your service. When you receive this small chest, please open it." The Siamese king ordered that the chest be opened. When it was opened, out sprang the image of a man created by sorcery and spells with a gun in his hand threatening to shoot the king. However, the ligaments which held the parts of the body together broke into pieces and the bewitched creature collapsed. Seeing this, His Majesty became angry and said: "The king of Ramaradt is like a faint-hearted woman because he wants to do devilish tricks but dares not be worsted by weapons." Both kings then were quiet for a year or two. The shavers practiced their skills on common people and also on the mandarins. They were so expert in their work and were praised so much that their fame reached the ears of their king. Through time His Majesty became dispassionate and no longer had bad memories of the king of Ramaradt. He had the shavers summoned to shave his head and chin, which they did very conscientiously. But after the shaving had been going on for some time, one of them stropped one of his razors until it was very sharp with the intention of cutting the king's throat. But when he was about to do it, he started to tremble so violently that all his strength left him. His Majesty asked why he was trembling so, and he threatened that if he concealed the truth, he would kill him. He was thus forced to reveal that all four of the shavers had been sent by the king of Ramaradt to kill His Majesty by cutting his throat when shaving him. The Siamese king became very angry at the king of Ramaradt when he heard this. Nevertheless, through his innate mercy he did not wish to mistreat the shavers whose identity had been revealed, but instead sent them back to their king with a letter. Its contents were as follows: "The gods have given me life and have made me king over my subjects. Why do you seek through treachery, sorcery, and devilish tricks to seize them from me and to deprive my subjects of their king? If you are of royal character, come and war with me; but if you are a small-hearted woman, then remain on your land." 76v

When the king in Ramaradt realized what had occurred by means of the shavers who had returned and from the missive they brought, he was greatly surprised, especially since the bewitched image had not killed the king of Siam but had fallen to the ground without evincing any power whatsoever. This was particularly astonishing since prior to that time, it had killed all who opened the chest. He became of the opinion that His Majesty was a supernatural being or in possession of extraodinary luck. Consequently, he resolved to make a sincere peace and close alliance with him.

As a sign of his inclinations toward the treaty, he wanted to send all kinds of rare goods which were at that time unknown in Siam. He asked the shavers what games or melodies there were in his country which were unknown in Siam. They answered that they had not seen any game or any diversion in Ramaradt which Siam did not also have, except *schoppen* or *schongelen*.[58] Also, they had not found any brahmans in Siam who were able to prevent misfortune or the casting of spells over the courts of kings, cities, and countries. The king of Ramaradt therefore sent two learned brahman priests with a letter in a friendly tone to the king of Siam asking that His Majesty forget all that had gone before and accept him as a brother. He also instructed the brahmans that they should make the game of *schoppen* or *schongelen* known in Siam and to establish it there.[59] The Siamese king accepted the brahmans, the letter, and the proffered peace, and sent a letter in reply establishing a friendship between both kings which has been maintained to the present day, renewed every two to three years by means of letters engraved in gold. Since then, various brahmans have come to Siam from many places, especially from Ramaradt, and have continued to be held in great esteem among the kings, princes, the royal family, and the community.

At that time the Moorish[60] traders from the Coromandel Coast came with their cloth, which practice continues to the present day. *Schoppen* or *schongelen* is still found today, because there are special places set out for playing it. There are special feast days held yearly which go on from one day to the next for a long time.[61]

But to shorten the story of this king Phrachao Ramathibodi, a short summary will be given of his life and his praises recounted in a few words. With regard to his luck, it was such that he dared to go among his enemies unweaponed. Many [such] kings and princes as those from Pattani, Kedah, Perak, etc., came to visit him and to fall at his feet. They submitted willingly to his domination. Some have still remained tributary states. He was a fighter

58. Since there is no equivalent in English. I have preferred to leave these words untranslated. Both refer to swings made of a board suspended by two ropes on which one can swing to and fro. (Note by Andaya)

59. Compare the Thai text mentioned in note 54, above.

60. I.e., Indian Muslims.

61. On the "Swing Ceremony" (*trīyambavy trīpavāy*), see H. G. Quaritch Wales, *Siamese State Ceremonies* (London, 1931): 238–47.

by nature, of great wisdom and foresight, merciful, had great concern for his soldiers, for the community, and the ecclesiastics. He performed many good 77
deeds toward the brahmans, and built and improved many cities, temples, monasteries, and houses for the religious and the poor from his own treasury without asking help or subsidies from anyone. He also rebuilt the royal palace which is still standing in the same place. His Majesty was such a great lover of foreign nations that he sent various missions to entice them to his land. He liked the foreigners and showed them friendship and great favor. In order to prevent anyone from suffering annoyances, being charged too much or being cheated, he imposed regulations and did not want them to be transgressed. The officials followed these with such care that all foreigners departed from the country satisfied. He also disliked having any beggars going along the streets, but wanted each family to maintain its poor relatives. Through temporary lack of means, the richest mandarins had to extend moderate subsidies. Under His Majesty's rule no theft was known and whoever was caught being unfaithful was punished with a severe death. In general, he commanded that the old laws and the religion should be maintained, and because he possessed so much luck and principal virtues, he was the most loved of all of his descendents and successors. He filled the kingdom with peace and experienced the most fruitful and most fortunate time of all the Siamese kings. The community was prospering and thriving, the land was fruitful. No sadness or grief was heard of. He was the first who established the large feasts and the game days, which were renewed this year by the present king. In sum, after having spoken of His Majesty, he was in many ways like Solomon. He ruled thirty-eight years and died, much to the grief of all who had known him.

NO PHUTTHANGKUN, THE TWELFTH KING OF SIAM, RULED FIVE YEARS.[62]

The son of the late king succeeded his father in the kingdom, being twenty-seven years old. He did not want to accept the name *phra* since he said the gods, but no human being, had the right to it. Thus he was called No Phutthangkun. In the beginning of his reign this king was very merciful, but His Majesty's goodness was abused, especially by the mandarins. Everyone thought that after the death of his father he was freed from subjection and did not have to obey his son or to show him any royal honor. When His Majesty noticed this, he changed his former character and ruled with a severe hand. He was a war-loving ruler of great wisdom and prudence, solicitous

62. VV: Noophout thae Coun; หน่อพุทธางกูร, King Borommaracha. *LP* gives him a reign of four/five years, C.S. 891–895 (A.D. 1529/30–1533/34), while *RA* and others give him a reign of similar length in the years C.S. 871–875 (A.D. 1509/10–1514/15).

and liberal. He was especially careful to place pious, sincere men in all judicial positions. He was a great enemy of bad judges and punished them with death. During his rule and his course of life he was so steadfast that no setback
77v dismayed him, nor was he gladdened by prosperity. He had no favorites but showed both high and low, spiritual and temporal, equal favor. His commands were carried out without alteration, and whosoever (through personal motives) did not implement even the smallest point or showed any disobedience was punished as a criminal. He was so fair in the administration of justice that he cut off the forefinger of his right hand because his finger had sinned against his own command in the following manner. His Majesty was strolling in a certain room in the palace when he saw that the walls were spotted in many places with lime. He asked his chamberlain who had smeared the walls. The chamberlain answered that the *maletten* (in our language, pages)[63] had done it with lime, which is sometimes present in too large a quantity in the *sirih* leaves. Thus the king said, "The first one who takes out the lime from the *sirih* leaves again and throws it against the wall shall have his forefinger cut off." A few days after that the king was sitting in one of the rooms of the palace. He wanted to chew some *sirih pinang* but seeing that there was too much lime in it, he took some of it out of the *sirih* with his forefinger and wiped it on the wall. When His Majesty realized that he had forbidden this himself, he took a *keris* and cut off his finger (so it is said) saying, "You have sinned against my command and that is why I reject you as unworthy."

He was attracted to, a lover and champion of, foreign nations and took great care that they were well-treated. He warred often with Lan Chang[64] and Pegu, and at the end of his life he was victorious. He went personally with a strong army to the borders of Pegu and conquered a city called Choulock.[65] On his way back he contracted smallpox and died after having ruled five years. During his lifetime it was generally a troubled and never a fruitful time.

WORARATSADATHIRAT, THIRTEENTH KING OF SIAM, RULED FIVE MONTHS.[66]

The son of No Phutthangkun succeeded to his father's kingdom when he was five years old. He was named Woraratsadathirat. Through lack of a more qualified person, this child was chosen as king because the late king had no

63. Apparently a rendering of *mahatlek* (มหาดเล็ก).

64. Lan Xang, i.e., the Kingdom of Luang Prabang.

65. Unidentified.

66. VV: Woo-Rhae Rassae Thae Thieraya; variously rendered as พระรัษฎาธิราช (*PN*) and พระรัษฐาธิราช *(RA)*, and not named in *LP*. *LP* places this reign in the years C.S. 895–896 (A.D. 1533/34–1534/35), while *RA* and others in C.S. 875–876 (A.D. 1513/14–1514/15). *RA* alone gives its exact length as five months.

brothers or older sons. He did not live longer than five months. He was killed by his cousin (who was distantly related and who ruled the kingdom as regent).

PHRA CHAIYARACHA, FOURTEENTH KING OF SIAM, RULED THIRTEEN YEARS.[67]

The previously mentioned regent was crowned king (when he was thirty-five years old) with the concurrence of all the mandarins. He was named Phra Chaiyaracha. This king was very merciful, wise, and pious. He waged war often with Cambodia and was victorious. He was soft and steadfast in his rule. A lover of good justice, he was not quick to punish but had all wrongdoers properly examined. He had no time for flatterers or evilmongers. He performed many good works for the religious and the poor. He built and improved many temples and residences of the religious. Among others, His Majesty built the large and marvelous temple Phra Chi Chiang,[68] about which 78
a lot can be written. In order not to get off the subject, however, only as many stories as are reasonable and are relevant will be told. Returning once again to the rest of the story that the king was loved by and familiar with everyone,[69] he removed from his land the fraudulent practice of small or false weights and measures. Rice and all foods could only be sold by large, signed *tsioupen*[70] or measures. His Majesty experienced a fruitful and fortunate time. He had a rich and prosperous community. Toward the end of his life the king went with a powerful army to the borders of Cambodia and captured the city of Lamphun.[71] On his return home he died of natural causes, having reigned thirteen years.

67. VV: Prae Tsieyaia Raetjae; พระไชยราชาธิราช. *LP* assigns his reign to the years C.S. 896–908 (A.D. 1534/35–1546/47), a total of 12–13 years; while *RA* gives it the 13–14 years C.S. 876–889 (A.D. 1514/15–1527/28).

68. The building of this *wat* is the first event in his reign mentioned in the *RA*, 77, and *LP* chronicles (s.v. C.S. 900, A.D. 1538).

69. Note Pinto's comment on this king, reproduced by W. A. R. Wood *(A History of Siam*, reprinted ed.. Bangkok, 1959, 106): "This prince lived in the reputation of being charitable to the poor, liberal in his benefits and recompenses, pitiful and gentle towards everyone, and above all incorrupt in doing of justice and chastening the wicked; his subjects spoke so amply thereof in their lamentations, as if all that they said of it was true; we are to believe that there never was a better King than he, either amongst these Pagans, or in all the countries of the world."

70. *Tsioupen*: Simon de La Loubère (*A New Historical Relation of the Kingdom of Siam*, London. 1693; reprinted Kuala Lumpur, 1969, 72) mentions that the Siamese "have a Pitcher called *Canan* in *Siamese*, *Choup* in *Portuguese*..." J. B. Pallegoix (*Description du royaume Thai ou Siam*, Paris, 1854, t. I, 257) explains that the "*khanan* ou coco légalisé qui équivaut a un fort demi-litre."

71. An apparent contradiction here: Lamphun is hardly near the borders of

PHRA YOT CHAO, FIFTEENTH KING OF SIAM, RULED THREE YEARS.[72]

The son of the late Phra Chaiyaracha became king when he was ten years old.[73] He was named Phra Yot Chao. He was a young prince of great promise. Everyone believed that he would become like his father in every respect since strong indications of and evidence for this seemed to be provided by his character and daily actions. He enjoyed the hunt immensely, riding on horseback through the forests, meadows, and fields, elephant fights, handling of weapons and other knightly exercises. The land was fruitful everywhere during his reign and was not affected by dearth. However, he only lived for three years and was killed by his father's concubine, called Mae Si Suda Chao,[74] using poison and sorcery. The aforementioned concubine was delighted with a sorcerer who came daily and read old stories and foreign histories in the king's language. In order to help the sorcerer advance, she decided with him to bewitch the young king and then to kill him. Toward this end the aforementioned concubine brought the sorcerer daily to the king's bedchamber and secluded places under the pretext of reading and telling enjoyable stories and memorable matters to the young prince. And when the sorcerer had demonstrated his devilish art to his king, the aforementioned concubine brought His Majesty the poison, saying that it was medicine with which he could become cured. And thus his royal spirit fled, to the great sadness of his subjects.

PHRA KHUN CHINNARAT, SIXTEENTH KING OF SIAM, RULED FORTY DAYS.[75]

The sorcerer remained in the king's palace and with the help of the aforementioned concubine made himself king against the will of all the

---

Cambodia! *LP* has him capture Lamphun in C.S. 908 (A.D. 1546/47), and makes no reference to warfare in the east. [The reference to Kamboja, translated here as Cambodia, may refer to northern Siam; see Vickery (1976: 228–9).]

72. VV: Prae Joodt t' Jaeu; referred to as พระยอดฟ้า by *LP* with a two-year reign, C.S. 908–910 (A.D. 1546/47–1548/49); by the same name with a specific 2 year 6-month reign by *PN*, C.S. 889–891 (A.D. 1527/28–1529/30); and with a reign of 1 year 2 months in *RA*, C.S. 889–891. Wood, *History*, 108–110, calls him Keo Fa.

73. *RA* gives his age as eleven years.

74. VV: Mee-soo-Seda t'Siau; in other chronicles, แม่อยู่หัวศรีสุดาจันทร์.

75. VV: Prae Con tsinne-radt; i.e. ขุนวรวงศา, who somewhat earlier in his career bore the title of ขุนชินราช, the detailed story of which is given in *PN* and *RA* under the date of C.S. 890–891 (A.D. 1528/29–1529/30), his reign being placed there for a space of five months (roughly July–November) of C.S. 891. *LP* gives it a length of forty-two days in C.S. 910 (A.D. 1548), from June 11 to July 23.

mandarins and to the displeasure of the common man. He called himself Phra Khun Chinnarat. However, the mandarins decided among themselves to kill him. Toward this end they ordered Okphra Thainam (then Captain-General of the Cavalry) and the Okluang Ratchayut (who was also a brave captain) to the theater where the elephants were kept.

In the meantime some of the mandarins went to the king and announced that an extraordinarily beautiful elephant had been seen in the vicinity of the abovementioned theater. They earnestly advised him to go there and try to capture the elephant. The king let himself be persuaded and went immediately with his entire retinue to the theater. At the first entrance stood the captains Thainam and Ratchayut, each with a loaded gun. When the king approached,
they fired and shot him down. He reigned forty days. This deed being 78v
accomplished, his body was thrown to the dogs. The aforementioned concubine (who had helped him gain the crown) was killed with a sword and thrown into the river.[76]

PHRA THIANRACHA, SEVENTEENTH KING OF SIAM, RULED SIXTEEN YEARS.[77]

The cousin or nephew[78] of Phra Yot Chao was crowned king with the agreement of the mandarins, so that the crown remained under the former house. He was about forty-two years old and named Phra Thianracha. He was a very merciful king, very studious, and more inclined toward the improvement of his laws and religion than towards the secular state. Justice was performed honestly in his time. He carried out many good works for the religious, especially the brahmans and the poor. He improved the temples more than he did the fortresses of his kingdom because he was by nature no warrior. He was liberal, experienced a very fruitful time, and during his lifetime possessed seven beautiful white elephants.

This king had given his daughter in marriage to Okya Phitsanulok, but the married couple had little in common so that there were often quarrels and disagreements. Finally, in one of these quarrels Phitsanulok hit his wife on the head and she started bleeding. The aforementioned wife wiped off the blood with a handkerchief and sent it in a golden cup from Phitsanulok to Ayutthaya to the king, her father, together with a letter of complaint about

76. A variant account of this event is given in *PN* and *RA*.

77. VV: Prae theen Nae Rhae tsiae; พระเฑียรราชา or มหาจักรพรรดิ์. *LP* assigns him a reign of 20 years, C.S. 910–930 (A.D. 1548/49–1568/69); while *PN* and *RA* give him 24 years, C.S. 891–914 (A.D. 1529/30–1552/53).

78. Dutch *neef* can mean either cousin or nephew (Note by Andaya). Mahachakkraphat was the younger half-brother of King Chaiyaracha, and therefore the cousin of Phra Yot Fa.

how badly she had been treated by her other half.[79] Because of this, the king became angry with his son-in-law Okya Phitsanulok. Calling his men to arms, he sent them to the province of Phitsanulok to kill the aforementioned Okya. Okya Phitsanulok, having heard from rumors what was in store for him, did not dare to wait for his father-in-law's might but left his government and fled to Pegu. The king of Pegu, learning of Phitsanulok's arrival, had him treated well. When Phitsanulok saw that he was pleased, he began to beseech the King of Pegu to war with Siam. But His Majesty refused to do such a thing saying, "The Siamese king has not done me any wrong, nor have I any pretensions to that kingdom."

Okya Phitsanulok, however, remained filled with the desire for revenge and in order to stir the king of Pegu to war with Siam, he announced that the king of Siam had just recently acquired seven beautiful white elephants. Of these, he said, several were born on the borders of Pegu; therefore, His Majesty has rights to them. Send ambassadors and demand two to three of these elephants, and when this is refused, you will have a just cause. This proposal was approved by the king. He therefore sent envoys to the king in Siam to procure two or three white elephants. When His Majesty realized what the king of Pegu was asking, he immediately denied the envoys' request and curtly sent them back home. On the envoys' return to their king, they reported what had occurred. Consequently, His Majesty resolved to war with Siam. He gathered his forces, brought many people under arms, and made Okya Phitsanulok field marshal of all of his foot soldiers with the promise that, if they conquered the city of Ayutthaya, Phitsanulok (in conformity with his many requests) would enjoy the Nopphathat temple as a reward.[80] Having received prior warning of Pegu's intentions and expedition, the Siamese king was so terrified that he wanted to lay down his royal position and become a monk. However, his mandarins were against this, since the son who was to succeed His Majesty was a carefree young prince of little promise. Therefore, they encouraged the king and earnestly advised His Majesty to take up the defense, arm his people, and call in the assistance of the Pattani people in
79 order to stop the Peguan forces.

When the king saw that he had to fight, he complained bitterly of his misfortune, especially since for many years he had intended to lay down his crown and to take up the duties of a monk. And when this did not happen, he prepared for battle. He summoned the Pattani people to come with as large

79. A similar tale is told of the son of King Nandabayin (1581–99) of Pegu: see G. E. Harvey, *History of Burma*, (London, 1967) 179–80; and Nai Thien, "Intercourse between Burma and Siam as Recorded in the Hmannan Yazawindawgyi," *JSS*, 8, 2 (1912): 36–37; reprinted in *Selected Articles from the Siam Society Journal*, V (Bangkok, 1959): 124–25.

80. Another reference to this *wat* see note 24, above.

a force as was possible. Within a short time the king of Pattani appeared personally with his youthful army in Ayutthaya. In the meantime the Siamese king became sick and became weaker daily so that there was not much hope for his recovery. The rumor spread that after his father's death, the king's unqualified son would become king. Wanting to take advantage of the situation, the Pattani people went with 300 armed soldiers (among whom was also the king) to the palace, intending to overrun the place, kill the old and the young kings, and help make the Pattani people gain the highest honor in Siam. The Siamese mandarins, seeing the fierce Pattanis approach, shut the gate of the palace, placed themselves on the defense, sent the *braspintados*[81] (who were the king's serfs) out through the back of the court and killed all the Pattani people throughout the whole city to the very last man.[82] However, the Siamese king died the next day after he had ruled sixteen years.[83] This caused great dejection among the royal family and the community.

About this time the king of Pegu arrived with his army, destroying everything in his path. He stopped in Phitsanulok, on the one hand in order to rest his people, and on the other hand to assess the state of the Siamese. When His Majesty learned of the turmoil and defeat of the Pattani people, as well as the death of the king, he was greatly grieved. He said to himself, "I am undoubtedly the cause of all this evil. Much innocent blood has been spilt on my account and that beloved king has without a doubt died of sorrow. Therefore, I intend to return and to leave in peace a man who has not committed any wrong against me nor my country or state, nor has tried to." But when the king was ready to break camp and to leave with his army, His Majesty also became ill and died of fever.[84] The Pegu army thus piteously and sorrowfully returned once again to their country. Since they had destroyed the countryside and many cities on their way, they had a shortage of supplies and had to improvise drastically in order to survive. When news arrived of the death of the Pegu king and the departure of the army from Siam, everyone was very happy because the war, which everyone was so afraid of, had ended by itself.

81. *Braspintado* (Portuguese), "painted arms"; i.e., the แขนลาย, concerning which see La Loubère, *A New Historical Relation*, 96–97.

82. For a Pattani version of these events, see A. Teeuw and D. K. Wyatt, *Hikayat Patani*: *The Story of Pattani* (The Hague, 1970): vol. II, 157–61, 231–35.

83. According to *LP*, the Pattani attack occurred in 1563 and the king's death in 1568 or early 1569.

84. This is King Bayinnaung who, however, did not die until 1581; G. E. Harvey, *History of Burma*, 174.

PHRA MAHIN, EIGHTEENTH KING OF SIAM, RULED SEVEN YEARS.[85]

The son of Phra Thianracha became king in his father's place when he was twenty-seven years old. He was named Phra Mahin. He was the least intelligent, most unsolicitous, and most incapable king known in the Siamese kingdom. He had no training in things political or spiritual. He let everything deteriorate under his rule – cities, forts, temples, monasteries, pyramids,[86] residences of the religious people, yes, even his palace became dilapidated without being repaired. He occupied himself with nothing but (poetically speaking) Bacchus and Venus, which caused him and his subjects such harm that he was finally killed with poison by his father's concubine and his land completely destroyed by the Peguans. The Okya Phitsanulok (of whom much has been said in the recounting of the life of the previous king) had returned to Pegu with the Peguan army, and although he was greatly hated because of the miserable outcome of the aforementioned expedition and the death of the Peguan king, he remained in a position of respect and favor with the young king, who with the death of his father inherited the kingdom and
79v crown. This Okya Phitsanulok often sent spies, with the knowledge of the Peguan king, to the Siamese borders in order to observe the disposition, character, and actions of the young king Phra Mahin closely. After receiving good information, he advised the Peguan king to resume the war once again. His Majesty let himself be convinced easily, but his mandarins and soldiers were not in favor of this. However, he called his people to arms and gathered a powerful army. He made Okya Phitsanulok commander of his foot soldiers once again, and they headed toward the frontiers of Siam. He burned, ravaged, and destroyed all the places that his father had missed and killed all the Siamese that he came across. Although the rumor, in fact the truth, came to the king in the city of Ayutthaya that the Peguan king was on his way with a large army, His Majesty could not be persuaded by either his mandarins or by anyone else to rouse himself to the defense. Consequently, the enemy gained a great advantage; they finally appeared around the city of Ayutthaya and attempted to besiege it. But the Peguans were driven away, not by the king's army, but by the height of the water (which yearly covers Siam). They retired to the provinces of Phitsanulok, Kamphaengphet, and the surrounding fertile high grounds, where they settled until the water receded and the land was once again dry. Okya Phitsanulok then brought his forces together and once

85. VV: Prae Nae Hin; พระมหินทร์ in all the Thai chronicles. *LP* puts him on the throne for a single year in C.S. 930–931 (A.D. 1568/69–1569/70); while both *PN* and *RA* give him two separate reigns, in C.S. 914–916 (A.D. 1552/53–1555), and 917–918 (A.D. 1555/+56–1556).

86. Dutch *piramiden*: the reference clearly is to religious monuments, *cetiya* and *stupa*.

again came to the royal city of Ayutthaya. The uncaring King Phra Mahin, having seen the Peguan army for the first time, placed himself in a defensive posture against the second Peguan expedition as a result of the urging of his mandarins. These defenses rebuffed the Peguans numerous times. Okya Phitsanulok, who had been the instigator of the war, fell into such disfavor with the Peguan king and his soldiers that he was in danger of death. Thus Okya left the Peguan army and hid at Phaniat (which was the place where the elephants were kept).[87] He stayed there until he met some Siamese with whom he sent a letter to his wife's mother, named Phra Suwat (who still lived in the king's court), to complain bitterly about the thoughtlessness of his wife as well as his said state. He requested that she write him about the present situation in the city. This woman was of great wisdom and courage and took great pity on her son-in-law Phitsanulok. She advised her daughter to be reconciled with her husband, to which the daughter finally consented. In the meantime there were several letters sent by Okya Phitsanulok to the court, and from his mother-in-law in the court to him. In this way he gained complete knowledge of the state of affairs in the city.

The king of Pegu (who was at the end of his war supplies, especially gunpowder, as a result of the many skirmishes with the Siamese) decided to depart and abandon the city of Ayutthaya. But Okya Phitsanulok, observing that this was his intention, sent a letter to His Majesty in which he sought pardon and assured him of victory if he would just remain a short time. The Peguan was glad to receive the letter and had Okya Phitsanulok summoned and pardoned him. And although His Majesty clearly understood from Phitsanulok the distress and the state of affairs in the city, it was only with great reluctance he resolved to stay, principally because the burdens of the war grieved him, disturbed his people, and there was little or no gunpowder left in the army.

Phra Suwat, learning of the Peguan king's intentions and the distress of
the army through a letter from her son-in-law Okya Phitsanulok, sent a chest
with gunpowder (disguised to appear as if there were a dead body in it) to the
Peguan army with a letter to the king that he should not leave but stay, and
that the whole land stood open for him. When the king received the 80
aforementioned chest and letter, he was both greatly astonished and overjoyed.
He changed his plans and resolved to remain with his army. The
aforementioned woman, Phra Suwat, was able to send to the Peguan army
several chests of gunpowder in the manner mentioned above. She conspired
and brought Okya Chakri (the Siamese king's commander) to her side.[88] Chakri

87. The elephant kraal (*phaniat*) of Ayutthaya was located northeast of the city: see Tri Amatyakul, *Guide to Ayudhya*, 58–61.

88. VV: Sicrij. The "Siamese king's Commander," head of the Mahatthai, usually bore the title of *chakri*.

made a sortie with just a few men so that he would be sure to give no opposition to the Peguans and would fall into their hands. By this means, he, the king, and Okya Phitsanulok would then be able to agree on the way of delivering the city of Ayutthaya.

The Peguan soldiers encountered Okya Chakri, made him and his followers prisoners, and brought Okya Chakri before their king. Chakri reported the state of affairs in the city to His Majesty and Okya Phitsanulok. After he had been in the Peguan army for several days, had arranged everything with the king, and had designated how he should storm and seize the city, he again returned to Ayutthaya. Upon arriving back in the city, he put himself in chains, placed his neck in a block and came bound before the Siamese king. He pretended that he had been seized against his will and that, chained and shackled, he had escaped. His Majesty was pleased to have his commander back again and inquired about the state of the Peguan army. Chakri replied (in order to make the king more careless and negligent) that everything was under control because the Peguan king had come to the end of his supplies and intended to abandon the city of Ayutthaya and return to his land. These reasons greatly pleased the king. Okya Chakri said, "You know what your post is; take care as you have done so far and perform all of your duties." After a few days the king of Pegu brought his forces together and stormed the city of Ayutthaya on many sides, but especially at the king's palace. Okya Chakri (who had command there) did not pack his gunpowder in tightly and did not shoot accurately. When the Peguans approached the court of the king, he opened the gate and let them in.

The Siamese king was so careless that he still stood and watched a cockfight when the Peguans had already captured the court. However, he was led to a certain room in the palace by Phra Suwat (about whom much has been said previously) and poisoned by her. He was thirty-four years old and had been king for seven years.

This woman Phra Suwat and her daughter came before the king of Pegu and Okya Phitsanulok and were both pardoned. After the king of Pegu had conquered the city of Ayutthaya, His Majesty was acknowledged as king of the whole Siamese kingdom. All the governors from distant and nearby provinces came to the court of His Majesty to pay homage. And after the king had brought everything under his sway, His Majesty made Okya Phitsanulok king with the condition that the Siamese kingdom would remain a tributary of the crown of Pegu and that the kings would always send one or two of their sons, or in the case of the lack of male offspring, the closest relatives, as hostages to Pegu. This is why the Siamese kings have become subjects of the Peguan Majesty. After this event the king of Pegu returned to his country with the rest of his forces, taking with him as hostage Phra Naret [Naresuan], the oldest son of the newly-made Siamese king, being a young prince of thirteen years of age.

PHRA MAHATHAMMARACHA, NINETEENTH KING OF SIAM, RULED TWENTY-TWO YEARS.[89]

Okya Phitsanulok was fifty-four years old when he became king and was named Phra Mahathammaracha Phrachao Song Queen.[90] He was a merciful king and very industrious. His Majesty enlarged the city of Ayutthaya, giving it the form which it still has to this day, and erected a stone wall around it. He also built the five high towers in the king's palace. He lived during a prosperous time so that the ravaged lands began to grow and flourish again. The population, which had been seriously reduced and impoverished by the Peguan war, began to increase and prosper again. He was a war-loving ruler and warrior, but nevertheless he respected Peguan power, not so much because 80v
of fear as the fact that his kingdom was bare of inhabitants and many places were destroyed.

After Phra Naret [Naresuan] had been a hostage in Pegu (as has been mentioned previously) about two years, he was reviled by the king, threatened with death because in many royal exercises, such as horseback riding, hunting, elephant fights, etc., he was better than the king of Pegu. The young prince was so deeply disturbed by this contempt and the threats that he fled secretly in the night with his retinue (about 300 Siamese nobles) to Phitsanulok. They burned and destroyed many Peguan places through which they passed. When the king learned of the flight of his hostage, he had him pursued by two war leaders named Weengh Ceu and Ceu Thaen[91] with 5,000 soldiers, with orders to bring Phra Naret back as a prisoner. Phra Naret, realizing that the Peguans were on the march and had come to Phitsanulok, went out with the inhabitants of that province to meet them and defeated both war leaders, vanquishing many Peguans and gaining 3,000 prisoners. The rest saved themselves by flight and returned to Pegu where they brought their king the sad news.

Phra Naret remained in Phitsanulok, on the one hand out of fear of his father, the Siamese king, and on the other land, out of fear that the Peguan king through anger would send another general to destroy and conquer the land. He nourished himself with the hope that he, being there in person, would encourage the inhabitants to resist the Peguan force. The king in Pegu, learning that Phra Naret was residing in Phitsanulok, sent his brother

89. VV: Prae Maehae d Harma Raetsiae; พระมหาธรรมราชา. *LP* assigns his reign to the years C.S. 931–952 (A.D. 1569–1590). *PN* and *RA* assign it to the years C. S. 918–940 (A.D. 1556–1578).

90. Probably Song Khwae, the old name for Phitsanulok.

91. The chronicles say the Peguan king sent Mang Thu, Mang On or Anan, Mang Abara or Achara or Asara, Cò Thang and Saming Phattaboet "to go down to the provincial cities along the way and had them dispense supplies to take care of the troops until they should reach the frontier of the Royal Metropolis of Ayutthaya" (*RCA*: 86, ll. 26–7).

Sarrathij[92] with 10,000 armed soldiers to fight Phra Naret and, if it were feasible, to take him prisoner. Phra Naret and the inhabitants of Phitsanulok and the neighboring provinces were warned of Sarrathij's expedition. The common people became so afraid that they did not dare wait for his arrival but fled together to the city of Ayutthaya; however, they were followed to that city by Sarrathij. When Phra Naret learned that Sarrathij only had a small force with him, he was displeased with the untimely flight of his people. In order to recover from the ignominy and shame suffered by the retreat and to humble the arrogant Peguan, he assembled his forces, attacked Sarrathij at the temple of Wat Mahaphram,[93] routed his people, and seized 2,000 elephants and thirty horses. Sarrathij fled with the survivors to Pegu. But when he arrived there, his brother who had sent him out died, and His Majesty's oldest son, named Maha Uparacha,[94] succeeded in his place. Phra Naret went to the city and gave permission to his people to return to their abandoned homes. This prince was about eighteen years old when he appeared before his father, the Siamese king.

When the Siamese king received his son Phra Naret, he was very upset and saddened. And although His Majesty was informed by his son of the cause of his flight and what had occurred since his departure from Pegu, he was nevertheless not happy. He would gladly have maintained the peace with the Peguan. He pointed out to Phra Naret the needs of the country, the destruction of many places, the poverty of the people, and the small number of his soldiers. But Phra Naret (although young in years) remained undaunted and could not at all understand the peace his father had made with the king of Pegu, namely that Siam would remain a tributary state. He bravely encouraged his father and put forward his reasons, saying that he had enough power and people not only to resist the Peguans but even to win his country and crown.

The king of Pegu was very angry and grieved at the flight of Phra Naret and everything which followed. He sent envoys to Siam and demanded his hostage. His Majesty appeared inclined to agree, but could not persuade his
81 council nor his children, so that the envoys returned without having accomplished their mission. Although the king [of Pegu] reminded him of his promise and of the condition under which he had accepted the Siamese kingdom from his [king of Pegu's] father, and that therefore he should fulfill his duty or otherwise be warred against, the envoys were unsuccessful in obtaining the young prince who had once been held hostage. The king of Pegu, seeing that neither friendly means nor threats were of any avail, called together 70,000 armed soldiers. He appointed three valiant war chiefs as

92. Tharrawaddy? Cf. Wood, *History*, 134.

93. VV: Wad Mae Hae Pram; probably Wat Phra Ram, วัดพระราม.

94. I.e., the crown prince, *uparja*, อุปราช.

heads, who were his father's brother, called Phya Bassein, and two mandarins, Phya Prome and Tharrawaddy,[95] to lead the assembled force to the frontiers of Siam to fight the king and his son Phra Naret. Having received word of the Peguan king's intention and of the approaching army, the Siamese king also prepared for battle, but faintheartedly since there were not many war materials available. This was a result of the former destruction of the Siamese kingdom and because of the few years of peace. However, the young prince would much rather have seen him do otherwise, and urged his father to prepare for the Peguan in order to stop him at the Siamese frontiers, thus sparing the country a second ravaging or total destruction. The prince, however, was not able to accomplish his purpose, while the king of Pegu prepared for battle with the Siamese king. The Peguan army went unhindered through the entire country, ravaging and destroying many places once again and essentially left nothing which could be of use for its needs. It besieged the city of Ayutthaya and summoned the Siamese prince Phra Naret to battle. The king and his mandarins did not find it advisable that the prince should leave with his army and do battle; they considered it better that the Peguan force appear before the city of Ayutthaya (which was then newly walled-in and fortified in the Indian fashion) because they might destroy themselves. But the prince could not understand such a thing at all, nor wanted to suffer the shame of having been challenged and provoked by the Peguan field generals. Finally, with the king's consent he gathered his forces and with his people attacked and put the Peguan army to flight. He captured the three war leaders and at the same time captured thirty elephants and 100 horses. Many Peguans were slain, and those who could escape fled to Pegu and brought the news to their king. His Majesty was very upset and grieved over the defeat, but he kept quiet for many years.

Phra Naret gained that great victory when he was about twenty years old. He was held in esteem and honor by everyone. This prince was a war-loving leader and gladly followed up the victory over the Peguan, restoring the Siamese kingdom to its former freedom and reputation. But the king his father considered that he was sufficiently freed from the Peguan yoke. Consequently, he considered it better to keep still and to wage a defensive war against Pegu, because the ravaged lands and cattle in the country would be able to flourish once again and be restored.

When the king in Cambodia learned of the destruction and weakening of the Siamese kingdom, he also wanted to take advantage of the situation. He sent a certain number of people to the province of Nakhon Ratchasima[96] (bordering on Cambodia) and yearly went raiding on the Siamese river with

95. VV: Phia Praem ende Sarrathij; unidentified. Cf. Wood, *History*, 134, the references there in the context of an invasion of 1584.

96. VV: Corrassima, which is known as either Khorat or Nakhon Ratchasima.

a small boat. Great damage was done, and many Siamese prisoners from Bangkok and the surrounding areas were taken to Cambodia.

81v The king in Siam, unwilling to tolerate the wrongs perpetrated by the Cambodians any longer, assembled a large army, not only to stop the king in Cambodia but also to conquer his country and make it subject as in the past. After having appointed his son Phra Naret as Commander-in-Chief, he sent the assembled force under capable war leaders overland to Cambodia, intending that Phra Naret would follow in a few days with the rearguard. After he had done this, the Siamese king received news that Maha Uparacha, king of Pegu, was en route with his entire force to besiege the city of Ayutthaya. Among his Peguan soldiers were all the Portuguese, Moors, and Turks who were then in Pegu.

As a result Phra Naret had to cancel his planned expedition, occupy the frontiers which bordered Cambodia, and call back his vanguard in order to offer resistance to [the] Uparacha.

The king of Pegu appeared with a mighty army before the city of Ayutthaya. Phra Naret arrived with the Siamese army at a certain ruined temple (the remains of which are still visible today) called Crengh or Nong Sarai[97] to meet the Peguans. As soon as the armies appeared opposite each other, Phra Naret and Uparacha (each clad with royal garments and sitting on war elephants) caught sight of each other and were so aroused that they both left their armies and rode without their troops toward one another as if they had gone mad. But the elephant on which Phra Naret sat was much smaller than that ridden by Uparacha. When the princes approached one another, the smaller elephant was so terrified by the larger animal that he swung his head around trying to retreat. Phra Naret was thoroughly frightened and said to his elephant, "Father of our Country, if you leave me now, you will also be abandoning yourself and your [good] fortune, for I fear that after this you will no longer possess any honor and no prince will ride you. Think, you now have control over two kings and can make me victorious. Look also at our poor people. Think how miserably they will be defeated and scattered if we flee the field. But if we stand fast, through your courage and the strength of our limbs, victory will be ours. And after the victory you will share the honor with me."

While the prince spoke, he sprinkled the head of the elephant three different times with water blessed and consecrated for this occasion by the brahmans. He cried so that his tears rolled over the elephant's trunk. The wise animal was so encouraged by the words and the water and tears of the brave prince that he raised his trunk, turned his head toward the enemy, and ran as if mad toward the Peguan king. It was frightening and amazing to see

97. Nong Sarai is located in the province of Suphanburi, northwest of the city in Si Phrachan district. VV is the only source apart from the Luang Prasoet chronicle which locates this event here: cf. *RA*, 377–78.

how this animal fought. The larger animal tried continually to force him back with his tusks. Finally, the smaller animal surprised his enemy, went past him a little ways, and then gave him such a terrible blow with his trunk that the larger animal squealed loudly and frightened the Peguan king. The Siamese king seized this opportunity to vanquish the Peguan king by hitting him on the head with his staff (with which he guided the elephant) and stabbing him with his lance until the latter fell to the ground dead. He then captured the elephant. His bodyguards (who followed soon after) stabbed the Portuguese who sat behind the Peguan king to cool him with a fan and to guide the elephant. When the Peguan army saw that their king had fallen, they quickly retreated in confusion and were pursued with great courage by the Siamese. Many were taken prisoner and many were slain and scattered like chaff in the wind. Several thousands were left behind, and since they had 82
to retreat through ravaged areas, very few returned to Pegu.

Phra Naret achieved this great victory when he was thirty-two years old and thus prevented the vassalage of his father's kingdom. Since then the Siamese kings have never been subject to any other prince of this world. After the victory over Maha Uparacha and the Peguan army, the Siamese king assembled his forces and sent a sizeable number of soldiers to Cambodia under the leadership of the Okyas Chakri and Kalahom to be followed by his son Phra Naret and the rearguard. Arriving at the borders of Cambodia, Chakri let no opportunity slip by to seize a place, thus thinking to do a great service for his king and his prince.

When Phra Naret appeared there, he became enraged at Chakri's action and had him skinned alive, saying, "The king, my father, and I have sent you here, but not in order that you might do battle and place our forces in danger. You have tried to compete with me for favor so that when we return victorious, you and I would both be conquerors. That is why you must die."

Phra Naret continued on with his force destroying many places in Cambodia and finally conquering its king. He made the king of Cambodia and all of his children prisoner, but he let the oldest son remain in Cambodia to govern the land with the promise that he would never rebel but would remain the subject of the Siamese crown. After having done this, Phra Naret returned to Siam and brought back the vanquished king and three of his children as prisoners.

The Siamese king held the conquered king and his three children prisoner for only a short time. With the approval of his son Phra Naret, the Siamese king finally restored the Cambodian king to his former position and sent him back once again to Cambodia under the following conditions: that his sons remain as hostages, and that he should do homage yearly to the Siamese majesty.

Shortly after the Siamese king Phra Mahathammaracha Phra Chao Song Queen had freed his kingdom from the Peguan yoke, brought the rebellious Cambodian king to obedience, and restored peace in his land, His Majesty left this world. He was king in Siam for twenty-two years and died at the age of seventy-six years.

PHRA NARET RACHATHIRAT, TWENTIETH KING OF SIAM, RULED TWENTY YEARS.[98]

After the death of the aforementioned king, the mandarins beseeched Phra Naret to accept the crown and the control of the kingdom. They put forward the arguments that, in addition to his services, he was the oldest son during his father's rule and was *fai na*, or first prince and closest heir.[99] But Phra Naret did not want to accept the crown and said that he had shed too much blood and would be too severe in his rule. Therefore, he wanted his brother Phra Anut,[100] who was *fai lang*,[101] or second prince, to be crowned king. Phra Anut and the mandarins well understood that Phra Naret had raised these objections to test them and that anyone who showed an inclination toward this suggestion would place his life in danger; therefore, they all persisted in their original proposal. Phra Naret compared his late father's mercy to his own extreme attitude. But the more he raised his objections, the less the mandarins dared select his brother, the *fai lang*, as king. Phra Naret said
82v finally, "Do you then really want me as your king?" His brother and the mandarins answered together, "Be our king; we will be as slaves to Your Majesty (as is proper)." Phra Naret replied, "Then I want all of you to obey me, fulfill the laws of the land, and maintain them unbroken. Anyone who commits the least transgression shall be prosecuted." He ordered the royal boats to be made ready and the mandarins to go by boat with him to the Phaniat (the place where the elephants are kept and the kings are crowned) in order to proclaim him king and swear their oaths of allegiance to him.

On arrival at Phaniat, Phra Naret's rowers made an error in the process of landing, which he left unpunished at that time. He was crowned with the proper solemnities when he was thirty-five years old and was called Phra Naret Rachathirat. After having been crowned, he had all the rowers in his boat, as well as those in the other royal boats (about 1600 men), burnt alive in that same place. He told his mandarins that he wanted them to remember this as an example of his rule and then returned to court.

98. VV: Prae Naerith Raetsia Thieraij; พระนเรศวรวรราชาธิราช. This reign is commonly assigned to the years A.D. 1590–1605.

99. ฝ่ายหน้า, i.e., the prince of the "front" palace, the usual residence of the designated heir to the throne. See Wales, *Ancient Siamese Government* 26–27, 29–32.

100. I.e., *anucha* (อนุชา), "younger brother," in this case the prince who was to succeed Naresuan. See f° 84, below p. 233, where the full form of his name is given as Anuchathirat Phra Ramesuan, อนุชาธิราชพระราเมศวร.

101. ฝ่ายหลัง; i.e., the prince of the "rear" palace. See Wales, *Ancient Siamese Government*, 27, 29–32.

Phra Naret Rachathirat was called "Raja Api"[102] by the Malays and the "Black King" by the Siamese. His reign was the most militant and severe of any that was ever known in Siam. Many stories and living eyewitnesses report that in the twenty years of his rule he killed and had killed by law more than 80,000 people, excluding those who were victims of war. Whether on an elephant, on horseback, in a perahu, or even on his throne in a meeting with his mandarins, he was never without a weapon. He always had a quiver resting on his lap and a bow in hand. When he saw someone who did the least thing which did not please him, he shot an arrow at the offender and asked that person to bring the arrow to him. He often had pieces of flesh sliced off from those (even among mandarins) who committed the smallest mistakes and had them eat their flesh before his very eyes. He made others eat their own feces. He always said, "This is the way you Siamese must be ruled because you are obstinate people of abominable nature and in a rotten state. But I shall do these things to you until I make you a respected nation. You are as the grass on the fertile field: the shorter you are mowed, the more beautifully you grow. I will have gold strewn in the streets and let it lie there for months. Whoever looks at this gold with greed will die."

Sometimes at night and at odd hours be would go with a small perahu and row up and down the river. He also went at odd hours with a small company along the streets to hear which rumors were about and to learn whether something would be advantageous or disadvantageous to him. He was the first to make the mandarins come creeping before the king and lie continually with their faces downward, a practice which is still in existence today. However, he did not want this humility from strangers or foreigners. He was fond of foreigners, especially the Dutch. He was the first Siamese king to send envoys and letters to Maurice, Prince of Orange, in The Netherlands.[103] Whenever he held audience for foreign envoys, he did not want them to alter their national customs and follow the slavishness of the Siamese. He said, "You are the representatives who have been sent to me by my brothers. Therefore, I

102. I.e., the "fire king."

103. On the opening of these relations, see W. Blankwaardt, "Notes upon the Relations between Holland and Siam," *JSS*, 20, 3 (1927): 245–46; reprinted in *Selected Articles*, VII, 18. George Vinal Smith (personal communication, 5 October 1973) informs me that "Van Vliet must be mistaken in saying that King Naresuan sent the first envoys and letters to Maurice. Possibly he intended to, but he died in 1605, long before the ambassadors left Ayutthaya. The first mention of the intention to send ambassadors appears in a January 6, 1606 entry in Van Warwÿck's journal – this information coming from Speck (Specx) who was still in Ayutthaya with Lambert Jacobsz Heÿn from 1604 – but by then Ekathotsarot already had become king. In any case, Specx, Heÿn and the ambassadors left Ayutthaya in 1607, as they did not arrive in Pattani until Oct. 4, 1607 (K.A, 966, Letter, L.J. Heÿn, Pattani, to Bewinthebberen, Feb.3, 1608)."

do not wish that you pay me any more honor nor show me more reverence than that which you are accustomed to giving to your rulers."

He asked the envoys if they knew the Siamese, Peguan, and brahman languages, and if they did, they had to speak to him directly. If they could not, he ordered one of the mandarins to serve as interpreter so he could speak with the envoys. He threatened to kill the interpreters if they changed the sentence or did not give a proper rendering. The foreigners at this time
83 were treated with such respect that the officers brought them gifts so that the foreigners would not bring any complaints against them to the king. The mandarins lived in great fear of His Majesty. When they were summoned, they put their homes in order as if they were going to their deaths, for they were always full of dread that they would not return.

Many memorable things are told about this king, but they will not be mentioned here to avoid going on too long. Although brevity has been promised, another thing must be added. One evening when His Majesty was on a perahu in the river, he was caught in a great rainstorm before he was able to return to the palace. Consequently, he went to a small house where an poor old woman lived and entered unrecognized with great commotion. The woman was very frightened and said, "My son, don't you know, that our king is often close by?" In reply His Majesty said vehemently, "Mother, and so what if he should hear it? What would it matter if he kills me. That would be my misfortune which strikes many people unexpectedly." The woman fell at his feet and pleaded dejectedly that he not speak of the king in such a way. She said, "The gods have provided us with His Majesty; therefore, he never does things which are bad. He is an avenger of the gods and the implementer of their sentences against our evil. We must obey those who have been placed here to rule us."

The more the woman tried to silence the king with such reasons, the more vehemently His Majesty bellowed. Finally, the woman asked that he leave her house because she did not want to become a party to his misdeeds. The king said that he would, but first demanded a drink of *arak*[104] because he had become cold from the rain. The woman answered, "Son, you know of course that this is the fast and that as long as it lasts, no one may buy or drink *arak*. But if you want dry clothes such as those I am wearing, I will give them to you. I will wash and dry what you have on. In the meantime go rest and sleep a little."

The king accepted the clothes offered to him, had his clothes washed and dried, but would not desist from his wish for *arak*. He said that he did not want to be bound by the strict laws of the king. Finally, the woman filled a tiny little jug with *arak*. She swore that she had bought the *arak* before the start of the fast and had not drunk any of it since then. She offered it to the king and made him promise that he would not report her to anyone. After he

104. A fermented alcoholic drink, which here could refer to either palm wine or rice wine. (Note by Andaya)

had drunk, the woman led him to her little mat to sleep while she dried his washed clothes. When the king awoke, he put on his dried clothes, thanked the woman, and said his farewells. The woman said, "Son, remain here until daylight or go home with your boat quietly so that you do not make too much noise for the king and have something evil befall you."

His Majesty answered, "I will do that," and left the old woman and her poor little house. He then returned with his little perahu to his bodyguards, who were waiting with their perahus not far from that little house.

The next day His Majesty sent a royal ceremonial perahu (on which was a small pyramidal house) to the poor woman's simple little house where he had lodged at night. This was the same perahu and the same little house that carried the king's mother or first wife on great feast days. Besides this, the clothes which Their Majesties had worn were also on board. He instructed his servants that after presenting these clothes to the old woman, they were to conduct her with the royal perahu to court and bring her before him. When the old woman saw the royal servants coming towards her, she became frightened and started trembling, thinking that His Majesty had heard what 83v
had happened in her home that night. Although these servants reported why they had been sent, the woman could not believe that she would remain unharmed. Furthermore, out of fear she beseeched the servants in a pitiful manner to tell the king that she had died. Meanwhile she wanted to save her life by fleeing to the monks. The servants, however, paid no heed to the woman. Since she did not want to go willingly, they respectfully seized her, clothed her, brought her on the perahu to court, and then presented her to the king. When His Majesty saw the woman, he took her by the hand and told her that he was the person who had lodged and been cared for at her little house that night. "And because in time of need you accepted me for your son," said the king, "henceforth I will call you Mother and love you for this."

His Majesty ordered a place for the old woman in the palace, and had her served and cared for till the end of her days as if she had been his own mother. At her death she was also cremated as a queen.

As has been said before, the king Phra Naret Rachathirat was a warlike hero. His Majesty also had many conquests and gained many victories, which will be mentioned generally to avoid being too lengthy. In the thirty-seventh year of his life and during the second year of his reign, he gathered a large army and went to Pegu. He conquered and destroyed many places, plundering over a wide area throughout the country and carrying away many treasures and prisoners from that kingdom. From there His Majesty went to Ava, where he also demonstrated his power by defeating and destroying many places and plundering the large city of Hongha.[105] He carried away that powerful king and brought away many treasures and people. On his return from Pegu and

105. This may be a confused reference to the old name for Pegu, Hongsa. See also note 106.

Ava, he warred with the kingdoms of Müang Hang,[106] which bordered on Pegu. He besieged Thongh Houw, at that time a large and famous city.[107] He swore that he would be victorious and that the city would fall into his hands within a few days. Through lack of rice and other necessities, however, he had to break the siege and leave the city. On the way from Thongh Houw, the king swore an oath that he would not enter the city of Ayutthaya until he had conquered and entered Thongh Houw.

Meanwhile, the king learned that the Cambodian king was once again rebelling, despite his having left three sons in Siam as hostages. He went there with his army, but when the Cambodian king was warned of the king of Siam's approach, he went personally to His Majesty and voluntarily surrendered himself and his country. His Majesty made peace with him on the condition that the latter send gold and silver flowers yearly to His Majesty in the city of Ayutthaya in Siam and arrange to have other hostages sent at the death of his children. From Cambodia the king continued on to Champa, where he conquered many places and forced the king to make his kingdom a tributary state of the Siamese crown.[108]

On his return from Champa the king warred with and conquered the kingdom of Lan Chang,[109] Chiang Mai, as well as many places in Müang Hang and the independent highland cities of Chiang Mai,[110] Lakhon [Lampang], Lao, and Kreng.[111] After that His Majesty departed from that region with his army and arrived at the city of Ayutthaya. But since he had sworn an oath (as was mentioned above), he did not enter the city. After spending a short time at various places in the vicinity, he left with his army for Tenasserim (which was then in rebellion against him), conquered that city, and again bound it to the Siamese kingdom. After that the king remained a long time in Phetchaburi and the surrounding areas. In the last year of his life he left once again with his army to go to Müang Hang in order to fight the city of Thong Houw. On his arrival there, His Majesty became ill and died shortly thereafter at the age of fifty-five. He was king for twenty years but did not reside more than two years in the city or Ayutthaya. The rest of the eighteen years was spent in war in the abovementioned places. The period of his reign was a prosperous and blessed one.

106. This and the preceding seem to refer to Naresuan's campaigns in Pegu and the Moulmein-Tenasserim littoral in 1593 and 1600.

107. I.e.. Toungoo, attacked in the campaign of 1600 but not conquered.

108. *RA* (182) states that the king and his forces returned directly from the capture of the Cambodian capital in 1594.

109. By this time, the capital of Lan Chang had been moved to Vientiane.

110. Chiang Mai here is rendered with two different spellings: Jangoma and Tsieengh Maeij.

111. Probably a reference to the Karens.

Before his death the king wanted his older brother (who was in the wars
with him) to swear that he would not leave Thong Hauw until he had
conquered it, and that his body would not be burnt; instead, at the conquest 84
of Thong Hauw, his body was to be bound to the head of his elephant, which would then be led through the city of Thong Hauw in order that his promise might still be fulfilled after his death. However, the king's brother was so little bound by the oath (which he should have carried out) that as soon as His Majesty was laid to rest, he disbanded the army and came with the entire force to the city of Ayutthaya. He brought with him the dead body of the king, which was burnt in a royal manner according to the custom of the land.

Many countries and cities which the king conquered and seized remained in subjection till the end of his life, such as Cambodia, Champa, various cities in Muang Hang, Lan Chang, Chiang Mai, the cities Chiang Mai,[112] Lakhon, Lao, and Kreng. But because no occupation or military force was left in these places (as in the European manner), these places broke away from the Siamese kingdom after His Majesty's death and were never again brought back to obedience, except for the cities Lakhon and Lao, as will be seen in what follows.

PHRA ANUCHATHIRAT PHRA RAMESUAN, TWENTY-FIRST KING OF SIAM, RULED FOR SIX YEARS.[113]

The brother of Phra Naret Rachathirat became king when he was forty-five years old. He was called Phra Anuchathirat Phra Ramesuan. In view of the severe rule of the former king, the new ruler was a good king of great wisdom and judgment, but not warlike. In his lifetime he carried out neither offensive nor defensive wars, although both possibilities arose on different occasions. These were due to the many princes and potentates who had been brought under Siamese domination through the warlike arms of his brother but who had now broken away (as was mentioned above). Furthermore, he was not devout, only slightly fond of the monks, but he conducted himself in a moderate fashion. His Majesty found great pleasure in going on the hunt, going horseback riding, fighting on elephants, and took delight in sailing from one place to another, etc. He was greatly inclined toward strangers and foreign nations. In order to attract them to him, he introduced the ordinances established by Phra Chao Ramathibodi to which the officers who served the foreigners (such as the Phrakhlang and his subordinates) had to conform; in

112. See note 110 above.

113. VV: Prae Anoet Tsiae Thieraij Praerha Mij Zoon; i.e. พระอนุชาธิราช พระราเมศวร. This king, usually referred to as Ekathotsarot, is considered to have ruled from 1605 to 1610 (ขจร สุขพานิช, "สอบศักราชปีรัชกาลสมเด็จพระเอกาทศรถ," *ศิลปากร* 11:2, July 2510, 76). *RA* assigns his reign to the years C.S. 955–963 (A.D. 1593/94–1601/02).

short, he lightened many burdens, and renewed the abovementioned order. He had many royal qualities but was more covetous than any of his predecessors. He was concerned solely with ways of enriching his treasury. Toward this end he introduced many oppressive laws. He demanded that all subject lands and cities under the Siamese crown list their slaves. After that he had the people counted in all of these places (except for the principality of Pattani, which did not wish to undergo such a thing). If someone possessed more slaves than he reported, these unreported slaves were given to the king so that His Majesty acquired many slaves, which make up a large part of Siamese wealth, splendor, and fame. He had the fruit trees counted everywhere in his kingdom: palms, pinang, rose apple, pomegranate, lemon, tamarind, tsiampacke [?], durian, mango, mangosteen, jackfruit, etc., and placed a tax on each of them. Thus their owners had to deliver a *fuang*, a Siamese coin worth 3¾ *stuivers*, yearly to his treasury officers or tax collectors, which amounted to a large sum when brought from all over the country. He also introduced a practice in which whenever a mandarin (at least those who received their court titles or signs of honor from the king) died, his possessions went to His Majesty. His Majesty also divided all those born and settled in his country (even though they were not slaves) under heads (called *nai* in Siamese) like district masters. The result of this was great subjection and slavery, because no one since has been free of servitude and has always been under the obedience of his *nai*. Whatever the *nai* commands them to do must be carried out or be staved off with gifts. The latter practice enables the nobles to often enjoy great profit while it burdens the commoner and the
84v poor. Whenever the kings undertake to build or repair things, every chief mandarin, such as the Okyas Awang,[114] Phitsanulok, Phonlathep,[115] Phrakhlang, etc., must contribute funds on account of their offices. What is contributed rarely comes from their own personal treasury, but from their subordinates, who are delegated to collect as much as they can. For example, the Phrakhlang has sixty-four council members and lesser officials (called in Siamese *Yaeu penningh-ans)*.[116] Whenever His Lordship has to contribute funds or provide assistance, even if it were the building of houses, *balais*,[117] *perahus*, etc., the *Yaeu penningh-ans* must contribute their quota and offer a helping hand. This is also the case with regard to all mandarins and *nais* or district masters. The sweat of the poor and the foreigners is necessary so that the kings or nobles can be remembered for building or repairing magnificent edifices. That is a major reason that the foreigners are extremely annoyed. Every one pinches and pares, plucks and fleeces wherever possible. He who

114. I.e., ออกญาวัง, head of the Department of the Palace or Royal Household.
115. I.e., พลเทพ, head of the Department of Fields, or Agriculture.
116. Perhaps -อยู่เป็นนิ่งอัน, i.e., "those who are silently present"?
117. In Malay, a *balai* is a reception hall. (Note by Andaya)

knows anything about the Siamese government would not be surprised at this, since its laws are based on it and everything legitimized by it. The burdensome customs introduced by this king not only continue to the present but become more burdensome daily. However, to come to an end, we will break it off here. His Majesty ruled six years and died when he was fifty-one years old. There was never a prosperous time in his reign, and it was, on the contrary, a period of continued trouble.[118]

PHRA INTHARACHA, TWENTY-SECOND KING OF SIAM, RULED NINETEEN YEARS.[119]

Son of the late king, he succeeded his father in the kingdom. He was called Phra Intharacha. This king was wise, very merciful, and generous by nature. He was not warlike, but very studious, devout, fought continually against idolatry, improved the religion and laws of the land, and shared many good things with the poor and the monks. He built and repaired more temples, pyramids, and living quarters for the monks than any of his predecessors as far as it is known. He willingly saw to it that his mandarins were well dressed and had good houses. Toward this end he had various houses built for his factors who were still present there. His Majesty was considered so holy that the Siamese claimed that he had no enemies in the world nor could he acquire any. The contrary, however, appeared to be the case, for His Majesty was seized in his palace by the Japanese living in Siam. These desperate villains would not free him until he offered them many benefits and swore that he would never retaliate for their wicked deed. He was strongly inclined toward foreigners, especially the Dutch, but became an enemy of the Spaniards because of the hostile acts of Don Fernando de Silva,[120] who, it is said, was thrown into the Siamese river.

118. Note that VV here makes no mention of the "phantom" king Phra Si Saowaphak, who is thought to have reigned for one year and two months in 1610–1611: see ขจร, *loc. cit.*; cf. *RA*, 221. On the basis of Dutch and English archival evidence nearly contemporary with the events concerned, George V. Smith (personal communications, October 5, 1973 and April 29, 1974) argues (a) that King Ekathotsarot was still alive on Oct. 5, 1610; (b) that King Songtham succeeded to the throne prior to Nov. 19, 1611; and (c) two English sources give 1610 as the date of King Ekathotsarot's death. None of these sources mentions King Saowaphak.

119. VV: Prae In Terrae tSiae (อินทราชา); i.e., King Songtham, whose reign, according to ขจร, extended from 1611 to 1628. Cf. *RA*, 221, 423–425, where his dates are given as C.S. 964–989 (A.D. 1602/3–1627/28). Van Vliet's own *Historiael Verhael* (1958): 18–19, dates his death on December 12, 1628, after a reign of nine years (according to the French version) or nineteen years (according to the Dutch version).

120. Don Fernando de Silva was the captain of a Spanish yacht from the Philippines. In August 1624, the Dutch ship the "Cleen Zeelant" (or Cleijn Zeelandt) arrived in

His Majesty built the first warships and galleys in Siam, which were unknown before his rule. He conducted two difficult wars against Lan Chang and Cambodia, but unfortunately after several defeats he made peace with the king of Lan Chang and went with two powerful armies to Cambodia. He sent one by water and went with the other by land. After his armada had been in the Cambodian river for some time, it withdrew without having accomplished anything. Now that the fleet had retired, the Cambodians were able to prepare an ambush for the army coming by land. They lured the Siamese with false guides, attacked the army, and put it to flight. His Majesty lost his brother and four of five [thousand] men. The king of Cambodia captured 450 horses, 250 live elephants, and 700 prisoners.

During his lifetime the Siamese king had three white elephants, of which two were born in his reign. About a year before the death of the king, His Majesty had gone to the Phaniat to capture elephants. After he had been sitting there for a short time, a white elephant of amazing appearance came walking into the theater of its own accord. Its right tusk was close to its chin and the other reached about halfway down its chest, which was completely swollen; the tail was cut off at the base and there was a black spot on the elephant's coccyx. Among the mandarins was a Siamese Peguan named Okphra Krit,[121] who began to weep when he saw the elephant coming in. When he was asked why he wept, he said, "That animal has a strange shape, and conveys a peculiar feeling of foreboding." In secret he told Okluang Chut[122] (then Shahbandar of the Moors), "Because the right tusk is completely gone, our king will soon die. Because the left tusk has no point, but looks like a tooth, all the valiant war commanders and upright mandarins will be snatched away in the prime of life, and the country will be without war leaders or capable mandarins. Because the elephant has a black spot, a person shall become king who is more lowly and more wicked than the one we have now. He will rule in neither a majestic manner nor a decent one. As regards the shortened tail, the mandarins will be like the king in character. Concerning the misshapen chest, the following king and mandarins will appear outwardly beautiful, but be full of deception and will bring displeasure to all because of their bad

---

the Chao Phrya River from Batavia. At that time the Spanish yacht was also in the river, and because the Dutch and the Spanish were then at war, de Silva attacked and captured the "Cleen Zeelant." King Songtham was enraged that the Spanish had violated the neutrality of his river. He raised his own naval might (after diplomacy failed) and attacked and took the Spanish yacht. Both sides suffered losses; the king returned the "Cleen Zeelant" to the Dutch (but not the goods, until many years later) and imprisoned the Spanish. This episode seems to mark the beginning of the Ayutthaya-Spanish conflict that lasted well into the 1630's (G. V. Smith).

121. VV: Oprae Kridt: unidentified.

122. VV: Oloangh tsiut; probably ออกหลวงจุฬาราชมนตรี who usually held this position.

government, changed actions, and greediness. The captive elephant, it is said, was taken as a tamed elephant, but died on the 16th day of its capture. It was buried in a poor grave by the followers of the Okya Kamphaeng Kalahom Yommarat[123] and Khun Kamphaeng (Lieutenant-Colonel of the Cavalry). All those who put this monstrous animal into the ground died a miserable death shortly afterwards.

The very same year the king became ill. During his illness, His Majesty asked the advice of his mandarins as to who should succeed him after his death: his brother or his oldest son. Some felt that in conformity with the laws of the land, the brother; others said that the son should become king. Some left it to the strong will of the king, saying, "Both princes are capable, and we will obey whomever His Majesty wishes to present this dignity to and serve him as his slaves." The king resolved it by himself and made a will in which his son would inherit the crown and succeed him. He did not, however, make his decision known publicly.

The king's sickness became so bad that His Majesty was overcome and reached the end of his days. He was thirty-six years old and was king for nineteen years. During His Majesty's rule, there were never difficult, but always prosperous times.

PHRA-ONG CHETTHARACHA, TWENTY-THIRD KING OF SIAM, REIGNED EIGHT MONTHS.[124]

The son became king (against the laws of the land) when he was fifteen years old. He was named Phra-ong Chettharacha. He was a prince of extreme behavior and of a hard nature; it was feared that he would govern strictly. He was uncaring, lustful, showed himself to be inconsiderate, and devoted more attention to his own pleasures than to the governing of the kingdom.

The brother of the late king (or uncle of the young king)[125] was the rightful heir to the throne, but having been denied it, he abandoned the secular world and donned religious robes. He did this principally to spare his life, which had been threatened. However, His Highness closely observed the character and activities of the young king. He also understood why the mandarins and the community disliked His Majesty. When the opportunity presented itself, he abandoned his monkly duties, went to Bangkok, secretly gathered as many

123. VV: Oya Caphijn Calahom Jumerat en[de] Con-Caphijn. A confused title, suggesting that its holder, ออกญากำแพง, was acting head of both the Kalahom and the Department of the Capital (กรมเมือง, the head of which usually bore the title of ยมราช).

124. VV: Prae Ongh Tsit Terrae Tsiae; พระองค์เชษฐาธิราช or เชษฐราชา. ขจร, *loc. cit.*, assigns him a reign period of eight months in 1628–29. Cf. *RA*, 425–27; and *Historael Verhael*, 20 ff., and Giles' translation in *Selected Articles*, VII, 36 ff.

125. Concerning this prince, Si Sin, see Wood, *Ancient Siamese Government*, 173–75.

people as he could, and opposed the king. When His Majesty learned of his uncle's intentions, he gathered a powerful army together with the Japanese soldiers and sent Okya Kalahom and Okya Thun[126] (Lieutenant-Colonel of the Japanese) to fight the prince. Learning that the Japanese and the king's army were coming to do battle with him, the prince dared not wait in Bangkok, but fled to Phetchaburi. The Okyas Kalahom and Thun followed His
85v Highness, put his people to flight, and took him prisoner. The king was happy to learn of the defeat and capture of the prince; nevertheless, after deliberating, His Majesty decided not to kill His Highness, but to let him die by lessening his food daily. He left him to this fate in Phetchaburi.

In order to execute the king's sentence, a deep well was dug in which His Highness was put. Each day he was given less and less food until he became so weak that there was nothing else he could do except wait for his death. But the ecclesiastics liked the prince very much because of his good character and virtue. They dug a pit several rods away from the hole where His Highness was and made something like a mine underground. They came at night, rescued him from the miserable well, put a dead body in his place and clothed it with the prince's clothes. When the guards came to the well in the morning, they thought that the prince in his weak state had died during the evening. They filled the well and went happily to the city of Ayutthaya to bring the news to the king. The monks nursed the prince back to health, and when His Highness was well and restored to health, he had the news spread that he was still alive, miraculously rescued from death. He felt that this would be considered a miracle and that he would therefore acquire a large number of followers. But his hopes were dashed. When the king learned that the prince was still alive and had gathered a reasonable force, he again sent the Okyas Kalahom and Thun with an adequate number of soldiers and Japanese to Phetchaburi. These Okyas routed the prince's forces, took His Highness prisoner and brought him to the city of Ayutthaya, where the king sentenced the prince to death. His Highness said that he was resolved to die, but he asked that he might speak to the king once. This was granted. When the prince appeared before His Majesty, he gave the king much memorable, pithy advice and in closing said that the king should not trust the Okya Kalahom too much, nor should give him too much power. He added, "The Kalahom will be as cunning as a fox in seizing the crown from your head, in putting an end to your life as well as those belonging to your father's house, and in dominating the kingdom like a lion." However, the young king paid no heed and commanded that the execution be carried out. The prince was brought to the miserable graveyard where he was made to lie on a red carpet. He was then hit on the chest by a piece of sandalwood, and he, as well as the sandalwood club and the carpet, was thrown into a well. He was twenty-six

126. I.e., Okya Senaphimuk. Cf. Van Vliet's more detailed account of this episode in the *Historical Account* (see pp. 267–69).

years of age and a prince of great stature. If His Highness had gained the crown, he would have surpassed his brother in many of the cardinal virtues.

Having defeated and killed that laudable prince, his lawful uncle, the king became yet more careless, proud, [and] vain, in addition to being tyrannical and arrogant toward his mandarins, thus causing great aversion toward him. The Okya Kalahom, on the other hand, treated everyone with friendship. Then the Kalahom's brother died. In order to cremate the body with great pomp, the Kalahom invited many mandarins, who accompanied him for several days in order to make the funeral celebrations complete. One day the king sat on his throne and asked, "Where are all the mandarins and why don't they come to court? They haven't been to court now for some days." When His Majesty was told in answer that the mandarins were accompanying the Okya Kalahom in the cremation of his brother's body, the king became angry and said, "I intended the Siamese kingdom to have one king and that office would be mine. Is the Kalahom the second king? I never knew that. But let him and his followers come to court, and I will have them enjoy the fruits of their service."

One of the mandarins present secretly left the court and went to the Okya Kalahom to warn him of the grave danger that they all faced from the king.
The Kalahom appeared to be very disturbed by the news and said he preferred 86
to die and placate His Majesty's anger with his blood but added, "If I, the most notable of all of you, die, what then will become of you?" After the mandarins had put forth various proposals, they swore to support the Kalahom in everything. They resolved that the Kalahom should strengthen himself with the king's army (which was principally in his hands) and that each of them would join it with his slaves and subjects. Having done this, they separated and returned home resolved to carry out their plans. In the evening the Kalahom appeared with a sizable number of soldiers at the Deer Gate[127] of the city. The mandarins joined him and went together to the king's palace, stormed it, and conquered it. When His Majesty learned what had occurred, he jumped onto a fleet-footed elephant alone without any followers, swam it across the river, and fled seven miles above the city to a ruined temple where he remained.

When Okya Kalahom learned whence the king had fled, he sent some of his people there to take him prisoner and bring him to the city. Having appeared in the city, the king was sentenced to death by the mandarins on recommendation from the Kalahom. The latter said, "Because you fled from your palace and abandoned the crown and the royal dignity, you do not deserve to rule over us." His Majesty was immediately seized and brought to the place where the prince, his uncle, had been killed and was killed in a similar manner. He ruled eight months.

127. Unidentified.

In the beginning of His Majesty's rule a white elephant was born in the city of Ayutthaya. The soothsayers gave various explanations for this, but the prophecies proved wrong and things happened completely differently.

PHRA-ONG ATHIT SURAWONG, TWENTY-FOURTH KING OF SIAM, RULED THIRTY-EIGHT DAYS.[128]

On the recommendation of the Okya Kalahom, the brother of the king who had been put to death was crowned king with the approval of the mandarins when he was ten years old. He was named Phra-ong Athit Surawong. The Kalahom was placed as guardian and regent of the kingdom because of the minority of the king, but he did not want to accept it. However, he was moved to accept the regency by the pleas of the mandarins, who said that His Grace was a direct descendant of the great and just king and second cousin of the present ruler. Finally, under protest, he accepted the guardianship and was acknowledged and declared such by the royal family.

After the king had been on his throne for several days, the Okya Kalahom wanted to be dismissed from his functions, saying, "When His Majesty comes of age, neither my life nor my position will be assured, because there is a possibility that false friends or denunciators will put my activities in the wrong light and so denigrate my person that I will not be able to avoid the king's wrath." He added that it was not proper that such a powerful kingdom and all of them should be ruled by a king in his minority. For various reasons he considered it better that a provisional king be crowned who would rule the kingdom until the child became of age and was capable of ruling. Furthermore, the crowned king should lay down his crown and deliver it to the rightful heir. In the meantime the child should be placed with the monks to be educated in the virtues. Having considered the Okya Kalahom's proposal, the mandarins could not agree to his dismissal from his duties but crowned him king under such conditions which His Highness himself had previously stipulated. However, he did not want to accept the crown but allowed himself to be persuaded by the pleas and numerous entreaties of both the high and low.

A few days after having accepted the royal office the Okya Kalahom proposed to the mandarins that the sharing of royal dominion could not be tolerated. He said that such limited power would have dangerous consequences, because when the young king reached the highest dignity, he might come to distrust the Okya Kalahom through false advice. The young king would always find cause to reproach him for his government and then he would be in extreme danger. Therefore, he did not want to assume the

128. VV: Prae Ongh Athit Soerae Wongh; i.e., พระองค์อาทิตยสุรวงศ์. ขจร., *loc. cit.*, assigns to him a reign of 38 days in 1629. Cf. *RA*, 427; and Giles, 61–71, where the length of his reign is given as 36 days.

royal crown nor the burdens of government, but wanted to be removed from both of them. The mandarins could not allow any of this, but in order to assure that their lives and positions would be secure and that the kingdom would be properly governed and have one and not two kings, they thought it best to do away with the child. However, the provisional king wanted no such thing, saying that the innocent child had done nothing wrong and hence his blood should not be shed. But through the persistence of the mandarins, he finally consented to have the child condemned in the same manner as his brother, the late king, and his uncle, the lawful king. He had the young king taken from school and brought to the miserable graveyard where he was beaten across the chest with a sandalwood club and thrown into a well with his brother and uncle. He was king for thirty-eight days. 86v

PHRA-ONG SI THAMMARACHATHIRAT, TWENTY-FIFTH KING OF SIAM, HAS BEEN RULING ELEVEN YEARS.[129]

After the death of the young prince, the provisionally crowned king Okya Kalahom (as was mentioned above) was declared sole and absolute king and crowned when he was thirty years old. He was called Phra-ong Si Thammarachathirat. This king and the two murdered kings were close relatives because the father of the two murdered princes and the present king were children of a sister and brother. The mother of the great king and the father of the present king were full sister and brother. However, whether the blood relationship in the reported circumstances was brought into play should be judged by one who knows better. The present king was very majestic in the beginning of his rule and was merciful toward his mandarins and lesser subjects. He was also very considerate; if any complaints came before His Majesty, he did not condemn nor judge the guilty hastily but commissioned the impartial to investigate the disputed matter, with orders that the examiners should not be swayed by the individual on trial but by the gods, the king, and by justice. But debauchery and vainglory so corrupted his former nature and understanding that the more powerful he became on the throne, the quicker he became in passing judgment.

In the beginning of his reign, he waged war against Lakhon [Lampang] (a city bordering Lan Chang and Ligor),[130] which cities had broken away from

129. VV: Prae Onghsrij d'Harmae Raatsiae Thieraija; พระองค์ศรีธรรมราชาธิราช; i.e., King Prasat Thong, whose reign extended from November 1629 to August 1656 (Giles, 113–14).

130. This statement does not make sense as written: Lampang (Lijcoon) does not border Ligor (Lijgoor, Nakhon Si Thammarat); and "cities" in the next phrase requires an earlier plural not in the text. As Prasat Thong also did wage war against Ligor, a fact certainly well known to Van Vliet, we must assume that he misplaced the close of his parentheses, which should follow "Lan Chang".

the crown during the troubles. However, he conquered Lakhon and again bound it to the kingdom. He expelled the Japanese living in Siam who had served him during the usurpation, but he recalled them within a short time. His Majesty also dealt with the Portuguese in a hostile fashion and treated them as if they were prisoners. After that, however, he sent ambassadors to Malacca and letters to Manila to offer peace to the Portuguese and the Spanish. His Majesty was reconciled with the Portuguese but no answer came from Manila. He sent emissaries to the kings of Acheh[131] and Arakan to establish firm peace with their majesties. These kings, especially the king of Acheh, did not oppose it, but it subsequently proved to be a friendship of words without any real substance behind it.[132]

The kingdom of Pattani refused to pay homage, and so in the fifth year of his reign, His Majesty sent a powerful army there. His armies, however, were repulsed. Thus His Majesty had all the war galleys repaired and new ones built in order to attack Pattani once again. But through the mediation of the king of Kedah and Siamese monks, a treaty and a peace finally resulted.[133] In the third year of his reign he had two young princes killed, one seven years and the other five years old, both sons of the great king and brothers of the young murdered king. The mandarins who opposed his plans suffered injuries at his own hands and had their houses and properties pillaged.

In the third year of his reign the golden tower of the Nopphathat suddenly collapsed without a crosswind, thunder, or lightning. He had it quickly erected
87 again, but before this tower was totally restored, the scaffolding (beautifully and durably made of bamboo) also collapsed unexpectedly during a rainstorm. As a consequence, strange omens were seen but were kept secret by the soothsayers.

In the fourth year of his reign the white elephant born during the reign of the young king died. In that same year a round-tailed elephant was born in the environs of the city of Ayutthaya. There are many stories told about the death of the white elephant and the birth of the round-tailed elephant, but these are heathen fables; therefore, I beg to be excused from relating them.

In the seventh year of his reign he had Okya Phitsanulok put to death under some trumped-up charge, despite the fact that the latter had helped him in gaining his royal office and in setting the crown on his head. He survived the 1000th year,[134] which was considered to bring great fortune. In

131. On this, see Hans Georg Penth, "An Account in the Hikayat Atjeh on Relations between Siam and Atjeh," *Felicitation Volumes of Southeast-Asian Studies Presented to Prince Dhaninivat*, (Bangkok. 1965): I, 55–69; and the same author's additional notes on the same subject in *JSS*, 55, 2 (1967): 287–90, and 57, 2 (1969): 355–59.

132. In the Dutch text, *op stroije beenen over ende wedergegaen heeft*, literally, "to go hither and thither on straw legs." (Note by Andaya)

133. See A. Teeuw and D.K. Wyatt, *Hikayat Patani*, I, 16–18; II, 249–53.

134. See O. Frankfurter, "A Proposed Change in the Siamese Era Chulasakaraj 1000 (A.D. 1638)." *T'oung Pao*, 2nd ser., 8 (1907): 99–104.

this year he also renewed the great feast days that had been introduced by the fortune-fated King Phrachao Ramathibodi. This act was held in great respect by the mandarins and the monks.

He was the first who made the mandarins so slavish that they come to court every single day and are allowed to visit each other in their houses or sequestered places but are not permitted to speak to one another except in a public meeting place. It is said that he had the walls of Ayutthaya wholly renovated and the palace and city greatly improved. He has built, renewed, and repaired more temples, towers, and pyramids than any of his predecessors. In order to reach the end of this story, I will note his nature in brief. He is warlike in the Siamese fashion, of great wisdom, eloquent and friendly of speech, very religious and devout, and has great love for the monks and especially the learned. He is a lover of foreign nations, and in order to attract them to him, he has lightened many of their burdens, and improved, renewed, and corrected the ordinances introduced by the eleventh king and continued by the twenty-first king. But he is proud, haughty, glorious, beautiful in his raiments, colorful, and although quick to judge, is quickly transformed from anger to mercy so that few are put to death by the law. He is inclined toward drink and excesses. After he became king, he took his wife's mother and sister for his wives and had children by all three of them. He is more feared than any other king before him. No one dares contradict him, not even the monks who have always been outspoken with previous kings. He is more avaricious than any other former Siamese king. He had temples torn down and their foundations dug up to search for gold and silver. The king called No Phutthangkun introduced the practice that for every ten measured lands which the mandarins owned, they had to pay a tical's weight in gold to His Majesty at their death. The king Phra Anuchathirat Phra Ramesuan introduced the practice in which one-third of the mandarin's personal possessions would go to His Majesty at their death. But this king wants everything. If a mandarin dies, his wives and children are taken into custody. One mandarin will often spy on another in order to discover whether anything is being concealed. Widows and orphans show great gratitide whenever the king extends to them a small section of their properties. It appears that His Majesty cannot consider himself rich until he has gathered all the treasures into his own treasury and has had everything squeezed out of the community.

Previously I mentioned[135] that Phra Chaiyaracha, thirteenth king of Siam, built the temple Phra Chi Chiang, from which place many miraculous things are reported to have occurred. Since these tales are too fabulous, I beg to be excused from relating them. This temple was at one time the largest and the highest of the entire kingdom, but it has been knocked down as a result of lightning and thunderstorms through the years. Many kings undertook to

135. See above, note 68.

87v rebuild this temple, but as soon as work began, they had to abandon it because the foremen and laborers were struck by numerous illnesses and died pitifully. It was also said that the brahmans and the monks have a prophecy that this temple can only be repaired by a king who is descended from the pure old family and rightful line of the Siamese kings. A few months ago the ruling king demolished the temple to its very base and had a large copper heathen image which was located there pulled back several rods so that another temple like the last could be built over the image. There are various opinions concerning the redoing of this temple. Many people say that the king will complete this work, and scrupulously give as a reason that His Majesty is like the first founder of the Siamese kingdom in so many ways. This is acceptable, but it is not intended so by the Siamese people since the former builder of the temple ruled the kingdom as a guardian, killed the young king of five years (after the child had ruled five months) and usurped the crown. However, the brahmans say that they have seen in the signs in the heavens, that His Majesty would not complete the newly-begun temple but would die before its completion, principally because the rebuilding was not begun out of pure devotion, but out of His Majesty's hope of finding great treasures in the demolition of the former temple. But what will come of this, only time will tell. The king has now ruled ten years and seven months, but his reign has never seen a prosperous time. On the contrary, it has been troublesome times, and the soothsayers remark that this will continue till the end of his life.

My Lord, there are still many worthwhile things to write about, such as the sickness of the great king, the expelling of the prince, His Majesty's brother, the succession and the death of the young kings, as well as the usurpation of the crown. During my presence here, I have investigated almost all the particulars and have put part of them down on paper.[136] But circumspection prevents me from completing what I have begun. However, permit me to present this to you as a beginning. If I should have the undeserved honor of receiving Your Lordship's pleasure with this my unworthy work, I would industriously put everything in order and compile it succinctly and truthfully. Meanwhile I humbly request that Your Lordship be so kind as to accept this in a kindly manner from he who is and remains,

In Ayutthaya in the Siam Comptoir, 8th February 1640
Under it was written, Your Lordship's humble servant
and was signed, Jeremias van Vliet

136. Undoubtedly what was to become, towards the end of the same year (December 1640), Van Vliet's *Historiael Verhael*: see the Iwao 1958 edition, 190.

HISTORICAL ACCOUNT OF KING PRASAT THONG

1640

Historiael Verhael der Sieckte ende Doot van Pra Interra-Tsia 22en Coninck in Siam, geintituleert Faeij loangh tiaeuwtrongh thantsiangh Pheeuck ofte den grooten rechtvaerdigen Coninc vanden witten Elephant. Item hoe den regherenden Coninck, Pra Ongh srij (wiens titulen zijn Pra tjaum Pra-sathongh Pra Tsiauw tsiangh Peeuck, Pra tjsaeuw tsiangh thongh dengh, Pratjaeuw tsiangh Chobolt, often Coninck van den gouden thoorn, insgelijcx rooden, witten, ende rontgestaerten Elephant) de Croone looslijck geuzurpeert, ende zich selven in verscheijden saecken, nopende de regeringe des Rijcx gedragen heeft.

Historical Account of the Illness and Death of Pra Interra-Tsia, 22nd King of Siam, titled Faeij loangh tiaeuwtrong thantsiangh Pheeuck, or the Great and Just King of the White Elephant, and of how the now reigning King, Pra Ongh Srij (whose titles are Pra tjauw Prasathong Pra Tiauw tsiang Peeuck, Pra tjsaeuw tsiangh thong dengh, Pratjaeuw tsiangh Chobolt, or King of the Golden Throne, as well as of the Red, White, and Round-tailed Elephant), usurped the Throne and of the Manner in which he conducted himself in several matters concerning the Governance of the Kingdom.

Dedicated to the Honorable Anthony van Diemen, Governor-General over the state of the United Netherlands in the East Indies.

TRANSLATED BY

ALFONS VAN DER KRAAN

EDITED AND INTRODUCED BY

DHIRAVAT NA POMBEJRA AND CHRIS BAKER

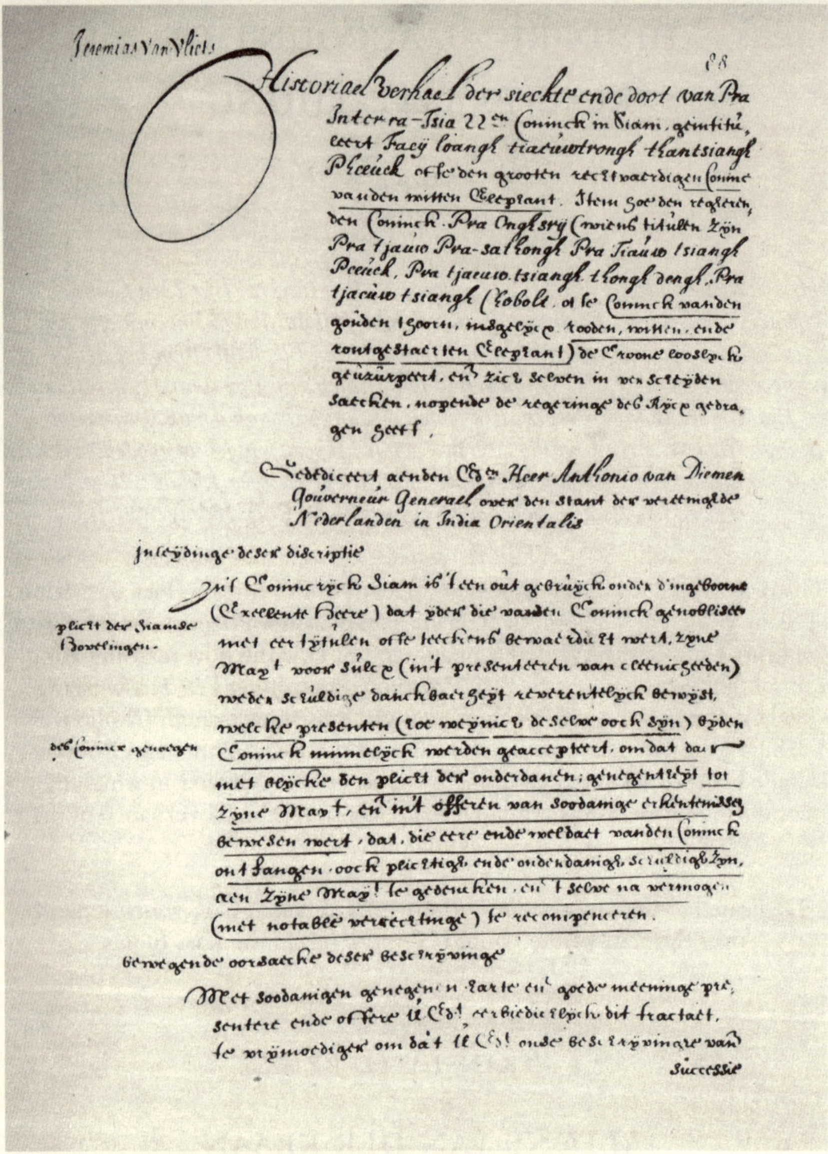

Jeremias van Vliet

88

Historiael Verhael der sieckte ende doot van Pra Interra-Tsia 22en Coninck in Siam, geintituleert Facij loangh tiacuwtrongh thantsiangh Pheuck oft de den grooten rechtvaerdigen Coninc vanden witten Elephant. Item hoe den regeerden Coninck Pra Onghsrij (wiens titulen zijn Pra tjauw Pra-saltongh Pra Tiauw tsiangh Peeuck, Pra tjauw tsiangh thongh deangh, Pra tjauw tsiangh (Robolt) of de Coninck vanden gouden throon, insgelijcx rooden, witten, ende rontgestaerten Elephant) de Croone looselijck geusurpeert, en zich selven in den selfden saecken, nopende de regeringe des Rijcx gedragen heeft.

Gededicteert aenden Ed. Heer Anthonio van Diemen Gouverneur Generael over den staet der vereenighde Nederlanden in India Orientalis

Inleydinge deser discriptie

plicht der Siamse Bovelingen.

Int Coninckrijck Siam is 't een out gebruijck onder d'ingeboorne (Excellente Heere) dat yder die vanden Coninck genobliseert met eertytulen ofte teeckens beweerdiget wert, Zyne Mayt voor sulcx (int presenteeren van eerlnige geeden) weder schuldige danckbaerheyt reverentelijck bewijst, welcke presenten (hoe weynich deselve oock zijn) byden Coninck minnelijck werden geaccepteert, omdat daer met blijcke den plicht der onderdanen; genegentheyt tot

des Coninck genegentheyt

Zyne Mayt, en int offeren van soodanige erkentenisse bewesen wert, dat die eere ende weldaet vanden Coninck ontfangen, oock plichtigh ende onderdanigh schuldigh zyn, aen Zyne Mayt te gedencken, en 't selve na vermogen (met notabele vereeringe) te recompenseren.

bewegende oorsaecke deser beschrijvinge

Met soodanigen genegenen harte en goede meeninge presentere ende offere U Ed. eerbiedelijck dit tractaet, te vrijmoediger om dat U Ed. onder beschrijvinge van successie

First page of the manuscript

INTRODUCTION

Dhiravat na Pombejra and Chris Baker

THE MANUSCRIPT AND NEW TRANSLATION

THE CLOSING DEDICATION of the *Historical Account* reads: "Written at the Netherlands factory in Iudia, capital of the Kingdom of Siam, and concluded on the last day of December 1640." It was probably presented to Antonio van Diemen in Batavia when Van Vliet travelled there in May 1641. A French version, translated by the historian Abraham de Wicquefort, was published in Paris in 1663. Apparently the Dutch version was never published. In 1904, W. H. Mundie, owner of the *Bangkok Times*, translated the French version into English on behalf of Prince Damrong. Mundie's translation was printed as a book in 1904 and reprinted in the *Journal of the Siam Society* of 1938.

Prince Damrong asked Khun Wichitmatra to make a translation into Thai, but only nine pages were completed and printed in 1934. Nantha Woranetiwong translated the whole of Mundie's work, which was distributed at the cremation of Sangat Janthraphai in 1965 as *Jotmaihet wan walit* (The records of Van Vliet), and tagged the "complete version" (*chabap sombun*) to distinguish it from Khun Wichitmatra's fragment. Kachorn Sukhabanij later edited this translation, correcting the names by reference to the Dutch original, and adding notes. This version was distributed at the cremation of Sengiam Banharuanphot in 1965.

In 1934, the Japanese scholar, Seiichi Iwao, discovered the Dutch manuscript in the Royal Archives at The Hague. The manuscript had been bought at auction by the Dutch colonial historian Jhr. M. C. de Jonge in 1843 and deposited in the Archives in 1883. In 1956, Iwao published a facsimile version of the original Dutch manuscript, and in 1958, a transcription of the Dutch side-by-side with a transcription of the French. Iwao noted that the Dutch manuscript was not written in Van Vliet's own hand. He also detected that the French translation (and hence also its descendants, Mundie's English version and Nantha's Thai version) was both incomplete and sometimes inaccurate.

The version presented here is an entirely new translation based on the Dutch manuscript as transcribed by Iwao (1958). It includes all the material omitted by earlier versions and hence is significantly longer (30,000 words compared to 27,800 words in Mundie's English version of Wicquefort). It is also very different in many details.

Wicquefort probably used a different Dutch manuscript from that found by Iwao. Wicquefort's versions of several of the proper names are very different, and would be difficult to derive from the orthography in the Iwao manuscript. Moreover, in several cases the proper names in the Iwao transcription are easier to trace back to a probable Thai origin than those in the Wicquefort version. Hence it seems likely that the Iwao MS is more "original" and that Wicquefort either worked with a copy which had already been shortened, or abridged it himself.

The passages which Wicquefort omitted were generally those not concerned directly with Siam. Mostly these are passages in which Van Vliet draws comparisons between the events in Siam and historical events drawn from classical literature, the Bible, and the recent European history of his day. Many of these are full sections. Some are individual sentences or paragraphs. In one case, in Section 17, he (or the publisher) omitted, probably by mistake, a paragraph which was integral to the narrative.

Iwao added section numbers to aid comparison between the Dutch and French versions. These were not part of the original manuscript, but we have retained them here for ease of reference. Wicquefort/Mundie/Nantha omitted all the section headings, and the following passages:

Section	Material omitted by Wicquefort/Mundie/Nantha
1	(complete)
2	(complete)
3	from "I make this request also..." onwards
4	except the sentence in the first paragraph "If the great and just King..."
7	from "It seems that His Majesty..." onwards
17	(complete)
35	first sentence
36	reference to Pilate in third paragraph
36	last sentence "And so also this King..."
39	sixth paragraph, quotation from Calahom, "Father... befallen you."
39	eighth paragraph "He was treated..." to end of the quoted verse
47	fourth paragraph "This election..." to end of section
48	second and third paragraphs and intervening quote, "Some of the Mandarins... wisdom and prudence"
49	final paragraph of section
50	final paragraph of section from "These cruel execution..." onwards

56	reference to "God's righteous vengeance" in last paragraph
61	reference to God in opening sentence
65	(complete)
66	(complete)

Mundie's English translation of Wicquefort's French was both complete and relatively faithful. But Wicquefort's translation from Dutch to French was not only incomplete but also loose and inaccurate. Some of the mistakes (such as dates) could be the result of errors by copyists and printers. But in some instances, Wicquefort seems to have completely misunderstood the Dutch original. A prime example is Section 59 on the expedition to Lanna. Besides, throughout Wicquefort was intent on conveying more the general sense of Van Vliet's story rather than providing an exact translation. This obscured something of the style in which Van Vliet presented the story. Wicquefort also edited the text in some subtle ways. Most importantly, he seems to have systematically tempered the violence in Van Vliet's account.

In this new translation, Alfons van der Kraan has set out to provide a very complete and accurate rendering of the original which omits nothing and preserves as much as possible of the style of Van Vliet's narration.

Mundie titled his translation "Van Vliet's Historical Account of Siam in the 17th Century." We have changed this, partly to signal the new translation, and partly to more approximate the (long) title of Van Vliet's original.

THE STORY

Van Vliet's *Historical Account* traces the story of the royal succession from the dying days of King Songtham in 1628 to the consolidation of King Prasat Thong in 1629–30, with some notes on the aftermath through the 1630s. This is a summary of the story with the future King Prasat Thong appearing as "P."

> P (first cousin of the King and head of his household) encourages dying King Songtham to nominate his 15-year old son as successor, rather than Songtham's brother Phra Si Sin. P gets support of Yamada, head of the resident Japanese. Songtham dies. Three main supporters of the brother are killed and fence sitters purged.
>
> The son succeeds as Chetthathirat. P becomes Kalahom. P and Yamada conspire to imprison Si Sin, but he escapes and raises revolt in Phetchaburi with the help of a royal relative of supernatural power, Mongkhon. The revolt is defeated by a Yamada ruse. Si Sin predicts P's ambition before he is executed. Mongkhon surrenders and mockingly displays his invulnerability before allowing himself to be killed.

Flashback to P's origins: cousin of Chetthathirat; dissolute youth; severely punished for disrupting First Ploughing Ceremony; almost executed for plotting to kill King's brothers; redeemed himself in war on Cambodia; imprisoned for seducing a Court lady; released and rose to head of royal household.

P purges more noble enemies and announces his ambitions for the throne by performing king-like funeral ceremony for his father. Young King Chetthathirat responds to this provocation. P asks senior mandarins to take sides, winning over two powerful senior aristocrats: the "Moor" Okya Kamphaengphet and the Phrakhlang. P storms the palace. Chetthathirat flees but is captured. He predicts more bloodshed before being executed along with his mother. Another purge.

P blocks Kamphaengphet's ascent to the throne. Yamada blocks P's ascent to the throne. Another Songtham son is crowned as Athittayawong with P as Regent. P now moves against the two remaining senior nobles who have been his allies. He has Kamphaengphet jailed and then executed on the grounds he had openly aspired to the throne. He maneuvers Council to send Yamada to quell a revolt in Ligor.

P becomes Regent and forces the Council to choose between him and the 11-year old King Athittayawong, who is executed. P is crowned. Athittayawong's beautiful mother is executed for refusing to become P's queen. Two female attendants suffer the same fate for showing remorse.

Yamada captures Ligor. P arranges for him to be poisoned. Yamada's son and other Japanese are forced to flee from Ligor.

P now consolidates. He sends armies south to quiet Ligor and Pattani, and north to preempt any further revolt involving Lanna and Burma. He executes five surviving sons of Songtham, drugs a sixth into imbecility, and places the final two sons under house arrest. He sends envoys to Cambodia, Ava, Malacca, and other regional centers to establish his credentials. He executes his last remaining ally, Phrakhlang (now Okya Phitsanulok). He purges other nobles and imposes rules to prevent noble conspiracies. He is an effective ruler.

THE PLOT

This new translation shows how much Wicquefort (and hence Mundie and Nantha) drained the story of its drama. Wicquefort toned down the violence and reduced all the orations to reported speech. But this translation shows how Van Vliet composed the work as a tragedy in the dramatic tradition of his era.

Most of the sections omitted are passages where Van Vliet draws parallels with incidents from classical or more recent history, and cites relevant quotations from the classical repertoire. These references suggest something about the literature which was probably brought for reading on the long ship journeys and kept in the factories. This library seems to have included: the Bible; the classical historians of ancient Greece, Rome, and Persia (probably including Herodotus and Euripedes); Aristotle; Machiavelli; and recent histories of Turkey, Persia, the Spanish conquest of Peru, and elsewhere. These references show Van Vliet's wish to present himself as a Renaissance man of learning. The construction of the story shows Van Vliet's absorption of the dramatic conventions of his day.

The plot opens with the death of a king so good that the scales of fate must now tilt in the other direction. A host of bad omens add to this premonition of bad times. Van Vliet then adds a "fatal flaw" which triggers the subsequent violence: P manipulates the succession against law and convention. In fact, this is Van Vliet's own interpretation (shared by Schouten). There is no evidence that there was any strict succession law in Ayutthaya, and the contest between the former king Songtham's son and brother was absolutely typical of other Ayutthaya successions. Noticeably, Van Vliet does not present any of the Thai characters as championing this idea of a succession "law." It is only himself as narrator, and the Japanese Yamada Nagamasa, who argue for this principle.

The plot then develops through a series of deceptions. Phra Si Sin is tricked into removing his monastic robe so he can be captured. In a double deception, his army at Phetchaburi is persuaded to fight a mock battle, and then double-crossed. In the storming of Chetthathirat's palace, the Phrakhlang pretends to support the King in order to play the Trojan horse role of opening the palace gates from the inside. P tells Kamphaengphet he will be released from jail but instead has him killed. Yamada is tricked into going to Ligor and then poisoned. His followers are then lured into fighting with one another.

The plot is prophesied and punctuated in a series of orations by those on the point of execution. Wicquefort reduced these to reported speech; here they are restored to their properly dramatic role in the plot. The first of these by Phra Si Sin accurately forecasts the outcome: "He [P] will cunningly sneak in, take the crown from your head, and put you to death along with all those who are of the blood of the King, your father, in order to put himself on the throne and rule the Kingdom." The magical royal soldier Mongkhon then dies cursing P as "a murderer of the Prince, a bloodsucker, a spoiler of a flourishing Kingdom, a disturber of the peace." Chetthathirat goes out with the words, "I greatly fear that the murders will not cease and that you will be the scourge of the Kingdom and its people." His mother follows vowing, "I prefer to die with him rather than receive my sustenance from your bloodstained hand." Kamphaengphet dies with a repetition of the prediction: "Your thirst for blood has not been sated because you, yourself, aspire to the crown. You will be like a scythe to the King's children and you will bring ruin to the Kingdom." Athittayawong ends more pathetically with the cry, "Why do I have to be killed? I am not yet eleven years old." And his mother repeats the vow of her predecessor, "Even if I was to keep my life, I would not give my pure body to an upstart bloodhound like you." Phrakhlang/Phitsanulok dies cursing P for his deceptions, "Where are your royal promises, the promises you renewed only recently, and which you have confirmed with the tasting of my blood?"

These orations predict the story that P will litter the stage with royal bodies, and indeed the violence steadily rises in scale and callousness from the first purge through to the systematic elimination of Songtham's remaining descendants. Yet the denouement is very far from a classical tragedy. The bloody rise of Prasat Thong leads not to disaster but a stable reign. In the finale, Van Vliet concludes Prasat Thong "has been a wise, careful, and mighty Prince who has possessed his Kingdom in prosperity and peace."

Van Vliet's political morality is right out of Machiavelli. This was perceptively recognized a long time ago by Sombat Chantornwong (1976). Sombat summarized the plot of the *Historical Account*, adding footnotes with quotations from Machiavelli's *The Prince* and *Discourses* which match the twists in the plot. Van Vliet's debt to Machiavelli becomes much more explicit in this new translation for two reasons. First, this translation includes the references and historical allusions which were omitted from the Wicquefort/Mundie version. Van Vliet cites Machiavelli at one point (Section 48). He also makes repeated use of one of Machiavelli's own favorite historical examples, the story of Antoninus Caracalla (Sections 35, 48, 65). Van Vliet's whole style of historical reference is reminiscent of Machiavelli's own (though that of course is not unique). Second, the Machiavellian morality of Van Vliet is explicit in the final two sections, which were omitted from the Wicquefort/Mundie/Nantha version. Van Vliet's concludes that Prasat Thong "is neither tyrannical nor bloodthirsty, because the judgment has to be made that His Majesty has not condemned anyone to death other than for reasons of state and to secure his Kingdom."

The last phrase is the important part: "for reasons of state and to secure his Kingdom." Machiavelli's *The Prince* prescribed a very specific political morality: princes had to act according to the dictates of statecraft, not the morality of the ordinary man. In the *Historical Account*, characters other than Prasat Thong are condemned by Van Vliet's Protestant morality: the Japanese in Ligor, for instance, die because of "God's righteous vengeance." But the judgment on Prasat Thong is very different. He succeeds, despite his violence, "principally through the unfathomable disposition of the almighty God." The rise of Cesare Borgia, described in Chapter 7 of *The Prince* is reminiscent of Van Vliet's story of Prasat Thong: he makes allies, then turns against them; he uses people, then has them killed; he purges scores of potential enemies. Borgia ultimately failed, but Machiavelli attributed this to bad luck (his father died and Borgia himself fell ill at the crucial moment), and presented Borgia as a model for a rising ruler. Machiavelli explained: "Those who become princes through their skill acquire the principality with difficulty, but they hold on to it easily" (Chapter 6). On the political use of violence, he rationalized:

> Therefore, a prince must not worry about the reproach of cruelty when it is a matter of keeping his subjects united and loyal; for with a very few examples of cruelty he will be more compassionate than those who, out of excessive mercy, permit disorders to continue from which arise murders and plundering; for these usually harm the community at large, while the executions that come from the prince harm particular individuals (Chapter 17).

In keeping with this idea, P all through the plot justifies his actions on the grounds that he is the only person able to impose strong and undivided rule. Machiavelli famously debated whether it was better for a ruler to be feared or loved, and concluded it was a greater priority to be feared. Van Vliet concluded that Prasat Thong "governs in such a manner that his power is secure, and he always makes sure that he is more feared than any of his predecessors ever were." Machiavelli also advised that a ruler should avoid being hated in order to diminish the potential for successful conspiracies. To this end, "he should appear … to be all mercy, all faithfulness, all integrity, all kindness, all religion." Van Vliet's Protestant conscience seems to take him a little beyond this pragmatism. In Section 17 (missing from the Wicquefort/Mundie/Nantha version), Prasat Thong's grandmother, who throughout plays the dramatic role of the voice of conscience, warns him not "to transgress too gravely against the Gods and the ecclesiastics, [as] he would no longer enjoy the blessings from Heaven and the intercession of the priests." In the longest and most eloquent of the pre-death orations, that of Phra Si Sin, Van Vliet seems to argue for a more positively benevolent rule:

> If then you wish to be a beloved King, be not careless, do not lead a dissolute life, but embrace righteousness, and note that virtue is an impregnable fortress, a flowing stream that never runs dry, a fire that is never quenched, a burden that will never become too heavy, a treasure that will never diminish, an army that will never be defeated, a guide that will never go astray, a friend who will never be disloyal, a reputation that will never be tarnished. And in order to give true proof of the sincerity of your royal heart, venerate the Gods and honor the house of your father. Acquire a good reputation, give joy to your friends, increase their affection for yourself, and then good people will serve you by inclination, while the wicked will disperse of themselves. For it is a great advantage for a King to make himself beloved for his goodness and feared for his justice.

STORY AND HISTORY

Van Vliet wrote his account of the rise of Prasat Thong using the framework of Renaissance tragedy and delivering a message right out of Machiavelli. Yet at the same time, the work tells us something about the process of creating historical knowledge in Ayutthaya.

Van Vliet noted at the end of the *Short History* (p. 244) that "During my presence here, I have investigated all the particulars [on Prasat Thong's rise] and have put part of them down on paper." Yet he had not been in Ayutthaya over the years 1628–30 when the main events of the *Historical Account* took place. In the passage on elephants in the *Description* (p. 176), he noted that Okya Phitsanulok "himself has told me everything that has been described above." We can imagine that he gained most of his information from such senior nobles remembering the recent past. While his presentation of the narrative owes a lot to European literary conventions, there are also obvious affinities with the style of storytelling in the unabridged versions of the royal chronicles and in the various "testimonies" taken down from Ayutthaya prisoners in Ava after the sack of 1767. These works mix narrative and dialogue in a similar way, allocate a similar role to portents, and devote lots of space to great stories like the death of Okluang Mongkhon. We can imagine that Ayutthaya's historical narratives took their first shape in the kind of recent accounts which Van Vliet recorded, and later became distilled, selected, and compressed into the written forms known mainly from the chronicles. This suggests two things. The oral tradition of recording and transmission was a key part of this process of creating "history" in Ayutthaya, and the participants included many members of the nobility, not just the official court scribes.

Historical Account of the Illness and Death of Pra Interra-Tsia, 22nd King of Siam, titled Faeij loangh tiaeuwtrong thantsiangh Pheeuck,[1] or the Great and Just King of the White Elephant, and of how the now reigning King, Pra Ongh Srij[2] (whose titles are Pra tjauw Prasathong Pra Tiauw tsiang Peeuck, Pra tjsaeuw tsiangh thong dengh, Pratjaeuw tsiangh Chobolt,[3] or King of the Golden Throne, as well as of the Red, White, and Round-tailed Elephant), usurped the Throne and of the Manner in which he conducted himself in several matters concerning the Governance of the Kingdom.

1. INTRODUCTION TO THIS DESCRIPTION.

In the Kingdom of Siam, Excellent Sir, it is an ancient custom that everyone who is favored by the King with titles or distinctions reverentially acknowledges these honors by presenting His Majesty with some small gifts, which, however insignificant they may be, are kindly accepted by the King. Such gifts symbolize the duty of the subjects towards His Majesty. They show that those who receive honors and benefits from the King, are duty bound in return to think of His Majesty, and (with accomplishments of note) to repay him to the best of their abilities.

2. REASONS FOR THIS DESCRIPTION.

It is in this spirit that I respectfully present and offer this treatise to Your Honor, emboldened, as I am, by Your Honor's kind acceptance of my *Short History of the Kings of Siam*, on which occasion I gave the undertaking to bring to light the events related here. Please then, Noble Sir, accept my insignificant work as if it were a small flower and regard it as a token of my grateful affection. I humbly pray that Your Honor will pay more attention to the truthfulness of the story than to the unvarnished language, because an

1. ฝ่ายหลวงเจ้าทรงธรรม...ช้างเผือก *fai luang chao songtham … chang phuak*, the king, King Songtham … of the white elephant.

2. Wicquefort mistranscribed this as Phra Ongly, which Mundie glossed as Phra Ong Lai. Giles then decided that Phra Ong Lai had been Prasat Thong's pre-regnal name. This then went back into Thai as พระองค์ไล.

3. พระเจ้าปราสาททอง พระเจ้าช้างเผือก พระเจ้าช้างทองแดง พระเจ้าช้างโคบุตร *Prachao prasatthong prachao chang phuak prachao chang thongdaeng prachao chang khobut*, King Prasat Thong, king of the white, bronze, and *khobut* elephants. The last term, *chang khobut*, is a class of special elephants with a voice, yellowish skin, and tail hair all considered to resemble a cow; and also only slightly uptilted tusks.

elegant style of writing is hardly to be expected from a poorly educated Merchant.

3. EXCUSES FOR THE ABSENCE IN THIS TREATISE OF AN ACCOUNT OF THE SITUATION IN THE KINGDOM OF SIAM.

By way of introduction to the subject matter of this treatise, it would be pertinent before commencing my account to give a short and clear description of the position of this Kingdom, of the character of its people, of their religion, and of the state of their political government. But since this has already been ably done by my predecessors, and since during my presence at Batavia in 1638 (upon the urging of the late Director, Phillip Lucas), I myself have written such an account,[4] I request to be excused from having here to repeat this exercise. I make this request also so as not to tire Your Honor with unnecessary verbosity, especially because I do not doubt that the aforementioned accounts of the situation in Siam have been duly presented to Your Honor. But to arrive at the matters I intended to bring to light, I will (in passing and not as a matter of necessity) touch upon a few historical precedents (pertinent to this treatise), praying that Your Honor will not be saddened by reading of these events.

4. HISTORICAL PRECEDENTS PERTINENT TO THIS TREATISE.

The very learned Anthonio de Guverro rightly says that nothing on this earth is more certain than that all human affairs are uncertain. Even though Aristotle says that people should undertake all matters with a definite outcome in mind, the Emperor Marcus Aurelius[5] reminded his friend, Corbino, of something the vain and ambitious have experienced all too often; namely, that just when they think they have put their affairs in perfect order, and just when they reach the highest peaks of happiness, that just at that time, their lives are violently taken from them. Truly, the course of life is unpredictable and this has been shown to be the case also in this Kingdom. If the great and just King of the White Elephant[6] had tempered his natural affection for his family, and especially for his eldest son, and if, instead, he had acted in accordance with the written laws of his land, he would have let the Crown pass to his lawful brother, the legitimate heir to the throne.[7] In Aurelius the

4. Meaning the *Description*.
5. Marcus Aurelius Antoninus, Roman emperor 161–180 AD.
6. King Songtham.
7. Van Vliet believed that Siamese "laws" stipulated that the brother of a deceased king, rather than the eldest son, had the prior right of succession. Evidence of any such law, however, has not survived.

Roman Empire had a more cautious Emperor, because aware of the character of his licentious son, Comodus,[8] he opposed his succession, expressing the wish that the Senate banish his son from Rome. But God Almighty, intending to punish the people of Rome, robbed the Senators of their reason and judgment so that they (out of gratitude for the achievements of Aurelius) entrusted the Empire to Comodus.

This happened also in the case of the late Siamese King (whose name has been mentioned). If His Majesty had been careful enough to have chosen the legitimate heir, if he had adhered to the rightful rules of succession, the peace of his Kingdom would not have been disturbed, and the Crown would have remained within his patrimonial lineage. But the Lord leads the hearts of Kings in whichever direction he wants. It is worth noting, in this connection, that Saba, the Queen of Arabia,[9] having witnessed in Jerusalem the great wisdom with which King Solomon governed his Kingdom, told Solomon that she had become convinced that God must love Israel to have given it a King like him. And yet, the severe governance of Rehabeam (Solomon's son)[10] brought great turbulence and division to that blessed Kingdom, which led the prophet Esaia[11] to observe rightly that God had summoned all the righteous and saintly people prior to the ill-fated day. For as long as Solomon was alive, no lamentations were heard nor tears were seen in the land; but because plagues were about to descend on Israel to punish Rehabeam for his apostasy, the King was called to appear before his maker.

This example applies to the unfortunate Kingdom of Siam, because as long as Faeij loangh,[12] or the great and just King,[13] governed this Kingdom, there was prosperity in the land and happiness within the royal family and at the Court. But after Pra Onghthit[14] had succeeded his father, great misery came over this erstwhile flourishing Kingdom. And even though the Lord Solomon had predicted the rending of his Kingdom, the troubles when they

8. Marcus Aurelius Commodus Antoninus (r. 180–192), Aurelius' son, famous as the populist megalomaniac portrayed in the film *Gladiator*. Most histories suggest his succession was initially welcomed in the hope he would follow in the footsteps of his popular father.

9. The queen, more commonly known as the Queen of Sheba, who mythically visited Solomon's Court around 950 BC carrying vast quantities of gold and seduced him, though he suspected she was a goat-demon.

10. Rehoboam succeeded his father Solomon as ruler of Judah around 930 BC, after which Judah was torn apart by revolts.

11. The biblical prophet usually spelled Isaiah.

12. ฝ่ายหลวง, *fai luang*.

13. King Songtham.

14. The king known as Chetthathirat. "Thit" may simply be a shortening of Chetthathirat which Van Vliet renders as "thit Terratsia" in Section 15. It might also be พระองค์ทิต, meaning he had formerly been a monk.

came were not just accidents of history, but were due to God's providence. The same is true for the Kingdom of Siam. Fate, says the learned Justus Lipsius,[15] rules the world and cannot be avoided, even if it has been predicted. This is apparent from the lives of Julius Caesar and Henry the Fourth,[16] both of whom had been foretold the hour of their deaths, and yet they were unable to escape their ill-fated assassins.

Signs of impending disaster and misery had been noted also in this Kingdom. About a year before his death, the King was out in the field trying to catch elephants when suddenly a monstrous beast of extraordinary appearance emerged from the forest. It resembled a white elephant; its right tusk was missing and only half of its left tusk remained; its chest was raised and covered with tumors; its tail was stunted and on its back there was a large black mark.[17] The appearance of this terrible monster was a premonition of His Majesty's imminent death – and yet, even though his death had been foretold, the King was unable to alter his destiny, which clearly shows that, also in the case of this Kingdom, misfortune followed its fateful course.

But leaving aside all these speculations, I will endeavor in the pages that follow to give an orderly account of His Majesty's illness and death and also of the cunning way in which the now ruling King usurped the throne, murdering and exterminating the lawful heirs and their supporters.

5. PORTENTS OF THE KING'S ILLNESS AND DEATH.

Towards the end of the Year of the Rabbit, when the eleventh waning moon had almost passed,[18] a change in the King's temper became evident. While formerly he was good-humored, agreeable, and kind to his subjects and servants, he now became unbearably peevish. He severely chastised some of his servants for minor misdemeanors, while he threw others into prison so that even the greatest of Mandarins did not dare any longer to approach him in order to speak to him of the important and necessary affairs of his Kingdom. This caused great sadness amongst the subjects because the King was much loved for his merciful nature, and the sudden change in his disposition aroused fears that His Majesty's end was drawing nigh.

15. Belgian neo-Stoic revivalist, 1547–1606, who tried to reconcile the idea of fate with the Christian concept of the will of God.

16. The French king, Henri IV, r. 1589–1610.

17. Stories of apparently auspicious elephants which then revert to ordinary status, or reveal defects, or break their tusks are a recurrent omen of royal disaster (see for instance *RCA*: 19, 22). However, the chronicles do not have such a story about King Songtham.

18. The last day of the eleventh month in CS 989, a year of the rabbit, is equivalent to 7 November 1627.

6. THE KING FALLS ILL AND DESIRES TO KNOW THE FEELINGS OF THE MANDARINS REGARDING THE SUCCESSION.

At the beginning of the twelfth and last moon of the Year of the Rabbit,[19] the King had a fainting fit, and it was soon evident from the course of his illness that there was no hope of his recovery. This was why the King (at the instigation of Oija Sijworra Wongh)[20] resolved to choose his eldest son (a Prince, 15 years of age, and of bad character) as his successor and to repudiate his lawful brother, who, according to the old laws of the Kingdom, should have succeeded. Nevertheless, in order to give some appearance of justice to this choice, His Majesty, through Oija Sijworra Wongh, desired to know the feelings of the Mandarins and had them summoned to an assembly expressly for that purpose.

Hiding his intention, the King asked them for their views. Most of the Mandarins remained silent, but some of them (on the advice of Sijworra Wongh) said that the King's son should inherit the Crown and govern the Kingdom. These Mandarins said that they believed the Prince to be old enough to succeed, arguing that the King's brother, having his own heirs, was likely to pass the Crown to one of his own sons in consequence of which the Crown would be alienated from His Majesty's direct lineage. But others, and principally Oija Calahom,[21] Oija Kheeu,[22] Opra taijnam,[23] Opra sirsij ancrat,[24] Opra tjula,[25] and Oluangh thamtraij locq,[26] were of the view that the King's brother[27] should succeed, and they had the courage to say that the

19. The first day of the twelfth month in CS 989, a year of the rabbit, is equivalent to 8 November 1627.

20. Okya Si Worawong, the future King Prasat Thong. Below (Section 16), the title Okya Si Worawong is described as belonging to "the head of the King's household." Possibly this means Okya Wang, head of the palace or *monthianban* department (see Appendix I), part of whose title is given in the Three Seals Law (*KTSD*, I, 237) as *Siwiriyaphongwongsa*.

21. Okya Kalahom, see Appendix I.

22. Giles suggests this is Okya Kien, ออกญาเกียน, head of the *Krom dang thongsai* unit of the military, sakdina 1600 (*KTSD*, 1: 305). Another possibility is ออกญาเกียรติ, one of two Mon nobles at the time of Naresuan.

23. Okphra Thainam, ออกพระท้ายน้ำ, an official in the military branch, more usually given an Okya rank (*KTSD*, 1: 280).

24. Giles suggests this is Okphra Si Naowarat, ออกพระศรีเนาวรัตน์, an officer in *Krom tha khwa*, right division of the port department, sakdina 2400, generally a Muslim (Malay, Indian or Persian).

25. Okphra Chula Ratchamontri, head of the right (Muslim) wing of the port department, sakdina 1400 (*KTSD*, 1: 233).

26. Okluang Thamtrailok (ธรรมไตรโลก), an official in Kalahom, sakdina 3000 (*KTSD*, 1: 279).

27. Phra Si Sin.

ancient laws of the Kingdom should not be corrupted in this manner. The rest referred the matter to the will of the King, saying that both Princes had all the qualities required in a good monarch, and that they would faithfully obey and serve as King whomsoever His Majesty should appoint to succeed him.

7. THE KING CHOOSES HIS SON TO SUCCEED HIM AND REPUDIATES HIS BROTHER, CONTRARY TO THE ANCIENT LAWS.

Following his own will and the advice of Oija Sijworra Wongh, the King by testament nominated his eldest son as heir to the Kingdom, even though this was contrary to the laws. At the hour of his death, he commanded Sijworra Wongh to make known his last will immediately after his decease, charging him to assist the young Prince on his attainment of the Crown, to watch over his actions, and to care for the well-being of the Kingdom. It seems that His Majesty, driven by fatherly affection for his children, wanted the Crown to remain within his family. For even though his lawful brother (a Prince, 26 years of age, and much loved on account of his kind disposition) should have inherited the Crown, and have succeeded to the Kingdom, the King (notwithstanding the Prince's requests) had never wanted to declare him his successor. He preferred his eldest son to wear the Crown, rather than to have him serving his brother.

8. DECEITFUL REPRESENTATION OF THE KING'S DISPOSITION BY OIJA SIJWORRA WONGH.

During the illness of the King, Oija Sijworra Wongh caused all approaches to the Palace to be so well guarded that no one could approach without his permission, so that there was not a single Mandarin who was able to see His Majesty during this time. All orders and commands were borne to the assembly of Mandarins and to the Council by the mouth of this one Minister. And in order to mislead the brother of the King, his supporters, as well as the Mandarins who sought to uphold the written laws of the land, Sijworra Wongh pretended day after day that the King's disposition was improving and that it was more likely that he would recover than that he would die.

9. THE KING BECOMES CAUTIOUS AND REINFORCES THE PALACE WITH JAPANESE AND ARMED SOLDIERS.

The opposition of some of the Mandarins to the King's preferred succession made His Majesty cautious and caused him concern, especially because Oija Calahom (General of the King's elephants and infantry) had taken the side of the Prince, his brother. In order to remove all obstacles that might prevent his son succeeding, the King, through Oija Sijworra Wongh, secured the support of Oija Senaphimocq[28] (Colonel of the Japanese who, about 600 in number, reside in the Siamese Kingdom). This was done, the aforementioned Oija swearing a solemn oath promising to help to put the King's son on the throne; and in order to give proof of his affection, Senaphimocq secretly lodged a good number of his armed Japanese in and around the Palace. Oija Calahom (who was more fearful of the King's death than of his recovery) sought to enlist the support of Oija Senaphimocq and his Japanese in order, with their help, to advance to the throne the Prince, His Majesty's brother. But at this meeting, Senaphimocq (instructed by Oija Sijworra Wongh) cunningly used words which, while promising nothing, nevertheless did not extinguish all hope that (at a time of need) the Japanese would render assistance. At the same time, not content with having fortified the Court with the Japanese in addition to the King's ordinary guards, Oija Sijworra Wongh had another 4,000 armed soldiers secretly brought into the Palace, while he arranged for another 10,000 soldiers to be held in readiness just outside the city. And in order not to arouse suspicion and to lull the opposition to sleep, he spread the rumor that the King had recovered his health and that he had called up all these soldiers because he was planning a campaign.

10. THE KING'S DEATH AND EULOGY.

After Oija Sijworra Wongh had cleverly arranged everything in accordance with the wishes of the King, and when the succession of His Majesty's son had been secured, the King (to the great sadness of his vassals and subjects) departed this world. This happened in the Year of the Great Snake, on the 22nd day of the first waning moon.[29] The King died in the flower of his life, 38 years of age, after having reigned 19 years, almost the whole time in peace. By several women he had begotten nine sons and eight daughters, most of whom, at the time of the King's death, were still in their minority.

This King was wise, beneficent, and liberal, not martial by nature, but studious, pious, and greatly concerned with the worship of their Gods, as well as with their ecclesiastical orders and the laws of the Kingdom. He was very charitable towards the ecclesiastics and the poor; he built and repaired more temples, pyramids, and living quarters of the ecclesiastics than any of

28. Okya Senaphimuk or Yamada Nagamasa. See Appendix IV.

29. At this point the manuscript has a marginal note: "Being the 12th of December, 1628 in the late afternoon." The exactness of this timing suggests it is the date and time of Songtham's death as remembered at the time. The main text is clearly wrong as there cannot be 22 days in any moon. This may be a copyist's error, and the marginal note may have been inserted by someone who noted the mistake. However the rest of the date is correct. 12 December 1628 is the *first* waning day of the first month in CS 990 which is a year of the great snake.

his predecessors.[30] It pleased him to know that his Mandarins were prosperous, and to see them splendidly dressed, well attended and magnificently housed. He had of his own bounty several houses built for members of his household. He loved justice, upright judges, and all good men, and he took such great care of his subjects, and even of the foreigners who resided in the Kingdom, that (amongst the Siamese) he was regarded as saintly and fortunate. He was so highly respected by neighboring Kings that they dared not attack him, for which reason it is not to be wondered at that he was given the epithets of great and just.[31]

11. THE KING'S DEATH IS ANNOUNCED TO THE MANDARINS AND THE SON APPEARS AS KING.

As soon as the thread of the King's life had been severed, Oija Sijworra Wongh called all the Mandarins to the Palace, who, ignorant of His Majesty's death, all appeared – not a single one being absent. Tearfully, Sijworra Wongh told them that the King had departed this world less than an hour ago (even though many suspected that His Majesty had been dead a long time, but that his death had been kept secret), and that it had been His Majesty's wish that his eldest son should succeed him and that he, Sijworra Wongh, should assist and advise his son in the governance of the Kingdom. Thereupon the son showed himself to the Mandarins on the throne as King and rightful heir to the Kingdom. This Sijworra Wongh confirmed by reading out the will of his father. All the Mandarins then recognized the young Prince as King, some of them by inclination, others out of fear of his powerful supporters and of the soldiers that the Minister had brought into the Palace.

12. THE MANDARINS WHO HAD SUPPORTED THE KING'S BROTHER ARE ARRESTED AND SOME OF THEM ARE EXECUTED.

All the Mandarins who were known to have favored the late King's brother, and all those who had not clearly declared themselves when the late King wished to know their feelings about the succession, were seized at once and thrown into severe imprisonment. Their slaves were taken from them and their houses and goods were given over to pillage. At the same time, the young King, acting on the advice of Sijworra Wongh, had three of the principal Mandarins taken from prison. Accused of having conspired against the lawful heir to the Kingdom, they were taken to Thacham,[32] one of the gates to the

30. Confirmed by *KCKK*: 97.

31. "Songtham" means righteous, behaving according to the *thamma*. This may have been a popular, descriptive referent, for his official name seems to have been either Intharacha (see Vickery 1976) or Tilokanat (*KCKK*: 95).

32. Probably Tha Chang, literally the elephant landing. This gate was on the

Palace, where they were cut in half through the middle. After the executions, their heads, hands, and feet were hacked off and put on stakes which were displayed in front of the various gates to the Court. As an additional punishment, all their property was confiscated, which the King caused to be distributed amongst his favorites.

13. THE WEALTH, POWER AND STANDING OF THE EXECUTED MANDARINS.

The three Mandarins who were thus executed were amongst the most powerful, wealthiest, and wisest Lords in the entire Kingdom. His Majesty, the deceased King, had held them in high regard. One was Oija Calahom, General of the elephants, a man of means, who possessed more than 2,000 slaves, 200 elephants, and many beautiful horses. He was one of the six greatest Mandarins. The second was Opra Taijnam, General of the cavalry, who only two months before his execution had still been Barckelangh,[33] a post he had held for five years, during which time he had amassed great wealth. The previous King had honored him above all others for his virtue and eloquence. The third was Oloangh Tham Traijlocq, who had been Governor of Tanassarij,[34] an old and venerable man. These Lords were killed not for any faults on their parts, but because of the hatred that their antagonist (who enticed the young King) bore them, and also because of their prominence and wealth. Not suspecting that misfortune was to befall them, the three Lords nonetheless faced death with great patience and fortitude, mindful, as indeed they were, that mankind is fated to suffer.

14. THE RELEASE OF THE IMPRISONED LORDS AND THE MEASURES TAKEN AGAINST THOSE WHO HAD HESITATED.

Two of the imprisoned Mandarins, namely, Oprasir Sij Ancrat and Opra Tjula, were also taken to the Thacham gate, where they were bound and pinioned in order to taste the undeserved bitterness of death. But Oija Senanphimocq, Colonel of the Japanese, protected them with his body, embracing both of them, thus preventing the blows from raining down on them. He then sent a messenger to Oija Sijworra Wongh requesting that they be pardoned – a request that was granted. Through the intercession of the ecclesiastics, the lives of the other prisoners were also spared, but they were deprived of their titles, offices, and property and continued to languish

---

western side, close to the Front Palace (*KCKK*: 197–201).

33. Okya Phrakhlang, the minister for the treasury and foreign affairs, usually called the Berckelangh by the Dutch and Barcalon by the French. He was in an ideal position to engage in trade and accumulate riches.

34. Tanaosi, Tenasserim.

in severe imprisonment. After some time, several still were executed, while others were banished, and others still were released of their bonds. Those Mandarins who had spoken ambiguously in respect of the succession, and had referred the matter to the King to appoint whomsoever he pleased, were also deprived of their property, offices, and titles and thrown in prison. There they remained until the young King took pity on them and had them released.

15. THE YOUNG KING IS CROWNED AND HIS VASSALS SWEAR THE OATH OF LOYALTY.

The day after the King's death was announced, the young King called to the Court all the Mandarins as well as all the late King's servants and slaves so that His Majesty could be crowned. He obliged them to do him homage and to take the oath of fidelity by drinking the water of allegiance which the Brahmin priests had expressly consecrated for that purpose. The King was named Pra Onghthit Terratsia.[35] Thus it might be said that with but little spilling of blood and without great upheaval, the young Prince had quietly succeeded his father. The very day of his accession to the throne, His Majesty pardoned several Lords who had been imprisoned or exiled by the King, his father. He also released many criminals from their chains and bonds, acts of mercy that brought him a good reputation at the very commencement of his reign.

16. HIS MAJESTY DIVIDES THE CONFISCATED GOODS AND APPOINTS OIJA SIJWORRA WONGH TO THE OFFICE OF CALAHOM.

The young King having thus been crowned and confirmed on the throne, Oija Sijworra Wongh advised him to dispose of the vacant offices of the Lords who had been punished in favor of a number of able persons respected by the people. He added that if the King was to show his bounty to the Mandarins (those who were deserving), he would place his royal state on a more secure footing. But the Minister wished above all that His Majesty should carefully examine the character, walk of life, and past actions of the person who was to become Oija Calahom for reason of the great dignity and importance of this office. For while disloyal Ministers could cause the King a great deal of trouble, it was especially dangerous in the case of the Oija Calahom because this Minister was in control of most of the army. Sijworra Wongh made it sufficiently plain that, even though an appointment as Oija Calahom would mean a reduction in status for him, he would be prepared to accept the office for the love he bore the King and out of a desire to secure the Kingdom.

The thoughtless King approved this advice, and at once gave the confiscated property of those who had been executed, banished, or disgraced to Mandarins

35. Phra-ong Chetthathirat.

who Sijworra Wongh named to him, and who were dependent more on that Minister than on His Majesty. Apart from the office itself, the King gave most of the property of the executed Calahom to this Minister, and in addition he appointed the brother of the new Calahom to the now vacant position of Oija Sijworra Wongh, the head of the King's household. In making these appointments, His Majesty in effect had placed the governance of the Kingdom in the hands of the new Calahom, who, from this time onwards, came to believe that he was destined one day to ascend to the throne.

17. EVIL INTENTION OF OIJA SIJWORRA WONGH (NOW CALAHOM) TOWARDS THE REJECTED PRINCE, EVEN THOUGH HIS HIGHNESS HAD BECOME AN ECCLESIASTIC.

The elder Prince,[36] the brother of the deceased King, had forsaken all worldly affairs during the late King's reign and had donned ecclesiastical robes, partly because having been excluded from the Crown, he had no hope to ever attain it, and partly also because he had reason to fear for his life. Even though it is an ancient Siamese law and ecclesiastical privilege that a secular ruler may not violate a priestly person dressed in ecclesiastical robes, Oija Sijworra Wongh (who was now Calahom), in the name of the late King, had summoned the Prince to the Court. There he had locked him into a room, intending to keep him imprisoned in order to dispatch him upon the death of the King. But the grandmother of Sijworra Wongh (now Calahom), who was the bravest and wisest woman in the entire Kingdom, advised against this plan, saying that it was too dangerous because the King was still alive; that it was not certain that he would die, and that if the King should regain his health, he, Sijworra Wongh, would be in grave peril for reason that His Majesty would want to avenge the injury done to his brother. She also warned that if Sijworra Wongh was to transgress too gravely against the Gods and the ecclesiastics, he would no longer enjoy the blessings from Heaven and the intercession of the priests. Dissuaded by these arguments, Sijworra Wongh released the Prince (who did not realize just how close he had come to misfortune) and sent him home with the excuse that the King had fallen into a deep sleep, for which reason he was not allowed to speak to His Majesty. The Prince accepted this as the truth.

18. OIJA SENAPHIMOCQ, COLONEL OF THE JAPANESE, BETRAYS THE PRINCE AND DELIVERS HIM INTO THE HANDS OF THE KING.

Having been crowned and confirmed in the Kingdom, the young King several times summoned his uncle, the elder Prince, to come to the Court,

36. Phra Si Sin.

only to be refused each time. This made Oija Calahom (formerly Oija Sijworra Wongh) very uneasy, for which reason he consulted with Oija Senaphimocq. By means of gifts and promises of great riches, he persuaded him to bring the Prince to the Court, and by means of some kind of ruse to make sure that he appear there dressed not in ecclesiastical robes, but in secular attire. Senaphimocq swore to carry out this plan.

Arriving at the Prince's residence, Oija Senaphimocq commiserated (but insincerely) with him about the King's death, His Highness' misfortune, the deaths, banishment, and imprisonment of many excellent Lords and venerable Mandarins. With great diffuseness he told the Prince of the young King's careless life, his severe governance, and of the power and authority of Oija Calahom (formerly Oija Sijworra Wongh). He protested to the Prince that he himself and several other Mandarins were so distressed about the situation that they had often secretly deliberated amongst themselves as to the means by which they could kill the young King and Oija Calahom, and raise His Highness to the throne. He added that if the Prince could be prevailed upon to come to the Court with him, he would use his Japanese soldiers and his other supporters to deprive the King of the Crown and expel him and Oija Calahom from the Kingdom. He would then help His Highness attain the royal dignity and the governance of the Kingdom.

The Prince believed the words of Oija Senaphimocq, dressed himself in ecclesiastical robes, and accompanied him to the Royal Palace. Arriving at the gate to the Palace, His Highness saw many armed Japanese guards, a sight that served to strengthen his confidence in the trustworthiness of the Oija. At this moment, when the Prince least suspected it, Oija Senaphimocq carried out his act of treachery. He told the Prince that his supporters were already inside the Palace awaiting his arrival, and that it was necessary that he should appear before them not as a person of religion, but as a martial hero. Giving this as a reason, Senaphimocq advised His Highness that he should take off his yellow robes and dress in the manner of a Prince. Following the advice of the traitor, the Prince changed his attire and entered the palace accompanied by Senaphimocq and some armed Japanese. But here misfortune overcame him. Scarcely had the Prince entered the Palace than he was seized and bound, and in this condition he was brought before the young King. His Majesty and Calahom, very pleased that they had ensnared their antagonist in this manner, thanked Oija Senaphimocq profusely for his treacherous act and made him very considerable presents.

19. THE PRINCE IS CONDEMNED TO STARVE TO DEATH, BUT MIRACULOUSLY ESCAPES.

The King and his Council condemned the Prince to death, but because neither His Majesty nor any other judge is allowed to shed His Highness' blood, they decided to send him to Piprij.[37] There he was to be placed in a subterranean pit, the intention being to cause him die of hunger by diminishing every day his victuals little by little. They established good order for the guarding of the pit, and appointed a number of royal commissioners who visited the Prince three times a day in order to make their reports to the King, and to be witnesses to the end of His Highness' life.

At about the same time the Prince was thus condemned to die a cruel death, one of his near relatives, a certain Oloangh Mancongh,[38] left the Court and withdrew with his brother secretly to Piprij. There he made representations to the ecclesiastics pointing out the injustice of the sentence passed on the Prince and begging them to assist him in his design to rescue His Highness from the hands of his executioners. But the ecclesiastics, fearing the wrath of the King and concerned also about the large number of soldiers who were conducting the Prince to his execution, were reluctant to take the matter in hand openly.

But considering that His Highness was the rightful heir to the Kingdom, that he himself had worn ecclesiastical robes (to safeguard his life), that he had always maintained the temples, and that he had always valued and supported their religion, the ecclesiastics decided to take pity on him. Assisted by Oloangh Mancongh, his brother, and their slaves, the ecclesiastics under the cover of darkness dug another pit from which a passage was made underground (as in a mine) to the one in which the Prince had been put. One night, when Oloangh Mancongh, driven by a strong desire to free the Prince, was digging all by himself, he came so close that he could hear the Prince sigh and say: "Oh, that I could only have a drink of water before my end, which is fast approaching."

Elated, the Oloangh ran to the ecclesiastics to tell them that the Prince was still alive. After some deliberation on the appropriate course of action, and with the approval of the Priests, Oloangh Mancongh strangled one of his slaves, whereupon they all went to the pit that had been dug. They lowered the lifeless body into the pit, pulled His Highness out of his miserable hole, and dressed the dead slave in the Prince's clothes. This having been done, the guards, who the evening before had seen the Prince in a very bad way, did not doubt that it was him when the following morning they saw a dead body at the bottom of the pit. Unceremoniously, they filled in the hole without even touching the body, whereupon they happily returned to the city of Iudia to announce to the King and his household that His Highness was dead. With his uncle out of the way, His Majesty was convinced he had overcome

37. Phetchaburi. In the chronicles, Phra Si Sin is not seized and imprisoned in this way but decamps to Phetchaburi and raises a revolt (*RCA*: 210–11).

38. Giles suggets this is Okluang Mongkhon, ออกหลวงมงคลรัตนราชมนตรี, head of tax collection in the capital, sakdina 2400 (*KTSD*, 1: 257).

all his enemies, that no one would now be able to challenge him, and that he would be able, henceforth, to possess his Kingdom in peace.

20. THE PRINCE GATHERS A MIGHTY ARMY AND IS CROWNED KING OF SIAM.

The ecclesiastics took such good care of the Prince that in a short time he recovered his former health and strength. This delighted the Priests so much that some of them shed their monk's robes and took up arms, whereupon they travelled the land far and wide visiting various noble Lords and prominent citizens to tell them of the Prince's miraculous deliverance. This was against His Highness' wishes, because he would have preferred to have kept secret his deliverance until the tyrannical government of the young King had rendered him odious with the nobility and the people, as this would have strengthened his party. Nonetheless, many powerful and prominent people secretly made their way to Piprij.

Oloangh Mancongh, who was highly esteemed and respected throughout the Siamese Kingdom for his physical strength and his martial skills, went in person to the neighboring towns and gathered to the cause of the Prince a large mass of people. Before long, the Prince had an army of about 20,000 soldiers (among whom there were many Lords, Nobles, and Courtiers) with which he secured the city of Piprij. There he proclaimed himself King of Siam. He distributed amongst his followers all the offices of the Court and dignities of the Kingdom. He appointed Oloangh Mancongh Supreme Commander of the army. He made this appointment mainly because the Oloangh had saved him from the jaws of death, but in part also because he was of royal blood, and because he was an experienced soldier who, through magical practices, was invulnerable to iron, steel, or the arm of man. Soon the Prince had subjected all the towns in the vicinity, so that it seemed that there was every likelihood that more and more people would come over to his side, and that he would become master of the entire Kingdom. But fate had ordained otherwise.

21. THE YOUNG KING SENDS SUCH A LARGE FORCE AGAINST THE PRINCE THAT HIS HIGHNESS IS DEFEATED AND IS TAKEN PRISONER.

Upon learning of the Prince, his uncle, being alive and at liberty, of his proclamation and of the rising of several towns, the King at once caused all roads to be closed off, thus preventing the further movement of people to the rebellious area. Soon he had gathered a considerable army, consisting of 15,000 to 20,000 soldiers and 700 to 800 Japanese, commanded by Oija Capheijn[39] (Supreme Commander) and Oija Senaphimocq (Colonel of the

39. Okya Kamphaengphet. The Dutch spelled Kamphaengphet as Capheim or Capheijn in other documents.

Japanese), which he sent out to confront the enemy. Upon arrival in the Piprij area, the commanders of the King's army found the affairs of the enemy in such good condition that they dared not attack, but instead sent to the young King for reinforcements. In the meantime, some units belonging to the hostile armies repeatedly engaged each other in ambushes and skirmishes in consequence of which many soldiers lost their lives.

Acting on the advice of Oija Calahom (and with foreknowledge of Oija Capheijn), the Colonel of the Japanese contacted the Supreme Commander of the Prince's army and (deceitfully) told him that he and his Japanese soldiers wanted to come over to his side and join the troops of the Prince. After several conferences, they came to an agreement that on a certain day, which they fixed on, both sides should take to the field for the purpose of giving battle. However, they should charge each other without bullets in order not to kill or wound anyone, and in the course of this mock battle, Senaphimocq, pretending to be compelled to do so, was to surrender himself and be made a prisoner. The Prince accepted in good faith the agreement between Oloangh Mancongh and Oija Senaphimocq, an agreement they had confirmed by tasting each other's blood. But the Japanese was to betray him for the third time. When at the appointed hour the two armies came out into the field and fell upon each other, the Japanese, powerfully assisted by the Siamese, attacked so ferociously that Oloangh Mancongh was forced to retreat with the loss of many of his troops.

Meanwhile, the young King had been sending ever more soldiers to Piprij with the result that the Prince had insufficient forces at his disposal to oppose the King's army. He resolved to withdraw his army to Lijgoor,[40] but in order to reach his destination quickly, His Highness went ahead with only a small suite. But Oija Capheijn, having received news of the Prince's flight, ordered him to be pursued and captured, something which Oloangh Mancongh desperately tried to prevent. He attacked the advancing army of the King, but after a hard fought battle, Oloangh Mancongh was defeated with the loss of some of the greatest nobles and many of his best soldiers. This victory enabled Oija Capheijn to press his pursuit of the Prince, who, indeed, was captured about halfway to Ligoor, whereupon he was taken to Iudia with many of his followers.

22. THE PRINCE IS CONDEMNED TO DEATH FOR THE SECOND TIME, BUT BEFORE DYING A MISERABLE DEATH HE WARNS THE YOUNG KING OF IMPENDING DISASTER.

The young King and his Council condemned the Prince to death for the second time, but when His Highness was told of the verdict, he earnestly requested that before dying he might see His Majesty in order to tell him

40. Nakhon Si Thammarat.

several things of importance. Permission being granted, he addressed the young King more or less as follows: "Before Your Majesty appears your lawful uncle, the legitimate heir to the Kingdom, and yet, because of the misfortune it has pleased the Gods to send upon me, a vanquished Prince who only awaits the hour of his death and cannot escape it. Nevertheless, a brave man does not hate life as long as he can possess it, nor does he fear death when it comes, because death is but a door with which one closes the house in which all the difficulties of this miserable world are sold. That is why I reject life and welcome death, even though my close family relationship to Your Majesty yields me cruel and bitter fruit. But with all that, I prefer being conquered in this fashion to being the conqueror and treating Your Majesty as Your Majesty is now treating me. I only beg of you that the wounds that soon will be inflicted upon me will serve as a warning to Your Majesty. For the best and most important service that one can render a friend is to give him good advice in important matters. If then you wish to be a beloved King, be not careless, do not lead a dissolute life, but embrace righteousness, and note that virtue is an impregnable fortress, a flowing stream that never runs dry, a fire that is never quenched, a burden that will never become too heavy, a treasure that will never diminish, an army that will never be defeated, a guide that will never go astray, a friend who will never be disloyal, a reputation that will never be tarnished. And in order to give true proof of the sincerity of your royal heart, venerate the Gods and honor the house of your father. Acquire a good reputation, give joy to your friends, increase their affection for yourself, and then good people will serve you by inclination, while the wicked will disperse of themselves. For it is a great advantage for a King to make himself beloved for his goodness and feared for his justice. Finally, I again implore Your Majesty to take warning from my suffering and to profit by it. For I am prepared to meet my doom, which I had not anticipated, and which I cannot avenge, as long as my death will serve to confirm you in your royal state and in the peaceful possession of your Kingdom. But I fear that Your Majesty will soon suffer the same fate that you are now inflicting upon me. If Your Majesty wants to avoid the misfortune that threatens you, beware of Oija Calahom, because ever since his childhood he has been full of malice and treachery, for which reason the King, your father, many times had cause to punish him. He will cunningly sneak in, take the crown from your head, and put you to death along with all those who are of the blood of the King, your father, in order to put himself on the throne and rule the Kingdom."

These remonstrances made no impression on the young King, nor did they stir him to feel pity for the Prince, his lawful uncle. On the contrary, His Majesty remained resolved that the Prince should die and ordered the execution to be carried out. Thereupon the vanquished Prince was led away to the temple named Wat Pramin Khopraja (situated opposite the Court).[41]

41. Wat Phramen Khok Phraya.

There he was placed upon a piece of red cloth, whereupon his chest was dashed in with a piece of sandalwood, a manner of execution used in Siam only for those of royal blood. They wrapped up the body and the sandalwood club in the cloth, and the whole was thrown into a well where the body was left to decompose. Such was the end of this wretched Prince who was the rightful heir to the throne of this mighty Kingdom. But this is fate. He was a Prince in the flower of his life, 26 years of age, of good character and of great promise, who, if he had come to the throne, would have surpassed in virtue the late King, his brother.

23. THE SUPPORTERS OF THE EXECUTED PRINCE ARE ALSO KILLED.

The death of the Prince was much lamented by many of the Mandarins and by the people at large, rich and poor alike. But they had to mourn him in secrecy. They had to be very careful that no one saw them shed tears, because many people of note who had supported His Highness were killed, whereupon their property was confiscated. In this way, Mandarins and soldiers alike were reduced to slavery. All this was done so thoroughly that within a very short time the entire party of the Prince had been reduced to nought.

24. THE FLIGHT, IMPRISONMENT, MIRACULOUS ACTIONS, AND DEATH OF THE SUPREME COMMANDER OF THE EXECUTED PRINCE.

Oloangh Mancongh, the former General of the Prince's army, was reduced to despair by the defeat and death of his Lord. But having been forewarned that the King's men were searching for him everywhere, he fled from one place to another. Finally, he secretly entered the city of Iudia under the cover of darkness with the intention of surprising Oija Calahom in his house and beating him to death. But Oija Calahom was by accident detained at the Court that night so that the project was unsuccessful. For that reason, he went to his own house and took away his first wife and one of his concubines and fled with them to Pra Sopsacce-Cram[42] on the frontier with the Kingdom of Pegu. There he dwelt for some time, living very poorly on fishing, hunting, and the fruits that God provided.

At last his place of retreat (even though it was very remote) was discovered, and while he was out hunting, his women were caught and brought before the magistrate of the district. Upon learning that his women had been taken from him and were being held by the magistrate, Oloangh Mancongh decided that for him, too, the time had come to renounce all pleasure. He went to the nearest town, revealed his identity, and voluntarily surrendered himself, requesting only that he be taken to Iudia.

42. Prasop Sakaekrang, ประสบสะแกกรัง. The Sakaekrang is a tributary which falls from the Tanaosi range and joins the Chaophraya near Uthai Thani.

Forewarned of Oloangh Mancongh's supernatural strength and the advantages he derived from black magic, the magistrate caused him to be locked in irons, which were attached to seven different parts of his body.[43] But Mancongh laughed scornfully, telling his captors that it was vain to put in irons and bonds one who had surrendered himself voluntarily. "For," he said, "if I had any desire to live, it would not be in the power of any one of you either to seize or to keep me. And with these words (to the amazement of all the bystanders) he snapped his bonds as easily as if they were made of dried-up hemp rope. He then went on: "If I wanted to show my strength and powers, I could cause many of you to lose your lives. But I wish to die; therefore, take me to Iudia free of bonds so that the tyrannical King and Oija Calahom, those murderers of the Prince, may satiate themselves with my blood, for which they have long been athirst."

The young King was very pleased to learn that Oloangh Mancongh had arrived in Iudia, because His Majesty loved him for his black magic and his courage. Desiring to save Mancongh's life, he sent to him Oija Calahom, who, pretending to act of his own volition, sought to prevail upon him to offer his services to His Majesty, telling him that if he took the oath of fidelity to the King, his life would be spared. But Oloangh Mancongh did not want to listen and said: "The King, Sir, is no more, and the young King and you have murdered the Prince, his lawful successor. For that reason, I too want to die. I prefer death to serving this unlawful King, who, along with you, Calahom, and all your followers, is a murderer of the Prince, a bloodsucker, a spoiler of a flourishing Kingdom, a disturber of the peace. I shall not take the oath of fidelity."

After Calahom had reported to His Majesty what Oloangh Mancongh had said, the King sentenced him to death by the sword. But having been led to the usual place of execution, Oloangh Mancongh made an address to the bystanders in which he represented to them the dangers that threatened the Kingdom and foretold many of the misfortunes that later came to pass. He concluded his address by referring to his strength and his knowledge of black magic, adding that if there were still people who did not know of his powers or who doubted the truthfulness of what he had said, he would give them proof in their presence. With these words he laid down to be executed, but the executioner was unable to even make an incision with his saber, let alone cut his body in two. Every time the executioner struck, the blow sounded as if it had been delivered on an iron anvil, so that after a while the saber became blunted.

Then Oloangh Mancongh rose, snapped the ropes with which he was bound, seized the executioner by the throat, and strangled him. That done he demanded water, over which he pronounced some words, drank some of it, poured some of it on his body, dipped the index finger of his right hand in

43. The normal practice was to fasten irons onto five parts of the prisoner's body.

it, and made a mark on his left side just above the short rib. (Those who are executed by the sword in Siam are struck in the left side, just above the short rib, so that the intestines slip out of the body.)[44] Then he lay down and ordered the second executioner to strike him on the place marked, threatening that if he missed, he would not hesitate to lay him out by the side of his comrade. The executioner struck his blow, but the fear of missing made him err so that the blow was not mortal. Oloangh Mancongh then demanded a kris and gave orders to be stabbed in the heart or else he would kill also the second executioner. Such was the end of this terrible man who was greatly feared by the King and all the Court. Overjoyed with his death, His Majesty and Calahom said quite openly that now at last the party of the Prince was lost and ruined, because with the death of Oloangh Mancongh, the vengeance of the Prince had also died.

25. THE KING IS RUINED BY SENSUALITY, WHILE OIJA CALAHOM CURRIES FAVOR WITH SINCERITY.

Right from the beginning of his reign the young King abandoned himself to all kinds of sensuality, dissoluteness, and debauchery. Seeing himself delivered of his enemies, he rendered himself insupportable to the Mandarins by his pride and arrogance and odious to the people by his cruelty, having none of the good qualities of the late King, his father. His Majesty was greatly feared, and the general view was that he would grow into a severe and aggressive Prince, a view that was substantiated by his amusements and behavior. For the King took great pleasure in seeing elephants fight, in horse riding, in handling weapons, while at the same time his pronouncements were harsh and his demeanor severe, all of which served to alienate the affection of the people around him, although no one dared to say so openly.

His Majesty was so thoughtless that he did not pay any attention to what happened amongst the Mandarins and the people. Instead, he left the governance of the Kingdom to Oija Calahom, being unable to imagine that anyone would dare to trouble him, dispossess him of his Kingdom, and usurp the throne. Making the most of this opportunity, Oija Calahom complained every day in the Council of Mandarins of the King's bad disposition, his dissoluteness, debauchery, and even of his cruelty and tyranny. He represented to them how troublesome he found the governance of the Kingdom, but that he had so much respect both for the last commands of the late King and for the obligations laid upon him by the ties of blood that he remained firmly resolved to do his duty. He would continue to labor with all his might for the preservation of the King's reputation and for the prosperity of the Kingdom. These daily discourses, his courteous manner as well as the goodwill Oija

44. Text in parentheses was written into the margins of the original manuscript.

Calahom showed to everyone ensured that he, much like Absalom, made himself beloved by the Mandarins and the people alike. The result was that he became so important a figure at the Court that everyone sought his favor, which more often than not, people sought to buy with gifts. On feast and ceremonial days so many people called on him that it seemed as if he were the second King and the absolute ruler of the Kingdom.

26. OIJA CALAHOM: HIS ORIGINS, LIFE, WANTON BEHAVIOR, PUNISHMENTS SUFFERED, AND RISE TO PROMINENCE.

In order for subsequent events to be more clearly understood, it is necessary to speak briefly of Oija Calahom's origins, of his reckless behavior in his youth, of the punishments he suffered from time to time, and of the means by which he regained his prominent position at the Court. Calahom's father was the lawful, eldest brother of the mother of the great King,[45] and was called Oija Sijdama Thijra-ija.[46] Although this is a royal title, he held no office and did not share in the administration of the Kingdom. He was a good-natured man and courteous in his manner, for which reason he was beloved by many people. And although the late King conferred many favors upon his lawful uncle, he also on occasion put him in severe imprisonment in order to punish him for the crimes and evil deeds of his son.

From his earliest youth, Calahom was brought up at the Court, where at first he was a Mahat-leck,[47] or page of the great King.[48] When he had reached the age of thirteen, he became Omonsij and supervisor of the royal pages. He was spirited and courageous, but at the same time he led a dissolute life, amusing himself by getting drunk and committing theft, in consequence of which he was several times caught red-handed in the company of sharps and thieves. To punish him for his evil deeds, the King chastised him; on one occasion personally giving him several cuts to the head, and on other occasions throwing him into severe imprisonment. But every time this happened, His Majesty's mother and his father's sister interceded on Calahom's behalf, whereupon the King ordered him released and again received him in favor. At the age of sixteen he was made Pramon Sijfarapha,[49] or captain of the pages, but he continued his reckless life until, at the age of eighteen, he

45. King Songtham.

46. Okya Si Thammathirat, ออกญาศรีธรรมาธิราช. Van Vliet probably misunderstood that this was a "royal title" rather than a high noble rank.

47. *Mahatlek*, royal page.

48. King Songtham.

49. Wicquefort transliterated this as Pramonsy Saropha, which Mundie glossed as Phra Mün Sri Sorarak. Giles (370–1) has a long but inconclusive discussion. There were four *chamun*, heads of the *mahatlek* with 1000 sakdina: Sanphet Phakdi, Si Saowarak, Wai Woranat, Samoe Chairat. Si Saowarak looks the most likely.

committed a crime that merited the punishment of death. Here is the story of the affair.

It is an ancient custom in Siam, established for many centuries, that when the paddy has been harvested and the fields have been cleansed of vermin and weeds by the fire that is put to the stubble, and before the plough is put to the fields, the King goes out into the country in great state and with a large suite. He does this in order to clear the fields of evil spirits so that the fruits of the land will not be damaged and a bountiful harvest will ensue.[50] If the King did not carry out this ceremony, the land would remain barren that year. Having been consulted on this subject, the mathematicians and soothsayers said they had seen in the course of the stars that if the young King himself carried out the ceremony and if he did not delegate the cleansing of the land to one of his Mandarins, he was fated to die within three years.

Accordingly, the commission was given to one of the Lords of the Court, a certain Oija Poelethip, the Grand Storekeeper of the Kingdom,[51] who, however, was prevented from carrying out the ceremony by a sudden and unexpected death. Having been consulted on this accident, the mathematicians said they had seen signs in the stars indicating that a similar fate would befall all his successors, and that, in order to prevent this from happening, the commission should be given to a person of lowly rank. The reason they gave was that the devils had become too proud because too much honor was done them. This had annoyed the Gods, who were displeased also by the prospect that the Kings and the Grand Storekeepers of the Kingdom should lower themselves by personally driving the devils from the fields.

On receiving this advice, the King and his Council thought it well, with the consent also of the mathematicians and the ecclesiastics, to make use for this purpose of a private person, who, under the title of Oija Kheeukhau,[52] would conduct the entire ceremony. This Oija, who was not permitted to perform any other functions, lived away from the Court and did not leave his compound until the day the fields were to be cleansed. On that day he went to the Court and presented himself to the King, who had him clothed in royal robes, whereupon a royal crown shaped like a pyramid was placed on his head. Thus attired, the Oija was placed in a small house, also shaped like a pyramid, and carried out of the Court on the shoulders of a number of men, accompanied by a large suite of musicians, Mandarins, courtiers, as well as commoners. Although his suite was smaller than is customary for the King, everyone was required, on pain of severe punishment, to honor him as if he were the King.

50. The ceremony of *raek na*, the first ploughing, is a Brahmanical court ceremony which usually takes place in the sixth month of the lunar calendar.

51. Unusually, Wicquefort omitted the Thai title and instead substituted "grand Pourvoyeur du Royaume." This is Okya Phonlathep, see Appendix I.

52. Probably Okya Kieo Khao (เกี่ยวข้าว), rice harvesting.

He receives no other income than that which he draws from the fines that are paid to him by those who fail to honor him like a King. Those who approach him along the way, those who fail to close the doors of their houses as he passes, those who leave their shops or stalls in the open street, or remain seated when he passes, all these people are robbed of their money. So many fines are levied that the Oija normally receives about 3 catties in Siamese coin, or about 360 guilders.

As soon as he has left the Court, he has that day all the power and authority of the King, for which reason the real King, for the duration of the day, does not leave his Palace and does not let himself be seen by anyone. When the Paddy King arrives in the fields, everyone who is so inclined is permitted to attack and do battle with his people and the people in his suite, as long as they do not touch either his person or the members of his bodyguard. If the Paddy King, after a furious battle, emerges victorious, the Siamese believe that the coming rice harvest will be abundant. If, on the contrary, the Paddy King suffers a defeat and is driven from the fields, they believe that the devils will render the fields infertile and that the coming harvest will fail. Sometimes a great battle ensues on this day, and normally a few people are cut down. At nightfall the Paddy King returns to the Court, reports to the King, lays aside the crown and the other royal ornaments, and goes back to his poor little house. If, on that day, he has received a lot of money in fines, he can live very comfortably for the whole year; if this is not the case, he has to live soberly.

Now Oija Calahom, when he was still Pramon Sijrapha and about 18 years old, found himself in the country one day when this ceremony was being performed. He was with his brother (who is now feijna[53] or Prince) and both were mounted on elephants and accompanied by their slaves. Calahom attacked the Paddy King and his bodyguard so furiously that it seemed as if he wished to kill all of them. The bodyguards protected their Paddy King, bravely throwing rocks at their assailants, one of whom injured the brother of Pramonsij. This so enraged Calahom that he drew his saber, and attacked the Paddy King with such fury that the latter was forced to flee with all his followers. Not content with this, Oija Calahom went after them, severely injuring all those he caught up with.

Arriving back at the Palace, the Paddy King complained to the King about the violence that had taken place, whereupon His Majesty, greatly angered by Pramonsij's evil deed, summoned him to appear at the Court. But fearing the King's anger, Pramonsij did not dare to appear before him and sought sanctuary amongst the ecclesiastics. The King, however, regarded the matter so seriously that he ordered the arrest of Oijasij, the father of Pramonsij, and

53. *Fai na* or *chao wangna*, Prince of the Front Palace. Thai sources do not concur with this. The royal chronicles say that Phra Sisutham(maracha) was of such bad character that his brother did not appoint him *chao wangna* (*RCA*: 215, ll. 36–41).

threatened to have him executed if his evil son did not immediately present himself at the Court.

Hearing this, Pramonsij appeared before the King and begged for mercy. But His Majesty ordered the pages to seize him, whereupon he personally gave him three cuts in each leg, from just above the knee to his toes. The King then had him thrown into a dungeon, where he was locked in irons that were placed on five parts of his body. There Pramonsij remained for five months until, at the intercession of Tjau Croa Maha-dijtjan[54] (widow of the late King Pra Naridt or the Black King),[55] he was released. But even though the King restored him to favor, Pramonsij could not forget the bad treatment he had received. He thirsted for vengeance, which he desired to wreak principally on two of the King's younger brothers, Pra Onthongh and Pra Sijsingh,[56] even though he knew very well that the King loved his brothers dearly. To this end, Pramonsij invited to his Watracham house[57] (which he had received from the King) four of his companions; namely, Oloangh Pijbon (later became Oija Coraissima and is now deceased),[58] Choen Sisab-Chan (presently Opra Tyila),[59] Choenpra Eptjongh (now Oija Poucelouq),[60] and Omom Tjongh Naij Tjauwangh (nowadays Oija Barckelangh).[61]

After he had entertained them well and after the arrack had made them merry, Pramonsij told them he wanted to avenge himself on the King's brothers (whose residences were located in the same encampment) over the injuries which His Majesty on several occasions had inflicted upon him. The four lords agreed to support him and they undertook, at a date to be fixed, to enter the houses of the King's brothers at night and to kill both of them. Thereupon they all swore an oath of loyalty, which they confirmed by tasting each other's blood.

But the conspiracy having been betrayed five or six days after it was formed by one of the slaves of Pramonsij, the King sent for him and asked him why

54. Ziau Croa Mady Tjan in Wicquefort. Probably something like Chao Khrua Maha-dichan, เจ้าขรัวมหาดิจันทร์ or Manichan, มณีจันทร์. The chronicles' account of Naresuan is so martial and masculine that no royal women are mentioned.

55. Phra Naresuan (r. 1590–1605).

56. Phra-ong Thong and Phra Si Sin.

57. Presumably meaning a house located near a temple called Wat Racham or similar (unidentified).

58. The text in parentheses following these four names was written on the margins of the manuscripts. Okluang Phibun, the Okya of Nakhon Ratchasima (Khorat).

59. Perhaps, Khun Sisap Khan, Okphra Chularatchamontri, head of the right-hand department of the port dealing with westward trade, sakdina 1400 (*KTSD* I: 233); usually a Muslim.

60. Perhaps, Khun Phra Aphaiwong, Okya Phitsanulok.

61. Perhaps, Okmun Chong, a *nai changwang*, head butler in the royal household; now the Okya Phrakhlang.

he had conceived such a despicable plot against his beloved brothers. Pramonsij denied the accusation, swearing solemn oaths to that effect. But the King, convinced of the truth of the report, flew into a rage and took a Japanese sword with which he surely would have hacked him in two, if the sword had not been caught by a supporting beam. Pramonsij tried to get away, but the King ordered him to be seized, whereupon with his own hand he gave him several cuts across his shoulders and back. Then he had him thrown, with his accomplices, in the dungeons among the common thieves. Oija Sij, the father of Pramonsij, was also arrested, but he was released after one month when his innocence had been established.

Some years later, the King decided to raise two powerful armies for the purpose of waging war against Cambodia in order to recall that country to its allegiance.[62] One of the armies, led by the King himself, was to advance on Cambodia overland, while the other army, commanded by Oija Oubrat (Oiya Oubrat is the head of all the nobility and is Stadholder of the Kingdom)[63] and Oija Barckelangh, was to attack by sea. Seizing the opportunity, Pramonsij beseeched the aforementioned Oijas to intercede on his behalf with His Majesty so that he might be released from his bonds and expiate his crime by the brave actions he promised to perform during the war. Touched by the entreaties of these Lords, the King released Pramonsij along with his accomplices after they had been incarcerated for more than three years and sent them by sea to Cambodia. And in truth, though this enterprise was not a success, Pramonsij so well acquitted himself that, on the recommendation of the Generals, the King once more restored him to favor, allowing him to return to the Court, and honoring him with the title of Sompa Moon.[64]

But for all that, Pramonsij did not change his way of life, for he debauched the concubines of the Prince, the King's brother. Upon hearing of the offense, the King flew into a rage and sentenced him to death, only to pardon him upon the intercession of various people at the Court. Nonetheless, Pramonsij spent another three years in severe imprisonment until, upon the intercession of his father and the King's mother, he was released. Since that time he has bettered his life and has served the King so well that, in recognition of his spirit and intelligence, His Majesty appointed him Oija Sijworra Wongh,[65] the superintendent of the Court. Thereafter His Majesty contracted the illness that was to claim his life. During his illness, when Sijworra Wongh was almost

62. On Songtham's unsuccessful Cambodian campaign, see *Short History*, p. 236.

63. The passage in parentheses was written in the margin of the manuscript. "Stadholder" was the title used by the Princes of Orange as titular heads of state of the Dutch Republic. This is Okya (Maha) Upparat, see Appendix I.

64. Sompan Meon in Wicquefort. Unidentified.

65. ออกญาศรีวรวงศ์ Okya Si Worawong. Perhaps this is Okya Wang (see Appendix I), part of whose name in the Three Seals Law is ศรีวริยพงษ์วงศ์, Si Wiriyapongwong (*KTSD* I: 237).

constantly in the King's presence, he to all intents and purposes became His Majesty's sole adviser. And during this time, he cunningly organized everything in such a way that, in the end, he became Oija Calahom under the young King, by which means he was to usurp the throne, assume the royal dignity, and exterminate almost the entire royal family.

27. CALAHOM DECEIVES THE KING TO THE MISFORTUNE OF MANY AND TO THE ADVANTAGE OF HIS FAVORITES. HE BURNS HIS FATHER'S BONES, EXPERIENCES THE KING'S WRATH, AND IS THREATENED WITH DEATH.

Through cunning design, Oija Calahom undertook to render odious to the young King many of the oldest, most distinguished, wealthiest, and most respected Mandarins. He succeeded so well in this plan that the deceived King came to hate many of the Mandarins, whereupon he had some of them executed, while he banished others, and stripped yet others of their offices, benefices, titles, and property. The King then distributed the vacant places and the confiscated goods to Calahom's creatures and favorites, in consequence of which Calahom came to be both feared and beloved.

Calahom's father had died some time before the death of the great King.[66] And his youngest brother having departed this world some time after, Oija Calahom, in arranging his funeral, caused the bones of his father, whose body had already been burned in accordance with Siamese custom, to be brought and had them burned over again. This is an honor reserved only for the King, or for the Prince who succeeds, irrespective of whether this occurs through force or election (in case of the absence of a rightful heir of royal blood) – he alone is entitled to burn the bones of his parents with royal ceremony.

In order to honor Oija Calahom, most of the prominent Mandarins and many Priests attended the funeral of his brother and father. The ceremonies lasted three days, and (contrary to Siamese custom) they were carried out with greater magnificence than had ever been observed for a Mandarin. The King's mother (who had already become suspicious of Calahom's distribution of the Kingdom's offices to his favorites and partisans) took advantage of this opportunity to render him an object of dislike to her son. Acting in concert with the enemies of Oija Calahom, she put all his actions in such a bad light that the young King was without difficulty led to regard him with suspicion. Convinced that the authority of the Minister put his own in the shade, the King resolved to rid himself of his erstwhile favorite. But he executed his plan with such imprudence and precipitation that he drew upon his own head the misfortune with which he had threatened the other.

66. King Songtham.

On the third day of the funeral of Oija Calahom's brother and father, the young King seated himself on his throne. Urged on by his mother, he indignantly demanded to know what had become of all the Mandarins, why they had not come to the Court as usual and appeared in their usual places at the audience in his presence. Oija Barckelangh (a partisan and creature of Oija Calahom), who had come to the Court every day to observe the King's humor, replied that Oija Calahom was occupied with the cremation of the body of his brother and the bones of his father, and that the Mandarins had been invited to be present at the ceremonies. Thereupon the King, foolishly giving way to anger, retorted vehemently: "I thought that the Kingdom of Siam had only one King, and I imagined myself to be the legitimate and solemnly crowned King to whom all the inhabitants of the Kingdom, whatever their rank, owed honor, respect, and obedience. But it seems that I am King in name only and that Calahom is the real King, because the Mandarins have renounced the service they owe me; they have abandoned me and have attached themselves to Calahom. But I will root out that den of iniquity. When Calahom and his accomplices come to the Court, I shall give them their just deserts, Calahom in particular. He will never again have such a large following, and I will ensure that after his death his body will not be honored in the same way as he has honored the remains of his father and brother." With every mark of respect and submission, Oija Barckelangh tried to explain the reasons why Calahom had held the ceremonies. But the King accused him of being one of Calahom's accomplices and threatened to put him to death as well. His Majesty then caused his guards and servants to be put under arms, whereupon he angrily left the throne room, failing to reflect (so it seems) that, upon hearing of the threats he had made, Calahom could be expected to form a strong party with his supporters.

28. CALAHOM LEARNS OF THE KING'S THREATS AND LAYS A PLOT WITH HIS ACCOMPLICES.

Oija Barckelangh secretly left the King's Court and hastened to find Oija Calahom, to whom he related everything he had heard concerning the threats the King had made regarding Calahom and his supporters. Oija Calahom gave evidence of being greatly astonished and began to sigh and to bewail himself in such a way that the Mandarins (a large number of whom were with him) pressed him to tell them the reason for the great change that had come over him. He then told them with much eloquence of the King's intentions, adding that he was ready to die if his blood could soothe His Majesty's wrath and reconcile him towards them all. "But," said Oija Calahom, "if the King threatens to put me to death, me, who has been his favorite, whom he has so tenderly loved, and who is the most prominent of his Mandarins, if he can do this to me, what misfortunes might not await all of you? And how will you save yourself from the hand of this tyrant? And how will you prevent him from carrying out his evil designs? And please consider, I pray you, what will be the state of the Kingdom after he has caused us all to perish? For you all know how young and inexperienced the King is; you know of his recklessness, his ill humor, his debauchery, and his cruelty. And if such is his character now, what will he become after he has put to death most of his Mandarins and when he will no longer be guided by their wise counsel? It is impossible to doubt that if these things were to take place, the Kingdom will become involved in civil war, and perhaps in a foreign war as well; and that could end only in the complete destruction of the State, causing us to fall under foreign domination."

Accompanying his arguments with tearful lamentations about the impending doom that threatened all of them, Calahom so moved the assembled Mandarins that he succeeded in winning them over to his side. Right then and there they made a league amongst themselves (confirmed by drinking each other's blood) by which they solemnly undertook to use every means at their disposal to prevent Calahom, or any one of their number, falling victim to the King's tyranny.

29. THE CONSPIRATORS SEND BARCKELANGH TO THE COURT TO GAUGE THE KING'S INTENTIONS.

In order to assure themselves of the intentions of the King, and to find out if it was through rage and passion that he had made those threats, the Mandarins resolved to send Oija Barckelangh to the Court. Barckelangh (a resolute and eloquent man, brought up at the Court, where for many years he had been Captain of the Pages of the late King), was to go and see His Majesty, and try to obtain from him merciful forgiveness for Calahom and his friends.

30. BARCKELANGH TRIES TO DEFEND CALAHOM BUT, INSTEAD OF LISTENING, HIS MAJESTY THREATENS CALAHOM A SECOND TIME.

On his arrival at the Court, Oija Barckelangh boldly told the King why he had come, and sought to persuade him that he was badly informed as to the intentions and actions of Oija Calahom and the Mandarins. But he found that the King was in such a rage that he refused to hear him out. Instead, the King said roughly: "Barckelangh, you, too, are one of Calahom's accomplices. Once I thought better of you, but now I see that you and Calahom are walking along the same path, and that both of you have become traitors. Therefore, I will soon give you your just desert. But first, let Calahom come to the Court so that I can give him the punishment that he deserves."

31. THE CONSPIRATORS DISPERSE AND RALLY THEIR FORCES, WHILE BARCKELANGH RETURNS TO THE COURT TO ALLAY THE KING'S SUSPICIONS.

Seeing the King in such a rage, Barckelangh became fearful and left the Court. He reported his experiences to Calahom and the Mandarins, and advised them that they should all go home, rally their slaves, horses, and elephants, and assemble their forces at Petou-tsjaeij (the heart-gate).[67] From there they were to march on the Palace in order to attack and occupy it, and to take the King prisoner. Calahom and his supporters approved this advice, whereupon they all went to muster their forces. Barckelangh, however, boldly went to the Court once more, ostensibly to reiterate to the King his plea of mercy for Calahom, but in reality to allay the King's suspicions, to find out whether the plans for an attack had been discovered, and to see what defensive measures were being taken.

32. OIJA CALAHOM AND HIS BROTHER WIN OVER OIJA CAPHEIJN, THE KING'S GENERAL, WHO ABANDONS THE KING AND ADOPTS THEM AS HIS SONS.

Oija Capheijn (a Moor by origin and religion)[68] was one of the most powerful Mandarins in the Kingdom. He was a man of great authority and respectability, richly endowed with earthly possessions, and commanding a personal force of more than 200 elephants, 2,000 slaves, and a large number of horses. Since Oija Capheijn had not attended his funeral festivities, Oija Calahom feared that he might join the King and resist him and his accomplices. To prevent this happening, Calahom (with his brother Oija Sijworra Wongh) called on Oija Capheijn at his house, complaining bitterly of the threats the King had made against him and against all the Mandarins who had attended his funeral ceremonies. He added that he was more than willing to suffer an undeserved death, but that he was greatly saddened by the thought that if he should die, great misfortune would befall many excellent Mandarins who would be executed, even though they were entirely innocent. He went on to say that this unjust decision of a tyrannical King could be averted only by courageous opposition, whereupon he told Oija Capheijn of the action he and the Mandarins, through sheer necessity, had resolved to undertake against the King.

67. Here, as in the *Description* (see p. 114, fn. 57), Van Vliet seems to muddle up the near homonyms, heart and victory. This is probably ประตูศรีไชยศักดิ์ (*pratu si chai sak*), the gate of auspicious and mighty victory, on the north side of the palace.

68. The identification in parentheses was totally omitted by Wicquefort/Mundie. Capheijn or Capheim appears often in Dutch sources for Kamphaengphet, so this would be the Okya Kamphaengphet. Other sources corroborate the facts given in the next few lines that this provincial lord commanded considerable military power.

Calahom had said all this so earnestly and intensely that Oija Capheijn was moved to pity. Seeing this, Calahom and his brother threw themselves at his feet, begging him: "Father, please accept us as your sons and protect all those who have been unjustly condemned by a thoughtless King. Save our lives and free us from this careless tyrant. If you act thus, we will strive to make you King and faithfully serve you. This is the only way to preserve the Kingdom of Siam, which otherwise will perish through the unhappy rashness of the King."

Unaware of what was in Calahom's heart, Oija Capheijn made the two brothers rise and adopted them as his sons. Thereupon they swore fidelity one to the other, which they confirmed by drinking each other's blood. Having in this fashion made sure of this powerful Mandarin, Calahom went home to arm his own people, with whom he soon joined his accomplices at the appointed place.

33. OIJA CALAHOM AND HIS ACCOMPLICES STORM THE PALACE, WHILE HIS MAJESTY, MISLED BY BARCKELANGH, TAKES TO FLIGHT.

While Oija Barckelangh was deceiving the King with tearful requests for a pardon for Oija Calahom and the Mandarins, Calahom assembled his troops and marched straight to the Palace. He arrived there in strength. Not only did he bring his own forces and those of his accomplices, but also the soldiers of the King, whom he had been able to muster because he held the office of Captain-General of the Elephants and Cavalry. Hearing unusual noises in the distance, the King startled and, in an astonished tone of voice, asked Barckelangh: "What does this mean? Has Calahom betrayed me, and is he coming to attack the Palace?" But Barckelangh assured His Majesty of the contrary, and in order to allay all suspicion he said: "Please, Your Majesty, take my body as a pledge. If Calahom should undertake the slightest thing to undermine your authority, Your Majesty can order to have my body cut in two pieces and fed to the animals."

The careless King was so much put at ease by this that he completely neglected to issue orders to his men to put themselves in a state of defense. In the meantime, Calahom steadily approached, and when at last he reached the Palace, he attacked at once with great fury. Hearing this, the King lost courage altogether, and gripped by great fear, he ordered the guards and all other persons who happened to be at the Court to resist the attackers with all their might. Realizing that he was now in mortal danger, Barckelangh told the King that he wanted to see for himself what was happening, promising to return at once and make a report to His Majesty. Still not doubting the loyalty of Barckelangh, the King allowed him to go.

But as soon as Barckelangh had left His Majesty, he went to the main gate of the Palace, where he knew Oija Calahom had assembled his force of soldiers, slaves, and Japanese. He opened the gate and led the soldiers to the room where he had just left the King, intending to take him prisoner. But the King, fearing capture, had withdrawn to another part of the Palace, so that Barckelangh failed in his object for that time. Outside the Palace there was fighting on all sides, because many of the attackers did not realize that the gate had been opened. Calahom, however, had entered the Palace with his people and the Japanese and was frantically searching for the King. The Japanese soldiers cut down all who tried to resist, so that terrible carnage resulted and much blood was spilled.

The King, his guards, and Court servants resisted bravely, so that in some parts of the Palace fighting continued until daybreak. Realizing that Barckelangh had deceived him, and seeing also that there was no hope of resisting the powerful attack of the rebels, especially the Japanese, His Majesty bemoaned (albeit too late) his imprudence and credulity. At last abandoning the Palace, the King mounted an elephant and, without any entourage, fled across the river which flows through the town, taking refuge in the temple Nomplij Mecamjongh,[69] which is situated above the town and bears a great reputation for sanctity. Here he remained several days, living very soberly among the priests.

34. OIJA CALAHOM TAKES THE PALACE AND DISTRIBUTES REWARDS TO HIS FAVORITES.

Seeing himself master of the Palace at the break of day, Calahom at once secured the King's jewels and treasures. Immediately, he distributed a number of sabers richly inlaid with gold and silver and many other valuable gifts to his favorites and to all those who had distinguished themselves in battle. He raised many slaves and other humble people to positions of wealth and power, whereby he ensured their everlasting gratitude and loyalty.

35. OIJA CAPHEIJN SEATS HIMSELF ON THE THRONE AND REQUESTS TO BE CONFIRMED AS KING, BUT OIJA CALAHOM OPPOSES IT.

Oija Capheijn (like Absalom, King of Israel; Amuratus, Sultan of the Turks; Anthonino Caracalla, Emperor of Rome; Prahartes, King of the Parthians; and many other illegitimate tyrants), was gripped by a lust for power.[70]

69. Probably a *wat* in the Makham Yong area to the northwest of the city. The chronicles locate this capture at (Pa) Mok Noi (*RCA*: 213).

70. Van Vliet may be tossing off stray references here. Caracalla qualifies as a usurper and is mentioned twice again below. Absalom, also mentioned again below, rebelled against his royal father, David, but failed and never had a chance to be a tyrant. The three minor Ottoman Sultans named Murat in the fourteenth to sixteenth centuries succeeded legitimately and ruled unremarkably. Similarly the four rulers of Parthia (Persia) named Prahates in the second and first centuries BC all succeeded their fathers.

Knowing that the King had disappeared, and that he had either fled or had died in the fighting, Capheijn (so it seemed) trusted the word of Calahom and his brother Sijworra Wongh that they wanted to make him King. Accordingly, he seated himself on the throne, placed the crown on his head, took the royal pillow under his arms, held the royal sword and the golden fan,[71] and presented himself as King. Oija Capheijn said to Calahom: "My son, fortune has favored us today! Come, and greet the father you have chosen and who has adopted you for his son. Render me the honor that you owe me as your King in order that all the other Mandarins who are present at the Court will follow your example, recognize me as their King, and confirm me in the possession of the Kingdom. If you do this, I shall make you Prince and declare you heir to the Kingdom of Siam."

Seeing Oija Capheijn on the royal throne, wearing the crown and the royal regalia, Oija Calahom startled and became angry, for he had begun to imagine himself in that position. Nevertheless, hiding his displeasure and maintaining a friendly countenance, he said to Oija Caphein: "Lord Father, it is still too early to take possession of the throne and have yourself declared King because we don't know what has become of the King, whether he is alive or not. Moreover, the late King has other sons, one of whom is 11 years old. Let us choose him and crown him King because, by acting thus, we ensure that the royal dignity passes to the rightful heir, which means that no one can accuse us of having taken up arms in order to usurp the crown."

Oija Capheijn replied: "Son, the throne of the Kingdom of Siam is too sacred and too venerable for it to be occupied by a mere child, but at the same time the throne cannot remain vacant. If you, who has chosen me as your father, do not wish to crown me, and recognize me as King, approach and receive the dignity from my hands. I will place the crown on your head and proclaim you King." But pretending to be disturbed and surprised, Calahom refused the honor. He begged Oija Capheijn (in order to avoid scandal and misfortune) to vacate the throne, so that they could act together and search for the fugitive King. Seeing that he would not be able to attain his design, Oija Capheijn stepped down from the throne and joined Oija Calahom.

36. THE FUGITIVE KING IS CAPTURED, CONDEMNED, AND TOGETHER WITH HIS MOTHER DIES A MISERABLE DEATH.

After a long search, the fugitive King was located at the temple of Nomplij Mecam Iongh. There he was seized and forcibly taken to the Palace, where the assembled Mandarins, at the suggestion of Oija Calahom, declared him unworthy of governing for the reason that he had abandoned the Palace, and

71. One of the royal regalia, associated with the "coolness and sublime comfort attributed to divine kings" (Wales 1931: 100).

by so doing had exposed the Kingdom to grave danger. The Mandarins, however, went a step further. They decided that by fleeing the Palace, the King had not only forfeited his right to rule, but also his right to live, whereupon they sentenced him to death.

Seeing that the whole assembly was inclined to put the King to death, Calahom pretended to oppose it, saying that His Majesty's life should be spared. But nonetheless, he allowed himself to be overruled by a majority of votes. When the sentence of death was pronounced, the King did not display any signs of sadness, saying he had not expected anything else from his treacherous Mandarins. He reproached Barckelangh for the treason he had committed, complained bitterly to all the other Mandarins of their rebellion, and lamented the bad advice Oija Calahom had given the deceased King, his father, regarding the succession. Then, addressing Calahom directly, he said: "You, Calahom, came into this world at an evil hour because you have poisoned the King, my father, and, by your machinations, you have caused the death of my uncle, the Prince. And now you want to also shed my royal blood. If my execution were to satisfy the Kingdom and put an end to the murders, my death would at least be bearable, but I greatly fear that the murders will not cease and that you will be the scourge of the Kingdom and its people. But in the end, the Supreme God of all Gods will avenge my death and make you pay for the evil you have done."

After speaking thus, the King begged the Mandarins to spare his mother's life and requested to be allowed to speak to her before he died. Hereupon Oija Calahom summoned the King's mother, whose name was Praongh Narit,[72] to appear before the assembled Mandarins. After denying all responsibility and, like Pilate, washing his hands, Calahom bitterly reproached her, saying that she was the cause of all the revilement he undeservedly had suffered, of all the misfortunes that had occurred, and of all the blood that had been shed. And because she had borne so wicked a son, whom she had led to his doom, she did not deserve to live. Calahom added that if she was prepared to forsake her son, cast aside natural love, and approve the sentence of death that had been passed upon him, he would preserve her life and give her maintenance in accordance with her royal rank.

The Queen bore all this opprobrium with equanimity, and with firm resolve she wisely replied: "The King, My Lord, has come to the end of his days. Owing to the misguided counsel with which you inspired the late King, our son ascended to the throne and received the ill-fated crown. But since your cruelty and ambition have now destined him to such a sad end, I prefer to die with him rather than receive my sustenance from your blood-stained hand. The fear of the pains of death will not compel me to deny my son whom I

72, Kachorn (see Vliet 2003, p. 298, fn. 1) suggested this might be พระองค์อัมฤทธิ์, Queen Amarit.

have borne in my body, to whom I have given birth, and whom I have nursed with care. I will not cast aside natural love, even if I was to suffer as many deaths as my body has tender parts, because if I were to sink so low as to deny my son, your bloodthirsty disposition would soon cause you to put me to death. I have lived but few years, but I have lived long enough to have wandered in the field of wretchedness and to have tasted the bitterness of life. Therefore, I do not want to avoid death for it will be but a pathway to a peaceful rest. Having given life to my son, I want to end my life with him."

The King and his mother were taken to the old ruined temple of Wat Pra Minkho Praja,[73] where the executioners laid them down on a scarlet cloth, whereupon they used a sandalwood club to dash in their chests. The bodies were contemptuously cast into a well where they were simply left to rot. On arriving at the place of execution, the King, who had ruled eight months, loudly lamented his misfortune and also that of his mother, who, innocent of any crime, for his sake was about to taste the bitterness of death. He also recalled the prophecy of the Prince, his lawful uncle, who not long ago had been executed on his orders at the same place and in the same manner as he himself was now about to die. But the Queen remained undaunted, saying to her son: "Have courage, and in the hour of death show that you are a true King. The Gods have not wanted a different destiny for us." And so also this King suffered the fate that so often befalls tyrants and murderers of blood relatives. For instance, when Ismael, the second son of Techmas, King of Persia, had killed all his brothers, all Princes and all the Lords he suspected, he himself, after six months, was poisoned by his sister.[74]

37. THE KING'S SUPPORTERS ARE ALSO KILLED AND EXTERMINATED.

Many of the great Lords and nobles who had remained loyal to the young King were killed. Others who had not joined Calahom's side and had not helped him attain his design were sent into exile. Others again were stripped of their offices, benefices, and means. The slaves and the confiscated goods were divided amongst Calahom's favorites, so that in a short period of time great changes occurred in the Siamese kingdom because many great Lords fell from their powerful positions into slavery, while others were raised from humble positions to occupy the highest offices.

73. Wat Phramen Khok Phraya.

74. Tahmasp I, the second shah of the Safavid dynasty in Persia, succeeded in 1524 at the age of 10 and ruled until 1576. He was followed by his son, Ismail II, who executed many of his family and followers, and was himself killed within a year.

38. THE BROTHER OF THE EXECUTED KING, AGED 10 YEARS, SUCCEEDS TO THE THRONE. OIJA CALAHOM BECOMES GUARDIAN OF THE CHILD AND REGENT OF THE KINGDOM.

The young King having been executed, the Oijas Calahom and Barckelangh, unaccompanied by bodyguards, slaves, or followers of any kind, took to a small boat in the middle of the night. Under the cover of darkness they made their way to the house of Oija Senaphimocq, the Colonel of the Japanese, in order to covertly inquire into his feelings regarding the succession. Calahom put it to him that the Kingdom could not exist without a King; that the great King, father of the one just deceased, had only left several small children; that it would be dangerous to entrust the royal dignity to a Prince so young; and that it would be a pity to have the whole Kingdom governed by a mere child. He begged Oija Senaphimocq to consider whether, in order to avoid all misfortunes and difficulties, it would not be better provisionally to elect and crown as King one of the most prominent Mandarins, who would govern the Kingdom until the children had come of age, whereupon he would renounce the dignity and hand over power to the most able of the Princes.

The Japanese, discerning Calahom's intentions, replied as follows: "If one of the Mandarins was to be elected King, you would be that person because you are of royal blood and, in addition, you are so accomplished that, in all fairness, we would not be able to go past you. If we were to elect you as King, it would seem to the whole world as if we had killed the young King out of passion, and that you had served him unjustly in order to have an opportunity to seize power illegally. And if we were to elect another Mandarin, it is greatly to be feared that when the Prince comes of age, he will not want to resign the Crown and that, in order to secure his rank, he will exterminate the entire royal family. Please consider that two Kings (whose deaths I regret) have already perished and that much blood has been shed. Surely, the time has come for the killing to cease and for peace to be restored to the Kingdom and its people. Therefore, let us crown the young Prince as King and appoint you guardian of the child and Regent of the Kingdom so that you can support the young child with wise counsel and, through resolute leadership, properly govern the Kingdom. For as long as the lawful bloodline of the great King exists and for as long as I can prevent it, the Crown will not be alienated from the rightful lineage."

Oija Calahom (unable to do anything else) approved the sentiments of the Japanese regarding the crowning of the young Prince, but declined to be chosen guardian and Regent. But nonetheless, at the suggestion of the Japanese he went to the Royal Palace, and the following day he summoned all the Mandarins to come to the Court. At the assembly, Calahom explained at great length that Siam could not be left without a King. He reminded the Mandarins that there were still Princes, sons of the great King, and brothers of the one recently executed, among whom there was a youth of good prospects about ten years of age, and proposed that this young Prince should receive the royal dignity and be crowned King. The assembly, and especially Oija Japan, approved this proposal, whereupon the boy was taken from school and crowned as King under the name of Praongh Athit Soerawangh.[75]

The venerable Lords, as well as the people generally, took great pleasure in this investiture in the hope that peace would now be restored to the Kingdom and that the bloodshed would cease. In view of his royal blood and his family relationship to the young Prince, Oija Calahom, at the same assembly and with the consent of the entire royal family, was made guardian of the young King and Regent of the Kingdom. Outwardly unwilling to accept this post, Calahom agreed to act in this capacity only after great protestations and the humble entreaties of all and sundry.

39. CONCERNED ABOUT OIJA CAPHEIJN'S WEALTH AND POWER, OIJA CALAHOM CUNNINGLY PLOTS THE DEATH OF HIS ERSTWHILE ALLY.

With the succession of the second young King and with his acceptance of the post of Regent of the Kingdom, Oija Calahom's star was clearly in the ascendancy. He realized, however, that he would be unable to reach his goal and attain the royal dignity if he did not soon remove the two great obstacles that stood in his path, namely, Oija Capheijn and Sinaphimocq. Calahom was of the opinion that Oija Capheijn aspired to the Crown, because after the Palace had been taken, he had seated himself on the throne and had adorned himself with the royal regalia, whereupon he had earnestly requested that Calahom crown him and declare him King. Calahom was hostile also to Sinaphimocq. As long as the bloodline of the great King existed, the Japanese refused to allow the alienation of the Crown from the rightful lineage. Moreover, the Oija had mourned the young King's death in Calahom's presence, and with the power he derived from his command over his Japanese soldiers, he would be able to prevent a change in the succession.[76]

Therefore, Calahom began to think of ways to put Oija Capheijn out of the way so that he would not be cunningly able to combine with the Japanese and use his status, wealth, and power to thwart his plan. Accordingly, Calahom disclosed his purpose to Oija Barckelang and together they resolved that

75. Phra-ong Athit Surawong, otherwise called Phra Athittayawong (r. Aug.–Sept. 1629).

76. This passage is significantly different in detail from the Wicquefort/Mundie version, particularly on the role of Yamada. Here and in the previous section, Yamada insists on the importance of legitimacy by bloodline, while the Thai participants show no similar concern. Here, too, Yamada's critical control of armed guards is emphasized.

Calahom would approach the young King, accuse Oija Capheijn of capital offenses, and when inquiries were made, Barckelangh would confirm the truth of the accusations.

Thereafter, Calahom went to the King and told His Majesty at great length that Oija Capheijn had been the principal instigator of the flight and death of the late King. He alleged that Oija Capheijn had incited the Mandarins to take up arms, and that he had forced some Mandarins to join the rebellion by threatening them with his slaves and elephants. He said, further, that after the young King had fled, Oija Capheijn had seated himself on the royal throne, that he had dressed himself in royal garments, and that he had several times requested to be proclaimed King, but that they (referring to their own persons) had prevented him from carrying out this evil scheme. Oija Capheijn, he said, had been a secret supporter of the executed Prince, who (when he had been sent to defeat the Prince) had wanted to join forces with His Highness, which surely he would have done if the Japanese Colonel had not stopped him. Oija Capheijn, he continued, had greatly regretted the death of the Prince, and he had dared to say that his murder would not remain unpunished and unavenged. All these things, said Calahom, permitted no other conclusion than that Oija Capheijn was an enemy of the children of the great King and their family, and that he had been a secret supporter of His Majesty's brother, the executed Prince.

After Oija Barckelangh had confirmed these false accusations, Calahom advised the King that, for the sake of the security of his person and the preservation of the Kingdom, it was necessary to do away with Oija Capheijn. The young king, who was a mere child, gave his approval, whereupon Oija Capheijn was arrested and put in prison, where he was locked in chains which were attached to seven parts of his body. His house was given up to pillage and his slaves were distributed among Calahom's favorites, so that in a very short space of time he was stripped of all his power.

But even though Oija Capheijn was now in severe imprisonment, he was not unduly disturbed thereby, firmly trusting as he did in the sworn friendship of Oija Calahom, who, he imagined, would surely deflect the King's wrath. Repeatedly he said that he was certain that his enemies had deceived the young Prince, that the Prince was misinformed about his activities, and that his son, Oija Calahom, would soon have him released from his bonds.

Eventually, Oija Calahom of his own volition went to see Oija Capheijn (at the place where he was imprisoned), pretending to be hugely astonished. He consoled the prisoner, urged him to be patient, and told him in great detail that Kingdoms ruled by children are always unfortunate. After Capheijn had complained about his arrest, about the King's harsh procedures against him, and after he had requested Calahom's intercession with His Majesty, Oija Calahom hypocritically replied: "Father, please cheer up and do not seek the help or advice of anyone. I swear by the oath with which we are bound to each other that before the sun sets you will be freed from your heavy bonds and be released from prison. It is certain that the King, our Lord, has listened to malicious slander and that your enemies have misled him. I know everything and I shall inform His Majesty of your honesty and good character, and I will ensure that from now on you will be freed from misfortunes of the kind that have presently befallen you." With these words Calahom took his leave.

Trusting Calahom's word, Capheijn remained behind in his prison confident of a good outcome. But death was closer than he himself realized, because about two hours before sunset he was released from his bonds and taken outside the Court to the Thacham gate[77] by the side of the river, where he was to be executed. Realizing that he was about to die and that Oija Calahom had deceived him, Oija Capheijn became angry and bravely declaimed against him. Loudly lamenting the deceit and treachery of Calahom, he said: "For shame, you accursed villain. Have you chosen me for your father[78] in order to shed my innocent blood, bring disgrace to my house, pillage my wealth, enslave my wives and my children? Now I see what you have been carrying in your perfidious heart. Even though you have treacherously done away with a King, your thirst for blood has not been sated because you yourself aspire to the crown. You will be like a scythe to the King's children, and you will bring ruin to the Kingdom."

After Oija Capheijn had spoken these earnest words and after his anger had subsided a little, he requested to be allowed to plead his innocence before the King, or failing this, to be brought to trial so that he could be judged in accordance with the customs of the country. But all his entreaties were in vain. Instead, he was hastily tied up, placed upon the trunk of a banana tree, and struck on his left side so that his intestines slipped out of his body. They pierced his neck with a rattan, and in this way they hung his body on a bamboo gallows so that all the people could see him. He was treated as if he had been a conspirator against the King. In truth, the words of a certain Latin poet pertain to this history:

> Amongst people who together
> Strive for a royal name,
> One finds neither faith nor concord.
> For those who thirst for the highest power
> Cannot regard as equal any other person,
> For they desire that all make way for them.

77. Tha Chang gate.

78. See Section 32 above where Calahom and his brother pleaded with Capheijn to "please accept us as your sons" in order to win him to their side.

The Japanese, Oija Senaphimocq, had not been at the Court that day, but when he learned that Oija Capheijn had been killed, he was very displeased with Oija Calahom. He was unhappy that Calahom had not prevented the execution, or at least, that he had not sent for him so that he could have interceded with the King on Capheijn's behalf (he did not know that Oija Calahom had been the false accuser and the cause of the execution). Upon hearing the news, Sinaphimocq immediately went to the Court. In an act of compassion, he had Capheijn's body taken down from the gallows and had it buried, weeping bitter tears for the death of his friend. Although Calahom was very displeased with this act of mercy, he dared not show his feelings because the Japanese was a man of great authority, a man, moreover, who wielded great power on account of the loyalty of his Japanese soldiers.

40. THE RICHES OF OIJA CAPHEIJN ARE DIVIDED BETWEEN CALAHOM AND BARCKELANGH. HIS WIVES AND CHILDREN ARE ENSLAVED AND ARE CONDEMNED TO SERVITUDE.

The immovable property of the executed Oija Capheijn, as well as his elephants, horses, war materials, gold and silver (which was buried, in accordance with Siamese custom), and the slaves that had been absent at the time of the looting, fell into the hands of the Oijas Calahom and Barckelangh. In this way Calahom acquired the means to make new friends and to strengthen the attachment to his cause of those who had already chosen his side. The first wife of Oija Capheijn and her daughter, as well as several of his concubines and their children, were brought to the Court, where they remain to this day as servants of the Queen. The remaining women and children were enslaved. Several of the sons were also taken to the Court, where they were distributed amongst several Mandarins, whom they still serve. None of Oija Capheijn's wives and daughters has ever married, nor have any of his sons risen to any rank, office, or position of power.

41. CALAHOM PLOTS AGAINST OIJA SENAPHIMOCQ, ALBEIT FRUITLESSLY.

It did not escape the attention of Oija Calahom that Oija Seaphimocq had dared to show compassion to the body of Oija Capheijn, even though the latter had been rejected by the King and had been executed at his command. He became cautious because he began to suspect that these two lords had been closer to each other than he, or anyone else, had supposed. He became fearful of the revenge of the Japanese, and in order to enhance his security, he adopted a friendlier posture towards all the other Mandarins with a view to winning their affection.

The Japanese, Oija Senaphimocq, absented himself from the Court for several days and avoided the company of Oija Calahom, because he now understood the duplicitous role he had played in respect of the execution of Oija Capheijn. But unable to endure Senaphimocq's absence, Oija Calahom resolved to visit him at his house in order (as may be supposed) to complain about the difficulty of his position, the King's youth, the fact that he had to execute His Majesty's will, for which reason he was unjustly hated, and to emphasize that he was innocent of Oija Capheijn's death. But the Japanese refused Calahom entry to his house; in fact, he closed the gate and declined to see him, an insult which Calahom bore with patience, even though it gave him a lot to think about.

42. CALAHOM'S FURTHER ACTIONS AGAINST SENAPHIMOCQ MEET WITH SUCCESS.

At that time the Honorable Sebalt Wonderaer (then a free merchant and Captain of the yacht Peerl, and presently Receiver-General of East India Company revenues at Batavia) arrived in the Siam river, at the city of Iudia. This caused Oija Calahom to become concerned that Oija Senaphimocq and his Japanese, in order to avenge the death of Oija Capheijn, might seek the assistance of the Netherlanders, and with their help undertake something against his person and state. Therefore, Calahom, through the intermediary of Oija Barckelangh, warned the aforementioned Captain that, given the perilous state of the Kingdom, he should remain with his yacht in the defensive position it occupied and should refrain from joining forces with anyone. And as a sign of the confidence the King and Calahom had in the Captain, they presented His Honor with a golden saber from the royal treasury.

At the same time, Oija Calahom covertly caused the rumor to be spread that Oija Senaphimocq and his Japanese, with the help of the Netherlanders, were planning to mount an evil action, a rumor that caused such consternation among the Mandarins that they all took up arms against each other. However, Calahom's only purpose in spreading this rumor was to enter into dialogue with Senaphimocq, to placate his thirst for revenge, and to secure his friendship. But in view of the preparations the Japanese were now believed to be making, Oija Senaphimocq had become so suspect with the King and the Mandarins that (in order to have certainty regarding his intentions) he was summoned to appear at Court. But as the Siamese are wont to do, Senaphimocq excused himself by pleading indisposition, although it is more likely that it was fear that prevented him from appearing at Court.

Taking advantage of this convenient opportunity, Oija Calahom took courage and for the second time went to see the Japanese at his house. This time Senaphimocq opened the gate and received him. During the interview, Calahom advanced so many arguments and in such a persuasive and sincere way that Oija Senaphimocq yielded and put aside all the feelings of ill will and all the thoughts of revenge he had harbored. In addition, Calahom gave Senaphimocq such plausible assurances that he would soon rise to high office that they renewed their friendship and swore an solemn oath never again to stand in each other's way, but instead to assist each other in all matters. They confirmed this oath by tasting each other's blood.

43. CALAHOM PREPARES TO RID HIMSELF OF OIJA SENAPHIMOCQ, AND AT HIS SUGGESTION THE GOVERNOR OF LIJGOOR IS SUMMONED TO THE COURT.

Peace having thus been made between the two ministers, Oija Calahom at once thought of a crafty plan to remove the Japanese (who was the last and the greatest obstacle to the realization of his design) and put him out of the way. At the meeting of His Majesty's Council, and with the approval of the King, he proposed that some of the Governors be summoned to appear at the Court in the city of Iudia to take the oath of loyalty to the King and to do him homage. Due to the recent changes in succession, said Oija Calahom, unrest and disloyalty could easily break out in the distant provinces, and these dangers had to be averted by timely action so that the Kingdom would remain secure. Everyone at the meeting approved of this proposal, whereupon the Council decided that Oija Ligoor should thus be recalled.

Calahom knew full well that this Oija could not afford to be absent from Ligoor at this time for reason that the Patanese were threatening war, and also because many of the local people were about to rise in rebellion. He expected, therefore, that Oija Ligoor would refuse to come to Iudia and would ask to be excused. And if this happened, Calahom would have a pretext for accusing the Governor of disobedience and an opportunity to send Oija Senaphimocq to arrest him. Therefore, the Trakhausa-by-dij,[79] that is, an order under the great seal, was at once sent to summon Oija Ligoor to the Court.

Suspecting that something was amiss, and facing the aforementioned twin threats of invasion and rebellion, Oija Ligoor and his Council decided to postpone his departure. With the greatest humility the Oija asked the young King to be excused, assuring His Majesty at the same time that he recognized him as his lawful lord and the sovereign ruler of the Kingdom. With this message the envoy returned to Oija Calahom. At the King's Council meeting which was held shortly afterwards, Oija Calahom so skillfully managed to misrepresent Oija Ligoor's arguments and excuses that the aforementioned Oija was declared to be a rebel and a person who resisted the King's commands. For that reason it was decided to immediately send another Governor there and to arrest Oija Ligoor and forcibly bring him to the Court in order for him to undergo his richly deserved punishment.

79. *Tra kosathibodi*, the Phrakhlang's seal or a document carrying it.

44. CALAHOM TRIES TO SEND SENAPHIMOCQ TO LIGOOR, BUT PHIMOCQ PREFERS TO STAY IN SIAM.

This resolution having been taken, Oija Calahom reminded the Council of the importance of the Governorship of Ligoor, emphasising that Ligoor was one of Siam's principal provinces, that it had an excellent seaport, and so forth. He told the Council of the rebellion of the people of Ligoor, of the threats of Patani, and everything else he could think of that would further his design. A distinguished, vigilant, and courageous hero, said Calahom, should be dispatched to Ligoor to arrest the current Governor and send him to Iudia, to inspire the people of Patani with terror, and either to satisfy the complaints of the Ligoor people, or to forcibly bring them to submission. No one, Calahom suggested, was better suited to undertake this mission than Oija Senaphimocq, a proposal that was approved by the King and Mandarins.

However, the Japanese, Oija Senaphimocq, proved entirely unwilling, and in the most amicable way asked to be excused from having to undertake this commission. He wanted to stay in Siam because, so it seems, he had perceived Calahom's design. He suspected that Calahom wanted to be rid of him so that the power of his Japanese soldiers would not stand in the way of the realization of his ambitions.

45. CALAHOM TEMPTS SENAPHIMOCQ. HE ACCEPTS THE LIGOOR GOVERNORSHIP AND IS CONFIRMED IN THIS OFFICE.

The unwillingness on the part of Oija Senaphimocq to accept the Ligoor Governorship caused Calahom to become greatly concerned, for which reason he did all he could to persuade Phimocq, resorting to all kinds of ruses and trickery. He humbled himself before the Japanese as if he were a slave, and, contrary to the laws and customs of Siam, he visited him every day at his house. On these occasions, Calahom complained loudly about the heavy burden of governing the Kingdom, which, he lamented, for the most part had come to rest on both their shoulders. He told Senaphimocq that he was deeply sorry that Phimocq, when he came to the Court, had to humble himself before him (because he was Regent of the Kingdom, who represented the King on many occasions), even though this was a necessary custom intended to keep the other Mandarins in awe. Calahom said that he had proposed to the King to appoint Senaphimocq Governor of Ligoor partly in order to release him from this Siamese servitude, and partly also because he was the most valiant man in the Kingdom and the one best able to do the King's service in Ligoor.

This cajolery flattered Oija Senaphimocq so successfully that he began to hesitate. Observing this, Calahom quickly caused Senaphimocq, in the King's name, to be called to the Court, whither he was taken in great state, wearing (in the Siamese manner) the pyramidal crown of the Governor of Ligoor, an honor which never before had been done to any Governor. But noticing that Oija Senaphimocq took no pleasure in the magnificent crowning ceremony and that he preferred to stay at the Siamese Court, Oija Calahom bought his compliance with presents. In fact, he gave him so many gold and silver ornaments, goblets, sabers, and all kinds of other valuables that, according to some accounts (even though it is difficult to believe), the prao in which he had come was overburdened.

With these gifts Oija Senaphimocq (who is now Oija Ligoor) left the Court like a crowned King. But when he approached his house, there arose such a violent storm that (to everyone's amazement) within a very short time the river became so turbulent that it seemed that Oija Ligoor's prao, with all his new riches and marks of honor, would be wrecked. However, some of his Japanese soldiers, who were present in large number, jumped in the river and bore up the prao with their shoulders, and in that way they brought their Colonel to the bridge in front of his house, where he alighted without having made his feet wet. Nonetheless, most of the Siamese who witnessed this peril regarded it as presaging Oija Ligoor's fall and terrible demise, which not long after indeed came to pass.

46. OIJA LIGOOR LEAVES WITH MANY OF HIS JAPANESE SOLDIERS TO THE DELIGHT OF CALAHOM AND THE ROYAL FAMILY.

Urged on by Calahom, Oija Senaphimocq (who is now Oija Ligoor) was soon dispatched to Ligoor to take up his governorship. And, in order that he should have the requisite authority to carry out his brief, it was resolved that he should take with him just about all the Japanese soldiers that were in Iudia at the time. In this way Calahom relieved himself of many worries, while the Siamese Court rid itself of the unruly Japanese, so that everyone was pleased with the way in which this problem had been resolved. However, no one at the Court thought of the poison Calahom carried in his heart.

47. CALAHOM BECOMES PRESIDENT AND ABSOLUTE REGENT OF THE ENTIRE KINGDOM, AND BY MEANS OF A RUSE HE SENDS THE YOUNG KING TO SCHOOL.

Having rid himself (by the killing of Oija Capheijn and the departure of the Japanese Colonel and his unruly soldiers) of the principal obstacles (standing in the way of his goal), Oija Calahom covertly began to complain about the young King to his favorites and partisans. He insinuated that the young King had a bad disposition, that he was incompetent, adding that it had never been customary at the Siamese Court that such a powerful Kingdom, with all its provinces, cities, and subjects, should be ruled by a mere child. He told them how difficult it was to govern the Kingdom and said that, for various reasons, he desired to be relieved of this burden. The main reason, said Calahom, was his fear that when the King reached his majority, he would lend ear to those who envied him and to his secret enemies, who would not fail to denigrate his government during the regency. The result would be, he said, that he would be unable to evade the King's hatred and his punishing hand, so that he would be in mortal danger.

For that reason, said Calahom, it was necessary to put the young King in school with the ecclesiastics, who would be able to correct his disposition through exercises and by teaching him the way to virtue. In the meantime, a President should be chosen who, with the title of "King," would govern the Kingdom until such time as the child had come of age, when he would step down and transfer power to the rightful heir.

This cunning plan found much approbation among Calahom's favorites on the Council of Ministers. Some of the greatest Lords openly declared that in the interest of the prosperity of the Kingdom, the maintenance of public order, and the preservation of respect amongst the Kings of neighboring countries, it was urgently necessary to place the young King for some time in a monastery, and to elect and authorize Oija Calahom President and Regent of the Kingdom, with the title of "King." Not only did Calahom pretend to want to refuse this honor, he also insisted that he wished to be relieved of the burden of governing. But despite his insincere protestations, everyone at the assembly, some through affection and others through fear, insisted that the election be held. The young King was then taken to Wat Deun (which is the high synagogue), where the chief priest resides,[80] while Calahom was elected President, with the title of "King," an honor which the cunning fox only accepted after repeated protestations on his part and the humble entreaties of the entire assembly.

This election has again shown the truth of what many ancient writers have maintained; namely, that nearly all oriental nations cannot accept a multiplicity of Supreme Commanders, but that, generally speaking, they prefer the monarchical form of government where there is only one Lord. When Croesus, the King of Lydia,[81] gave his brother a share in government, one of the Lydian Lords said: "The sun is the cause of all that exists in the world. If there are two suns, there is a danger that they will burn each other, which will cause everything in the world to go to ruin." The Lydians are content to have one King, whom they regard as their savior; they cannot tolerate two Kings. The poet Homer expressed the same sentiment when he made Ulysses say:

80. Maybe Wat Doem (Ayothaya) but see p. 120, fn. 67.

81. Lydia was a polity in the west of modern Turkey. Croesus ruled around mid-sixth century BC and was famous for his wealth from gold mines.

That everyone should be a King is against law and reason;
It is best that only one King should rule over us.
Let us willingly obey the commands of the hero
The exalted Jupiter has placed above us.

When asked why a plurality of Princes was undesirable, Marcus Anthonius Simara replied that in case a government becomes tyrannical, there is less danger in being tyrannized by one Prince than by many. Seeing that the notables of the Siamese Kingdom used suchlike considerations to deem their lawful King unworthy of governing and to choose Calahom instead, it can justifiably be said that they joyfully brought in the Trojan horse.

48. IN VIEW OF HIS GOOD GOVERNANCE, OIJA CALAHOM IS DEEMED TO MORE DESERVING OF THE CROWN THAN THE YOUNG KING, FOR WHICH REASON HIS MAJESTY IS UNJUSTLY SENTENCED TO DEATH AND IS EXECUTED.

Having thus accepted the governance of the Kingdom, Oija Calahom acquitted himself at the beginning of his regency very worthily. He decided all matters with such prudence, moderation, and justice that many of the Mandarins (some in order to make their fortune, others because they wanted to flatter him, and still others out of fear) concluded that he was more deserving of the Kingdom than was the lawful King. Aware of this, the cunning Regent played his part with his customary craftiness. He told his favorite Mandarins that under a monarchical form of government there could not be a rival for the throne, and that in order to safeguard his life, he wanted to renounce the Crown. He said that when the young King reached his majority and assumed the throne, His Majesty was certain to come under the influence of undesirables and people ill-disposed towards his governance. The result would be, said Calahom, that the Mandarins would face great danger. Many of them would be brought to the end of their lives, while he himself would not be able to escape His Majesty's punishment, a misfortune that inevitably would entail the total ruin of his entire family.

Some of the Mandarins secretly held conferences to consider the Regent's proposal, and after debating the matter for a few days, they decided that some Councillors of State should pass a special resolution at an assembly that was to be held of all the officers of the Crown. This resolution set forth that there was great danger in suffering two sovereign Princes in the same Kingdom, since they threatened the entire state not only with civil unrest and foreign wars but with inevitable ruin. It seems that these Councillors were of the view that the royal throne is too narrow for two occupants, a view shared by Aristotle:

A plurality of Lords is undesirable.

Let us choose one as King and Regent, and
Let him be our highest Lord.

Machiavelli was of the same view. He maintained that a state can neither be established nor maintained if it is governed by rulers equal in power, because when one is as great as the other, it is difficult for them to reach agreement. It is better, said Machiavelli, that the wisdom and authority of a single Prince should decide all matters of state, and that he should be a speaking lawmaker.[82] The Siamese Mandarins and Councillors, too, were of the view that for the maintenance of the commonwealth it was preferable to do away with the young and incompetent King and to elect the Regent as King for reason of his manifest wisdom and prudence.

Even though the whole assembly (acting from various motivations) accepted this unjust proposition, the crafty Regent, pretending to feel compassion for the young King, at first refused to give his consent. Only after a great deal of persuasion by the assembled Mandarins (and outwardly unwillingly) did he give his permission for the resolution to be carried out. Thereupon, the unfortunate young King was taken from the school, stripped of his ecclesiastical garment, and taken to the same place where his uncle, his brother, and his brother's mother had been executed. There he was murdered to the secret sorrow of the most loyal Lords and citizens, after having been King for thirty-eight days.[83]

When the child reached the place of execution, he burst into tears and said: "Why do I have to be killed? I am not yet eleven years old. Is it not enough for this Council of Blood to have put to death my uncle, my brother, and his mother? Is it not enough that my Kingdom has been taken from me? Do they now want to spill my blood? Let the elected King be and grant me my life." These laments moved the executioners and bystanders to such pity that everyone had tears in their eyes. If it had been possible, some would have sacrificed themselves to save the King's life. Such was the end of this unfortunate King, whose reign had seen neither spring, summer, nor winter.

These events again confirm the truth of what Gagin has said, namely, that when people without piety and faith rise to a high state and want further to increase their power, they spare neither relatives nor friends. We have seen evidence of this in the actions of many tyrants. For instance, Anthonio Caracalla[84] killed his brother, Gatam, in the arms of his mother so that he

82. This seems to come from Machiavelli, *Discourses* I:9, which ends "All things considered, therefore, I conclude that it is necessary to be the sole authority if one is to organize a state."

83. Thirty-six in the Wicquefort/Mundie version.

84. Marcus Antonius Caracalla succeeded as co-emperor of Rome with his brother Geta in 211 AD. He subsequently killed his brother and possibly 20,000 others in an ensuing purge, and ruled until 217 before being murdered himself.

alone could rule the Roman Empire. But the sinners do not escape their punishment. Trobellius Polio writes that Gajus Marius[85] (a smith by his first trade), who at the time of Galieni was elected Emperor by the soldiers, was killed by one of the soldiers on the third day of his reign. This soldier, who had been his servant in the smithy, stabbed him, saying: "This is the sword that you yourself have forged."

49. THE KING WEDS THE ELDEST DAUGHTER OF THE GREAT KING AND GIVES THE SECOND DAUGHTER TO HIS BROTHER, WHOM HE DECLARES HEIR TO THE KINGDOM. HE KILLS THE MOTHER OF THE EXECUTED KING.

After the three successive Kings had been done to death in the manner that has been described, the cunning Regent (in the year 1629, at the age of 30) was declared absolute King and was crowned amidst great splendor and with many ceremonies. He was given the name of Pra Onghsrij d'Harma Raatsja Thijraaja.[86] In order to strengthen his claim to the throne, he took for his wife the eldest daughter of the great King, who was the sister of two of the executed Kings. She became his fourth wife, that is, she became the lesser wife among the four great Queens. He gave the second daughter of the great King to his brother, whom he declared a Prince of the realm and first heir to the Kingdom.

The new King also wanted to take for his concubine the mother of the youngest executed King, who was as beautiful a woman as Siam had ever seen. But she refused, and even though the King summoned her several times, she declined to come to the Court. But seeing that he was trying to compel her, the Queen at last went to the Court where she addressed him as follows: "The King, My Lord, is no more. My son, too, has left the world. I am tired of life and unworthy. But even if I were to keep my life, I would not give my pure body to an upstart bloodhound like you." The King was so offended by this refusal, reproach, and sharp reply that he at once had the aforementioned Queen dragged out of the Court to the bank of the river, where he had her cut in two pieces. The upper part of the body was fastened to a bamboo gibbet by means of a rattan that was stuck through the neck, a sad spectacle for all the people to see.

After the body had been displayed for two days, and on the prayer of the ecclesiastics, the King allowed it to be taken down, whereupon it was burned

85. Marius became emperor of the Gallic part of the divided Roman empire in 269 AD while Publius Licinius Egnatius Galienus ruled at Rome. He may have lasted two days or two months. Van Vliet may be confusing his name slightly with *Gaius* Marius, famous populist consul of Rome three centuries earlier, and uncle of Julius Caesar.

86. Phra-ongsi Thammarachathirat.

without much ceremony. He took all the other daughters and concubines of the great King, making concubines of those who were young and beautiful, and putting to death with great cruelty those who refused to go to him. The aged ladies and those who were past their prime were placed in separate quarters at the Court where they were fed very meanly.

50. THE KING ORDERS THE CRUEL EXECUTION OF TWO INNOCENT SISTERS.

Even though many people were grief-stricken at the vile murders of the three noble Kings, no one dared to shed tears publicly for the innocent blood that had been shed. Those who were suspected of mourning the Kings were in mortal danger. Two sisters who had served the youngest King's mother shed tears in the privacy of their own house for the deaths of the Queen and her son, the innocent young King. Upon learning of their grief, the King at once ordered the sisters to be dragged by their hair from their house to the bank of the river, where he had rattans stuck through their necks. After these rattans had been fastened to a cross-bamboo in such a way that their feet barely touched the ground, he had their bodies cut open on both sides as well as their mouths. Splints were then placed in their mouths to distend their jaws, and in this way the sisters were left to die agonizing deaths.[87]

Upon hearing of the suffering of his children, the father of the sisters hastened to the place of execution, where he loudly bewailed their imminent deaths. When the King was informed of this, he at once ordered the sorrowful father to be seized and cut in two pieces at the same place. After this had been done, the body parts were hung on a gibbet. These cruel executions caused such fear among all and sundry that no one dared to open their mouths or express any kind of lamentation or complaint. This sad tragedy is reminiscent of the Turkish Sultan Salijman. After this cruel Emperor, out of jealousy, had killed his son Mustapha (who had just returned from the Persian War), his youngest son, the brother of the one who had been killed, lamented the cruel murder, whereupon Sultan Salijman had him poisoned.[88] This caused such fear among the soldiers that everyone kept his mouth shut.

87. Wicquefort's rendering into French significantly toned down the level of cruelty in this and other descriptions of executions. For example, Wicquefort had the jaws gagged, not distended by splints.

88. Sultan Suleiman Khan I (r. 1520–66) killed his eldest son Mustapha in 1553. The story was recounted by Bartel Georgijevic, a Croatian who escaped from captivity in Turkey to live in the Netherlands and elsewhere in Europe, where he wrote several books on Turkish history and customs that became widely popular.

51. OIJA LIGOOR'S ACTIONS AT THE BEGINNING OF HIS REIGN.

Having so far dealt with the cunning, violent, and illegal succession of the King, we must now return to the Japanese, Oija Senaphimocq, and see what he did at Ligoor, before going on to examine the way in which the King exterminated both his followers and competitors for power. The incumbent Governor of Ligoor, having sure information as to what had transpired at the Siamese Court and aware that his successor was on his way, awaited him patiently and remained in his government. He did so partly out of fear of the King's wrath, and partly also because he hoped to place himself under the protection of his successor, so that if he were sent to Iudia, he might escape the punishment with which he had been threatened. Upon arrival at Ligoor, therefore, the new Governor found the former Governor at his post. The arrival of the new Governor caused such dread in Ligoor that no one dared to speak of rebellion or give even the slightest indication of disobedience. Nonetheless, the new Governor sought out all those who had instigated the disorders, disobedience, and rebellion, punishing some of them with death and others with confiscation of property, which he divided amongst his Japanese soldiers. In this way he quickly established his government and secured the province for the Siamese King. But at the earnest request of the former Governor, he kept him by his side, confirming him in his post as chief adviser.

52. OIJA LIGOOR INFORMS THE KING OF HIS ACHIEVEMENTS, AND HIS MAJESTY HYPOCRITICALLY PRETENDS TO BE PLEASED.

Unaware that the young King had been killed and that Calahom had been crowned King, Oija Ligoor hastened to report to Iudia on the situation in Ligoor, the measures he had taken to punish the rebels, and the means he had employed to secure the province for the Siamese Crown. Even though this resounding success displeased the newly elected King (who feared the Japanese), he insincerely pretended to be very happy with the way the Governor had carried out his brief. At the assembly of the Mandarins, he said that it was necessary to appropriately recompense so laudable a service. This needed to be done, said the King, so that it would become apparent that royal affection and benevolence awaited those who did well, just as royal justice awaited the wicked, and also to inspire other office-bearers to similar praiseworthy deeds. This proposal was approved by the whole Council. It was resolved that Oija Ligoor be required to take the appropriate oath of fidelity to the newly crowned King and that amongst many other gifts and marks of honor, a number of the most beautiful young women would be sent to him in the King's name, and with the intention that he should marry (in the Siamese manner) one of them.

53. THE KING SENDS THE PRESENTS TO OIJA LIGOOR, AND FEARING HIS POWER, HE COVERTLY KILLS HIM WITH POISON.

The presents and the young damsels were sent to Ligoor with great pomp and circumstance. But at the same time, the King caused Oija Barckelang to write to the ousted Governor that if he could get rid of the Japanese Governor and the majority of his unruly Japanese, he would be restored to His Majesty's favor and be reappointed Governor of Ligoor.

Although very pleased to receive the King's presents, Oija Ligoor was saddened to learn that the young King had been killed, and was unhappy also that Calahom, without soliciting his advice or counsel, had been elected King and had been crowned. He grieved openly and let it slip that the murder of the young King and the illegal election needed to be avenged. Nonetheless, after the first emotion had passed, he recovered his composure and pretended to rejoice in the succession, holding triumphal processions and other rejoicings to celebrate the occasion. At the same time, Oija Ligoor became so distrustful of the former Governor that he banned him from his presence, denying him entry to his house. He did not cease, however, to have contact with Opra Narit,[89] the former Governor's brother, allowing Narit to visit him from time to time.

Around this time it happened that, during an attack of the Patanese, Oija Ligoor received an injury to his leg. And since the injury was very painful, he made use of some preparations that Opra Narit had brought. These preparations not only soothed the pain, but also assisted in healing the wound, so that almost cured of his injury, Oija Ligoor decided to celebrate his marriage to the girl the King had sent him. But on his wedding day, amidst great rejoicing and glory, when happiness reached its peak, misfortune approached. When everyone was full of joy and merriment, when no one thought of misfortune, Opra Narit applied a poisoned dressing to Oija Ligoor's leg. The poison quickly took effect, and just a few hours later Oija Ligoor died, to the great sadness of his Japanese soldiers.

54. OCKON SENAPHIMOCQ, SON OF THE DECEASED GOVERNOR, ILLEGALLY TAKES HIS FATHER'S PLACE AND REBELS AGAINST THE KING.

The son of the Japanese, a youth about 18 years of age, well made and of good prospects, named Ockon Senaphimocq,[90] at his own initiative took his father's place as Governor of Ligoor. Suspecting that the former Governor had killed his father, he had him arrested and, in order to avenge the murder,

89. Possibly Okphra Marit, an official of Mergui.
90. Okkhun Senaphimuk.

sentenced him to death. But the former Governor knew well how to flatter the young Japanese. He gave him his eldest daughter in marriage and managed to remove all evil suspicions from his mind, whereupon they swore to assist each other under all circumstances and come what may.

After that, the father-in-law began to tell his new son, the Japanese youth, that the Siamese King had appointed his father absolute ruler over the province of Ligoor and that, this being the case, Ligoor was a hereditary possession to which he, as the eldest son, was entitled to succeed. The aforementioned youth and some other Japanese believed and accepted this talk, whereupon they put aside their grief at the death of their Lord and began to do everything in their power to secure Ockon Senaphimocq's succession. The young man began to fill some vacant offices, to distribute gold and silver jewelry, golden sabers, and other marks of honor to his favorites, and to appoint Oijas, Opraes, and such-like notables. He also set a day for his public coronation as King of Ligoor, a day during which he would be recognized as such by the people, who would then be required to drink the consecrated water of the oath of fidelity.

But at the same time, the former Governor of Ligoor incited against his son-in-law Ockon Cirwij Agwoot[91] (a terrible Japanese), the Captain of the Japanese soldiers. He told him that the youth did not deserve to be Governor and that he, the Captain, was more deserving of command. Ockon Cirwij lent ear to this talk and became desirous of the Governorship. He began to arm his followers and declared himself against the upstart Governor. In this way the Japanese were divided into two factions, factions which sometimes clashed, thinning the numbers on both sides.

55. OCKON SENAPHIMOCQ IS CROWNED KING OF LIGOOR BUT IS NOT ACCEPTED BY THE NOBILITY.

Having in this manner divided the Japanese against each other, the former Governor sought yet another means to destroy them. He began to incite opposition to the Japanese among the nobility and inhabitants of Ligoor by complaining of Japanese pride and willfulness, and by suggesting that they were rebels who had no right to the succession. If the Japanese were to succeed to Ligoor, the former Governor said, the King's name and authority would be besmirched for reason that the government of the province was not hereditary, but elective, and the election of the Governor depended entirely on the disposition of His Majesty.[92] He added the warning that unless the

91. Okkhun Sri Waiyawut in Wicquefort. Possibly ออกขุนศรีวัยวุฒิ.

92. This interesting piece of information proves that the Ayutthaya kings had the authority to appoint governors of Ligor, and at the same time it goes some way in explaining why Ligor rebelled against Ayutthaya.

people of Ligoor were careful and prevented the Japanese from realizing their intent, they would incur the wrath of the Siamese Court, which would expose them to the peril of the utmost punishment.

The people of Ligoor took such careful notice of these propositions that the entire nobility determined not to go to Court on the day appointed for the coronation, not to recognize the Japanese in any matter of state, and not to yield to them any superiority whatsoever. The Japanese, however, continued to make all the preparations for the coronation which they deemed necessary, but on the appointed day not one of the Ligoor nobility appeared at the Court, even though the Japanese had issued repeated invitations. Nonetheless, the upstart Japanese was crowned King of Ligoor. The Japanese recognized him, and they issued repeated proclamations ordering the nobles of Ligoor to come to the Court and render him homage and drink the water of allegiance. The people of Ligoor, however, refused to obey these orders. They said that Ockon Senaphimocq was a usurper and a rebel against the King of Siam; that they did not want to recognize him, nor respect or obey him until the King of Siam had lawfully authorized and confirmed him in his dignity.

56. TERRIBLE MURDER AND DESTRUCTION IN LIGOOR.

In consequence of the sly intrigues of the former Governor of Ligoor, the hatred between the two Japanese factions had intensified to such a degree that each party began to fortify itself against the other. Ready to attack each other at a moment's notice, they remained on the defensive. However, realizing at last that he had been deceived by the old Governor and that the latter had cunningly sought to effect the downfall of the Japanese, Ockon Cirwij Agwoot assembled his followers and joined the other Japanese. He then attacked the former Governor in his house, where he cut him down with his own hand, whereupon he proceeded to kill everyone he found in and around the house.

After this incident a terrible fight ensued between the Japanese and the people of Ligoor. Many were killed and cut down on both sides, but in the end the Japanese charged their enemy so desperately that the people of Ligoor took to flight, whereupon the Japanese burned and plundered the greater part of the town. Some time after this terrible massacre Ockon Senaphimocq invited those who had fled to return. He offered them the hand of friendship, promising that everyone who returned would be allowed to repossess their property (if it still existed), which they would be able to possess in peace and freedom. But the distrust was so great that, apart from a few Chinese, no one took up the invitation. The people of Ligoor stayed in the country and in neighboring towns so that the town of Ligoor remained a deserted and ruined place.

The upstart Japanese and Ockon Cirwy resumed their dispute over the supreme dignity and government, and consequently their respective followers often clashed so that many of them were killed. God's righteous vengeance caused the number of Japanese to dwindle. In the end, also the intrepid and ambitious Japanese, Ockon Cirwij, lost his life in a skirmish, much to the delight of his opponents. Seeing that little advantage was to be derived from Ligoor, and reflecting also that the Siamese King would not allow them to rule over the province, the Japanese left the town and withdrew to Cambodia. And so to the delight of the King, the Mandarins, and all the people, the Kingdom of Siam at last was relieved of this gang of lawless, desperate villains.

57. THE DOWNFALL OF THE JAPANESE AND THEIR FLIGHT FROM SIAM.

Delighted with the downfall and flight of the Japanese, the King and the Court were not too concerned about the murder and destruction in Ligoor. Even though these villains had behaved in a very cruel fashion, upon the return to Iudia of some of them from Cambodia and from other places, none of them suffered even the slightest punishment. But nonetheless, people looked askance at them and shunned their company.

In the meantime, the junk of the poisoned Japanese Colonel had returned from Japan with a large capital. This junk, as well as all the other possessions of the Japanese, had been seized by the King, mainly (as many suspected) to irritate them or to make them so discontented that they would leave the land of Siam. But fearful of desperate action on the part of the Japanese, His Majesty restored the junk and its cargo to them and allowed them to divide the proceeds amongst their ranks. In addition, he sold the Japanese one of his own junks and granted them permission to trade freely. But instead of being grateful, the Japanese villains continued to thirst for vengeance. Some of them intimated that they were going to pay the King a visit in his throne room and carry out an act of desperation, as indeed they had done at the time of the great King.[93]

But having been warned of the evil resolve and desperate intent of the Japanese, the King decided to surprise them. On the night of October 26, 1630, when the land around Iudia was inundated by water from the river, he ordered the Japanese quarter to be set ablaze. In addition, heavy cannon fire was brought to bear upon the Japanese so that they were forced to retreat in their junks. But since they were too few in numbers to adequately defend both junks, they embarked in just one of them and retreated down the river, fighting all the way. The King pursued them down the river and, with the loss of many Siamese lives, expelled them from the country. A few Japanese who had remained in Iudia or had been trading in the interior, were seized,

93. A reference to the attempt by around 500 Japanese (according to the chronicles), including both traders and palace guards, to seize the palace in the early months of King Songtham's reign (*RCA*: 208).

taken prisoner, or were killed, so that, through God's vengeance, most of those who had been disloyal and hostile to their lawful Prince were exterminated and destroyed.

58. THE LIGOOR REBELLION AND ITS SUPPRESSION BY THE SIAMESE KING.

Finding themselves delivered of the Japanese yoke, the people of Ligoor tried to free themselves also of Siamese servitude. They rose in rebellion and refused to recognize the King as their lawful Lord and sovereign, trying instead to separate from the Crown and establish an independent Kingdom. But the King sent an army of 10,000 Siamese soldiers, divided into three columns. Each column was commanded by a prominent Mandarin; namely, Opra Soupan Pontrock[94] in front with 3,000 men, Oija Thaijnam,[95] the commander-in chief, in the center with 4,000 soldiers, and Oija Ligoor (newly appointed to rule the province after its conquest) in the rear with 3,000 men.

This army captured the town of Ligoor, put down the revolt, and took prisoner seventeen of the principal leaders of the rebellion, who were taken to the city of Iudia. Without being heard and without any form of trial, the rebels had the soles of their feet burned on red hot iron plates, whereupon they were bound with heavy chains and buried in the ground up to their shoulders. All the passers-by had to knock them over the head with their knuckles, an act that is regarded in Siam as a great insult. But after they had been in this miserable position for twenty-four hours, and after they had received their deserved punishment, the ecclesiastics interceded on their behalf, whereupon they were taken out of the ground and released.

59. THE SIAMESE KING GOES TO WAR AND DESTROYS LICOON LAUW.

At this time the Kings of Tcheen Meij and Naan,[96] who were brothers, were on very bad terms with each other because the King of Tcheen, who

94. Mundie suggested this was Okphra Sakda Pholarit, and Giles noted this was a registrar in the service of the Upparat.

95. Okya Thainam, probably the Okya Decho Chai Thainam, see Appendix I.

96. Chiang Mai and Nan. According to the Nan and Chiang Mai chronicles, in 1615/6 the elders of Chiang Mai invited the ruler of Nan to become ruler of Chiang Mai. According to the Nan chronicle, Chao Si Song Muang Palasuk of Nan accepted the invitation and placed his younger brother, Chao Un Muang, as ruler of Nan. Nine years later, possibly 1624/5, Chao Un Muang "rebelled against the Burmese and fled to the South Country." He returned and briefly retook Nan, but was dislodged by a Burmese army and fled to Lanchang. In 1631/2, Suddhodhammaraja of Ava took Chiang Mai, hauled Chao Si Song Muang Palasuk away to Pegu, and installed Phraya Thippanet of Chiang Saen in his place. See Wyatt and Aroonrut (1995: 125–6); Wyatt

possessed the greater Kingdom, wanted to seize the territories of his brother. The King of Naan fled to Siam with many of his subjects. But after he had lived under the protection of the Siamese King for some time, about 500 of his Lauwan[97] followers went over to the side of Tcheen Meij. This caused the King of Siam some uneasiness because he feared that the King of Tcheen Meij, encouraged by the reports from the deserters, might stir up the King of Ava against him, and that these two Kings might combine to wage war against him.

For this reason he decided to preempt them. He raised an army of 90,000 men, foot and horse, accompanied by elephants, artillery, and all necessities, an army that, by the standards of the Indies, was well-equipped to reduce the Kingdom of Tcheen. He sent ahead Thiauphia Pouckelouck,[98] the commander-in-chief, along with the Oijas Calahom and Pitcheij[99] and a force of 9,000 soldiers to whom the captured Japanese were added. The King himself followed three days later with the rest of the army.

On leaving the Palace, the King swore a solemn oath to the effect that he would sacrifice the first four women he encountered and have their bodies cut in pieces so that he could have his proas smeared with their blood, fat, and intestines. Scarcely had His Majesty left the Court than he met four ill-fated women in a proa, and in their persons he immediately fulfilled the oath he had just taken. He then continued happily on his way, confident that he would be victorious over his enemies.

Upon learning that the King of Siam was approaching with a powerful army, the King of Tscheen Meij abandoned his Kingdom and fled with all his subjects without waiting for the help the King of Ava might have been able to send him. But in order to ensure that his advance would not remain fruitless, the King of Siam decided to attack and seize Lycoon Lauw,[100] ostensibly because the King of that province had paid tribute to the King of Tscheen Meij and had done him homage. The King again sent ahead Pouckelouck, the aforementioned Oijas, and their force of 9,000 soldiers, while he himself followed with the rest of the army.

(1994: 69–71). This section was totally misinterpreted in the Wicquefort translation and hence in all its descendants. This new translation makes this incident resemble the provincial revolts which occurred after future contested successions, including those of Phetracha and Taksin.

97. Probably the people often written nowadays as Lua or Lawa. They may be descendants of Mon-Khmer speakers who preceded the Tai in the Lanna hills. They still occupy the mid-slopes of the hills in Nan, where they are often swidden cultivators.

98. Chaophraya Phitsanulok. Wicquefort/Mundie omitted the "Phitsanulok." This is the only place where he is entitled as Chaophraya.

99. Phichai, possibly Phichai Songkhram, see p.55, fn. 30.

100. Probably Lampang, often called Nakhon in this era.

But Pouckelouck was so valiant that, without waiting for His Majesty to join him, he attacked the chief town on all sides, forced the gates, and set fire to the houses. This assault so terrified the defenders (even though there were about 20,000 able-bodied men in the town) that the King of Lycoon Lauw fled with most of his followers. The King was hotly pursued and taken prisoner, but on the way back to the captured town he became ill and died of sadness, so that the Siamese King did not get to see him.

When three days later the King arrived at Lycoon Lauw and learned that Pouckelouck had already captured the town and that the Majesty had died, he stopped his advance and rested his army. He ordered Pouckelouck to post notices along all roads and pathways stating that if the son of the deceased King was prepared to pay homage to the Siamese King, he was free to come and would be confirmed in the possession of his father's territory. But the Prince (apparently out of fear) did not appear.

After Pouckelouck had been in the town for ten days, he gave it up to pillage, carrying off with him all the valuables, artillery, ammunitions, victuals, as well as most of the inhabitants. He left about 1,000 old, infirm people with the body of the late King so that it might be cremated with the usual ceremonies. He then joined the Siamese King, whereupon His Majesty returned to Iudia with his army carrying a great deal of booty as well as over 10,000 prisoners. After Pouckelouck had left the town of Lycoon, the escaped Prince, the son of the deceased King, with many of his followers re-entered the destroyed place in order once again to take up residence.

The fugitive Lauws, who had been the cause of the war, were overtaken at Lijcoon Seuangh,[101] tied up, and taken to the King. His Majesty ordered the young men to be put in split bamboo and, in a standing position, to be placed on growing bamboo shoots in order to die an agonizing death. Some of them were still alive after four or five days. The old men, the women, and children were condemned to die by fire, but through the intercession of the ecclesiastics, they were pardoned, whereupon they were enslaved and divided up among the Mandarins.

60. THE KING EXTERMINATES HIS FOLLOWERS, AND IN ORDER TO SECURE HIS POWER, HE KILLS FIVE YOUNG PRINCES.

Having triumphed over the rebels and most of his enemies, the King rid himself of many of the wisest, most experienced, and most prominent Lords who had assisted him in the illegal usurpation of the Kingdom. He did this partly because he wished to establish his Kingdom on a solid footing, and partly also for fear that these Lords one day might exercise against him the same perfidy he had shown towards the previous Kings.

101. Nakhon Sawan.

In April 1633, during the third year of his reign, the King seated himself on the throne and asked the assembled Mandarins whether any of them had ever wanted to get drunk. When no one replied, His Majesty asked: "What kind of arrack do you people consider better, old arrack or arrack that has been newly distilled?" When some of the Mandarins ventured an opinion, the King said: "There are still two bottles of arrack of the great King. Is it better that we keep them, or shall we pour them out?" When he received no reply, he concluded to himself: "It is better that we pour out the old arrack so that its age and strength does not crack the bottles, and no one can drink it and get drunk."[102]

Oija Oubrat and Oija Jumerat[103] understood the King's intention and asked with great humility: "What harm can two poor, innocent children do who, together, have not yet lived twelve years?" The King, however, regarded this reply as a reproach and took great exception to it. He flew into such a rage that, with his own hand, he inflicted several wounds on their heads, had them thrown into the dungeons, disposed of their slaves, and gave their houses up to pillage. Without seeking anyone's advice or approval, he ordered the arrest of the two young Princes, sons of the great King, seven and five years of age. They were taken to the same place where the previous Kings had been killed, where, to the great unease and sadness of all the people, they were executed in the same manner, whereupon their bodies were contemptuously cast into a well. There the bodies remained for over a year until the decomposing remains were taken from the well and burned on the bank of the river, into which the ashes were thrown so that no memory of them would remain.

In the same year, three other sons of the great King, with very sad faces, were talking to one of the concubines of the deceased Majesty, a concubine the reigning King had taken for himself. As soon as His Majesty was told of this meeting and of the sad demeanor of the woman and the children, he sent at once for Oija Sicrij,[104] the current Barckelangh. He asked Oija Sicrij whether the Nimpha flower (which grows in the water) is still edible when the stems, upon breaking, appear stringy. Sicrij (who knew what the King wanted to say) replied that such flowers were most definitely injurious to health and that it was much better to pull them out roots and all so that the weeds should not spread further.

Thereupon the King told Sicrij what he had learned concerning the aforementioned concubine and the children, adding: "Even though they are still in their minority, these children dare to support each other and to talk with sadness about what has happened. What is to become of this when they

102. The Wicquefort/Mundie translation omitted the clause "no one can drink it and get drunk" and thus lost much of the force of this rightly famous quotation.

103. Okya Yommarat, see Appendix I.

104. Okya Chakri, the *samuha nayok* or upper minister in charge of the civilian wing of the administration; see Appendix I.

come of age? It is better to lay them out alongside the rest of them, so that in future they will not give us stringy stems or weeds." Hereupon the three boys (who together were about eighteen years of age) were apprehended, taken to the same place of execution, and killed in the same manner as their lawful uncle and their four brothers. The woman was cut in two[105] and her remains were thrown into the river.

There is now only one Prince still alive (a son of the great King's brother), whose father should have inherited the Kingdom.[106] But inasmuch as Pra Narit, that is to say the Black King,[107] blinded him almost completely with fire,[108] this Prince at the time declined the throne and agreed that the Crown should devolve upon his brother. The present King has confined this youth (who is now about thirty years of age) to the Palace since the beginning of his reign. He has a wife and several slaves to assist him, and every day he has to appear several times in His Majesty's presence.

In March of the year 1635 a terrible fire broke out which destroyed a large part of the city. The day after the fire had been put out, this Prince was given permission to go into the city in order to witness the destruction. But no sooner had he appeared in the street than he was approached by many people, who, with tears in their eyes, told him of their misery, rendering him more than usual honors, yes, rendering him honors normally reserved only for the King. When the King was told about this, he became so jealous of the innocent Prince that he resolved to kill him. But in order to ensure that this be done with a semblance of legality, he ordered some of the palace guards, those with tattooed arms, to provoke the Prince. Unable to tolerate the insult, the Prince hit the guard who had offended him under the chin, whereupon the guards went to report the incident to the King.

After His Majesty had sent for the Prince, he reproached him bitterly. "If you are this brave and audacious," the King concluded, "you cannot possibly respect me. If you can raise your hand against the tattooed, who are my slaves and soldiers, the protectors of my person, the keepers of public order, and

105. Here yet again Wicquefort seemed intent on toning down the violence, as he omitted the detail of being "cut in two."

106. Most likely this is the mysterious Phra Si Saowaphak, a son of King Ekathotsarot. In the later chronicles he is recorded as king for 14 months in 1610–11, before being deposed and executed by his brother or half-brother, King Songtham. However, he does not appear in other sources including Van Vliet's *Short History* and other sources like the *Khamhaikan chao krung kao*, and hence some historians have suspected he is a "phantom king" inserted into the later chronicles. However, this and other mentions by the Dutch (see Dhiravat, 2002: 148–9) seem to confirm his existence.

107. King Naresuan.

108. There is no mention of this incident in other sources, but his blindness is confirmed elsewhere (Dhiravat, 2002: 148).

the executioners of justice, then obviously I cannot rely on you. If you can do this, you can also raise your hand against my wives and children, and after you have done that, against my own person. For that reason, it is better that we prevent this evil from occurring by putting an end to your life."

And so the innocent Prince was also condemned death. But when he arrived at the place of execution, where he was to be put to death in the same manner as his uncle and cousins, he unexpectedly received a royal pardon that the King had granted on the intercession of his grandmother, his mother, and all the Queens.[109] Nonetheless, by administering harmful medicines, the King succeeded in robbing him of the greater part of his reason, his hearing, and his sight so that this unfortunate Prince was made totally unsuited ever to assume the royal dignity.

Finally, on February 18 last year,[110] seeking to eliminate all causes of further unrest, the King ordered the last two sons of the old King (sixteen and fourteen years of age), secretly and under the cover of darkness to be taken to the temple Praminkho Praja[111] (where their brothers had been killed), with the intention to execute them in the same fashion. But His Majesty's grandmother (who had advised him in respect of all the executions) and his mother, who are the two most powerful women in the Kingdom, as well as the two sisters of the young Princes, sought to intercede on their behalf. The King, however, would not listen to them, which prompted the King's mother to threaten to drown herself, while the Queens prepared to take poison.

This forced the King to suspend the executions. But since this time the Princes have not been allowed to reside in the Palace; instead, they have been allocated separate places across the river and opposite the Court. The eldest Prince has been given a low-class girl in marriage; they both have but few slaves and very little income. Every day they have to present themselves before the King, but when the King appears in public, whether on water or on land, they are obliged to join his following, richly attired and seated on sumptuous barges or riding beautiful elephants or horses. Usually, the Princes appear in close proximity to the King. Of this wretched royal dynasty only the Queen (who is the third wife of the King), her sisters, the two aforementioned Princes, and a few female cousins now remain; surely, a terrible fate for a house that, through a succession of excellent Kings, has been most noble, famous, and illustrious.[112]

109. King Prasat Thong's grandmother would have been the mother of King Songtham's mother; see Appendix III.

110. Presumably 1639.

111. Wat Phramen Khok Phraya.

112. The dynasty began with Maha Thammaracha, installed on the throne by the Burmese in 1569. The family probably originated from Sukhothai-Phitsanulok.

61. THE KING MAKES PEACE WITH VARIOUS PRINCES AND BRINGS TO OBEDIENCE THE REBELLIOUS PATTANESE.

It is worthy of note that this King who, principally through the unfathomable disposition of the almighty God, miraculously has gained possession of so large a Kingdom, nonetheless has governed his Kingdom with wisdom, courage, and prudence. At the beginning of his reign, when the principality of Patani refused to pay the customary homage to the Siamese crown, the King sent envoys to the Kings of Atchin[113] and Aracan in order to ensure that Patani should not receive assistance from these quarters. He made peace with these Kings and re-established the old alliances. And even though subsequent events have shown that these renewed alliances on all sides rested on legs of straw, His Majesty adroitly used the lull to press his case against Patani and bring the principality to obedience.

In the beginning of the year 1634, the King assembled a powerful army of about thirty thousand Siamese soldiers (reinforced with many foreigners residing in His Majesty's Kingdom, such as Portuguese mestizos, Japanese, Malays, and others), as well as elephants, horses, artillery, and victuals. The army was led by four principal commanders; namely, Oija Ligoor, the Commander-in-Chief, and the Oijas Barckelang, Calahom, and Rabisidt.[114] But due to poor leadership, inexperience in conducting military operations, and the staying away of Dutch assistance, they ran into difficulties and were forced to retreat with the loss of many of their soldiers.

This led the King to raise a second army, which was so formidable that the Queen of Patani[115] became fearful. In 1636, she availed herself of the mediation of the King of Queda[116] and sent her envoys to make peace and to pay homage to His Majesty in the customary manner, namely, by presenting him with the obligatory gold and silver flowers that are the tokens of reverential submission. And desiring to strengthen the repose of his Kingdom, to draw to it foreign commerce, and to safeguard the voyages of his junks to various places, the King made peace with all the Princes and European potentates that are known in the Indies. And even though the King had violently expelled the Japanese, before long he invited them to return, and in addition, he sent several embassies to Japan to make peace with that powerful Emperor. Notwithstanding the arrogant manner in which the Japanese treated the Siamese embassies, His Majesty in May of last year sent an envoy to the Japanese Emperor with a letter engraved in gold and (in the Siamese manner) an extremely valuable gift. But since that envoy has not yet returned, it is impossible to say what the outcome of this mission has been.

113. Aceh.

114. Okya Ramasit in Wicquefort, but also possibly Okya Ratchaprasit; see also p. 130, fn. 91.

The King of Chiampa,[117] since time immemorial, was also subject to the Siamese Crown. But when this King, some fifty years ago, asserted his independence, Pra Narit or the Black King, defeated him and compelled him again to pay homage. But after the death of this awe-inspiring King, Chiampa once again refused to acknowledge the King of Siam. Shortly after the present King came to the throne, he sent Tsakhausa Thijbijdij[118] to Chiampa with an appropriate present to remind the King of his duty, to renew the old friendship, and to invite him to send representatives to Iudia. The Chiampa King treated the envoys very well, and after a short time, he sent them back with the assurance that he recognized the King of Siam as his overlord and that he would send envoys hither to pay him homage. But since this promise remained unfulfilled, the King of Siam, in December last, sent another envoy to Chiampa with the aforementioned Tra and a small present in order to remind the King for the second time of his duty and to extend another friendly invitation to him. Only time will tell what will come of this.

At the beginning of his reign, the King was very hostile to the Portuguese residing in his Kingdom, keeping many of them in severe imprisonment. But in 1636, His Majesty sent envoys to Malacca and Manilla in order to renew the treaties of friendship with the Governors of these places and to offer them peace. In 1639 a Portuguese envoy arrived from Macau to make peace with the King, but from Manilla no reply has been received as yet. If the Macau envoy had not stayed in Siam during the past south monsoon, the King would have sent a second envoy to Manilla. The King sent also, at the beginning of his reign, envoys to the Kings of Ava, Pegu,[119] and Langsjangh,[120] which resulted in an exchange of embassies and the establishment of peace between the Siamese Kingdom and the aforementioned Kings. But the jealousy of Ava and Langsjangh was so much aroused by these peace treaties

115. Raja Kuning (r. 1635–88?). The dispute with Ayutthaya was begun by her mother, Raja Ungu, who died in 1635 (Teeuw and Wyatt 1970: 16–18, 179–84).

116. Kedah.

117. This looks like Champa but is clearly Cambodia, which Naresuan attacked in the 1590s and early 1600s. Some time after Naresuan's death, Cambodia renounced its dependence on Siam (possibly in 1618). In 1630, survivors of Prasat Thong's massacre of the Japanese in Ayutthaya took refuge in Cambodia and persuaded the King to help them in a revenge attack. In 1635, a Cambodian king was killed by his uncle, and this event may have triggered Prasat Thong's attempt to reassert influence. In the 1640s, the Dutch hoped to ally with Prasat Thong to take advantage of Cambodia's chronic dynastic disputes, but nothing came of these plans, and Vietnam asserted its influence instead (Kersten 2003; Dhiravat na Pombejra, 1984).

118. As a "Tra" is mentioned a few lines below, this is probably a copyist's error for tra kosathibodi, a document with the seal of the Phrakhlang.

119. King Thalun ruled both Ava and Pegu in this period.

120. Lanchang, possibly King Mom Kaeo.

that these Princes became very distrustful of each other and fearful lest others should unexpectedly attack them.

Nonetheless, all these initiatives clearly demonstrate that this King is a peaceful ruler, a ruler who seeks to effect the security of his realm, because in matters concerning the Kingdom's governance and prosperity, he is wise, cautious, and moderate. He governs his Kingdom to ensure its prosperity, well-being, and peace.

62. THE KING ORDERS THE EXECUTION OF OIJA POUCKELOUCQ, HIS MOST FAITHFUL SERVANT, WHO HELPED AND ADVISED HIM DURING HIS USURPATION OF THE CROWN.

After the King had subdued the principality of Patani and had made peace with the neighboring Kings and Princes, he rid himself of Oija Barckeleng, whom he had made Oija Pouckelouck. This Lord had faithfully served His Majesty from the time he was Calahom, and had warned him (when he was Calahom) that the young King intended to kill him. The King, therefore, not only owed him his life, but was also indebted to him for the reason that Pouckelouck had been the principal proponent of the King's usurpation of the Crown, a proponent who had assisted him with wise counsel, resolute action, and courageous deeds. For these reasons His Majesty had solemnly promised him that when he came to the throne, he, Oija Barckelangh, would become Feijna[121] or Prince of the Siamese Kingdom, an oath which had been confirmed by the tasting of each other's blood.

But the King did not keep his promise. When he assumed the royal dignity, he elevated his only brother to the rank of Feijna, or heir to the Kingdom, while he appointed Barckelangh to the rank of Oija Souor Colouck,[122] and some time later to the Governorship of Pouckelouck. The King did this even though the government of this province had always been reserved for sons of the King and Princes of royal blood. Barckelangh, however, was not satisfied with this dignity, and many times he reminded the King of the oath he had sworn. His Majesty (who knew full well that he owed the throne to Barckelangh's courage) repeatedly showed him his gratitude, but for the love he felt towards his brother, he was unable to fulfill his promise. Nonetheless, the King repeatedly assured Barckelangh that he would never harm him, and that next to his brother, he would always appoint him to the highest offices in the Kingdom.

But after the victorious conquest of Lijcoon, for which Barckelangh received all the honor, he grew so much in stature that he aroused the jealousy of the King's brother. This Prince, assisted by His Majesty's grandmother,

121. The *fai na* or *chao wang na*, Prince of the Front Palace and heir-presumptive to the throne.

122. Okya Sawankhalok.

their common mother, and some flatterers gradually brought Barckelangh so much in disfavor with the King that eventually he flew into a passion. Contrary to his oath and promise (which they had renewed only three months earlier), the King caused Barckelangh to be seized by force. The soles of his feet were burned on hot irons, his body was weighted down in five places, and then he was thrown into a filthy prison supervised by Oija Iumerat, his declared enemy. His house was pillaged and his slaves, horses and elephants were confiscated.

The King went to these extremes also because some mathematicians and astrologers had said that the stars under which Barckelangh had been born were so unusually favorable that they promised nothing less than sovereign power and a royal crown. And seeing Barckelangh gain in authority, power, and wealth, the King began to believe that this prophecy was about to be realized, and consequently he began to greatly fear and hate him.

In the end, the son of Pouckelouck, at that time about nine years of age, acting on the advice of the ecclesiastics, prostrated himself before the King, and supported by the Priests, begged for his father's life. This display so moved His Majesty that he promised to release Pouckelouck that very day and to send him home. But God's vengeance caused renewed bitterness in the King's heart so that the outcome was quite different. After the child had left happily, His Majesty began to drink heavily,[123] and after a while he asked Oija Iumerat what he thought should happen to Pouckelouck. Iumerat, who sought only to rid himself of his enemy, replied that when someone who has raised and nourished a serpent should accidentally tread on it, the serpent will not think of the past, but will strike and kill that person with its venom. The King was so pleased with this reply that he ordered Iumerat to kill his faithful servant and principal supporter.

Iumerat at once left the presence of the King. Meeting the ecclesiastics who were waiting for a pronouncement of the King in respect of Pouckelouck and fearful lest they should succeed in interceding on his behalf, Iumerat told them that the King had pardoned him, whereupon the ecclesiastics dispersed and went home. Iumerat immediately caused Pouckelouck to be taken from his prison, and for fear that the King should change his mind, he inflicted with his own hand a mortal wound, stabbing him in the right side of his chest. At the same time, Iumerat denied everyone access to Pouckelouck so that the execution could proceed.

Seeing that he could not escape death, Pouckelouck bitterly inveighed against the perjury of the King, saying: "You, faithless bloodhound, what a cruel reward do you give me for my loyal service. You are spilling the blood of the one who has saved your life, the one who has made you King. Where

123. Dutch sources of this period tell of the King's heavy drinking, leading to extreme volatility of temper. He was apparently worried about the coming age of calamity upon completion of 1000 years of the Lesser Era (*Chula sakkarat*) in 1638.

are your royal promises, the promises you renewed only recently, and which you have confirmed with the tasting of my blood? If I had known of your faithlessness, I would have gathered my forces and I would have drawn my sword. I could have made myself King and have punished you for your treachery."

Pouckelouck wanted to say more, but Iumerat took him to the place of execution, where he had his body hacked into three pieces. The priests burned Pouckelouck's remains, and on orders of the King, his ashes were interred in a grave of Siamese Princes. Even though His Majesty often mourned the passing of his friend, Pouckelouck's wife nonetheless was kept at the Court in a servile capacity. The surviving son, who had received a golden candle from the King, was stripped of this distinction. He was housed with relatives, where he was fed but meagerly, without ever being allowed to appear amongst the pages at the Court.

63. THE KING'S STRATEGY OF ENCOURAGING STRIFE AMONGST THE PRINCIPAL LORDS.

Oija Iumerat, the executioner of Oija Pouckelouck, from infancy was brought up by the Queen Mother alongside His Majesty himself (although both of them at that time were in humble positions). During the King's usurpation of the crown, Iumerat rendered him many valuable services with his wise counsel, for which reason the King appointed him Oija Sicrij, one of the highest and most dignified offices in the Kingdom. He carried out this office very satisfactorily for many years. His intelligence, civility, kindness, and his willingness to help Siamese as well as foreigners so increased his influence and authority that the King became concerned.

Sicrij and Pouckelouck (who had been killed), however, were envious of each other and covertly sought as much as possible to conspire against each other. Aware of this rivalry, and fearful of the power of these Lords, the King began to encourage this strife. In the end, Sicrij was accused because some of his followers, namely, three Oijas, three Opraes, and two Oloangs (when drinking at his house), had boasted that they (providing they helped each other) could knock the King off his chair and replace him with Sicrij. The King was warned of this, whereupon he summoned Sicrij and all those who had been at his house to appear before him. After the King had sharply interrogated them, he mounted a mad elephant intending to trample them all underfoot.

Pouckelouck, however, interceded on their behalf, whereupon His Majesty dismounted. Before leaving, the King ordered Pockelouck to tie up Sicrij and his followers and to bring them before him so that he could stab them all to death with his own hand. Seeing the King in such a great passion, and realizing that his life was in the gravest danger, Sicrij said humbly: "Brother Pouckelouck, save my life and beg the King to moderate his anger towards us." Responding to this plea, Pouckelouck approached the King's mother and a few ecclesiastics, who interceded with the King, whereupon Sicrij and the other accused were granted their lives. Nonetheless, they were all thrown into severe imprisonment and their houses were given up to pillage. In order to ensure that the looting of Sircrij's house should not spill over to the King's temple (that was under construction near Sicrij's place of residence) or to His Majesty's arsenal, Pouckelouck was sent hither with Oijas Barckelangh and Pitter Raetsja[124] to supervise everything. But even though Pouckelouck had pleaded for Sicrij's life, he was so embittered against him that he used an elephant to break down the wall around Sicrij's house, saying that he refused to pass through a gate through which a traitor had gone.

After Sicrij had been in prison for quite a long time, he vindicated himself through the ordeal of fire, which led His Majesty to believe that he had been innocent. The King then restored him to favor. He returned his women and slaves, and on the day that Pouckelouck was apprehended, he made him Oija Iumerat, placing Pouckelouck under his authority. But Iumerat chose not to remember that he owed his life to Pouckelouck. Instead, he sought vengeance for old wrongs, accusing him of many crimes, so that the King became ever angrier with Pouckelouck, in consequence of which he treated him in the manner we have just related. This I have set forth in passing in order to show how cleverly the King sets one Lord against the other.

64. THE KING FORESTALLS ALL CONSPIRACIES.

In order to ensure that no one should undertake faithless attempts against him, His Majesty has issued strict orders that all the powerful Mandarins (except when indisposed) appear at the Court each day. In addition, he has prohibited the Mandarins from visiting each other in their houses, and he has stipulated that they consult each other only in public places when everyone can hear what they say. In this way, the King seeks to prevent all secret conspiracies.

Moreover, the King's strict governance, his magnificent Court, his passion for public works, such as the renovation of the city and Palace, the building of temples and other great projects, all these things have so impoverished the Mandarins and community that no one has the means to stage a rebellion. In addition, the King changes the highest offices so frequently that none of the Mandarins are able fully to establish themselves in their posts. For instance, the Governors of the principal provinces are not permitted to leave for their respective provinces, but are usually required to remain in Iudia, where the King can keep an eye on them. In the meantime, deputies administer the provinces, often to the detriment of the community and the poor. In sum,

124. Probably Phra Phetracha, พระเพทราชา, head of the department of elephants, sakdina 5000 (*KTSD*, 1: 250)

the King governs in such a manner that his power is secure, and he always makes sure that he is more feared than any of his predecessors ever were.

65. RELEVANCE OF THIS TREATISE.

Although in the past many barbarian usurpations involving treachery and murder have ended in the violent downfall of the usurpers, it is unlikely, as far as a mere mortal can judge, that this upstart King will suffer a similar fate. His power is sufficient to resist the enmity of the surrounding Kings, Princes, and potentates, and at the same time this King is so absolute and so cunning in the governance of his realm that all associations that could lead to conspiracy are prevented and defeated.

Nonetheless, the righteous judgment of God and the power of the Almighty can destroy worldly vanities and cast asunder the usurpers, as will be demonstrated with a few brief examples. Apries, the Egyptian King, boasted that he was so firmly seated on his throne that even the Gods were unable to topple him. Not long afterwards he was taken prisoner and hanged by King Amasa.[125] Policrates, the King of Samien,[126] was fond of saying that he had never experienced misfortune; yes, that nothing bad could ever happen to him. When he threw a precious pearl ring into the sea, and when the fish that had swallowed the ring was sold to his cook so that it returned to him, Policrates became even more proud, thinking that nothing could ever go wrong. Yet this unfortunate man shortly afterwards was defeated by Orate, the General of King Darius,[127] and nailed to a cross.

Cralo, the King of Lydia,[128] seated on his golden throne, asked Solon: "Is there anyone in the world more fortunate than I am?" Solon replied that no one should deem himself fortunate until he has come to the end of his life.

125. Apries or Wahibre Haaibre ruled in Egypt around 588–569 BC, and was displaced by Amasis/Ahmose, who ruled until 526 BC. The story is told in Herodotus, *Histories*, II, 161.

126. Policrates was a famously tyrannical ruler of the Greek island of Samos, c. 538–522 BC, mentioned in the Bible and Herodotus. The story of the ring appears in Herodotus, *Histories*, III, 41–42.

127. Oroetes, a Persian governor of Sardis, attacked and killed Policrates of Samos in 522 BC. Darius then had Oroetes killed. The account appears in Herodotus, *Histories*, III, 120–8.

128. "Cralo" is in fact Croesus, the fabulously rich ruler of Lydia, who Van Vliet has already mentioned above. According to the historian Herodotus (Book I, 29–33), the Roman law giver visited Croesus, who displayed his treasure and was disappointed when Solon responded as Van Vliet describes here: "In truth, I count no man happy until his death, for no man can know what the gods may have in store for him." Herodotus continued with the story of his war against Cyrus the Great of Persia (580–529 BC), who Van Vliet spells as "Cijrum." Herodotus described (I, 88) how, after Cyrus had imprisoned him, Croesus remembered Solon's words.

Even though Cralo thought this a strange reply, not long afterwards he had occasion to experience the world's unsteady course. He began an unnecessary war against Cijrum, the King of the Persians and Medes. Cralo lost the war, was taken prisoner, and sentenced to be burned alive, even though, through the mercy of the victor, he was eventually set free. All this serves to show that there is no more certain rule in this world than that all human affairs are uncertain. Therefore, the old Germans appropriately said:

> Do not allow fortune to deceive you;
> It can twist, swim and fly.

God's laws and the uncertain course of the world usually ensure the righteous vengeance of equivalent retribution. This was the case with Adonibeseck,[129] whose thumbs and toes were hacked off for reason that he had done this to the seventy Kings he had taken prisoner. Absalom,[130] who drove his father David from the Kingdom, was defeated and killed by his father's General. All those who conspired against Julius Caesar died a violent death and were killed with the same dagger with which they had murdered him. The same happened to the murderers of the Emperor Gordiani.[131] None of the nine men who had killed him managed to escape: seven killed themselves with the daggers with which they had committed the murder, and Philippus (the chief steward of the Kingdom) and his son (the instigator of the murder of the Emperor) were both stabbed to death.

Anthoninus[132] murdered his brother, Gatan, and set himself up as Emperor of Rome, but when he had ruled for six years, his treacherous General, Macrinus, had him killed. After this murder, the soldiers of Macrinus elected him Emperor. But he neglected his good fortune, abandoned himself to sensuality, and after he had ruled but a short time, his General, Maximinus, (a barbarian from Thrace, who had been a cowherd in his youth), had him killed, whereupon he set himself up as Emperor. But the cruelties of this

129. Biblical figure who mutilated 72 kings.

130. The Bible's Second Book of Samuel recounts how King David's daughter was raped by a half brother who was then killed by another brother, Absalom. David banished Absalom, who later returned and was killed in a failed revolt against his father.

131. Gordianus III (r. 238–44 AD) of Rome was killed and succeeded by his Arabian prefect, Philippus.

132. This is the same story of Marcus Antonius Caracalla which Van Vliet mentioned in Section 48 above. Caracalla was probably killed by one of his own generals from Mauritania, who succeeded him as Marcus Opellius Macrinus in 216. He in turn was put to flight in a countercoup by Caracalla's family a year later, and eventually executed. These stories are told in Herodian, *History of the Empire from the Time of Marcus Aurelius*. They are also favorite examples of Machiavelli, used in Chapter 19 of *The Prince* and Chapter II:6 of the *Discourses*.

terrible tyrant made him so hated with the soldiers that in the end they fell upon him and beat him to death. After the cruel murderer Phocas,[133] who had killed the Emperor Mauritius along with his wife and children, had ruled the Empire for seven years, some of the most prominent Lords began to conspire against him, whereupon he was taken prisoner in Constantinople. The crown was taken from him and Heraclij, who succeeded him, ordered his hands, feet, genitals, and head to be cut off, whereupon the soldiers burned his torso to ashes in the market place. His brothers and many of his other relatives were also killed.

Atabaliba, the mighty King of Peru,[134] having been taken prisoner by the Spanish, was promised his freedom if he would fill the hall in which he was standing with gold and silver ornaments to the height of a man. Atabaliba did this so that he paid a ransom worth mere than two million ducats in gold, whereupon the Spanish proceeded to strangle him with a cord. But through God's will, all those who had a hand in the King's death met an untimely end, for which reason it is worth recalling the words of Euripides:

> Those who commit treachery and murder
> Shall not live even half their days.

It would be possible to give more examples relevant to this treatise. This, however, is unnecessary because Your Honor is better acquainted than I am with several outstanding works of history that are full of tales of this kind.

66. CONCLUSION TO THIS DESCRIPTION.

The events I have related show how this King, through crafty plots and many murders, has succeeded in usurping the Crown, and how after having acquired that Crown illegally, he shed a great deal of blood to confirm his possession of it. Nonetheless, it is worthy of note that in matters relating to government and well-being of his Kingdom, His Majesty has been a wise, careful, and mighty Prince, who has possessed his Kingdom in prosperity and peace.[135] It is true that the King is choleric and quick to condemn, but whilst severe in his governance, he is neither tyrannical nor bloodthirsty,

133. Phocas was a junior military officer who became Roman emperor by a coup against Mauritius in 602 during a campaign against the Slavs. He figures in Church histories because he eased persecution of the Christians. He was dislodged and beheaded in a coup by another general, Heraclius, in 610.

134. Atahualpa, the great Inca ruler, was killed by the Spanish conquistador Francisco Pizarro in 1532.

135. This whole section (and the previous one) was omitted from the Wicquefort/Mundie translation. The assessment of Prasat Thong is similar to that in the closing pages of the *Short History* (see p. 244).

because the judgment has to be made that His Majesty has not condemned anyone to death other than for reasons of state and to secure his Kingdom. For this reason his cunning usurpation will be forever memorable.

In carrying out my duty I have endeavored to give a truthful and accurate account of the crafty and violent succession of this King. I have described everything to the best of my knowledge. During the time I have lived in this Kingdom, I have diligently investigated all these matters and I have made inquiries into everything.[136] If I have missed anything (which I hope is not the case), I pray that Your Honor will understand that the fault rests not with me, but with the inadequacy of the information I have received. In the meantime, I trust that Your Honor will not take amiss my boldness in composing these poorly constructed lines, and accept my description as a token of my grateful affection. I hereby conclude this treatise, praying the Almighty that His Godly Majesty may bless Your Honor's praiseworthy government to the benefit of the Fatherland and Your Honor's pleasure, and ensure that Your Honor may long rule in health and prosperity. Amen.

Written at the Netherlands factory in Iudia, capital of the Kingdom of Siam, and concluded on the last day of December 1640.

Underneath was written:
Your Excellency's humble servant,
Jeremias van Vliet.

136. Van Vliet here hints a little about the way he composed this work.

APPENDIX I: STRUCTURE OF GOVERNMENT

VAN VLIET'S *Description* is the earliest known document to attempt a sketch of Ayutthaya's structure of government. Michael Vickery (1996) has used this material, along with other European accounts, to correct Quaritch Wales' over-literal analysis of the Three Seals Code. The account below depends heavily on Vickery's approach, but with more space than Vickery could devote to Van Vliet's data in the context of a very wide-ranging article.

Van Vliet mentions several senior officials and gives brief descriptions of their duties, but he offers no view of the overall framework of government. This can be reconstructed, as Vickery noted, using the Hierarchy Laws of the Three Seals Code.[1] The Laws list twenty positions with sakdina of 10,000, the highest ranking outside the royal clan. They appear in the Code in the order shown below. This reflects a fourfold division into civil, Brahman, military, provincial,[2] and then possibly some precedence within each. The Okya Maha Upparat stands above this division. Van Vliet's comments on each of these posts are collected below.

> *Okya Maha Upparat*: "first mandarin and *stadholder* of the king" (p. 145) and "the head of all the nobility of the kingdom" (p. 278). He appears to be a sort of standing regent, able to deputize for the king during absences. Van Vliet mentions that he is old and inactive (note that he is different from the *upparat*, or designated royal successor).

1. *Phra ayakan tamnaeng na phonlaroen* (พระไอยการตำแหน่งนาพลเรือน) and *phra ayakan tamnaeng na thahan hua muang* (พระไอยการตำแหน่งนาทหารหัวเมือง) in KTSD, 1.

2. This fourfold division is two times two. In the Three Seals Code, there is one law for the "civil" hierarchy and another for the "military and provincial." In the latter, the division into military and provincial is explicit. In the former, the division between civil proper and "Brahman" is implicit in the way the law is organized.

Civil

Okya Chakri: "chief of the army and the navy and minister of interior ... chief over the political, military, ecclesiastical, and civil affairs" (p. 122, 145). He was a kind of chief minister, with jurisdiction over both civil and military affairs, and also held the title of *onkharak*, head of the royal bodyguard.

Okya Yommarat: "chief judge for criminal and civil cases in Judia" (p. 145). Head of the *muang* (city) department.

Okya Phonlathep: "chief purveyor of the kingdom" (pp. 122, 145). Head of the *na* (fields) deparment. Also overseer of Mons in the kingdom.

Okya Phrakhlang (Kosathibodi): "chief of the king's warehouses, keeper of the great seal, and intermediary for the foreigners who are in the country ... counsel and leader of all foreign affairs at the court and keeper of the great seal" (pp. 122, 145). Head of the *khlang* (treasury) department.

Okya Wang: "president of the king's council ... president of His Majesty's secret council" (pp. 122, 145). Head of the *wang* (palace) department. Also overseer of the Lao in the kingdom.

Okya Phrasadet: Scarcely figures in Van Vliet's account. Prominent in La Loubère's 1687–8 account as "Governor of the City of Siam." Elsewhere described as being in charge of the Buddhist Sangha.

Brahman

Phra Maharat Khuru: Not mentioned directly, but Van Vliet describes the Okya Phrakhlang, Okya Yommarat, and the Brahmans as "the four or five greatest men of the country" (p. 147).

Phra Maharat Khuru Phra Rat: Not mentioned.

Military

Okya Kalahom: "general over the elephants and over the armed forces afoot and on horseback" (p. 145). Perhaps the most powerful post "because this Minister was in control of most of the army" (p. 264).

Okya Decho Chai: Not mentioned.

Okya Decho Chai Thainam: Appears in the *Historical Account*.

Provincial

The provincial hierarchy in the *Three Seals Law* lists two governors with Chaophraya rank and six with Okya rank (listed below). Four appear in Van Vliet's accounts. He noted: "The governors have also great authority, especially those of the four most important provinces, Poucelouck, Capheyn, Sorcelouck, and Suckothay. These governments are due to princes of the blood and only if these fail are they given to the greatest and most influential men as a great privilege" (p. 145).

Chaophraya Surasiphisomathirat: governor of Phitsanulok. "The province of Poucelouck is still looked upon as being the most sacred of the kingdom. The government of this province is still only given to princes of the blood and, failing these, most prominent men in compensation for great services" (p. 104).

Chaophraya Sithammarat: governor of Nakhon Si Thammarat.

Okya Krasetsongkhram: governor of Sawankhalok.

Okya Sithammasukkorat: governor of Sukhothai.

Okya Ramronnarongsongkhram: governor of Kamphaeng Phet.

Okya Petchrattanasongkhram: governor of Phetchabun.

Okya Kamhaengsongkhram: governor of Nakhon Ratchasima.

Okya Chaiyathibodi: governor of Tennasserim.

Van Vliet recorded about the Okya Wang, Phonlathep, Chakri, and Phrakhlang: "Each of these men has about one-fourth part of the administration of the country, and also receives one-fourth part of the revenue" (p. 122).

Van Vliet also recorded that Okya Maha Upparat, Wang, Phonlathep, Chakri, and Phrakhlang "have to represent the king and have to rule under the royal standard of the kingdom until a king is chosen" in the event of the king dying "before anybody had been chosen to succeed him and without leaving any legal heir" (p. 145).

APPENDIX II:

This table compares the list of Ayutthayan kings in David Wyatt's *Short History of*
Vliet's *Short History*. For a discussion, see Vickery (1976).

WYATT		LUANG
King	*dates*	*King*
Ramathibodi	1351–1369	Ramathibodi
Ramesuan	1369–1370	Ramesuan
Borommoracha I	1370–1388	Boromracha
Thong Chan	1388	Thong Lan
Ramesuan (return)	1388–95	Ramesuan (return)
Ramaracha	1395–1409	Phaya Ram
Intharacha	1409–1424	Intharacha
Borommaracha II	1424–1448	Borommaracha
Borommatrailokanat	1463–1488	Borommatrailokanat
Borommatrailokanat (Phitsanulok) Borommaracha III (Ayutthaya)	1488–1491	Borommatrailokanat (Phitsanulok) Borommaracha III (Ayutthaya)
Borommaracha III	1491–1529	
Intharacha II	1488–1491	
Ramathibodi II	1491–1529	Ramathibodi
Borommaracha IV	1529–1533	No Phuttangkun
Ratsada	1533–1534	son of above
Chairacha	1534–1547	Chairacha
Yot Fa	1547–June 1548	Yot Fa
Khun Worawongsa	June-July 1548	Khun Chinnarat
Chakkraphat	1548–1569	Thianracha Maha Chakkraphat
Mahin	Jan-Aug 1569	Mahin
Maha Thammaracha	1569–1590	Maha Thammaracha
Naresuan	1590–1605	Narai
Ekathotsarot	1608–1610/11	[Luang Prasoet chronicle ends]
(Si Saowaphak)	1610–1611?	
Song Tham (Intharacha)	1610/11–1628	
Chettha	Dec 1628–Aug 1629	
Athittayawong	Aug–Sep 1629	
Prasat Thong	1629–1656	

Based on Wyatt (1984: 312–13); Vickery (1976: 211–13); *RCA*.
d = days; m = months
Accession column under Luang Prasoet is in C.S. calendar (+638=AD)

TABLE OF KINGS

'hailand with the details available from the Luang Prasoet chronicle, and Van

?RASOET		VAN VLIET	
Accession	*reign*	*King*	*reign*
712	20	Ramathibodi	19
731		Ramesuan	3
732		Khunluang Pha-ngua	18
750	7d	Thong Chan	7d
750		Ramesuan (return)	6
757		Phra Ram	3
771		Nakhon In	20
786		Borommaracha thibodi	20
810		Borommatrailokanat	20
825–850 825–853			
		Intharacha	37
853		Ramathibodi	38
891		No Phuttangkun	5
895		Woraratsadathirat	5m
896		Chaiyaracha	13
908		Yot Chao	3
910	42d	Chinnarat	40d
910		Thianracha	16
930		Mahin	7
931		Mahathammaracha	22
952		Naret Rachathirat	20
		Ramesuan	6
		Intharacha	19
		Chettharacha	8m
		Athit Surawong	38d
		Si Thammarachathirat	

APPENDIX III: DYNASTIC TREE

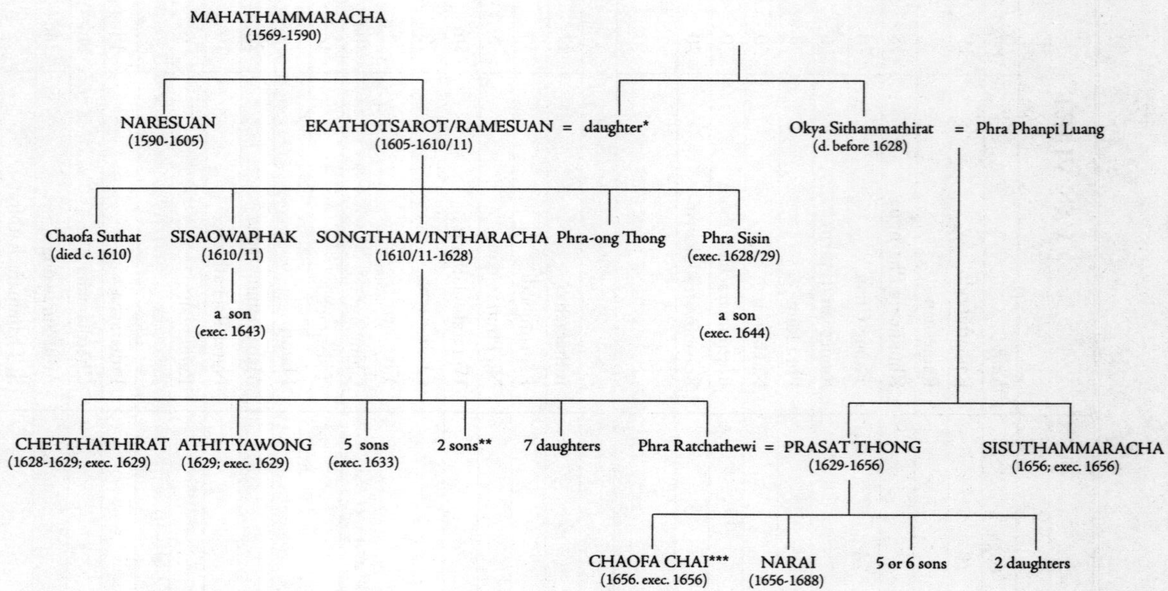

* A younger daughter of Okya Sithammathirat

**In 1642, the younger of two surviving sons of Songtham called "Thasai" rebelled against Prasat Thong and was executed. In 1644 Prasat Thong ordered the execution of the other son, Phra-ong Khamphra or the "orphan prince." He was spared after pleading by Prasat Thong's mother, but may not have lasted much longer.

***Only Narai was born of Phra Ratchathewi. Chaofa Chai and others were born of other consorts.

APPENDIX IV: YAMADA NAGAMASA

Yamada Nagamasa was probably born in 1590 in Sunpo (present-day Shizuoka). Around 1605, he may have been a palanquin-bearer for the local daimyo (feudal lord), Okubo Tadasuke of Numazu. In 1612 he traveled to Siam, but nothing is known of his early time there. By 1621 he had become one of the heads of the Japanese community in Ayutthaya. In that year, he sent letters to two members of the shogun's Council of Elders:

> I have been asked by the King of Siam to deliver a message to the great Shogun asking for his blessings and indulgences. As you are no doubt aware, the King of Siam has dispatched an envoy of two Siamese men, and Ito Kyodayi, according to your august wishes. The King here has also presented the envoys with letters of introduction, in which he asks that you grant them your favors. And one very small thing, please allow me to extend my personal courtesies, the envoys carry two sheets of decorative sharkskin and 200 *kin* [12 kilograms] of gunpowder as a present for you.

He signed himself "Yamada Nizaemon Nagamasa." The shogunate officials had no idea who he was, prompting a search in the records which came up with the birth details noted above. The official embassy that Yamada mentioned reached Edo in August 1621. The two officials reciprocated with gifts of white cotton cloth, and addressed Yamada with the suffix *no jo* used for a junior officer.

Yamada clearly kept up such personal connections with Japanese high officialdom in subsequent years. A letter he wrote to a personal attendant of one member of the shogun's Council of Elders on March 3, 1629 indicates that his role in relations between the two courts had become more important.

> Only just last year, as you surely recall, I presented you with a few small gifts and asked you to humbly deliver a message to the great Shogun [Tokugawa Iemisu] informing him of my fortunes.... Actually the King over here [Songtham] unfortunately passed away quite recently, and so the new King [Chetthathirat] has ordered his representatives to deliver a message of greetings

to the Shogun. Accordingly, three men Okluang Sakontek, Okkhun Wakehit, and Okkhun Yokohat, serving as envoys, and a translator named Gozaemon, will soon pay their respects. They are sailing in a merchant ship that I have prepared for them. On arrival they will deliver their king's message of greeting forthwith. Please pass on my kindest regards to the great Shogun, asking for his blessings and indulgences.

As a matter of fact, a merchant ship was supposed to be sailing to Japan in the summer of last year to deliver a message to the Shogun from the former king. Unfortunately though, owing to a series of delays at that time, the ship never left harbor. Anyway as in ordinary years, I will prepare merchant ships to visit you and ask that you grant them kind favors. Through all this, thank heavens, I have at last received a letter issued and sealed in vermilion from the Shogun himself, conferring upon me his trust in my efforts to carry out commerce and trade. Recently, I have suffered many hindrances and setbacks; nevertheless, I would like to give a few humble presents to both the great Shogun and the distinguished former Shogun [Tokugawa Hidetada] as a show of my keen respect and affection for their highnesses.

Again he sent presents to his Edo contact. This letter anticipated the arrival of a ship sent by Yamada which arrived in Edo on 13 September 1629 with an embassy from the new king, Chetthathirat, and presents from both Yamada and Kalahom (the future King Prasat Thong). When Chetthathirat's message was presented to the shogun, Chetthathirat himself was already dead. In the letter of reply Yamada was addressed as "Honorable Yamada Nizaemon," in a form of address implying high rank, but Yamada probably never saw this reply.

The above information from Japanese records will shortly be published by Professor Iwamoto Yoshiteru of Tohoku Gakuin University, to whom many thanks for permission to reproduce these excerpts here.

GLOSSARY

aguel	eaglewood (aquilaria), a tree producing a core of resin used as an aromatic
benzoin	benjamin, a tree resin used as an aromatic
chedi, cetiya	reliquary, shrine for holding relics
kuti	monk's residence in a *wat*
mondop	mandapa, hall, a shelter built over a Buddha image
nakhoda	shipmaster, captain
picul	= 61.76 kg
pinang	areca tree or nut
prang	Khmer-style temple tower
prao, proa, perahu	boat, canoe
sakdina	numerical ranking system of Thai nobility
shahbandar	harbormaster
sirih	betel tree or leaf
tra	seal, document carrying a seal
wat	Buddhist temple
wihan	vihara, assembly hall

Ranks (in ascending order)

Okphan	ออกพัน
Okmun	ออกหมื่น
Okkhun	ออกขุน
Okluang	ออกหลวง
Okphra	ออกพระ
Okya	ออกญา

BIBLIOGRAPHY

UNPUBLISHED RECORDS FROM ARCHIEF VAN DE VEREENIGDE OOST-INDISCHE COMPAGNIE (VOC), RIJKSARCHIEF, THE HAGUE (USED BY ALFONS VAN DER KRAAN)

Missive Philip Lucassen, Arties Gijsels, Adam Westerwolt, Joan Goossens, Jacob de Wit ende Cornelis van der Lijn aen den Coopman Jeremias van Vliet, Opperhooft op 't Comptoir Siam, 20 Mei 1637. Batavia's Uitgaand Briefboek. VOC 859.

Brief Gouverneur-Generaal Anthonio van Diemen aen den Grootmachtich Coninck van Siam, 12 Augustus 1636. Batavia's Uitgaand Briefboek. VOC 858.

Missive Gouverneur-Generaal Antonio van Diemen aen Van Vliet, overgebracht door Oppercoopman Hendrick Jansz Nachtegael, 25 Augustus 1637. Batavia's Uitgaand Briefboek. VOC 859.

Instructie voor den Coopman Hendrick Jansz Nachtegael, ende den voorderen Scheepsraet van het schip *Leyden*, seijlende van hier en recht door naer Siam, 25 Augustus 1637. Batavia's Uitgaand Briefboek. VOC 859.

Missive Gouverneur-Generaal Anthonio van Diemen aande Coopluijden Hendriq Nachtegael ende Jeremias van Vliet, met *Het Wapen van Delft* gezonden, 4 September 1637. Batavia's Uitgaand Briefboek. VOC 859.

Resolutie Siam Raedt, Hendrick Nachtegael, Jeremias van Vliet, Reijnier van 't Zum, Isaack Moerdijck ende Jan Jansen, 6 October 1637. Overgekomen Brieven 1637, Tweede Boek, vervolg. VOC 1125.

Een Treur-blij ende Ongeluck, des Oost-Indische Compagnies Dienaers in 't Jaer 1636 wedervaren, in 't Coninckljjcke Hof van Siam, in de Stadt Judia, onder de Directie van den Edele Jeremias van Vliet. Collectie Koloniale Aanwinsten, no. 47.

BOOKS, THESES AND ARTICLES

Baker, Chris. 2003. "Ayutthaya Rising: From Land or Sea?" *Journal of Southeast Asian Studies*, 34,1: 41–62.

Blankwaardt, W. 1927. "Notes upon the Relations between Holland and Siam." *JSS*, 20,3: 241–58; reprinted in *Selected Articles from the Siam Society Journal*, VII, Bangkok, 1959.

Boxer, C. R. (ed). 1935. *A True Description of the Mighty Kingdoms of Japan and Siam by Francois Caron and Joost Schouten.* London: Argonaut Press.

Breazeale, K. 1999. "Thai Maritime Trade and the Ministry Responsible." In *From Japan to Arabia: Ayutthaya's Maritime Relations with Asia*, ed. Breazeale. Bangkok: Foundation for the Promotion of Social Sciences and Humatities Textbooks Project.

Brummelhuis, Han ten. 1987. *Merchant, Courtier and Diplomat: A History of the Contacts between the Netherlands and Thailand.* Lochem: Uitgeversmaatschappij De Tijdstroom.

Brummelhuis, Han ten and Kleinen, John. 1980. *A Dutch Picnic in Ayutthaya 1636.* Amsterdam: University of Amsterdam.

Campos, J. 1940. "Early Portuguese Accounts of Thailand." *JSS*, 32: 1–28.

Caron, Francois and Schouten, Joost. 1986. *A True Description of the Mighty Kingdoms of Japan and Siam.* A Facsimile of the 1671 London edition in a contemporary translation from the Dutch by Roger Manley. Introduction and Notes by John Villiers. Bangkok: Siam Society.

Charnvit Kasetsiri. 1976. *The Rise of Ayudhya: A History of Siam in the Fourteenth and Fifteenth Centuries.* Oxford: Oxford University Press.

Chatthip Nartsupha et al. 1990. *Ayutthaya Historical Study Centre.* Ayutthaya: Ayutthaya Historical Study Centre.

Colenbrander, H. T. (ed). 1899. *Dagh-Register gehouden int Casteel Batavia vant passerende daer ter plaetse als over geheel Nederlandts-India.* Anno 1637. Batavia: Landsdrukkerij.

Collis, Maurice. 1982. *Siamese White.* Bangkok: DD Books.

Coolhaas, W. Ph. (ed). 1960. *Generale Missiven van Goeverneurs-Generaal en Raden aan Heeren XVII der Vereenigde OostIndische Compagnie*, Deel 1: 1610-1638. Den Haag: Nijhoff.

Cushman, Richard D. (tr.). 2000. *The Royal Chronicles of Ayutthaya.* Bangkok: Siam Society [*RCA*].

Damrong Rajanubhab, Prince. 1920. "Siamese History Prior to the Founding of Ayudhya." *JSS*, 13,2; reprinted in *Selected Articles from the Siam Society Journal*, III: 69–74. Bangkok, 1959.

Dhiravat na Pombejra. 1984. "A Political History of Siam under the Prasatthong Dynasty." Ph.D. thesis, SOAS, University of London.

Dhiravat na Pombejra. 1992. *Court, Company and Campong: Essays on the VOC Presence in Ayutthaya.* Ayutthaya: Ayutthaya Historical Study Centre.

Dhiravat na Pombejra. 2001. *Siamese Court Life in the Seventeenth Century as Depicted in European Sources.* Bangkok: Chulalongkorn University.

Dhiravat na Pombejra. 2003. "The Thaisai Prince's Rebellion of 1642: A Forgotten Event in Ayutthayan History." In *Dedications to Her Royal Highness Princess Galyani Vadhana Krom Luang Naradhiwas Rajanagarindra on her 80th birthday.* Bangkok: Siam Society.

Forbin, Claude de. 1996. *The Siamese Memoirs of Count Claude de Forbin*, ed. by Michael Smithies. Chiang Mai: Silkworm Books.

Frankfurter, O. 1907. "A Proposed Change in the Siamese Era Chulasakaraj 1000 (A.D. 1638)." *T'oung Pao*, 2nd ser., 8: 99–104.

Frankfurter, O. 1909. "Events in Ayudhya from Chulasakaraj 688–966." *JSS*, 6,3: 1–21; reprinted in *Selected Articles from the Siam Society Journal*, I: 38–62. Bangkok, 1954.

Gervaise, Nicolas. 1928 [1688]. *The Natural and Political History of Siam*. Trans. by H. S. O'Niell of *Histoire Naturelle et Politique du Royaume de Siam*. Bangkok: Siam Observer.

Gervaise, Nicolas. 1998 [1688]. *The Natural and Political History of the Kingdom of Siam*, trans. and ed. by John Villiers. Bangkok: White Lotus.

Giles, Francis H. 1938. "A Critical Account of van Vliet's Historical Account of Siam in the 17th Century." *JSS*, 30,2:155–240 and 30,3: 271–77; reprinted in *Selected Articles from the Siam Society Journal*, VII: 91–176. Bangkok, 1959.

Grimm, T. 1961. "Thailand in the Light of Official Chinese Historiography: A Chapter in the 'History of the Ming Dynasty.'" *JSS*, 49,1: 1–20.

Heecq, G. 1911. "De Derde Voyagie van Gijsbert Heecq naer Oost-Indien. *Marineblad: Bijblad op de Verslagen der Marinevereeniging.* Deel 25: 422–50.

Heeres, J. E. and Stapel, F. W. (eds). 1907. *Corpus Diplomaticum Neerlando-Indicum.* Vol. 1. Den Haag: Koninklijk Instituut voor Taal-, Land- en Volkenkunde.

Herbert, Thomas. 1663. *Relation du Voyage de Perse et des Indes Orientales, Traduit de l'Anglois de Thomas Herbert. Avec les Revolutions arrivees an Royaume de Siam l'an mil six cens quarante-sept. Traduit du Flamand de Ieremie Van Vliet.* Paris: n.p.

Inventarissen van Rijks-en Andere Archieven van Rijkswege Uitgegeven voor zoover zij niet Afzonderlijk zijn Afgedrukt. Deel 1. 1928. Den Haag: Algemeene Landsdrukkerij.

Iwao, Seiichi (ed). 1958. *Historiael Verhael der Sieckte ende Doot van Pra Interra-Tsia 22en Coninck in Siam, ende den Regherenden Coninck Pra Ongh Srij, door Jeremias van Vliet, 1640.* With French Translation of Part thereof, taken from Les Revolutions arrivées au Royaume de Siam par Ieremie van Vliet. Toyo Bunko Publications, Series D. No. 5. Tokyo: Toyo Bunko.

Kaempfer, Engelbert. 1971. *The History of Japan, together with a Description of the Kingdom of Siam, 1690–1692.* 3 Vols. Trans. by J. G. Schaucher. Glasgow: James MacLehose and Son.

Kaempfer, Engelbert. 1987 [1727]. *A Description of the Kingdom of Siam.* London; reprinted Bangkok: Orchid Press.

Kemp, Jeremy. 1969. *Aspects of Siamese Kingship in the Seventeenth Century.* Bangkok: Social Science Association Press of Thailand.

Kersten, Carool. 2003. *Strange Events in the Kingdoms of Cambodia and Laos (1635–1644).* Bangkok: White Lotus.

Kraan, Alfons van der. 1998. "On Company Business: The Rijckloff van Goens Mission to Siam, 1650." *Itinerario*, 22,2: 42–84.

Kraan, Alfons van der. 2003. "Anthony van Diemen: From Bankrupt to Governor-General, 1593–1636." Unpublished paper.

La Loubère, Simon de. 1969 [1693]. *A New Historical Relation of the Kingdom of Siam*. London. Reprint, Kuala Lumpur: Oxford University Press, 1969.

Leider, Jacques. 2002. "Arakan's Ascent during the Mrauk U Period." In Sunait Chutintaranond and Chris Baker (eds.), *Recalling Local Pasts: Autonomous History in Southeast Asia*. Chiang Mai: Silkworm Books.

Macleod, N. 1927. *De Oost-Indische Compagnie als Zeemogendheid in Azie*. Tweede Deel, 1632–1650. Rijswijk: Blankwaardt & Schoonhoven.

Mandelslo, Jan-Albert de. 1727. *Votages célèbres et remarquables*. Amsterdam: n.p.

Manguin, Pierre-Yves. 1991. "The Merchant and the King: Political Myths of Southeast Asian Coastal Polities." *Indonesia*, 52.

Mundie, W. H. 1904. *Historical Account of Siam in the 17th Century*. Bangkok. Reproduced as "Van Vliet's Historical Account of Siam in the 17th Century." *JSS*, 30,2 (1938): 95–154; and also in *Selected Articles from the Siam Society Journal*, VII, 31–90. Bangkok, 1959.

Nai Thien. 1912. "Intercourse between Burma and Siam as Recorded in the Hmannan Yazawindawgyi." *JSS*, 8,2; reprinted in *Selected Articles from the Siam Society Journal*, V. Bangkok, 1959.

Notton, C. 1939. *Légendes sur le Siam et le Cambodge*. Bangkok: Bangkok Times Press.

Pallegoix, J.-B. 1854. *Description du royaume Thai ou Siam*. Paris: Au profit de la mission de Siam.

Pelsaert, Francois. 1647. *Ongeluckige Voyagie van 't Schip Batavia nae de Oost-Indien, gebleven op de Albrohos van Frederick Houtman, op de hooghte van 28 graet by-Zuyden de Linie Aequinctiael, uytgevaren onder den E. Francoys Pelsert*. Amsterdam: Jan Jansz.

Penth, H. G. 1965. "An Account in the Hikayat Atjeh on Relations between Siam and Atjeh." In *Felicitation Volumes of Southeast-Asian Studies Presented to Prince Dhaninivat*. Bangkok: Siam Society.

Penth, H. G. 1967. "Zur Siam–Episode in der Hikayat Atjeh (Notes)." *JSS*, 55,2: 287–90.

Penth, H. G. 1969. "Zum Verhältnis Sayam–Atjeh im 17 Jahrhundert (Notes)." *JSS*, 57,2: 355–59.

Phiset Jiajanphong. 2003. *Phramahathammaracha kasatattirat* (King Thammaracha). Bangkok: Sinlapa Watthanatham.

Piriya Krairiksh. 1992a. "A Revised Dating of Ayudhya Architecture." *JSS*, 80,1: 37–58.

Piriya Krairiksh. 1992b. "A Revised Dating of Ayudhya Architecture (II)." *JSS*, 80,2: 11–26.

Piriya Krairiksh. 2000. *Sinlapa sukhothai lae ayutthaya: phap lak thi tong plian plaeng* [The art of Sukhothai and Ayutthaya: models in need of change]. Bangkok: 2000.

Pos, Arie and Lourciro, Rui Manuel (eds). 1997. *Itinerário, Viagem ou Navegação de Jan Huygen van Linschoten para as ändias Orientais ou Portuguesas. Gravuras e Mapas.* Lisbon: Comisão Nacional para as Comemorações dos Descobrimentos Portugueses.

Ravenswaay, L. F. van. 1910. "Translation of Jeremias van Vliet's Description of the Kingdom of Siam." *JSS*, 7: 1–108.

Reid, Anthony. 1993. *Southeast Asia in the Age of Commerce 1450–1680.* Vol. Two: *Expansion and Crisis.* New Haven: Yale University Press.

Satow, E. M. 1885. "Notes on the Intercourse between Japan and Siam in the Seventeenth Century." *Transactions of the Asiatic Society of Japan*, 13: 139–210.

Schouten, Joost. 1935 [1636]. In François Caron and Joost Schouten, *A True Description of the Mighty Kingdoms of Japan and Siam*, trans. by Capt. Roger Manley, ed. by C. R. Boxer. London: Argonaut.

Smith, George Vinal. 1977. *The Dutch in Seventeenth Century Thailand.* Center for Southeast Asian Studies. Special Report no. 16. DeKalb: Northern Illinois University.

Smithies, Michael. 1995. "Seventeenth Century Siam: Its Extent and Urban Centres According to Dutch and French Observers." *JSS*, 83,1&2: 63–78.

Sombat Chantornwong. 1976. "Khamson thang kanmuang khong van vliet ... ru withesobai khong prachao prasatthong [Van Vliet's political teaching or foreign policy of King Prasat Thong]." *Warasan Thammasat*, 6,1.

Sternstein, Larry. 1965. "'Krung Kao': The Old Capital of Ayutthaya." *JSS*, 53,1: 83–122.

Sternstein, Larry. 1966. "Notes on Krung Kao." *JSS*, 54,2: 211–220.

Sunait Chutintaranond and Than Tun. 1995. *On Both Sides of the Tenasserim Range: History of Siamese Burmese Relations.* Bangkok: Chulalongkorn University.

Tachard, Guy. 1981 [1688]. *A Relation of the Voyage to Siam Performed by Six Jesuits Sent by the French King, to the Indies and China in the Year 1685.* Reprint, Bangkok: White Orchid.

Teeuw, A. and Wyatt, D. K. 1970. *Hikayat Patani: The Story of Patani.* The Hague: Martinus Nijhoff.

Tri Amatayakul. 1957. *Guide to Ayudhya and Bang Pa-In.* Bangkok: Fine Arts Department.

Tri Amatayakul. 1972. *The Official Guide to Ayutthaya and Bang Pa-in.* Bangkok: Fine Arts Department.

Vickery, Michael. 1976. "Review of Van Vliet's *Short History*." *JSS*, 64,2: 207–36.

Vickery, Michael. 1996. "The Constitution of Ayutthaya: The Three Seals Code." In A. Huxley (ed.), *Thai Law: Buddhist Law. Essays on the Legal History of Thailand, Laos and Burma.* Bangkok: White Orchid..

Vivadhanajaya, Prince (tr.). 1935, 1937. "The Statement of Khun Luang Ha Wat." *JSS*, 28,2: 143–172; and 29,2: 123–36.

Vliet, Jeremias van. 1647. "Verhael ende Historisch Verhael van 't gene des Vereenighde Nederlandtsche Geoctroijeerde Ost-Indische Compagnie's Dienaers onder de directie van Jeremias van Vliet, in de jaren 1636 ende 1637 bij de Koninck van Siam in de Stadt Judia wedervaren is." In Francois Pelsaert, *Ongeluckige Voyagie van 't Schip Batavia naer de Oost-Indien*. Amsterdam: Jan Jansz.

Vliet, Jeremias van. 1648. "Een Treur-bly ende Ongeluck, des Oost-Indische Compagnies Dienaers in't jaer 1636, weder-varen, in't Coninckliјcke Hof van Siam, in de Stadt Judia, onder de directie van den E. Jeremias van Vliet." In: *Ongeluckige Voyagie, van't Schip Batavia, nae de Oost-Indien*. Amsterdam: Voor Joozt Hartgerts.

Vliet, Jeremias van. 1663. "Relation historiqve de la maladie et de la mort de Pra-Inter-Va-Tsia-Thiant-Siangh Pheevgk, ou du grand & juste Roy de 1'Elefant blanc, & des revolutions rrivées [sic] au Royaume de Siam, jusqu'à l'advénement à la Couronne de Pra Ongly, qui y regne aujourd'huy...." In Thomas Herbert, *Relation du Voyage de Perse et des Indes orientales. Traduite de l'Anglois de Thomas Herbert. Avec les revolutions arrivées au Royaume de Siam l'an mil six cens quarante-sept. Traduites du Flamand de Ieremie Van Vliet*. Paris: n.p.

Vliet, Jeremias van. 1692. *Beschrijving van het Koninkrijk Siam*. Leiden: Vliet, Jeremias van. 1692. *Beschryving van het Koningryk Siam, Mitsgaders het verhaal van den oorsprong, onderscheyd, politijke regering, d'ecclesiastique, en costuymelijke Huyshoudinge van d'Edelen en Borgerlijke Lieden: Als mede den loop der Negotie, en andere remarquable saaken des Koningrijks Siam*. Leiden: Frederik Haaring.

Vliet, Jeremias van. 1956. *Historiael Verhael der Sieckte ende Doot van Pra Interra Tsia 22en Coninck in Siam & den Regherende Pra Onghsry, 1640*. Toyo Bunko Publications, Series C, No. XIV. Tokyo: Toyo Bunko.

Vliet, Jeremias van. 2003. *Ruam banthuk prawatsat ayutthaya khong fan flit (wan walit)* [Collected writings of Van Vliet]. Bangkok: Fine Arts Department.

Wade, Geoff. 2000. "The *Ming shi-lu* as a Source for Thai History – Fourteenth to Seventeenth Centuries." *Journal of Southeast Asian Studies*, 31,2: 249–94.

Wales, H. G. Quaritch. 1931. *Siamese State Ceremonies*. London: Bernard Quaritch.

Wales, H. G. Quaritch. 1965 [1934]. *Ancient Siamese Government and Administration*. London: Bernard Quaritch. Reprinted, New York: Paragon.

Wheatley, Paul. 1956. "Langkasuka." *T'oung Pao*, 44: 387–412.

Wheatley. Paul. 1961. *The Golden Khersonese*. Kuala Lumpur: University of Malaya Press.

Wilaiwan Khanittanan. 2001. "Thai + khamen => thai lumnam chaophraya" (Thai+Khmer=>Thai of Chaophrya Basin), *Warasan sinlapasat* [Journal of Liberal Arts], 1,1.

Wolters, O. W. 1966. "The Khmer King at Basan (1371–3) and the Restoration of the Cambodian Chronology during the Fourteenth and Fifteenth Centuries." *Asia Major*, n.s. 12,1: 44–89.

Wyatt, David K. (ed). 1975. *The Short History of the Kings of Siam by Jeremias van Vliet.* Translated by Leonard Andaya from a transcription by Miriam J. Verkuijl-van den Berg. Bangkok: The Siam Society.

Wyatt, David K. 1967. "The Thai 'Kata Mandiarapāla' and Malacca." *JSS*, 55,2: 279–86.

Wyatt, David K. 1975. *The Crystal Sands. The Chronicles of Nagara Śrī Dharrmarāja.* Data Paper No. 98. Ithaca, N.Y.: Southeast Asia Program, Cornell University.

Wyatt, David K. 1984. *Thailand: A Short History*. London: Yale University Press.

Wyatt, David K. 1994. *The Nan Chronicle*. Studies on Southeast Asia No. 16. Ithaca, N.Y.: Southeast Asia Program, Cornell University.

Wyatt, David K., and Aroonrut Wichienkeeo. 1995. *The Chiang Mai Chronicle*. Chiang Mai: Silkworm Books.

กฎหมายตราสามดวง [Three Seals Law]. Bangkok: Khurusapha, 1984. [*KTSD*]

คำให้การขุนหลวงวัดประดู่ทรงธรรม (Khamhaikan khun luang wat pradu songtham), *แถลงงานประวัติศาสตร์ เอกสารโบราณคดี* [Historical reports, archaeological documents], 3,1, 1969. [*KKLWP*]

คำให้การชาวกรุงเก่า (Khamhaikan chao krung kao), [Testimony of the residents of the old capital]. Bangkok: Chotmaihet, 2001. [*KCKK*]

คำให้การชาวกรุงเก่า ฯลฯ (Khamhaikan chao krung kao), [Testimony of the residents of the old capital]. Bangkok: Khlang Witthaya, 1964.

ตำนานเมืองนครศรีธรรมราช [Chronicle of Nakhon Si Thammarat] in รวมเรื่องเมืองนครศรีธรรมราช [Collected articles on Nakhon Si Thammarat)]. Bangkok, 1962.

ประชุมจดหมายเหตุสมัยอยุธยา ภาค ๑ [Collected records of the Ayutthaya period, vol. 1]. Bangkok: Commission for the Publication of Historical, Cultural, and Archaeological Records, Office of the Prime Minister. 1967.

ประชุมพงศาวดาร [Collected chronicles], pt. 61. 2nd ed. Bangkok, 1972.

พระราชพงศาวดารกรุงศรีอยุธยา (ฉบับหลวงสารประเสริฐ และฉบับกรมพระปรมานุชิตชิโนรสและพงศาวดารเหนือ). [Royal Chronicles of Ayutthaya, Luang Prasoet and Pharamanuchit Chinorot editions], 2 vols. Bangkok: Khurusapha, 1961. [Luang Prasoet chronicle, *LP*]

พระราชพงศาวดารกรุงศรีอยุธยา ฉบับพระราชหัตถเลขา [Royal Chronicles of Ayutthaya, Royal Autograph edition]. Chonburi: Cremation of Tailong Phonprapha, 1969. [Royal Autograph chronicle, *RA*]

พระราชพงศาวดารกรุงศรีอยุธยา ฉบับสมเด็จพระพนรัตน์ วัดพระเชตุพน [Royal Chronicles of Ayutthaya, Phonnarat edition]. Bangkok: Khlang Witthaya, 1964; reprinted 1972. [Phonnarat chronicle, *PN*]

พระราชพงศาวดารกรุงศรีอยุธยา [Royal Chronicles of Ayutthaya]. Bangkok: Khurusapha, 1961.

พระราชวังและวัดโบราณในจังหวัดพระนครศรีอยุธยา [Ancient palaces and temples in Ayutthaya province]. Bangkok, 1968.

Wyatt, David K. (ed.) 1975. *The Crystal Sands: The Chronicles of Nagara Sri Dharrmaraja*. Translated by David K. Wyatt. [illegible]

Wyatt, David K. 19[illegible]. "The Thai 'Katā Mandhiraban' and Malay [illegible]". *JMBRAS* [illegible]

Wyatt, David K. 19[illegible]. *The Crystal Sands: The Chronicles of Nagara Sri Dharrmaraja*. Data Paper No. [illegible]. Ithaca, N.Y.: Southeast Asia Program, Cornell University.

Wyatt, David K. 1982. *Thailand: A Short History*. New Haven: Yale University Press.

Wyatt, David K. 1994. *Studies in Thai History: Collected Articles*. [illegible]

Wyatt, David K. and Aroonrut Wichienkeeo. 1995. *The Chiang Mai Chronicle*. Chiang Mai: Silkworm Books.

[illegible] Bangkok: [illegible]

[illegible] 1980. [illegible]

[illegible] Bangkok: [illegible] 2001. [illegible]

[illegible] Bangkok: [illegible] 1982.

[illegible] Bangkok, 1962.

[illegible]

[illegible]

[illegible] Bangkok, 1982.

[illegible] Bangkok, 19[illegible]

[illegible]

[illegible] Bangkok, 1980.

INDEX

Index entries give the "correct" spellings, not the many variants found in the text. As Van Vliet, King Prasat Thong, and Ayutthaya are present throughout the book, they have no index entries except to the descriptions of Ayutthaya and to Van Vliet's life.

Aceh 57, 94, 133–6, 313, 242
Adonibeseck 320
Alak, Okphra 149, 153
Angkor 191, 199, 202
Apries of Egypt 319
Arab, Arabia, Arabic 2, 3, 61, 138, 182, 257
Arakan 94, 109, 132–3, 242, 313
Aristotle 251, 256, 298, 298
Atahualpa of Peru 321
Athit Surawong (Athittayawong), King 190, 240–1, 250–1, 289, 297–8, 326–7, 328
Ava 109, 124, 126, 132, 134, 168, 231, 232, 250, 254, 307–8, 314
Ayutthaya, description of 1–17, 105, 110

Ban Chaophraya 71–4, 81–2, 177
Bang Pa-in 120, 210
Bangkhli 21
Bangkok 6, 64, 74, 81–3, 105, 109, 152, 199, 237–8
Banjarmasin 169
Bassein 225
Batavia 21–2, 25–32, 37, 39–41, 52, 56, 58, 77–82, 85, 87, 91, 97, 128, 129, 132, 142–3, 182–5, 236, 247, 256, 293
Bayinnaung, King of Pegu 219
Bengal 2, 19, 52, 106, 109, 132, 144, 148, 170
benzoin 21, 151
Boeretiet 45–9, 60, 65–7
Borgia, Cesare 252–3
Borneo 169, 172
Borommatrailokanat, King 188, 191, 207, 326–7
Borommoracha, King 326–7
Brahmans 59, 147, 196, 200, 264, 275
braspintado 47, 50–1, 55, 62, 64, 66, 69, 219
British Museum chronicle 181
Brito, Felipe de 21
Buddhism 20, 95, 108, 154–61, 189, 197, 243–4

Canton 138–41, 169, 202
Caracalla, Antoninus 252, 284, 299, 320
Caron, François 25, 28, 30, 42, 183
Castilians 68, 130, 141–2
Catholic 25, 38, 140, 161
Chai(ya)racha, King 157, 188, 215–7, 243, 326–7
Chaiya 109, 123
Chakri, Okya 60, 63, 66, 69–70, 115, 122, 131, 145, 221–2, 227, 310, 317–8, 324–5
chamberlain 53–5, 59, 62, 64, 66, 214
Champa 2, 104, 232, 233, 314 n.117
Chanthaburi 108, 150
Chao Ui 198–9
Chaophraya River 1, 23, 24, , 41, 71, 110, 130, 152, 271

Chettharacha/Chetthathirat, King 190, 237–40, 249–51, 257, 264, 266–71, 326–7, 328, 330
Chiang Mai 106, 121, 127, 168, 232–3, 307–8
Chiang Saen 196, 307
China 2, 19–20, 94, 97, 103–4, 121, 138, 169, 188, 196, 198–9, 202
Chinese 1–2, 7–8, 15, 20, 51–2, 70, 83, 104–6, 138–41, 149, 152, 167, 169, 177, 197–202, 305
Chinnarat, King 216–7, 326–7
Chong Chalung 208
Chularatchamontri, Okphra/Okluang 62–6, 71, 74–7, 80, 83–5, 88, 236, 259, 263, 275
Cochinchina 15, 106, 169
Commodus (Marcus Aurelius Commodus Antoninus) 257
Coromandel coast 48, 121, 133, 141, 144, 148, 167, 169, 170, 209, 212
Coronelli map 5–6, 8, 16, 24
Croesus, King of Lydia 297, 319
Cyrus of Persia 319

d'Alcrassa, Don Jan 140
D'Avilla, Sebastian Moutos 140–1
Damrong Rajanubhab, Prince 29, 247
Darius of Persia 319
de Choisy, Abbé 10, 17, 102
De Gusman, Luis 141
De Guverro, Anthonio 256
De Silva, Don Fernando 130, 140, 235–6
deer, deerskins 18, 21, 26, 56, 107, 136, 142, 150–2, 167, 169, 171, 177
dress 163
Dutch East India Company (VOC) 4, 20–5, 29, 31, 35, 37, 42, 45, 48, 51, 56, 61, 71, 98–9, 101, 103, 129, 141, 182, 185, 200, 293

eaglewood 21, 150
education 165
Ekathotsarot, King 18, 21, 46, 190, 202, 229, 233–5, 311, 326–7, 328
England 38, 42–3

Feroske, Taramatsu 57, 73
festivals 116–20, 159–60
food 162–3
Forbin, Count Claude de 17
Front Palace 4–12, 45, 263, 276, 315

Gaijus Marius 300
Galieni 300
Giles, Francis H. 128, 130, 192, 237, 240, 254, 255, 259, 267, 274, 307
Goa 139, 141
Golconda 3, 144 n.116
Gordianus III of Rome 320
Griswold, Alexander B. 181, 206

Henri IV, King of France 258
Hirado 25, 56, 183
housing 8–10, 162

India 2, 3, 19, 48 n.7, 98, 121, 139, 140, 144, 209
Indian Ocean 25, 31, 106
Indians 2, 3, 15
inheritance 164–5
Intharacha, King 208, 235–7, 326–7
Iskandar Muda 134 n. 100
Iwao, Seiichi 29, 56, 181–3 185, 186, 192, 247–8, 254

Jacobsz, Daniel 41, 45–6, 59, 67, 70, 77, 86
Jambi 104, 106, 169
Japan 3, 4, 20–3, 25, 28, 30–1, 42, 83, 94, 97, 136–42, 152, 169, 182–3, 313
Japanese 4, 15, 29, 30, 55–7, 70–4, 118, 122, 128, 130, 136–42, 149, 152, 169, 172, 235, 238, 242, 249–52, 261, 263, 266, 268–9, 278, 283–4, 288–96, 302–8, 313–4
Johore 21, 129, 134
Julius Caesar 258, 300, 320
justice 96, 107, 112, 153–5

Kabin(buri) 150
Kachorn Sukhabanij 181, 247
Kaempfer, Engelbert 7, 8, 10, 15, 16, 47, 120

Kalahom, Okya 18, 50, 60, 63–6, 130, 145, 227, 237–41, 248–9, 259–303, 308, 313, 315, 324
Kamphaeng(phet), Okya 237, 250–1, 268–9, 282–5, 289–96, 325
Kamphaengphet 108, 145, 151, 202, 207, 220
Kedah 123, 129, 132, 134, 212, 242, 313–4
Kelang 141
Khorat, see Nakhon Ratchasima
Khun Wichitmatra 247
Kreng 125, 226, 232, 233
Kui, Kuiburi 104, 152, 196, 199

labor 75–6, 149
lac 21, 151
Lamare map 5–8, 11–12, 14, 140
Lampang 126, 127, 129, 134, 232–3, 241–2, 308–9
Lamphun 215–6
Lanchang, see Lanxang
Langkasuka 192, 198
Lanxang 106, 121, 126–7, 168, 198, 232, 233, 236, 241, 314
Lao 94, 121, 149, 233, 237
Laurentsz, Joost 41, 45–6, 59, 67, 70, 77, 86
Ligor 21, 94, 108, 109, 129–31, 134, 141, 152, 169, 199, 241, 250–2, 304, 308
Lipsius, Justus 258
Lopburi River 6, 71
Lopburi 2, 8, 9, 203
Luang Prasoet chronicle 111, 125, 181, 182, 188, 191, 203, 226
Lucasz, Philip 27, 91, 183, 256

Macao 130, 140
Machiavelli, Nicolo 251–4, 299, 320
Maeklong 109, 152
Maha Uparacha of Pegu, 145, 224–8
Mahathammaracha, King 223–8, 326–7, 328
Mahathip Mahamontri, Okphra 153
Mahin, King 190, 220–2
Makassar 15, 169
Malacca (Melaka) 2, 21, 30–1, 97–8, 101–2, 139–41, 171, 184, 244, 250, 314
Malacca gum 121, 127, 151, 168, 169
Malays 15, 61, 122, 129, 149, 229, 313
Manila 140–1, 172, 242, 314
Marcus Aurelius Antoninus 256–7
marriage 158, 163–4
Martaban 109
Masulipatnam 133, 167
Mergui 19, 21, 52, 109, 133, 303
military 107, 109–10, 122–4
Moerdijck, Isaac 45, 69
Mon 3, 102, 259 n.22, 308 n.97
Mongkhon, Okluang 249, 251, 267–73
Moors 8, 15, 61, 75, 97, 122, 133, 148, 149, 153, 160, 167, 169, 170, 212, 226, 236, 250, 282
Muang Hang 232, 233
Mundie, W. H. 29, 244–55, 274, 282, 289, 299, 307, 308, 310, 321
Muslims 3, 4, 50, 62, 72, 80, 83, 129, 130, 160–1, 212, 259, 277

Nagapattinam 140
Nagasaki 21, 56, 137, 140
Nakhon Chaisi 202
Nakhon In, King 206
Nakhon Pathom 109
Nakhon Ratchasima 71, 97, 108, 168, 176, 225, 277
Nakhon Ratchasima, Okya 71, 325
Nakhon Sawan 108, 154, 310
Nakhon Si Thammathirat, Okya 325
Nakhon Si Thammathirat, see Ligor
Nan 307–8
Nandabayin, King of Pegu 218
Nantha Woranetiwong 247–53
Narai, King 11–12, 20, 41, 47, 118, 328
Naresuan, King 3, 12, 20, 46, 93, 124, 128 n.84, 190, 191, 223–33, 259, 277, 311, 314, 326–7, 328
No Phutthanangkun, King 213–4
nobility 144–9, 161–4, 234, 243
Nong Sarai 125, 226

Orange, Prince of 22, 38, 130, 142, 229, 278
Oroetes 319

Pahang 21, 129
Paliacatta, see Pulicat
Pasak River 1, 6
Pattani 20–1, 62, 93–4, 99, 104, 106–7, 123, 128–34, 152, 169, 198–9, 212, 218–9, 229, 234, 242, 250, 294–5, 303, 313, 315
Pecap 61, 70–2, 74–6, 80, 83, 84
Pegu 3, 93–4, 106, 109, 122, 124–8, 134, 149, 168, 214, 218–27, 230–2, 271, 307 n.96, 314
Perak 212
Phangua, King 204
Phaniat 221, 228, 236
Phanpi Luang, Queen 328
Phatthalung 109, 129, 146, 152
Phetchabun, Okya 325
Phetchaburi 2, 62, 152 n.137, 199, 232, 238, 249, 251, 267–9
Phetracha, Phra 318
Phichai (Songkhram), Okya 55–6, 149, 308
Phitsanulok 2, 47, 104, 108, 121, 127, 145, 151, 202, 207, 217–24
Phitsanulok, Okya 19, 127, 131, 166, 176, 217, 218–23, 234, 242, 250, 254, 277, 308–9, 315–8
Phocas 321
Phonlathep, Okya 122, 145, 149, 234, 275, 324–5
Phrakhlang, Okya 21–2, 29, 41–2, 46–88, 119, 122, 127, 129, 130–7, 145, 147–8, 153, 166, 170, 233–4, 250–2, 263, 277–93, 303, 310, 313, 315–8, 324–5
Phrasadet, Okya 130
Phrasadet, Okya 324
Phrommathep 187, 196–7
Phuket 21
Piriya Krairiksh 46, 120
ploughing ceremony 275–6
Policrates of Samos 319
Portuguese 1, 3, 15, 21, 30, 51–2, 61, 68, 72, 98, 122, 125, 130, 133–4, 139–41, 149, 161, 169, 170, 172, 226–7, 242, 313–4
Prachin 108, 150, 151
Prome 225
Pulicat 48, 170

Raden Ibrahim 50, 54, 58, 62, 73–4, 76, 77, 79, 83
Ramaracha, King 326–7
Ramarat 144, 170, 209–12, 326–7
Ramathibodi I (U Thong), King 106, 188–91, 199–203, 206, 326–7
Ramathibodi II, King 144, 188, 191, 207, 209–13
Ramesuan, King 203–5, 326–7
Ratchaburi 109, 152
Ratchamontri, Okphra 149
Ratchaprasit, Okya 130, 313
Ratchayut, Okluang 217
rayskins 21, 26
Rear Palace 12, 45
Reid, Anothony 17
Royal Autograph chronicle 188, 191

Sakaekrang River 271
Sakda Pholarit, Okphra 307
San Thome 140
sappanwood 21, 75, 139, 142, 151–2, 167, 169, 171–2, 199
Sarrathij 223–5
Sawankhalok 108, 145, 151, 207
Sawankhalok, Okya 315, 325
Schouten, Joost 7, 8, 11, 13, 21–2, 25–8, 37–9, 51–3, 71, 91–2, 95–9, 103, 108, 118, 183, 251
Senaphimuk, Okya, see Yamada Nagamasa
shahbandar 22, 50, 62–6, 71–2, 75, 77, 83–5, 88, 148, 236
Si Sanphet, Okya 153
Si Saowaphak, King 235 n.118, 311, 326–7, 328
Si Sin, Prince 237, 249, 251, 253, 259, 265, 267, 277
Si Suda Chao 216
Si Suthammaracha, King 20, 47, 118, 328

Si Worawong, Okya 259–66, 278, 282, 285
Sirisudhammaraja, King of Arakan 109, 132, 133
Sisombat, Okphra 149
Solomon, King 213, 257
Sombat Chantornwong 252
Songkhla 22, 109, 123, 129, 131, 134, 146, 152
Songtham, King 19, 79, 115, 120, 128, 130, 132, 134, 190, 235–6, 249–58, 261–2, 274, 278–9, 306, 311–2, 326–7, 328
Specx, Cornelius 99, 229
Sri Waiyawut, Okkhun 304–6
Suleiman Khan I, Sultan 301
Sukhothai 2, 3, 108, 115, 145, 151, 202, 207, 312 n.112
Sukhothai, Okya 115, 325
Sumatra 2, 104
Sumet Jumsai 46
Suphanburi 2, 203 n.35, 205, 206 n.44, 226 n.97
Surat 148, 167
Suwat, Queen 221–2
Swares, Casper 140
Swatow 139, 167
Syriam 21

Tachard, Guy 11, 13–4, 17, 102, 118
Taiwan 25, 82, 98, 141–2, 167
Taymon, Itoya 57, 73
Tenasserim 3, 21, 52, 62, 108, 109, 133, 141, 146, 148, 151, 153, 167, 169, 211, 232, 263, 271
Thainam, Okphra/Okya 217, 259, 263, 307, 324
Thajin 109, 152
Thalun, King of pegu 314
Thammaracha 190
Thammarachathirat, King 241, 300
Thammikarat Chao, Phra 187, 196–7
Thamtrailok, Okluang 259
Thianracha, King 217–8, 326–7
Thip Sombat, Okkhun 57, 59, 64, 70–7, 80, 84, 88
Thippanet, Phraya of Chiang Saen 307
Thong Chan, King 204–6, 326–7
Thong Hauw 232–3
Thong Su 51, 149
Tjoucko 51, 53–5, 59, 62, 64, 66, 69, 83
Toungoo 232
trade 20–5, 96–7, 121, 148, 150–3, 167–71
trial by ordeal 112, 153–5
Trompanit, Okmun 61, 64–5, 80, 83–6
Turkey 3, 251, 297, 301
Turks 3, 226, 284

U Thong, see Ramathibodi I
Un Muang, Phraya of Nan 307
Ungu, Queen of Pattani 129, 314
Upparat, Okya (Maha) 145, 146, 278, 307, 310, 323, 325
Uthaitham, Okya 51, 55, 59

Valentijn's map 71, 120
Valgarneira, Father Thomas 6
Van Diemen, Anthonio 22, 26–31, 38–42, 49, 52, 98, 183, 185–6, 195, 245, 247
Van Goens, Rijckloff 32, 42
Van Ravenswaay, L. F. 28, 89, 100, 109
Van Vliet, Jeremias, life of 25–32, 182–5
Vickery, Michael 153, 175, 216
Vientiane 106, 121, 232
Vijayanagar empire 2
Vingboons atlas 4
VOC, see Dutch East India Company

wang na, see Front Palace
Wang, Okya 59, 122, 145, 149, 234, 259, 278, 323, 325
Wat Ayotthaya 120, 201
Wat Chai Wattanaram 20, 46
Wat Chaophraya Thai 54, 120, 155
Wat Chi Chiang Sai 157, 215, 243
Wat Doem 120, 155, 201, 297
Wat Mahathat 12, 14, 55, 117, 120, 135, 152, 155–6, 158, 201, 218, 242

Wat Phra Si Sanphet 11, 13–4, 106, 116, 155–6
Wat Phramen Khok Phraya 270, 287, 312
Wat Phraram 13–4, 224 n.93
Wat Phutthaisawan 120, 201 n.24
Wat Ratchaburana 201
Wat Suwantharam 7
Wat Worachet 44–6
Wheatley, Paul 192, 199
Wichit Phasa, Okmun 48, 65, 71, 73–4, 81–3
Wicquefort, Abraham de 29, 184, 247–55, 274, 275, 282, 289, 299, 301, 308, 310, 311, 321
Wolters, O. W. 206
Wonderaer, Sebalt 293
Woratsadathirat, King 214–5

Yamada Nagamasa (Okya Senaphimuk) 238, 249–51, 261, 266–9, 288–9, 292–6, 302–5, 329–30
Yommarat, Okya 145, 147, 153, 155, 237, 310, 316–8, 324
Yot Chao, King 216, 326–7

Chris Baker is co-author of *Thailand: Economy and Politics* and *A History of Thailand*. Dhiravat na Pombejra teaches in the Department of History, Chulalongkorn University, and is author of *Siamese Court Life in the Seventeenth Century* and several studies on the Dutch in Siam. Alfons van der Kraan teaches in the School of Economics, University of New England, Australia, and has written widely on the Dutch East India Company. David K. Wyatt is John Stambaugh Professor Emeritus of History at Cornell University, and author of *Thailand: A Short History*.

